ATONEMENT AND COMPARATIVE THEOLOGY

Comparative / *Thinking Across*
Theology / *Traditions*

Loye Ashton and John Thatamanil, series editors

This series invites books that engage in constructive comparative theological reflection that draws from the resources of more than one religious tradition. It offers a venue for constructive thinkers, from a variety of religious traditions (or thinkers belonging to more than one), who seek to advance theology understood as "deep learning" across religious traditions.

ATONEMENT AND COMPARATIVE THEOLOGY

The Cross in Dialogue with Other Religions

CATHERINE CORNILLE, EDITOR

Fordham University Press NEW YORK 2021

Library of Congress Cataloging-in-Publication Data

Names: Cornille, Catherine, editor.
Title: Atonement and comparative theology : the cross in dialogue with other religions /
    Catherine Cornille, editor.
Description: New York : Fordham University Press, 2021. | Series: Comparative theology :
    thinking across traditions | Includes bibliographical references and index.
Identifiers: LCCN 2021027359 | ISBN 9780823294350 (hardback) |
    ISBN 9780823294343 (paperback) | ISBN 9780823294367 (epub)
Subjects: LCSH: Atonement. | Christianity and other religions.
Classification: LCC BT265.3 .A855 2021 | DDC 232/.3—dc23
LC record available at https://lccn.loc.gov/2021027359

Printed in the United States of America

23 22 21   5 4 3 2 1

First edition

CONTENTS

Rethinking Redemption

ATONEMENT AND COMPARATIVE THEOLOGY

Introduction

Catherine Cornille

At the heart of Christian faith is the extraordinary belief in the salvific efficacy of the suffering, death, and resurrection of Jesus Christ. In spite of, or because of, its central role in Christian faith and practice, the mystery of atonement remains one of the most intractable questions in Christian theology. Why did Jesus have to die? What is the evil that is conquered by his death? How does his death and resurrection effect the salvation of all? These are the questions that have occupied Christian theologians throughout history and that have given rise to a variety of theories of atonement, from the vicarious satisfaction theory of Anselm to the moral influence model of Abelard, and from the bait and hook account of Gregory of Nyssa to the happy exchange notion of Luther and the scapegoating theory of René Girard. Each of these theories is based on a different conception of God, evil, salvation, human agency, and the relative importance of the divine and human natures of Christ.[1] The various theories of atonement have been variously classified as classical, objective, and subjective theories (Aulén);[2] the Patristic, Anselmian, and Thomistic models (Stump);[3] the model of the cross as sacrifice, as victory, as forgiveness, and as moral example (MsGrath).[4] Many of the classical theories have been subject to important critique. The penal substitution theories of atonement have been generally rejected in contemporary theology as based on an outdated feudal understanding of retribution. Feminist and other liberation theologians have taken theories of vicarious suffering to task for their tendency to glorify suffering and surrogacy.[5] The overall metaphysical framework underlying many theories of atonement do not always accord with contemporary worldviews. And the traditional notions of evil and sin seem to have lost much of their purchase on modern anthropology. Despite this, the cross continues to speak to the imagination and enrich or inform the spiritual and social lives of Christians, and theologians continue to explore new ways of understanding the salvific meaning of the cross and of making sense of the doctrine of atonement. Thus, Kathryn Tanner has developed a model of atonement based on the incarnation,[6] Elizabeth Johnson has proposed a shift from a substitutionary understanding of suffering to one of accompaniment with the suffering of all creation,[7] Eleonore Stump offers a Marian interpretation of atonement as a "satisfactory remedy for both shame in all its varieties and guilt in all its parts,"[8] Charles Heffling interprets suffering as the inevitable consequence of the act of forgiveness,[9] and Ligita Ryliskyte rearticulates the intelligibility of the cross from the perspective of redemptive justice.[10] These theologians reinterpret atonement in light of new and enduring questions or challenges, while remaining largely within a Christian frame of reference.

The discipline of comparative theology presents a promising opportunity to reflect anew on the meaning of the suffering and death of Christ in conversation with other religious traditions. As Christianity has come to recognize the working of the spirit and the presence of rays of truth in other religious traditions, these traditions have become a source of inspiration for Christian theological reflection. In this volume, Christian comparative theologians with expertise in Hinduism, Buddhism, Daoism, Judaism, Islam, and African religions offer insights on the question of atonement gained from engagement with one of those religious traditions.

The theological insight and inspiration drawn from another religion may take different forms, from the reinforcement of one's own beliefs through analogical beliefs or practices in other religious tradition to the reaffirmation of their particularity, and from the reinterpretation of one's teachings in light of other hermeneutical frameworks to the recovery of neglected or forgotten texts or teachings or the appropriation of new ideas or practices.[11] The possibilities for learning from other religions are, of course, circumscribed by scriptural witness to the suffering, death, and resurrection of Jesus and by their interpretation in the Christian theological tradition. But this still leaves ample room for other religions to shed new light on the Christian understanding of atonement.

The mystery of atonement represents a topic for particularly fruitful collaboration among Christian comparative theologians engaged in different religious traditions. Not only does it concern the crucial question in Christian theology, but it also allows for various forms of critical and constructive engagement in the areas of anthropology, soteriology, and eschatology. The articles in this volume indeed deal with the conception of evil and sin underlying atonement, the symbolism of the cross, and the meaning of vicarious suffering and redemption. Though every contribution touches to some extent on each of these topics, they are here arranged according to the main focus or argument.

The articles in the first part of the volume deal predominantly with the question of the need for atonement. While Muslim thinkers have often accused Christianity of being overly pessimistic about human nature and lax about moral responsibility, questioning the necessity of a mediator of salvation who suffers and dies for the sins of others, Daniel Madigan points out that the Islamic tradition also has a strong understanding of the gravity of the sin of Adam and of the strong tendency of humans toward evil. Though the notion of original sin is indeed unique to Christianity (and Muslim critique of certain interpretations of it may be at times justified), Madigan also points to various areas of anthropology and soteriology where Muslim and Christian thinkers might agree. Thierry-Marie Courau draws inspiration from the Buddhist tradition, in general, and from Tibetan Buddhist texts, in particular, to interpret the notion of original sin in terms of the reality of craving and grasping. From this perspective, which views all suffering as arising from desire and attachment, the sin of Adam and Eve involves disobedience arising from a delusional conception of an autonomous self and from focusing all desire and attachment on "the smallest object." He then argues that the redemption of Jesus may be understood as a reversal of the deadly cycle of craving and attachment through the example of total obedience, self-emptying, and detachment.

In discussing various contemporary interpretations of atonement, Klaus von Stosch draws particular attention to the German thinker Thomas Pröpper, who understands the need for atonement in light of the human longing for the unconditional, which can only be fulfilled by a human who embodies God's unconditional love. He finds in the fifth *sura* of the Qur'an a verse that might help Christians to acknowledge the gnomic free will of Jesus, thus reinforcing his full humanity against tendencies to over-emphasize his divinity and impeccability. The idea that suffering may play a redemptive function, or that there may be a connection between suffering and salvation, is not foreign to many religious traditions. Bede Bidlack draws from the Daoist tradition to illustrate the recurrence and broader validity and power of notions of vicarious suffering and penitential practices. He discusses the rituals of Dust and Soot and internal alchemy as traditional Daoist expressions of the notion of suffering for the sake of one's ancestors and of the larger social context. Against current interpretations of the cross and atonement that tend to focus only on accompaniment, he suggests that Christian penitential rituals may be revalidated as contributing not only to one's own salvation, but also to that of the larger community of relatives and loved ones.

Part II focuses mainly on the scandal of the cross when seen in light of other religious traditions. Francis Clooney states that because of its shocking nature, early missionaries in India tended to de-emphasize the central importance of the cross in their dealings with Hinduism. However, the later Hindu saint Ramakrishna actually appropriated some of the Christian language of vicarious suffering in order to make sense of his suffering and death. The Hindu tradition may thus draw attention in particular to the redemptive role of contemplating the suffering divinity. The experience of suffering certainly plays a role in the narratives of Hindu divinities portrayed in the Ramayana, and sacrifice and blood feature prominently in Hindu ritual as well as in the mythology of divinities. Though confessing her own discomfort and even horror when hearing hymns glorifying the blood of Christ, Michelle Voss Roberts comes to a new understanding of and appreciation for the role of blood sacrifice through engaging Hindu deities such as Bhairava. This, in turn, leads her to a recovery of analogous ideas and feelings in the work of Julian of Norwich.

Daniel Joslyn-Siemiatkoski reflects on the scandal of the cross in dialogue with Judaism. He points to the fact that from a Jewish perspective, the cross may be regarded as an insult to God, whereas for Christians it became a marker of its separation from Judaism. In an attempt to develop a non-supersessionist approach to atonement, he draws from Heschel's and Moltmann's views of divine suffering to suggest a notion of covenantal belonging that would include both Israel and the Church. Though the suffering and the cross may represent a scandal for some, Elochukwu Uzukwu points to parallels in the experience of suffering, or "stretching," that healers in African traditional religions have to undergo in order to serve the larger community. A combination of suffering and prophecy is also evident in the self-understanding of many of the founders of African Independent Christian Churches. He discusses in particular the Antonine movement, which sought to bring about a purification and reorientation of Christianity in Africa, but whose foundress, Kimpa Vita, was burned at the stake by the official representatives of the Catholic Church.

The third part of the volume deals predominantly with attempts to re-interpret or expand the meaning of atonement and redemption in light of other religious traditions. One of the recurring critiques of the Christian concept of atonement is its tendency to abnegate moral agency and responsibility. In engaging the Jewish tradition, Marianne Moyaert raises up the problem of speaking of redemptive suffering in view of the Shoah. While acknowledging various important historical and contemporary Jewish critics, Moyaert still emphasizes the relevance of some form of substitutionary atonement in lifting the burden of preoccupation with personal responsibility and guilt that might otherwise threaten to crush individuals. In light of the Muslim critique of the moral depravity and arrogance that is associated with the notion of atonement, Ralston, for his part, shifts attention from the suffering and death of Jesus Christ to his resurrection. While the cross represents a sight of judgment of human sinfulness, the resurrection is a vindication of the life and teachings of Jesus, including his offer of forgiveness. It is also a vindication of all those who suffer unjustly and an expression of God's solidarity with those who work for justice. He argues that this emphasis on the resurrection rather than on the cross may serve as a bridge to Muslims, who also focus on the mercy and the forgiveness of God.

Mark Heim and Leo Lefebure point out that for Buddhism, the cross represents a problematic symbol, unintelligible at best and despicable at worst. Buddhist interpretations of the cross tend to emphasize its symbolic and exemplary function, rather than its penal and substitutionary functions. Rather than associating salvation with violence, Leo Lefebure approaches atonement from a Pure Land Buddhist perspective as a process of self-emptying by becoming one with Christ and one with God. The violent death of Christ is thus not regarded as essential or instrumental in the process of salvation. Atonement occurs in the collapse of theological and interpersonal dichotomies and in a movement toward compassion or love for others that is never completed in this world. For Mark Heim, the cross symbolizes the radical self-emptying of Christ, in accord with the notion of no-self and the emptiness of reality. While interpreting the cross from a Buddhist perspective, he also reaffirms the particularly Christian emphasis on the singularity of every individual and the inimitability of the event of atonement. The cross also stands for the identification of Jesus with the marginal, with the victim, and exposes our own tendency toward scapegoating. Though a Buddhist understanding of redemption will thus not replace traditional Christian self-understanding, it might at least preclude the glorification of suffering, or prevent any added personal suffering.

The comparative theological approaches to atonement presented in this volume offer only a sample of the insights that may be gained from constructive theological engagement with other religions. Each religion contains a wealth of texts, traditions, and teachings that may shed a different light on the question. This is evident in the diversity of approaches by comparative theologians dealing with any one tradition. Nevertheless, there is also a certain synergy in the work of comparative theologians dealing with particular religions, Christian-Buddhist comparative theologians stressing the symbolic meaning of the cross as a contestation of any reified conception of the self, Hindu-Christian comparative theologians focusing on the more aesthetic and contemplative dimensions of atonement, and Muslim-Christian comparative theologians struggling with how to deal with the preservation of the meaningfulness of atonement in light of a Muslim emphasis on personal accountability for sin and salvation. Every comparative theological exercise is inevitably shaped by the particularity of the tradition engaged.

Taken together, the contributions to this volume do not represent a unified approach. While many tend toward the exemplarist model of atonement, some reinforce the substitutionist model. Between the cross as symbol of the voluntary expiatory suffering for others and the cross as symbolizing self-effacement, non-attachment, and holy indifference, there continues to be a variety of ways in which the salvific power of the cross may be understood and experienced. It may serve as a symbol of hope or consolation, love or justice, solidarity, obedience, surrender, emptiness, reconciliation, freedom, or wisdom. This semantic indeterminacy illustrates the symbolic richness of the cross and the notion of atonement and the futility of attempting to capture it in a single theory.

Comparative theology does not aim or pretend to replace or supersede classical Christian theories of atonement. Neither does it seek to reduce traditional Christian views of atonement to the hermeneutical framework of another religion. Nor does it offer a comprehensive alternative theory or model. It mainly seeks to shed new light on certain aspects of the mystery. In focusing on particular dimensions of atonement through the lens of another religion, other dimensions may be missed or ignored.

It is the never-ending task of Christian theologians to attempt to make sense of the cross in changing historical and cultural contexts. The encounter with other religions offers a particularly fruitful context for rethinking traditional theories and conceptions of atonement and for broadening the horizons of interpretation. Because the ultimate goal is to inform and enrich the broader theological tradition, it is particularly important for comparative theologians to engage systematic theologians in mutually critical and constructive reflection on this most important article of Christian faith.[12]

Notes

1. These are discussed by Gustaf Aulén in *Christus Victor: An Historical Study of The Three Main Types of the Idea of Atonement*, trans. A. G. Herbert (New York: Macmillan Company, 1951), 143–59, and reformulated and summarized by Kathryn Tanner in *Christ the Key* (Cambridge: Cambridge University Press, 2010), 249.

2. Aulén, *Christus Victor: An Historical Study of The Three Main Types of the Idea of Atonement.*

3. Eleonore Stump, *Atonement* (Oxford: Oxford University Press, 2018).

4. Alister McGrath, *Christian Theology. An Introduction* (Oxford: Blackwell Publishers, 1994).

5. Rita Nakashima Brock and Rebecca Ann Parker, *Proverbs of Ashes: Violence, Redemptive Suffering, and the Search for What Saves Us* (Boston: Beacon Press, 2001); Delores Williams, "Black Women's Surrogacy Experience and the Christian Notion of Redemption," in *Cross Examinations: Readings on the Meaning of the Cross*, ed. Marit Trelstad (Minneapolis: Fortress Press, 2006).

6. Kathryn Tanner, *Christ the Key*, 247–73.

7. Elizabeth A. Johnson, *Creation and the Cross. The Mercy of God for a Planet in Peril* (Maryknoll, N.Y.: Orbis Books, 2018).

8. Stump, *Atonement*, 379.

9. Charles Hefling, "Why the Cross?: God's At-One-Ment with Humanity," in *The Christian Century* 130, no. 6 (2013): 24–27.

10. Ligita Ryliskyte, *"Cur Deus Cruciatus?*: Lonergan's Law of the Cross and the Transpositions of 'Justice over Power,'" (PhD diss., Boston College, 2020).

11. For an overview of different types of learning, see Cornille, *Meaning and Method in Comparative Theology* (Chichester: Wiley, 2019), 115–48.

12. I am deeply grateful to the Christian systematic theologians who have offered invaluable feedback to particular contributions in this volume: Dominic Doyle, Shawn Copeland, Jeremy Wilkins, Brian Robinette, Matthew Petillo, Elizabeth Antus, Frederick Lawrence, Matthew Kruger, Ligita Ryliskyte, Joy McDougall, Andrew Prevot, and Michael Himes.

Why Atonement?

Who Needs It?

ATONEMENT IN MUSLIM-CHRISTIAN THEOLOGICAL ENGAGEMENT

Daniel A. Madigan, S.J.

The place of the study of Islam within the "field" of Christian comparative theology is unique in various ways. Islam, like Rabbinic Judaism, offers a reading of the biblical and post-biblical tradition distinctly different from that proposed by the Christian tradition. Though it is of doubtful value to lump all three together under the rubric "Abrahamic," there is no escaping the fact that we inhabit the same world of discourse, and therefore Christian theology ignores these challenging voices to its own detriment.

Those of us in the "field" know how enriching for our theologizing is the careful attention we pay to the voice of the other, and this is particularly the case with Muslim voices, because Islam emerges from the Late-Antique religious matrix in which the key elements of Christian faith were still matters of active and often contentious debate.[1] Indeed, the Qur'ān and the early Islamic tradition bear witness to the fact that, in the seventh century, Christians had still not yet found a convincing, or even comprehensible, way to proclaim their faith in the God of Jesus Christ to the many who were prepared to believe in the God of Abraham and to recognize in the history of the People of Israel—including in the mission of Jesus—a privileged locus of God's engagement with humanity.

It is still the case today, sadly, that even the good-faith questions posed by Muslims, to say nothing of the polemical challenges that are often aired, tend to meet with the same unconvincing answers because our theologizing and our catechesis so often take place, if not in a closed circuit, at least in a world in which the major interlocutor is still too often the skepticism of modernity rather than the world of diverse living faiths. In the classroom, it becomes clear that what distinguishes Muslim students from Christians is not so much the particular questions they have about some central aspects of Christian faith, but the fact that the Muslims are ready to ask those (perfectly legitimate) questions out loud. The Christians often hesitate to probe too deeply lest the questions seem impious, or worse, lest they fail to find a convincing response.

Much of the vocabulary that clusters around the notion of atonement—"redemption," "expiation," "ransom"—finds little place in the Qur'ān and the Islamic tradition. To be sure, there are a number of words we might translate as "save" or "salvation," yet the configuration of these concepts is quite distinct from Christian Arabic usage.[2] As is well known, the Qur'ān denies at least the significance and perhaps even the very historicity of the death of Jesus. His cross—if, indeed, it was him on the cross—certainly plays no role in God's engagement with humanity. Although the Qur'ān recognizes both the murderous intent of Jesus's enemies, and his own readiness to accept the consequences of obedience to his mission, whatever took place seems to be read as a failure on Jesus's part, one that required divine intervention.[3] According to Ismaʿil Raji al-Faruqi, Islamic soteriology is "the diametrical opposite of that traditional Christianity. Indeed, the term 'salvation' has no equivalent in the religious vocabulary of Islam. There is no saviour and there is nothing from which to be saved. Man and the world are either positively good or neutral, but not evil."[4] For al-Faruqi, "*Falāḥ*, or the positive achievement in space and time of the divine will, is the Islamic counterpart of Christian 'deliverance' and 'redemption.'" Although he states it more forcefully than most, al-Faruqi's position is not unrepresentative of a substantial part of the tradition:

> Islam holds man to be not in need of any salvation. Instead of assuming him to be religiously and ethically fallen, Islamic *daʿwah* acclaims him as the *khalīfah* of Allah, perfect in form, and endowed with all that is necessary to fulfil the divine will, indeed even loaded with the grace of revelation![5]

Al-Faruqi sees this position as thoroughly modern and he encourages Christians to embrace it: "For modern Muslims and Christians the way out of the predicament of sin is in human rather than divine hands. Salvation is achieved by continuous education and each person must educate himself."[6] It is not just that the claimed atonement in Christ is deemed ineffective; in a "modern" mindset it is considered unnecessary. Damian Howard notes that Christian theology has already had experience with a similar condemnation of pessimistic views of sin in its engagement with secular modernity, which shares with al-Faruqi a similarly optimistic anthropology. We have responded, says Howard, "by stressing the value and goodness of human agency and the hope for humanity which comes in salvation through Christ."[7] However, he adds, the challenge for theology in this climate of perhaps inexplicable optimism about the human is "to ensure that the glory of the Cross is not lost from sight,"[8] that it is not simply jettisoned as surplus to requirement.

One of the most often repeated claims regarding the theological anthropology of Islam is: "There is no original sin in Islam." It is said by some, as we have seen, that there is no need of a savior, no need for atonement. These negations usually involve several elements. The following are some of the more important:

1. The Criticism that Christian theology is overly pessimistic and fails to recognize the goodness of God's human creation.
2. The charge that too much is made of the single transgression of Adam and his wife—such a small matter could not have had lasting consequences for all their offspring.
3. The questioning of any hereditary or social understanding of sin and guilt, with a concomitant stress on individual responsibility and culpability.
4. The affirmation that, like human transgression, divine forgiveness is a relatively straightforward matter. Forgiveness is a free act of divine sovereignty, costing God little, and so there is no need for a savior to effect for human beings something we are unable to do for ourselves.
5. The criticism that the supposed mechanism of redemption by the death of Jesus would only seem to multiply and deepen human sinfulness rather than heal it.
6. The objection that the Cross would seem to demonstrate the weakness rather than the power of God, who is inexplicably unable to save humanity without this maneuver.
7. The accusation that the Christian understanding of salvation short-circuits, as it were, the moral task and responsibility of the human person, that it leads too easily to an arrogant complacency about one's ultimate fate, and so to a passivity in the face of the world's needs.

As with most aspects of the Islamic critique of Christian faith, there are here salutary reminders about the possible traps into which Christian theologians may fall as we try to express what we believe about God and humanity. We do not want, after all, to merit the Qur'ān's accusation, initially leveled against unbelievers, that "these people have no grasp of God's true measure" (Q 39:67). Indeed, some Christian theologians also seek ways of understanding even the doctrine of atonement without any reference to original sin.[9] It may also be the case, however, that the Christian affirmation of original sin has some questions to pose to the Islamic tradition. Some of these points of mutual questioning will pinpoint irreducible differences in our theological anthropologies—differences that make us who we are and that cannot be abandoned. The close consideration of other questions, however, may uncover some more elements in common than we are accustomed to acknowledging.

This chapter has three tasks: to identify and acknowledge valid Muslim critiques of some Christian understandings of sin and salvation; to sketch a theology of sin and atonement that steers its way between the various pitfalls to which the Islamic critique points and yet remains true to Christian tradition; and to examine whether the Qur'ān's understanding of humanity's situation is as one-dimensional as some would suggest, or whether the Qur'ān might, in fact, offer some insights that would render a Christian theological anthropology somewhat more recognizable to Muslims. Rather than approach these three tasks one at a time in sequence, let me take each of the points of critique and attempt all three tasks with regard to each of them. It is important, however, to make five introductory points.

First, sin and redemption should not be thought of as sequential, but rather as concomitant. Our alienation from God, and God's activity to overcome that alienation so as to bring to fulfillment what God intended in creating us: both are continuing processes, and one does not simply finish when the other begins. As Rahner would put it, though we speak of them in temporal terms, one after the other, they exist in a circular relationship with each other. We cannot understand fully the nature of guilt except in the experience of being forgiven and of realizing from what we have been delivered.[10] This is why it is difficult to speak of original sin in isolation from atonement (literally at-one-ment, that is, making one). This is a key point to which we will return because an important element of the critique we are considering is an understandable dissatisfaction with the idea of sin having been completely dealt with, and of atonement as a *fait accompli*.

Second, as Charles Adams puts it, "The centrality of man's predicament as a sinner does not derive from logical considerations, nor even from the authority of revelation, but from the quality of life. If Christians speak of themselves as sinners, this is so because they feel themselves to be such."[11] That is to say, the *basic datum* for the doctrine of original sin is *not* the scriptural account of the sin of Adam and Eve, but rather the experience of human existence itself.[12] It might be more accurate to say that the sense of human alienation from God is the origin of the story of Adam and Eve's sin, rather than the other way around. This idea is much contested in the Islamic tradition. There, for the most part, the scriptural basis is paramount and usually taken to be historical; it is also perhaps less dramatic. However, as I discuss later, the evidence in the Qur'ān for a more complex view of human sin is often minimized.

Third, because the notion of original sin begins from reflection on humanity's existential situation, there will be many theologies of sin and of redemption, some more convincing than others. I do not attempt here to treat all of them, and certainly not to defend all of them.

Fourth, the discussion will privilege some of the most trenchant modern critics of the doctrines of original sin and atonement, not because they represent fully the Islamic tradition, but precisely because they are among the most searching and demanding.[13] The tradition obviously has various modes of conceiving of how humans might become one with God—the original and literal sense of at-one-ment—as well as conceiving of what it is that causes the alienation from God that needs to be overcome. Consideration of those will have to wait for another opportunity.

Fifth, I recognize that the readings of the Qur'ān offered here are not Muslim readings, and it is not the place of a Christian to enunciate an Islamic theology of sin and salvation. Nonetheless, I hope it becomes clear that a Christian reading the Qur'ān can recognize there some affirmations that seem to support at least some of what has been criticized in Christian theologies of sin and atonement.

The criticism that Christian theology is overly pessimistic and fails to recognize the goodness of God's human creation.

In his remarkable book on Christian ethics, Isma'il al-Faruqi dismisses the Christian understanding of sin as "an idealogical [*sic*] presupposition" rather than something based on observation. "Peccatism," as he dismissively calls the view of man as a sinner, "is not a view of man as he is, not a description of his reality, but the view of him which Christian dogma requires and then dictates."[14] Peccatism becomes an obsession with human weakness and goes hand in hand with "saviorism," the wrong-headed belief that humanity needs someone to effect what we are incapable of doing for ourselves, and that all that is necessary has been effected in Jesus. Al-Faruqi goes on to claim that the successively more exaggerated claims made for Jesus logically required a similar exaggeration of the evil from which he was believed to have saved humanity.[15] These are the key aspects of what he likes to call "Christianism" to distinguish it from the putatively original religion of Jesus.

Al-Faruqi neatly illustrates Adams's claim that "Muslims who do not find it important to give first priority in the religious lexicon to 'sin' can bypass the concept because it does not correspond to or express something essential in their perception of themselves."[16] Al-Faruqi would argue in response that, even though Christian theologians may have consistently maintained the "peccatist" position in theory, when it comes to practice, the general run of Christians follow what he would consider a more normal human ethic of worldly engagement and ethical self-improvement.[17] His observation is not far wide of the mark. Unfortunately, it did not prompt him to question whether his description of the "peccatist" position was accurate, or whether he might have needed to take more account of the Christian concepts of sanctification, and satisfaction for sin.

Eastern Christian theologies may have found a better balance between realism about human sinfulness on the one hand and a positive regard for God's human creation on the other. In seeking to explain some of the differences between Western and Orthodox theologies, Andrew Louth maintains that the East never lost sight of the primacy in God's intention and dealings with us of the "arc" that stretches from Creation to Deification. Humans departed from this arc, introducing sin, death, and destruction through the misuse of their freedom, and this needs to be dealt with. Thus a second, minor "arc" opens in the story, stretching from Fall to Redemption. However, there is always the risk that this minor arc can become the exclusive focus of the theologian's attention, at the expense of God's overarching purpose in creating human beings.[18] Perhaps what we see in al-Faruqi's critique is a reaction to such an overemphasis, particularly in the West, on the minor arc. The question remains, however, whether his vision takes seriously enough the amply demonstrated human alienation from God.

It is true that notions like Calvin's "total depravity" can lead to, or be mistaken for, fundamentally pessimistic views of human nature, views that ignore God's own judgment of creation that it was "very good"

(Gen. 1:31). Yet, that divine judgment is precisely what the doctrine of original sin seeks to protect. It insists that the alienation we sense between God and humanity has its origin not in God and God's good creation, but in human beings' free choices. The doctrine of original sin does not deny the innate dignity of the human person—a dignity that is, like human existence itself, entirely a gift. Rather, it underlines the difficulty humans have—and, we sense, always have had—in accepting and living that dignity.

In what does human dignity consist of? In being God's *khalīfa*, God's vice-gerent on earth; in being made in the image of God (according to Genesis and to a hadith). Although we have been given the ability to shape and to configure our world in various ways, both physically and spiritually—and this is what we commonly call "creativity"—we are not creators in an absolute sense. Both the Bible and Qur'ān limit the use of the verb "to create" to God alone. Our dignity is to be *muṣawwirūn*—those who can shape and give form to things that already have their existence, as we do, from the Creator. More to the point, it is our dignity that we are the only creatures on earth who are able exercise this kind of reflective and innovative, albeit derivative, creativity.

Yet within this dignity of being *muṣawwirūn*—creative creatures—there exists an inherent tension that makes it difficult to manage. We repeatedly try to dissolve the createdness-creativity tension by choosing one or other pole of it. We either seek a greater dignity—an autonomy apart from God and a god-like dominance over the rest of creation—or, on the other hand, we decline that dignity along with the responsibility it carries, and prefer to live as though we had not been given a share in God's shaping of the world. Each person experiences this tension in herself or himself and recognizes that it is of the nature of being human; it goes to our very origins—it is "original" in that sense. Notice that there is no external force of evil at the origin, only a free decision by human beings to decline the relationship God offers, and to mistrust God's intentions for us. It is here that we come to the second criticism.

The charge that the transgression of Adam and his wife is such a small matter that it could not have had lasting consequences for all their offspring.

If the sin of the first humans was simply a historical event of two people's disobedience against one of God's prohibitions, then indeed it would make little sense to imagine that it has such global repercussions. However, as I pointed out in the methodological matters previously, the starting point of the teaching on original sin is not the biblical witness but reflection on human experience. We can say that the biblical accounts in Genesis represent, as Karl Rahner would put it "an aetiological inference *from* the experience of man's existential situation in the history of salvation *to* what must have happened 'at the beginning' if the present situation of freedom actually is the way it is experienced."[19] The Adam and Eve story is not an eyewitness account, but a narrative that projects back to the very beginning of human decision-making the truth we sense about our own humanity in relationship to God.

The account itself signals to us that it is not an event in the realm of history—the knowledge of good and evil does not grow on trees (Gen. 2:9); snakes do not talk (Gen. 3:1); God does not walk in gardens in the cool of evening (Gen. 3:8). Nor does the account *explain* the origin of sin: Rather, it dramatizes it. It offers no theory as to why Adam and Eve would trust the words of the talking snake over the word of the God who created and blessed them, yet this is what it shows them doing. They are only too ready to believe that God is trying to keep them from having a clear vision of things and a higher dignity than that they already enjoy. The serpent easily convinces them that God is not to be trusted: Eating the forbidden fruit will not be the death of them; on the contrary, it will open their eyes and they could actually be like God, determining (literally, "knowing") good and evil (Gen. 3:5). Their act in eating that fruit was, in a sense, an act of despair:[20] They were made in the image and likeness of God (Gen. 1:26–27) but despaired of God's gift and came to believe that, if they wanted really to "be like God," they would have to unmask God's mendacity and take what was within their reach and rightly theirs. What they have rejected—what humanity senses it has rejected—is that peaceful relationship with God, that acceptance of God's self-communication,[21] quaintly expressed by the image of walking together in the garden (Gen. 3:8). They (we) have chosen rivalry over communion. When they are confronted with what they have chosen, they take another tack: They abandon even the dignity they had, and claim merely to have been unwitting pawns—the man in the hands of the woman, the woman in the hands of the serpent (Gen. 3:12–13).

Many Muslim interpreters have wanted to minimize the significance of the sin of Adam and his wife, not least because of a gradually developing orthodoxy about the impeccability of prophets, and the identification of Adam, perhaps surprisingly, as a prophet.[22] The emerging notion of the impeccability of Muḥammad had necessarily to also embrace his precursor prophets in order to be coherent. Because it was becoming unthinkable that a prophet would sin, then God's warning to Adam about the tree must only have been advice rather than command; so what the Qur'ān calls Adam's disobedience and error must really just have been a failure to take appropriate advice; what the Qur'ān calls his repentance could not have been repentance from sin because the Garden is not a place of testing that could result in sin. And so it goes.

Nonetheless, if we read the text without the prior commitment to a doctrine of impeccability, there are various elements in the Qur'ān's several retellings of the story that point to an awareness of the momentous nature of this first recounted human exercise of freedom.[23]

IBLĪS AND ARROGANCE

The sin of Adam is spoken of as a "slip" (Q 2:36). Humans are found forgetful and lacking in constancy (Q 20:115) and their lapse is followed immediately by repentance and forgiveness. However, the event is always linked in the Qur'ān with the influence of Iblīs. Perhaps we should say that Iblīs's sin of arrogance (*istikbār*—literally, considering oneself greater) is the first sin recorded, though he is not identified as human. Nonetheless, the arrogance that Iblīs demonstrated in his refusal to obey God and show respect for the newly created human being is precisely the attitude that the Qur'ān considers as fundamental to human sinfulness.

In fact, unbelief (*kufr*), "as man's denial of the Creator, manifests itself most characteristically in various acts of insolence, haughtiness, and presumptuousness."[24] The Qur'ān returns repeatedly to the figure of Pharaoh—his name occurs seventy-four times—and he becomes the archetypal enemy of God and humanity precisely in his arrogance—declaring himself to be his people's High Lord (Q 79:15–24; see also Q 26:24–29). Furthermore, Pharaoh leads his people into arrogance (for example, Q 20:79; 23:46).

IBLĪS'S TEMPTATION

Iblīs's whispering to Adam and his wife is recounted in two separate verses, tempting them in slightly different ways:

Satan whispered to the two of them so as to expose their nakedness, which had been hidden from them, and he said: "Your Lord only forbade you this tree so that you would not become angels nor become one of the immortals." (Q 7:20)

Satan whispered to him "Adam, shall I show you the tree of immortality and of a sovereignty that never decays?" (Q 2:120)[25]

These temptations are perhaps a little less strong than the suggestion of the serpent in Genesis 3:5 that, if they were to eat the fruit of the tree, Adam and Eve would become like God, knowing (that is, determining) what is good and evil. Nonetheless, Iblīs's offer in the Qur'ān, and the newly created humans' desire for it, are strikingly similar. Immortality and eternal sovereignty (*mulk*) are presented as being within reach, and God is said to be trying to keep us humans from them. The act of Adam and his wife in the Qur'ān, no less than in Genesis, seems to be a choice to treat God as a rival and to seek autonomy from God in an immortality and a lasting sovereignty that are not granted by God but grasped by humans in spite of God's prohibition.[26] Although many commentators will minimize Adam's sin, when the verses that speak of eating the fruit are read together with the verses that give the motivations for that transgression, it can be seen that disobedience of the first humans is anything but trivial.

The questioning of any hereditary or social understanding of sin and guilt, with a concomitant stress on individual responsibility and culpability.

The Islamic tradition is certainly right to insist that one person's act of disobedience is not to be imputed to another. If the story of the first parents were simply such a personal act, then there would be no reason to think it affects my moral status or yours, and this is a point where Christian theology needs to make more careful distinctions than it often does. Rahner is clear on this point: "Original sin in the Christian sense in no way implies that the original, personal act of freedom of the first person or persons is transmitted to us as our moral quality."[27] We rightly recoil from the idea that each newborn begins life with the personal moral status of a sinner, already carrying a debt incurred by her forebears. At the same time, however, it is almost impossible to conceive of a human being whose own freedom is not constrained in some way right from the beginning by the history and culture of sin into which she is born.

The Islamic tradition insists strongly on individual responsibility for wrongdoing and the impossibility of bearing another's burden:

> No burdened soul will bear the burden of another: even if a heavily laden soul should cry for help, none of its load will be carried, not even by a close relative. But you can only warn those who fear their Lord, though they cannot see Him, and keep up the prayer—whoever purifies himself does so for his own benefit—everything returns to God." (Q 35:18)

> Say, "People, the Truth has come to you from your Lord. Whoever follows the right path follows it for his own good, and whoever strays does so to his own loss: I am not your guardian." (Q 10:108)

> Whoever accepts guidance does so for his own good; whoever strays does so at his own peril. No soul will bear another's burden, nor do We punish until We have sent a messenger. (Q 17:15)

However, even if one accepts the importance of individual responsibility, frank reflection on our human experience leads us to recognize that even what seem our freest choices take place in an atmosphere and a history that has already long been marked by a rejection of God's offer, that the range of our choices and even our understanding of those choices is conditioned by our insertion in human community. Our freedom is not ours alone in isolation from other human beings.

In his *Political Theory of Islam* (1968), the Indo-Pakistani thinker Abul A'la Maududi describes the human predicament in ways that would be recognizable to someone holding a belief in original sin as we have been outlining it: the refusal of humanity to recognize its createdness, and its preferring to be like God.

> The pleasure of posing as a God is more enchanting and appealing than anything else that man has yet been able to discover . . . *The root cause of all evil and mischief* in the world is *the domination of man over man*, be it direct or indirect. This was the origin of all the troubles of mankind and even to this day it remains the main cause of all the misfortunes and vices which have brought untold misery on the teeming humanity.[28]

The desire to lord it over creation rather than to recognize our own creatureliness is the essence of human sin, and Maududi proposes that prophecy has always offered the cure for this, the warning to acknowledge only one Lord:

> The only remedy for this dreadful malady lies in the repudiation and renunciation by man of all masters and in the explicit recognition by him [of] God Almighty as his sole master and lord *(ilah* and *rabb)*. There is no way to salvation except this; for even if he were to become an atheist, he would not be able to shake himself free of all these masters *(ilahs* and *rabbs).*[29]

Although Maududi is surely right in his diagnosis of the fundamental human ill—the human desire to be god—he does not take full account of the extent to which such a desire conditions not only those who would wield quasi-divine power at the apex of political structures, but also the very cultural, political, and economic structures they control, in which we are all immersed and by which we are shaped. That is to say, everyone is involved in this deformation of our humanity, not just those in power.

Again, there are elements in the Qur'ānic accounts that might suggest that the sin of Adam and his wife goes beyond their personal transgression and involves humanity more broadly:

ADAM AND HIS WIFE UNDERSTAND THAT THEY HAVE
WRONGED THEMSELVES. YET THEY ARE THE FIRST-CREATED
SELVES FROM WHICH ALL OTHER SELVES COME.

They pray, "Our Lord, we have wronged our souls (or 'our selves' *anfusanā*): if You do not forgive us and have mercy, we shall assuredly be among the losers" (Q 7:23). The idea of sin as *zulm al-nafs* (wronging the self or the soul) is often appealed to in order to sustain an idea of isolated individual responsibility for sin. Yet in the case of Adam and his wife, the term *nafs* is freighted with meaning. After all, God has created humanity from a single soul or self *(nafs)*:

> O mankind! Be careful of your duty to your Lord, who created you from a single soul [*min nafsin wāḥida*] and from it created its mate [*zawj*] and from those two has spread abroad a multitude of men and women. (Q 4:1)

Adam and his *zawj* are not just any souls or selves; they are the selves at the origin of all selves, and those selves have been wronged. God's mercy and forgiveness are—like everything divine—eternal and unchanging, but it becomes clear as the Qur'ānic narrative continues that the history of human selves is filled with arrogance, with rejection, with *ẓulm* against God and God's creatures. The Qur'ān unmistakably depicts the origins of human history as marked by disobedience to God, and such disobedience is seen not only as an individual failing on the part of Adam and Eve: It was provoked by the bitterness of Iblīs, who had already been condemned for his arrogance in disobeying God for which he is to be expelled from the divine presence; and it has its sequel in Cain's murder of his brother.

IT IS DIFFICULT TO READ THE EXPULSION FROM THE GARDEN IN ANY WAY BUT AS A PUNISHMENT—A DISTANCING FROM GOD AND A MUTUAL ENMITY THAT AFFECTS ALL HUMAN BEINGS.

The same verb is used in banishing Adam and his wife as was used to banish Iblīs: *uhbiṭū / uhbiṭā / ahbiṭ*. In response to Adam's prayer for forgiveness in Q 7:23, God replies,

> All of you get out [*uhbiṭū*]! You are each other's enemies. On earth you will have a place to stay and livelihood—for a time. . . . There you will live; there you will die; from there you will be brought out. (Q 7:24–25)

Commentators argue that, because God's explicit intention in creating human beings was that they should live on earth, the expulsion from the Garden was perhaps not as punitive as it might seem; it was, they maintain, the expected sending to earth of the vice-gerent God had created. However, explanations that dissociate the disobedience from the expulsion often seem deliberately aimed at minimizing the significance of the disobedience of Adam and his wife by suggesting that there was no punishment, only immediate forgiveness.

THERE IS SAID TO BE AN ORIGINAL PURE NATURE ACCORDING TO WHICH GOD CREATED HUMANITY. WHATEVER NATURE THIS IS, IT IS SHARED BY ALL.

> So set your face firmly towards religion as a person of pure faith [*ḥanīfan*], consonant with the nature [*fiṭra*] according to which God created [*faṭara*] mankind—there is no altering God's creation. That is the right religion, though most people do not realize it. (Q 30:30)

It may well be that our original nature was innocent and not prone to sin or evil.[30] It may be the case that human beings were created with a natural tendency toward the recognition of the One God. However, it is clear even from the Qur'ānic narrative that human nature was from the very first moment capable of arrogance and disobedience and everything that follows from that. To recognize this is not to imply that human nature was defectively made. Rather, it is the very dignity and capabilities of the human being that made possible—perhaps even made likely—a sense of rivalry with the creator. This is what the Christian doctrine of original sin recognizes. Some say that human sin is only the result of forgetting one's true *fiṭra*, that the *fiṭra* itself remains pristine and unaffected.[31] However, it is difficult to see how fundamental to humanity this God-given nature could be if it can simply be forgotten. Is it not, rather, the choosing of an alternative understanding of the self in preference to the God-given self? If the *fiṭra* of the human being is, as I have suggested earlier, a combination of both creativity and creatureliness—both of which are God-given goods—then sinfulness would not involve so much a forgetting of one's nature, but rather an inability to handle the tension inherent in that nature, in being at the same time both creative and created.

In the traditions, the notion of *fiṭra* is often identified with the "natural religion" of Islam. In a hadith existing in several versions, Muḥammad is quoted as saying "No baby is born without being in the natural state [*fiṭra*]. It is his parents who make him a Jew or a Christian or a Polytheist."[32] Even if we accept that the *fiṭra* according to which God created humanity is principally a religious disposition, then according to this hadith one is apparently able to act against that innate disposition because of social context and pressure. Therefore, the *fiṭra* can scarcely be understood as something that would prevent us from inheriting the errors into which our forebears have fallen, nor from becoming involved almost congenitally in structures of sin.[33]

"INDEED THE SELF URGES TO EVIL." (Q 12:53)

Yusuf, or Joseph as he is known in Genesis, is one of the Qur'ān's great heroes. He refuses to excuse himself for the almost-consummated act of adultery with his Egyptian master's wife, Zulaykha, acknowledging the proneness—even more than the proneness, the driving, the urging—of the soul or self (*nafs*) toward evil. This is quite an admission, though the tradition tends to soften the impact by taking three references to the *nafs* in the Qur'ān—*al-nafs la 'ammāra bi-l-sū'* (the soul commands to evil, Q 12:53); *al-nafs al-lawwāma* (the reproaching soul, Q 75:2) and *al-nafs al-muṭma'inna* (the contented soul, Q 89:27)—and developing from those hints a typology of souls and states of soul that relativizes the self's urging toward evil, and makes it seem temporary or occasional. However, Yusuf's statement was more categorical. He did not speak of the soul insistently commanding to evil as though it were one of the souls, or a temporary state of soul. Rather, he seems to make a general statement about the soul or self:

> I do not absolve myself, for surely the soul is such as commands insistently to evil, and were it not for the mercy that my Lord has exercised . . .[34]
> My Lord is forgiving and merciful. (Q 12:53)

Yusuf expresses the perplexity and shame that all human beings experience—that there is something in us, profound enough to be called the self or the soul, that is at odds with the will of the Creator. Several other instances of the use of the term *nafs* make it clear that human life is constantly assailed not only from outside but by its own nature: tempted by whims and drives (for example, Q 53:23, 79:40), whispered to by the *nafs* in the same way the devil whispers. It is the *nafs* that convinced one of Adam's sons to kill the other (Q 5:30).[35]

The affirmation that, like human transgression, divine forgiveness is a relatively straightforward matter, requiring no savior figure.

Forgiveness is, so it is said, a free act of divine sovereignty, costing God little, and so there is no need for a savior to effect for human beings something we are unable to do for ourselves. Adam says in the Qur'ān, "If you do not forgive us and exercise mercy, we are assuredly among the losers" (Q 7:23). He recognizes as Yusuf does that there is indeed something we cannot do for ourselves. Only God's mercy and forgiveness can bring about a reconciliation with those who, through arrogant confidence in their own will and autonomy, have adopted a rivalrous attitude toward God. In the Qur'ānic narrative Adam's immediate repentance is met with an equally speedy forgiveness, and the account is considered settled. Polemicists ask why, if Adam repented and God accepted that act, there was any need for an atonement at all, at any price, let alone at the cost of an innocent life.[36]

This is a fair question and so a key issue for any understanding of atonement. Three aspects of it need to be addressed. First, it must be acknowledged that the underlying insight of the story is important: Divine forgiveness does not represent a change in God that is time-bound and so can be delayed. It is of the nature of God to be forgiving, and in that sense divine forgiveness is immediate. The question, however, is not whether divine forgiveness is complete and punctual, but rather whether human repentance is. The ongoing effect of the *nafs* that has been wronged in that first disobedience is well documented in the Qur'ān and in human experience.

Second, if the sin of Adam and Eve were simply the transgressing of a particular and perhaps even quite arbitrary divine prohibition, then it would be right to wonder why it is considered so catastrophic. However, what is being portrayed in mythical form in the Adam and Eve story is, in the Christian reading of the text, not simply a minor infraction against God's command, but rather the human rejection of God's free and loving self-communication. Even in the Qur'ān's account of the event, this "slip" is tied, as we have seen, to the desire for immortality and eternal sovereignty (Q 2:120).

Third, it is essential to affirm that the reconciliation Christians perceive to have been effected in Christ is the act of God, not the act of a "someone else" doing God's dirty-work for him. Christians must acknowledge that careless language on this matter can indeed make it seem as though God is somehow locked into a mechanism whereby God requires someone other than God's self to achieve a reconciliation. No; there can never be a condition or a process that locks God in. The only thing that could be said to condition God is God's being true to God's own nature.

Reconciliation in Christ is a free act of God—God freely acting out God's nature as merciful and self-giving. The mutual self-giving of the Father, the Son, and the Spirit is, of course, an eternal interrelation. However, in the incarnation, life, death, and resurrection of Jesus Christ humanity is drawn into this action and relation of mutual self-giving. Here at last is a human life lived completely according to the *fiṭra* (nature) God intended; here at last is one who does not treat God as a rival; who resonates completely and seamlessly with the Word through which all is created (Jn 1:3); who does "not consider equality with God something to be exploited for himself" (Phil 2:6); who does not feel he has to keep something for himself, but who in his living (and even in his dying) gives himself fully to expressing in his flesh and blood what God wants to express through him.

Much talk about atonement makes it seem to Muslim interlocutors—indeed, to any interlocutor—as though something is being done *for* God, or as though God needs something to be done in order "get over" his wrath and satisfy his wounded sense of honor. This is certainly one of the flaws in the many explanations that follow Anselm of Canterbury (d. 1109), who will be discussed further shortly. On the contrary, as the Nicene Creed puts it, God is doing something "for *us* human beings and for *our* salvation." As Christian faith would see it, in Christ there is now a renewed possibility of peace with God for every human person, if we choose to enter it, if we allow ourselves to be drawn by the spirit of God into that humanity that fully embodies what it is to be divine.

The criticism that the supposed mechanism of redemption by the death of Jesus would only seem to deepen sinfulness rather than heal it.

It is sometimes asked why, if the death of an innocent person were required to balance the sin of Adam, the death of his son Abel would not have sufficed?[37] Suggestions like this alert Christian theologians, perhaps, to how much talk about atonement suggests that this is an elaborate accounting procedure, a balancing of the books. Even if it were, Muslims understandably ask why the killing of Jesus is not thought to have marked the definitive break between humanity and God—a final bankruptcy, if you like—but rather is believed to have somehow made up the age-old "deficit" caused by the sin of the first humans by bailing them out with a massive injection of moral "capital."

It needs to be kept quite clear that, in spite of what can be the rather complex language of our theologies and the variety of understandings of atonement we develop, what is at issue is not a demand on God's part for the death of anyone. The death of Jesus was willed and carried out by human beings who could not bear and would not hear what he as God's Word was expressing.[38] What *God* willed and what God himself *carried out* was the enactment in a human life of the very nature of God. And God did this even though it was clear that it would provoke the same rivalrous violence that we sense has characterized human life since its beginning. It was not Jesus's killing that God willed, but rather Jesus's complete faithfulness to expressing mercy and compassion even when it was clear it would almost certainly lead to his death. It makes little sense to say that God willed the murderous rejection of his Word, as Muslims are not slow to point out.

In spite of the criticisms that can justly be leveled at Anselm's theories, he did recognize that God did not compel Christ to die, for in Christ there was no sin:

> Instead, Christ willingly underwent death—not by obeying a command to give up His life but by obeying the command to keep justice. For He persevered so steadfastly in justice that He incurred death as a result.[39]

Here I return to a point made briefly at the beginning: Because of the interrelationship of sin and salvation—a circular relationship Rahner calls it—we only fully understand them in the light of each other. For Christians, the depth of human rebellion against God and the full extent of God's mercy become visible together in the Christ event. Paul is often criticized for having deformed the religion of Jesus and having invented a new religion. Yet it was Paul who most clearly realized and expressed this insight about sin and redemption. In the moment of encounter on the road to Damascus—we could call it the moment of his *risāla*, his becoming an apostle—he came to a double realization: first, that the murderous rage he had thought of as righteous (Acts 8:1–3; 9:1; 22:3–4) was, in fact, directed against God, and second, how great was the mercy of God in forgiving him and commissioning him. *Pace* al-Faruqi, a lively sense of human sinfulness is not just an "ideological presupposition" upon which to construct an elaborate theory of atonement; rather it is the concomitant of a vivid sense of God's mercy.

One can certainly see in the Qur'ān a strong sense of sin. It certainly pulls no punches in its description of the almost universal human rejection of God's offer of guidance.[40] Romans 1:18–23 could very well be taken as a summary of Qur'ānic thought:

> The wrath of God is revealed from heaven against all ungodliness and wickedness of those who by their wickedness suppress the truth. For what can be known about God is plain to them, because God has shown it to them. Ever since the creation of the world his eternal power and divine nature, invisible though they are, have been understood and seen

through the things he has made. So they are without excuse; for though they knew God, they did not honor him as God or give thanks to him, but they became futile in their thinking, and their senseless minds were darkened. Claiming to be wise, they became fools; and they exchanged the glory of the immortal God for images resembling a mortal human being or birds or four-footed animals or reptiles. (NRSV translation)

What leads, perhaps, to the difference in our understandings of human nature and human sin is the difference in our understanding of what God is offering and what God has done to deal definitively with this state of affairs. In what seems to be the Qur'ānic way of thinking, God sends warning and guidance, threat and reminder to deal with a heedless and forgetful humanity, which is lost, following its own whims rather than the way that has been marked out for it. To put one's faith in that act of God's mercy places one at the beginning of a process of acting in accordance with that guidance and living toward resurrection and a divine judgment that will vindicate the faithful.[41] For the healing of the human condition Maududi prescribed obedience to the prophetic admonition to worship God alone. However, the malady he had rightly diagnosed—the human desire to be god—involves a rivalry with God that, Christians sense, no amount of divine commanding can resolve. As Paul recognized, any divine command is more likely to provoke human rivalry than to defuse it. In order to dissolve the rivalry and to dispel the notion that God is in some kind of power struggle with humanity, God allows God's self to be vanquished in this humanly conceived test of strength. God's glory consists not in beating humans at their own game, but in demonstrating personally and dramatically that God has a quite different "game" in mind. Love seeks not domination but communion, not victory but reconciliation.

It is certainly not out of order to question, as Muslim thinkers do, how pain and suffering inflicted on one person could atone for the moral failings of someone else, particularly when it is the guilty party who is inflicting the suffering, even to the point of killing. However, this question only makes sense if one thinks of atonement as compensation rather than as reconciliation. The death of Jesus is an essential element of atonement not because it was the price demanded by God, but because in that death Jesus was enacting the unconditional love that is the very nature of God. If we keep the focus on the fact that the atonement is something God is doing rather than something that is being done for God by someone else, and that what God is doing is "for us," as the creed says, then we may recognize in the death of Jesus the completeness of God's self-giving— God's self-communication—to us. God's communication is precisely a self-communication, not just an offer of knowledge or guidance, but an offer of God's very self. The offer comes undefended, disarmed, non-competitive; it holds nothing back. It is the human rejection of that offer that brings about Jesus's death. He notes (John 10:18) that his life is not taken from him by superior force; he freely lays it down, in the sense that he refuses to use force himself.

It is strangely fitting that this high-point in the history of the human rejection of God paradoxically becomes the central locus of God's reconciliation with us—the place where divine self-giving is joined to human self-giving in Jesus. Golgotha, where he is crucified, is a place accessible to all—no qualifications are needed to enter there. The point where, in the Christian understanding, God opens the divine life fully to humanity is not a place delimited by the sacrality of a temple, the perfection of law-observance, the learning of a synagogue, or the power of a palace. Humanity at its worst is at home there: jeering and cursing, brutalizing and violating, fickle and arrogant, as the gospels attest. There humanity does its worst, but its worst is not enough to vanquish divine love and close off the possibility of God bringing God's plan for humanity (that arc from creation to deification) to fulfillment. As Joshua Ralston explores in his essay in this volume, the resurrection is not a correction but rather God's vindication of the truth expressed in the Cross.

The objection that the cross would seem to demonstrate the weakness rather than the power of God, who is inexplicably unable to save humanity without this counter-intuitive maneuver.

The renowned Egyptian modernist thinker Muḥammad Rashīd Riḍā (d. 1935) accuses Christian missionary publications in his country of claiming that

> salvation from sin in the afterlife, and eternal life in the heavens, are only obtainable through the belief that God found no way to save mankind from the sin of his father Adam except by becoming incarnate in a human body, empowering over himself a group that was the most superior of

peoples, their crucifixion of Him, and His becoming cursed by the ruling of the divine law and shariʿa![42]

Put this way, of course, it does seem ridiculous. Who could believe such a thing without, as he puts it, extinguishing the light of his mind, and ruining the natural disposition of his soul?[43] Riḍāʾ has put his finger on a weakness in several Christian theories of sin and atonement, those that Eleonore Stump, in her extensive work on the subject, would classify as theories of the Anselmian kind, whether Catholic or Protestant.[44] What characterizes these theories is their insistence that the obstacle to God's forgiveness of human sin lies somehow in God. Because of God's justice, or honor, or goodness, God is actually unable to cancel the debt incurred by human sin. Human salvation, in Anselm's understanding, could not have been brought about unless humanity repaid what we owed to God. This debt was so large that, although only humanity owed it, only God was capable of repaying it. This seems to require that there should be a human being who is identical with God (the *Deus-homo*, in Anselm's language), and whose life, therefore, is so precious that, when it is given up, it can suffice to repay the debt owed for the sins of the whole world, and infinitely more besides.[45]

Here is yet another case in which classic Muslim critiques of Christianity identify a weakness in some Christian positions, a weakness that Christian theologians themselves come to acknowledge—not normally because of the Muslim critique, but because of the continual development of theology as reflection on the Gospel. It cannot be disputed that for the last millennium Anselm has shaped Christian thinking about the nature of human sin and the role of the Cross of Christ in dealing with it, and yet the Thomist theologian Eleonore Stump can argue from well within the Catholic theological tradition that Anselm's kind of interpretation of the atonement is irremediably flawed and cannot be salvaged.[46]

Unlike Anselm, but like many Muslim critics, Aquinas rejected the idea that it was impossible for humanity to be delivered from sin without the suffering and death of Christ. He maintained that there is nothing preventing God from forgiving sin without any "satisfaction" being paid:

> If [God] had willed to free man from sin without any satisfaction, he would not have acted against justice. . . . [I]f God remits sin, which has the formality of fault in that it is committed against himself, he wrongs no one: just as anyone else who, without satisfaction, overlooks an offense against himself acts mercifully and not unjustly.[47]

The incarnation, death, and resurrection of Jesus are not a pre-condition for God's exercise of mercy. Rather, they *are* the exercise of that mercy and its fullest expression. The free divine mercy expressed in the human life of Jesus encounters rejection by sinful humanity, a rejection that ends in his being killed. In his resurrection there is revealed the invincibility of that merciful love and the assurance that peace with God is still possible.

The accusation that the Christian understanding of salvation short-circuits the moral responsibility of the human person and leads to an arrogant complacency about one's ultimate fate.

This could be the most serious charge against many Christian understandings of salvation, and the point is well taken. Again al-Faruqi puts it starkly and repeatedly in his writings:

> While the redeemed life in Indian religion is not a life in space-time but in Nirvāna, life under the grace of Christ is either an *imitatio Christi*, i.e., a seeking of death at the hand of one's enemies; or monotonous proclamation of the news of the *fait accompli* redemption by Christ while awaiting the eschatological end of this-world as if it were a temporary, intermediate interlude, insignificant in itself, but important only on account of that to which it leads. In neither case is the only and final criterion of truthfulness to this-world realized, namely, whether or not man's vocation consists of diverting the causal threads of the cosmos towards a historical space-time reality in which all values are realized.[48]

> The only morality that can flow out of accomplished salvation necessarily robs man's life of its gravity, its seriousness and its significance.[49]

> In this scheme of things man remains a puppet. He is saved but not by his own agency, just as he had sinned, compelled by the necessity of creation being what it is. As a puppet, it is no wonder that the Christian who is a consistent saviourist is wide open to the spiritually fatal attacks of ethical complacency. It cannot be denied, for instance, that what European Christendom has allowed itself to do vis-à-vis the non-Christian world during the last five centuries . . . is an effect of that self-righteousness which saviourism breeds and nourishes.[50]

Thus, it takes something more than redemption, in the sense of forgiveness and release of ethical energies, to achieve salvation, in the sense of ethical felicity, or realizing value in space-time. It takes a life of danger, of disturbing the flow of space-time, of deflecting its threads toward value-realization, the bringing about of the *matériaux* of value and filling the world therewith.[51]

Rashīd Riḍā also derides the notion that salvation follows from unquestioning assent to the idea of atonement regardless of moral status:

Whoever . . . accepts this principle [of the atonement], is one saved, one who inherits the highest heavens, even if he kills, commits adultery, drinks alcohol, obtains the property of the people through deceit, treats worshippers unjustly, and is the bane of civilization.[52]

However, Christians too recognize that there are understandings of *sola fide* and *sola gratia* that lead to what has been called "grace-ism," and which might seem to be precisely what al-Faruqi is attacking in his dissatisfaction with faith as merely intellectual assent and with salvation as a *fait accompli*.[53] Thus, Scot McKnight:

Regarding this grace-ism, who has not heard that grace means "God's riches at Christ's expense" or that it means "pure gift" or "God's unconditional love" or, from a different angle, "God's mercy to those who don't deserve it." One also hears what follows: you don't have to do a thing, you don't have to worry, it's all been done for you, just sit back and relax in this unconditional grace of God.[54]

Addressing particularly an Evangelical Christian audience, Matthew Bates seeks to rethink the key terms of the language of salvation. In particular, he proposes understanding the key Pauline term *pistis* as "allegiance" in the sense of a way of living, rather than as "faith" thought of as simply an assent. The version of the Gospel that he says he consistently encountered growing up could easily pass as one of al-Faruqi's or Rashīd Riḍā's caricatures:

(1) we are all perniciously bent on trying to earn our salvation by doing good deeds; (2) yet all have sinned and fallen short of the glory of God—and that includes *you*; (3) but the good news is that Jesus died for your sins; (4) so if you will just believe this and pray along with me, then the free gift of eternal life is yours today. And now the warning: the only thing that you must not under any circumstances do is believe that you

can earn your salvation through good works, for this was the mistake of many Jews in Paul's day and is still the error of the Catholics today.[55]

Bonhoeffer's denunciation of what he calls "cheap grace" is invoked in Bates's critique. Discipleship has a cost:

> Cheap grace means grace sold on the market like cheapjack's wares. The sacraments, the forgiveness of sin, and the consolations of religion are thrown away at cut prices. Grace is represented as the Church's inexhaustible treasury, from which she showers blessings with generous hands, without asking questions or fixing limits. Grace without price; grace without cost! The essence of grace, we suppose, is that the account has been paid in advance; and, because it has been paid, everything can be had or nothing. . . . Cheap grace means grace as a doctrine, a principle, a system. It means forgiveness of sins proclaimed as a general truth, the love of God taught as the Christian "conception" of God. An intellectual assent to that idea is held to be sufficient to secure remission of sins . . . Cheap grace is grace without discipleship, grace without the Cross, grace without Jesus Christ, living and incarnate.[56]

This comparison of Muslim and Christian texts on this area of criticism shows that Christians do have a case to answer when it comes to taking seriously the moral task of the believer and the relationship of ethical action to salvation. This is the case particularly with Anselmian understandings of atonement, where the entire burden of obedience and faithfulness falls on Jesus and is imputed to others in what can look like a simple accounting transaction. Thomistic and other approaches, however, recognize the importance of human ethical cooperation with divine grace, not simply as a satisfaction owed to God, but with a strong sense of the transformation that is needed to deal with human guilt and shame, and to reestablish the bonds of human community ruptured by sin.[57]

Conclusion

Consideration of these quite forceful Muslim criticisms of the doctrine of Original Sin and of the Atonement that Christians believe God is effecting in Christ has highlighted a number of areas where the critique can often be justified: the excessive pessimism about God's good creation; the facile notions of an inherited moral status; the positing of some incapacity on God's part to forgive without an elaborate mechanism to supposedly resolve a debt of honor; the understanding of salvation as a *fait accompli* that absolves humanity from any further ethical struggle. What has also been shown is that diversity of opinion on these key theological questions does not simply divide along confessional lines. Christian theologians would share some of the same reservations Muslims express about ways of understanding these teachings. Similarly, some Muslim thinkers recognize well enough the concerns that Christian thinkers bring to questions of theological anthropology and soteriology: We all have to grapple with the origins of human sin; we all have the experience of being immersed in cultures and civilizations in which human sin is so deeply ingrained as to be almost inescapable; we all agree that God takes sin seriously.

At the same time, as people who claim to believe in a God whose self-definition rests centrally on mercy (Qur'ān 6:54; Exodus 34:6), we are necessarily faced with the question of how the two realities of mercy and sin are to be understood in relationship. We clearly differ about where and in what way the merciful God has acted decisively in history to deal with our alienation. For both traditions, God deals with human sinfulness through the divine Word. In one case, it is understood to be through God's word of clear warning, reminder, and guidance in the history of prophecy culminating in the Qur'ān, which delineates and smooths the path of faithful obedience. In the other, God deals with sin by bearing it in a humble identification with humanity through the Word incarnate, who himself has become the space of at-one-ment, where, as the Qur'ān might put it, "God is pleased with them and they are pleased with God" (Q 58:22; 9:100). There is clearly much more to be explored in our theological engagement, as we try to move beyond the shallow caricatures of one another's positions that have fueled centuries of polemics.

Notes

1. Klaus von Stosch's contribution to this volume explores some Christological disputes taking place in the Byzantine Empire at the time of Islam's emergence. Sophronius, Patriarch of Jerusalem at the time of the Muslim conquest of the city in 634 CE, had for some years been a major figure in Christological arguments that would seek a resolution at the Third Council of Constantinople in 680–81 (monoenergism and monotheletism. Von Stosch proposes a connection between some rather enigmatic words in the Qur'ān and the Julianist Christology in vogue at the time. However, to say that the affirmation that Jesus and Mary ate food is a particular reference to Julianist christologies— note that a similar point is made about Muhammad in Q 25:7—and that this reference can be read as "a very detailed response" to the prevailing tendencies in Byzantine theology is perhaps to claim too much.

2. See Maurice Borrmans, "Salvation," in *The Encyclopaedia of the Qur'ān*, ed. Jane Dammen McAuliffe (Leiden: Brill, 2001–08), 4:522–24. See also Daniel A. Madigan "Criterion" in ibid., 1:486–87.

3. For a presentation of both pre-modern and modern readings of the Qur'ānic verses in question, see Abdullah Saeed, *Reading the Qur'ān in the Twenty-first Century: a Contextualist Approach* (Abingdon: Routledge, 2014), 129–46. See also Joshua Ralston's essay in this volume.

4. Isma'īl Raji al-Faruqi, *Islam and Other Faiths*, edited by Ataullah Siddiqui (Leicester: The Islamic Foundation, 1998), 15.

5. al-Faruqi, "On the nature of Islamic *da'wah*," 316f., cited in Charles D. Fletcher, "Isma'īl al-Faruqi (1921–1986) and Inter-Faith Dialogue: The Man, The Scholar, The Participant" (PhD diss., McGill University, 2008), 225. See also Fletcher, *Muslim-Christian Engagement in the Twentieth Century: The Principles of Interfaith Dialogue and the Work of Isma'il Al-Faruqi* (London: I. B. Tauris: 2015).

6. al-Faruqi, "Islam and Christianity: Diatribe or dialogue," reprinted in al-Faruqi, *Islam and Other Faiths*, 242.

7. Damian Howard, "Christians and Muslims in Tomorrow's Europe," *Studies: An Irish Quarterly Review* 105, no. 419 (Autumn 2016): 299.

8. Ibid.

9. See von Stosch's discussion of Pröpper's Christological proposal in this volume.

10. Karl Rahner, *Foundations of Christian Faith: An Introduction to the Idea of Christianity* (New York: Crossroad, 1978), 93.

11. Charles J. Adams, "Islam and Christianity: the opposition of similarities," in *Logos Islamikos: Studia Islamica in Honorem Georgii Michaelis Wickens*, ed. Roger M. Savory and Dionisius A. Agius (Toronto: Pontifical Institute of Mediaeval Studies, 1984), 296.

12. Rahner, *Foundations of Christian Faith*, 110: "We arrive at the knowledge, experience and the meaning of what Original Sin is, in the first place, from a religious-existential interpretation of our own situation, from ourselves."

13. Some more classical critiques are presented in Joshua Ralston's essay in this volume.

14. al-Faruqi, *Christian Ethics: A Historical and Systematic Analysis of Its Dominant Ideas* (The Hague: Djambatan,1968), 221.

15. al-Faruqi, *Christian Ethics*, 229.

16. Adams, "Islam and Christianity," 296.

17. al-Faruqi, *Christian Ethics*, 219.

18. Andrew Louth, *Introducing Eastern Orthodox Theology* (Downer's Grove, Ill.: Intervarsity Press, 2013), 69–70.

19. Rahner, *Foundations of Christian Faith*, 114.

20. Michael Himes made this point in the symposium that was the origin of this volume.

21. Rahner, *Foundations of Christian Faith,* 114.

22. There is a great deal of popular literature on the impeccability of prophets, even though it is difficult to square with so many explicit statements in the Qur'ān. On the emergence of this orthodoxy, see Shahab Ahmed, *Before Orthodoxy: The Satanic Verses in Early Islam* (Cambridge: Harvard University Press, 2017), in particular 278–80 with regard to pre-Islamic prophets as typological prefigurements of Muḥammad.

23. Perhaps the covenant event of *a-lastu bi-rabbikum* (Q 7:172) should be considered the first act of human freedom. However, the Qur'ān presents that primordial event,

where God asks all humanity to bear witness that He is their Lord, as a prehistoric witness of faith that can be used against those who at the judgment would claim not to be responsible for their failures to acknowledge the authority of God.

24. Toshihiko Izutsu, *Ethico-Religious Concepts in the Qur'ān* (Montreal: McGill University Press, 1966), 120.

25. Note the occurrence in the two verses of the root *m-l-k*. In Q 7:20, it is presumed to relate to angels, though *Tafsir al-Jalālayn* notes that it can be read differently as *malikayn* "kings." In 2:120 it is the abstract noun *mulk*—power, authority, possession.

26. Note how this is echoed in the important Christological hymn of Philippians 2:5–11. In the garden, humans reach out to grasp what they think will make them "like God." Christ Jesus, says Paul, did not think that his identity with God was something to be grasped for himself (*harpagmon*). See Jean-Luc Marion, "Dieu et l'Ambivalence de l'Être," *Transversalités* (Paris) 125 (2013): 170.

27. He continues: "In Original Sin the sin of Adam is not imputed to us. Personal guilt from an original act of freedom cannot be transmitted, for it is the existentiell "no" of personal transcendence towards God or against him. And by its very nature of this cannot be transmitted, just as the formal freedom of a subject cannot be transmitted. . . . For Catholic theology, therefore, original sin in no way means that the moral quality of the actions of the first person or persons is transmitted to us, whether this be through juridical imputation by God or through some kind of biological heredity, however conceived" (Rahner, *Foundations of Christian Faith*, 11).

28. Sayed Abul A'la Maududi, *The Political Theory of Islam* (Lahore: Islamic Publications Limited, 1968), 8–13. Italics in the original.

29. Maududi, *Political Theory*, 15.

30. For a helpful description of the various ways this is conceived in Islamic tradition, see Yasien Mohamed, "The Interpretations of Fiṭrah," *Islamic Studies* 34, no. 2 (1995): 129–51. A more extensive treatment of some key thinkers is available in Ovamir Anjum, *Politics, law, and community in Islamic thought: The Taymiyyan Moment* (Cambridge: Cambridge University Press, 2012).

31. See, for example, Şaban Ali Düzgün, "The Capabilities Embedded in to the Human Nature/Fitra," *Journal of Islamic Research* 27, no. 3 (2016): 213–19: "In this context *fiṭra* is maximally great—so perfect and splendid that nothing greater is conceivable than it. It is the criterion according to which other criteria of life should be evaluated and checked."

32. Various forms of this hadith are recorded in *Saḥīḥ Muslim*, *kitāb al-qadr* (the book of destiny).

33. Human obstinacy in following the errors of the forebears is a recurrent refrain in the Qur'an. See, for example, Q 2:170: "And when it is said to them, 'Follow what God has sent down,' they say, 'No; but we will follow such things as we found our fathers doing.' What? And if their fathers had no understanding of anything, and if they were not guided?" See also Q 7:28; 7:70–71; 11:62, 87; 14:10; 21:53–54; 26:74–76; 31:21; 34:43; 37:69–70; 43:22–23.

34. Joseph's statement trails off here, referring to what had already been said in Q 12:24: "She wanted to have intercourse with him, and he wanted to have intercourse with her [and would have] if he had not seen the evidence of his Lord." Early Qur'ān commentators are quite graphic in their descriptions of how close they were to consummating

their desires. See, for example, Fudge's account of al-Tabrisī's discussion in Bruce Fudge, *Qur'ānic Hermeneutics: al-Tabrisī and the Craft of Commentary* (London: Routledge, 2011), 103–7.

35. For a broad description of the Qur'ān's understanding of human nature, see Mona Helen Farstad, "Anthropology of the Qur'ān," in J. D. McAuliffe, ed., *Encyclopaedia of the Qur'ān* (Brill Online, 2016), dx.doi.org/10.1163/1875-3922_q3_EQCOM_050509.

36. See, for example, al-Qarāfī's *al-Ajwibat al-fākhira* recounted in Diego Sarrió Cucarella, *Muslim-Christian Polemics Across the Mediterranean: The Splendid Replies of Shihāb al-Dīn al-Qarāfī* (Leiden: Brill, 2015), 207.

37. Ibid., 207–8.

38. For a discussion of contemporary criticisms of atonement theory as sacralizing violence, see the contribution of Leo Lefebure in this volume.

39. Anselm of Canterbury, *Cur Deus Homo*, Book I, Chap. 9. Anselm goes on to say, "But it can also be said that the Father commanded Christ to die when He commanded the thing in consequence of which Christ incurred death." That may just be logical precision, but later in the same chapter he goes a step further—far enough to reveal a serious flaw in his theory: "[Jesus] speaks of the Father's will not in the sense that the Father willed the Son's death rather than the Son's life but in the sense that *the Father was unwilling for the human race to be restored unless man performed some deed as great as Christ's death was to be*. . . . Therefore, the Son says that the Father wills His death, which He, the Son, prefers to undergo rather than to see the human race not be saved." Anselm of Canterbury, *Complete Philosophical and Theological Treatises of Anselm of Canterbury*, trans. and introduction by Jasper Hopkins and Herbert Richardson (Minneapolis: A. J. Banning Press, 2000), 312–14.

40. See Daniel A. Madigan, *The Qur'ān's Self-Image: Writing and Authority in Islam's Scripture* (Princeton: Princeton University Press, 2001), 102–3.

41. This rather exoteric understanding is not the only strand of Islamic thought by any means and one does not want to reduce the definition of Islam to a core of legal observances. A very significant strand of Islamic thought when considering "at-one-ment" is the unitive way of the Sufi, but that will have to wait for another time for deeper exploration. However, it should be noted that the kind of unity envisaged in that way tends to focus more on the unity of all existence than on the embodied "at-one-ing" of loving will and action between humanity and God that Christian faith would see as constituting the ultimate sharing in the divine life.

42. Muḥammad Rashīd Riḍā and Simon Wood, *Christian Criticisms, Islamic Proofs: Rashīd Riḍā's Modernist Defence of Islam* (Oxford: Oneworld, 2008), 137.

43. Ibid.

44. Eleonore Stump, *Atonement* (Oxford: Oxford University Press, 2018), 21–23 and passim.

45. Anselm, *Cur Deus Homo*, particularly Book II, Chapters 6–7.

46. Not all the current critiques of Anselm are as carefully thought through as that by Stump, *Atonement*, 23–27, 71–112. See also Elizabeth A. Johnson, *Creation and the Cross: The Mercy of God for a Planet in Peril* (Maryknoll, N.Y.: Orbis Books, 2018).

47. Aquinas, *Summa Theologica*, trans. Fathers of the English Dominican Province (London: Burns Oates & Washbourne, 1920), 3.46.2 ad 3.

48. al-Faruqi, "On The Raison d'Être of the Ummah," *Islamic Studies* 2, no. 2 (1963): 164.

49. al-Faruqi, "Islam and Christianity: Prospects for dialogue," *Sacred Heart Messenger,* (September 1967): 29–33; here 33. Cited in Fletcher, op. cit., 188.

50. al-Faruqi, *Christian Ethics,* 236.

51. al-Faruqi, "Islam and Christianity: Problems and perspectives," in James P. Cotter, ed. *The Word in the Third World* (Washington: Corpus Books, 1968), 177ff.

52. Riḍā, *Christian Criticisms,* 137.

53. See Joshua Ralston's essay in this volume.

54. Scot McKnight, Foreword in Bates, *Salvation by Allegiance Alone,* x.

55. Matthew W. Bates, *Salvation by Allegiance Alone: Rethinking Faith, Works, and the Gospel of Jesus the King* (Grand Rapids: Baker Academic, 2017), 21.

56. Dietrich Bonhoeffer, *The Cost of Discipleship* (New York: Touchstone, 1995), 43–45.

57. For an excellent treatment of this, see Stump, *Atonement,* 39–70.

Christian Atonement Enlightened by a Buddhist Perspective on Craving

Thierry-Marie Courau, O.P.

Atonement in Christianity is linked to many theological concepts and metaphors (reconciliation, justification, participation, restoration, redemption, ransom, sacrifice, forgiveness, payment, cleansing, expiation, appeasement, propitiation, substitution, and so on), all referring to salvation through Christ for all people. All are saved in Christ. Ephesians 1:7 states it thusly: "In him we have redemption through his blood, the forgiveness of our trespasses, according to the riches of his grace."

We need not return to numerous debates concerning atonement's conceptualizations or definitions to focus on the general concept of salvation as the process of making humans righteous. Christianity proclaims that justification is realized by way of atonement through Christ's blood, which is the consequence of Jesus's act of total obedience to the Father. However, we might ask ourselves, what are the real stakes of Christian salvation, and what are we saved from? In order to develop an understanding of this essential element of faith for our current times, I focus here on some central biblical texts on the subject along with key Buddhist concepts.

Among so many possibilities for addressing the topic of redemption in the scriptures, I chose to focus on three passages central to Christian soteriology: Paul's letter to the Romans, chapter 5; his first letter to the Corinthians, chapter 15; and his letter to the Philippians, chapter 2.[1] These texts represent the movement of salvation history: a humanity, continuously created by God, stuck in sin, and led to final salvation in Jesus Christ. This brings us back to the narrative of Genesis 2–3 and its symbolic account of the process of man's making of evil, the process of sin.

Then, I use an Indo-Tibetan lamp: the Lam Rim, i.e., the Progressive Path (to Enlightenment), a textual tradition at the heart of current Tibetan

Buddhist practices. Through it, I approach the fundamental Buddhist concept of *duḥkha*,[2] which offers an alternative reading to Christianity's vision of the origin of misfortune and death, as well as of the path toward happiness and life, realized in and by Jesus Christ. Although the experiences, contexts, and paths of Buddhist deliverance are distinct from those of Christian salvation, the diagnosis on humanity's responsibility for the rise of non-satisfaction points to at least two things: the identification of the problem as the act of craving-grasping, and its resolution as progress on the path of deliverance. Using this singular anthropological approach as a lamp on the Christian doctrine of redemption may shed new light on how humanity might approach and taste salvation today.

Salvation Realized in Christ

The fifth chapter of Paul's letter to the Romans is about salvation by faith. Humans receive grace that makes them righteous by faith (Romans 5:1). This is offered through the One who has established justice by giving himself up to death. The proof of the great love of God is in his having given the Son for the salvation of all. Humans need salvation because they are sinners. Because they have broken their relationship with God, they have lost life and have become subject to death (5:12). Reconciled with Him in the dead and resurrected Christ, they share in his life (5:10–11).[3] This is salvation.

> For if while we were enemies, we were reconciled to God through the death of his Son, much more surely, having been reconciled, will we be saved by his life. But more than that, we even boast in God through our Lord Jesus Christ, through whom we have now received reconciliation. (Romans 5:10–11)

The mystery of redemption and atonement is summarized in verses 12 to 21, with an insistence on a comparison between Adam's disobedience and Jesus Christ's obedience: "[A]s by the one man's disobedience the many were made sinners, so by the one man's obedience the many will be made righteous" (Romans 5:19).

Paul develops his concept of salvation in relation to the narrative of the sin of Adam. Reconciliation and redemption in Christ can thus not be understood without reference to this sin. If Adam prefigures Christ, it is for the purpose of creating contrast.[4] Here, Paul is building an opposition between trespass and gift, sin and grace, death and life. This opposition is accentuated by playing with the literary argument "one man": by one man comes sin (5:12ff); only one man fulfills justice (5:15ff). By one, all are introduced into sin and death. By one, all are made righteous and redeemed from death (5:18). This strengthens the free gift of salvation and grace of God through Christ for all. Christ died for humans who reside in death and are unable to save themselves. Redemption is accomplished through Christ by the total and gratuitous giving up of his human life, until death. Through this act, righteousness is realized and life is given to all humans:

> [L]aw came in, with the result that the trespass multiplied; but where sin increased, grace abounded all the more, so that, just as sin exercised dominion in death, so grace might also exercise dominion through justification leading to eternal life through Jesus Christ our Lord. (Romans 5:20–21)

In this chapter 5, there is an interweaving of justification, faith, free gift of grace, life, reconciliation, love of God, gift of the Holy Spirit, eternal life, access to grace, peace with God, and participation in God's glory. The love of God is for sinners (5:8). He gives them his life through Christ. Nothing is asked of humans in return. However, life given freely and without conditions to every person highlights the peculiar effect of sin: the break with God. The relationship between humans and God and between individuals themselves is hurt, damaged, spoiled, messed up, broken. So, humans are missing out on life. From this, a cry for salvation goes up to God.

Restorer of Relationship

If sin is, according to Paul's Adamic model, a human's act and process of hurting and breaking the relationship with God and others, how does "one man," Jesus Christ, have the ability to re-establish it, for all humans? This man is also God the Son, who receives everything from the Father. What Jesus lives in his humanity is received in his divinity, and vice versa. According to the Chalcedonian formulation, "Christ is a single subject: Son of God, made present in our humanity. He is not only associated with the human nature of Jesus. He is the only subject of existence and action. But its operations, its activities, are mixed: human and divine, in synergy and without confusion."[5] He is God as Son coming into humanity and totally assuming the human condition, living among a people whose relationship with God is wounded. He lives within sin's flesh without knowing sin (2 Corinthians 5:21). Having become a part of humanity, God the Son lives a relationship of total listening, of complete obedience to God the Father (Romans 5:19, Philippians 2:8).

One human's obedience is decisive for making redemption possible.[6] Jesus establishes for the "first time" a full, complete, living and loving relationship between humans and God where there had been between humans and God and among humans themselves, damaged, broken, and dead relationships. Potential loving relationships were exchanged from the "beginning" into relations of power, distrust, submission, and protest. A full and total obedience was only realized by and through this man in the most dramatic situation that can exist. Jesus's choice was between giving himself to an unjust death, despite having the power over the one who decided to put him to death (John 19:11) and continuing to live but in denial of himself, in denial of who he is and for whom he has come.[7] If he had denied himself, he would have broken his relationship with God who chooses, by his act of creation, to commit himself forever to his creatures. God's creative act is done through his Word, God the Son, God's love-recipient. In the acceptance of his death, Jesus's lived faith bears witness to the power of the life of the One whom he obeys, the One from whom he never ceases to receive all things, including love and righteousness. This acceptance in faith, in total dependence upon the Father, makes him righteous. The result is Jesus the Christ. From birth to death, a human never broke his relationship with God in any situation, including his cry of distress on the cross. In other words, he never knew sin during his human existence. On the cross, his cry is itself testimony to his relationship with God, even when the unacceptable happens (Hebrews 5:7). His obedience went to the extreme (Hebrews 5:8). And his obedience to the Father, totally listening to him, is also obedience to humanity, listening to it: to its distress, its chaos, its quest for life, its query for the meaning of life.

The shape of the world changes through Christ. God experiences humanity in its extreme weakness by coming into the flesh. The relationship restored, God's grace can flow in human nature without obstacle, re-establishing the potentiality of relationship between humanity and God. And humanity experiences God's power in Jesus's death, being introduced into the loving divine life by his resurrection. That this man, without sin and therefore in relationship with the Father, who receives all from the Father, accepts death in this way, without escaping, by choosing to welcome his murderers as he welcomes the Father, welcomes all humanity in him and leads them to the Father. Drawing a comparison with contemporary cosmology, we could say that humanity is carried away in his wake, immersed in his life, as a black hole irrevocably attracts all within its reach. Totally attentive to God, totally available, he is the unreserved recipient of the fullness of the Father's love, even in death. Through his death, the life that was in the Son spreads among the multitude (Hebrews 5:9). "God's love has been poured into our hearts through the Holy Spirit that has been given to us" (Romans 5:5). The whole of humanity is touched by this life and grace, whether consciously or not. The creature is forever related to Creator through the death and resurrection of Christ.

The First Human

In Romans 5, Paul plays with the expression "one man" for opposing obedience to disobedience, Christ's obedience to Adam's disobedience. However, in his first letter to the Corinthians, he focuses on Adam, the "first human": "The first man, Adam, became a living being."[8] This sentence appears in a section on the relation between the physical and the spiritual, concerning the resurrection of the dead (1 Corinthians 15:35–56):

> It is sown a physical body; it is raised a spiritual body. If there is a physical body, there is also a spiritual body. Thus, it is written, "The first man, Adam, became a living being"; the last Adam became a life-giving spirit. But it is not the spiritual that is first, but the physical, and then the spiritual. (1 Corinthians 15:44–46)

Here, humanity in its physicality comes first. The first human is no less the whole of humanity, humanity in its physicality, designated under the name Adam. Paul's Greek text can literally be translated as "Adam in a living psyche" (Ἀδὰμ εἰς ψυχὴν ζῶσαν).

The apostle then considers the "last Adam," Adam of last times, Adam of the *eschaton*:[9] "Adam in a life-making spirit [Ἀδὰμ εἰς πνεῦμα ζῳοποιοῦν]." The lack of reference to "the human" here leads commentators to link the eschaton's Adam to Christ. But the broader context suggests that Paul has not only Christ in mind but humanity in its spiritual future, its future in the life of the Spirit. This move is less an opposition between "the first sinner" in his "disobedience" and the righteous one in his obedience than a contrast between the human beings in their physicality first and then their life in Christ's spirit, as shown by both prior and following verses.[10] The spiritual (πνεῦμα) is related to breath and to life. Subsequently, Paul uses another opposition, not between "first" and "last" (1 Corinthians 15:45), but between "first human from earth, dusty" and "second man, from heaven":[11]

> The first man was from the earth, a man of dust; the second man is from heaven. As was the man of dust, so are those who are of the dust; and as is the man of heaven, so are those who are of heaven. Just as we have borne the image of the man of dust, we will also bear the image of the man of heaven. (1 Corinthians 15:47–49)

Some commentators likewise associate this figure of the second man of heaven with Christ. However, the general intention of Paul in this whole passage of 1 Corinthians 15 is surely, and more largely, to convey to his audience the perspective of a transformation of the mind for a life under the Spirit's breath, both after death and now. Whatever the relevance of translations and commentaries including ours, we only want to underline here how the contrast between the figure of Adam and the figure of Christ is traditionally strongly related to salvation, life, redemption, and atonement. It is therefore important to understand the figure of Adam to better understand the stakes of salvation through Christ.

Adam and the Breath of Life

In contrast to the man who reestablishes right relationship in the last days, in the fullness of time, the image of the "disobedient" humans formed from dust, who break the relationship with God, is put forward.[12] Paul Ricoeur called the second Creation story, Genesis chapters 2 and 3, a "mythical symbol." It lies at the root of Augustine's theory of original sin, showing how all humans, past and present, commit evil.[13] The myth does not explain the origin of evil, but rather describes, by means of symbolic language, how human beings hurt relationships and the consequences that result.[14]

The personal name Adam (*adam* Ἀδάμ) appears in the Septuagint for the first time in Genesis 2:16, when God addresses the human whom he is putting into the garden in Eden (2:8.15).[15] He gives the whole garden to humanity without reserving anything for himself. Here, by addressing all of humanity with a personal name, he gives him a proper existence.

God enters into a relationship with his creature. Every human being discovers when he is addressed by his name that he is someone for someone. He feels he exists. Strictly speaking, every one of us comes into existence through the establishment of a relationship. This is God creating through his Word, i.e., in a continual address and commitment. Prior to this moment, God was forming (2:7–8) physical humanity from dust through breath, but still not creating the human being by his word. Thus, Adam in the Septuagint (and consequently in 1 Corinthians 15 and Romans 5) corresponds first to all of "physical" humanity in relationship with God.[16]

In the Hebrew Bible, the use of the name Adam is different. God addresses the human with the personal name Adam (*adam* אָדָם) only in Genesis 3:17, after the eating of the fruit by the two beings when he assigns blame and delineates the inevitable consequences of their act. Prior to this personal name attribution, the Hebrew Bible retains the generic term for human (*ha adam* הָאָדָם), maintaining a direct link to ground-earth (*ha adamah* Genesis 2:7)[17] and to dust coming from it.[18]

"Physical" humanity is from earth, dusty (*choïkós* χοϊκός) by nature.[19] Paul's understanding of this comes from Genesis. All humans are made from the dust (χοῦς) of the earth (γῆ).[20] The human being becomes alive only because God produces, gives birth, generates (ἐνεφύσησεν) on his face (πρόσωπον), on the soil-earth's dust-formed figure, a wind, a breath (πνοή) of life (ζωή).[21]

For Genesis 2, the breath of life generated by God is only given to humans, and not to animals, even though the human calls them "living beings" (ψυχὴν ζῶσαν), marking a common psyche-nature with him.[22] But this received breath of life denotes something special: It signifies and nourishes the relationship between creature and Creator. It comes from nothing but the will of God, who creates humanity through the communication of life by breath (2:7) and address (2:16), through the communication of the life that is in God and from God—God's very own being. The life that humanity receives can be seen in the figure of the tree of life which is located in the middle of the garden and, like all other trees there, is good to eat. This second mention of life is located two verses after the first one (2:9). The pairing of soil-earth and life forms a chiasm (verses 7 and 9) around God who is planting a garden in Eden and placing the human there (verse 8).[23]

Likewise, two other verses create a chiasm describing how the stream and the river flow to water and to irrigate the earth (2:6) and the garden (2:10). Ground, life, good food, water: these constitute the garden where

God is putting the human, where God is meeting him (3:8). All the goods of the garden are offered unconditionally and unreservedly to the human. They may eat anything, without exception, according to God's word (2:16). The divine word, though, designates a grave danger, a potential disaster. It is the counterpart of the total gift. With the gift comes the potential to confuse the gift with its opposite: its loss, its absence, its shadow. A shadow is without its own existence but has real effects. Here, the gift is the nourishing life with all his goods. If the creature is not nourished by life, death ensues. A voluntary act can cause death by attempting to take hold of life rather than receiving it. This is dying by death, by the impossibility of accessing life, which cannot be possessed. Formed from dust, the human figure is really alive only through the breath of life (πνοὴ ζωῆς) bearing the word. In the absence of this life, there remains only an appearance of personality through the dusty form. Made of dust, a heap of particles, the human remains only the dead cluster of fragments—of "pixels," lifeless. This deadly condition is the place from which the cry for salvation arises.

The prospect of salvation is co-emergent with the creation of human by God. By the word of God offering to human the whole of the trees in a delimited space, a habitable and cultivable place, the text shows us that God is, in fact, offering himself totally, but in a measured way adapted to humans. By choosing to establish a relationship with human beings— to communicate life to them, to speak to them, to meet them—God assumes responsibility for them. He commits himself to accompanying them as they are, never to break this relationship, so that they may once again taste the unique joy of living at home, in the place that befits them, the garden, the life that can only be received and never seized.

How Does Life Disappear and Death Arise?

What is the process leading to death? After receiving the word that maintains the singularity of God and his unity with humanity (Genesis 2:17), the latter is differentiated into two spousal beings, called to face one another for the sake of helping each other (2:18–24). Seduced by a lie, one of them is entangled in a discussion where, though seeking to defend God, life and death become confused, leading them to death. This entails "an anonymous discourse that stifles the word and reduces men to flesh without words"[24] (3:1b–5). Separated from God, one becomes distracted and lured by other attractions:

> So, when the woman saw that the tree was good for food, and that it was
> a delight to the eyes, and that the tree was to be desired to make one wise,
> she took of its fruit and ate; and she also gave some to her husband, who
> was with her, and he ate. (Genesis 3:6)

Though there is an immense gift to receive—all the trees of the garden,
the divine life—the human gaze falls upon a very small and ridiculous
object, appearing as seductive, good to seize. In appropriating it for oneself, it seems possible to succeed and dominate. Yielding to greed, taking the object and eating it, he gives it to his partner, without even a
word.[25] And the two, united in wordless deed, eat it (3:6). The other-than-
human, God, the One who was continually giving himself through his
Word, giving himself as their life to be received, has now been transformed into an object to conquer—and with this transformation comes
a transformed orientation toward all else as well. The act of taking and
ingesting that which was to be recognized as irrevocable otherness is the
act of taking and devouring the word received from God. Destroying the
distance with the Creator, human makes life vanish. The Word which
gives existence to another, to others, has been eaten, devoured. There is
no longer God's word crossing the human's heart. There is no longer a
recipient for the Word. There is no longer a listener, an obedient one. Existence becomes a path of destruction, of death.

A relationship of fear is established with God (3:7–8). In the garden,
having experienced their capacity to destroy for the sake of their own
cravings, being afraid of themselves, humans are afraid of God when he
comes to meet them at the time of the evening breeze. They are hiding
from Him. The human voluntarily renounces his relationship with God
(3:8–10), a renunciation born of the fear of being oneself, of being human,
weak, and fallible. This is the fruit of the confusion between what life is
and what death is. Wanting to be like the Other (God) leads them to de-
vour the Word that distinguishes them from him. For spousal creatures
called upon to agree, to live harmoniously, the dissolution of this distinction transforms their relationship into confusion, producing inner divisions in their own relationship. Everything collapses at the same time.
The two separations making life possible disappear. God has been introducing diversity into humanity. This diversity, this distinction, was to be
the basis of all friendship, the basis of all human relationships (2:24). God
is maintaining the distinction between Creator and creature through his
Word. But from the human side, both distinctions, once held together

in harmony, are now replaced with internal division, fear, dissimulation, and accusation, reflected in all manner of external divisions. Paradoxically, the craving to find an exit to this confusion only increases it, leading to war, destruction, and death (3:11–19).

What is designated by Genesis's mythical symbol shows a causal chain, a process. The fantasy of omnipotence, the naive possibility of control and domination, is elaborated in the course of a debate born from a doubt that turns into a seductive and fallacious proposition, which is represented by the figure of the serpent. The figure of the human, facing it alone, represents vainglory and pretension, a refusal to call for help. This verbal exchange leads to confusion between life grasping and life receiving. Confronted by God, who refuses to be conformed to their confusion and who comes to them without judgment, human beings enter into a pattern of fear and denial. Freedom disappears. Accusations fly. Division follows. Death appears. This experience of confusion and division, and its associated consequences, is called knowledge of good and evil, of happiness and misfortune (Genesis 3:22). Reality, the unity of distinctions, becomes fantasy, fragmented and broken. Judgment once based on listening and discernment, on the wisdom to co-respond and maintain right relationship, becomes craving to be similar, to compare, to possess that of the other, to rivalry. Everything ends in accusation, in lying and domination, and in broken relationships (3:15–18). Relationship with God, with oneself, with other humans, and with the natural world is now damaged, leaving human beings in fear and in search of control. The divine project of a dialogue of love is replaced by a discourse of domination. This capacity to damage relationships is the human condition everyone knows from birth.[26] This reality, which Augustine referred to as "original sin," penetrates all lives and leads to the call for salvation.

The Buddhist Concept of Craving

Our understanding of the Genesis narrative may benefit from the light shone upon it by the Buddhist concept of craving-thirst (*tṛṣna*). This concept leads us to be more sensitive to the ease with which we can build a fantasy world based on our longing for and grasping of seductive objects. The Buddhist concept of thirst (*tṛṣna*) is itself strongly related to the notion of *duḥkha*, which I examine through the Tibetan Lam Rim's texts.[27] I chose these texts because they are an organized and progressive presentation of the Indo-Tibetan Buddhist traditions of The Great Vehicle.[28] They point to the central core of all Buddhist thought.

Lam Rim focuses on the basic human condition of *duḥkha*, a term that can be translated as unease, pain, suffering, frustration, dissatisfaction, non-satisfaction, and beyond it also to its solution. Like many other Buddhist texts, Lam Rim has narrative, practical, performative, doctrinal, and symbolic approaches and dimensions, but all focus on resolving this issue. For the sake of its practice, Buddhism developed a vision of the flow of existences (*saṃsāra*) based on the theory of the fructification of greedy action (*karman*).[29] This vision establishes a relation between past act and present fruit and between present act and future fruit. In this view, the perceived world is the fruit of *karman*, action undertaken with thirst.[30] The fruits of these actions are new existences marked by *duḥkha*. Existences arise, flowing one after the other, one into the other (*saṃsāra*).[31] In one existence, consequences of past actions manifest in sensations perceived as pleasant, unpleasant, or neutral. From these, then, the human mind produces further consequences resulting from the thirst which animates the person, such as the search for enjoyment and the development of appetites, the refusal of losses and the rejection of inconveniences:

> When you reflect on how you have no lack of experience with the wonders and sufferings of cyclic existence, you should become disenchanted. You indulge in pleasures in pursuit of satisfaction, yet, with worldly pleasures, you are never satisfied no matter how much you enjoy them. Hence, time after time your craving grows, and on that account, you wander for ages through cyclic existence. For an immeasurably long period of time you will experience intolerable suffering, which those pleasures will not ameliorate in the least. The *Friendly Letter*:
>
> "Just as a leper tormented by maggots
> Tums to fire for relief
> But finds no peace, so should you understand
> Attachment to sensual pleasures."[32]

For the Buddha, the fundamental origin of *duḥkha* is thirst (*tṛṣṇa*; this corresponds to the second Truth[33] of the Nobles[34]). It is the main cause, present everywhere alongside other mental states described by the Buddha. It is the motor of a vicious, self-sustaining circle. Thirst seeks an object that promises happiness, but when it is attained and consumed, happiness flees and the thirst remains. It is as if one were thirsting for water but had only the salty ocean to drink. Drinking this water only increases one's thirst and leads to a greedy appetite to quench a thirst that has increased tenfold. This longing only reproduces itself and keeps the sentient being in this cycle of non-satisfaction. There is an inseparable link between dissatisfaction and the craving that seeks to fight, reject, and ignore it.

The result of any act performed with this thirst is *duḥkha*. The mind's contact with objects arouses an emotion, setting in motion a craving, an active thirst for grasping of objects that cannot satisfy it. The process then repeats itself in ever-changing ways. All of this activity produces a suffering world that does not exist in itself but is only a mental creation. This is why every birth is *duḥkha* (first Truth of the Nobles). *Duḥkha* is not seen in contrast to a world that would otherwise be good. The only true good, if we keep this word, is the disappearance of the non-satisfaction, the cessation of *duḥkha*. The third Truth of the Nobles, called "Truth of the cessation (*nirodha*) of *duḥkha*" describes this disappearance as the "cessation and detachment without rest of thirst, its rejection, its renunciation, its liberation, its absence of attachment." The cessation of craving requires understanding of its origin:

> Unless you reflect on the origin of suffering until you have a good understanding of the root of cyclic existence, which is *karma* and the afflictions, you will be like an archer who does not see the target you will miss the essential points of the path. You will mistake what is not a path to freedom from cyclic existence for the path and exhaust yourself without result.[35]

The Trio of Craving-Grasping-Existence and Their Extinction

An explanation of the arising of *duḥkha*, of the creation of a painful world by the human mind,[36] of suffering or non-satisfaction that does not exist in itself, is best articulated through the Buddhist concept of dependent arising (*pratītyasamutpāda*).[37] The four Truths of the Nobles and *pratītyasamutpāda* are strongly linked, each being used to explain the other.[38] In the presentation in twelve members of dependent arising, amongst them, a trio deserves our particular attention: craving (*tṛṣṇa*), grasping (*upādāna*), and existence (*bhava*).[39] These three factors—craving, grasping, and existence—are engines (actualizers) for creating new existences (actualized), which are all *duḥkha*.[40]

The active dimension of any existence, then, has three aspects: thirst or the presence of greedy appetite, the search for enjoyment, and the action that puts into motion a state of becoming. This is illustrated by the metaphor of sexual union and procreation. If the three are not dissociable, the first two are passive and the third is active. First, thirst represents the five aggregates of appropriation (*upādānaskandha*) in their concupiscent activity (*kāma*), nourished by imagination once an object is seen and craved.[41] Second is longing-attachment, appropriation, as the one who runs everywhere in search of enjoyment. Third is the action that will result in existence (*bhava*) to come. Any action carried out in pursuit of enjoyment will produce new existence. Passions and actions constitute what is the process for future existences (*karmabhava*).[42]

This suffering of beings through innumerable existences arouses the compassion of the numerous buddhas and bodhisattvas.[43] They commit themselves to show beings how to break free from the craving-grasping-existence phenomenon. They show that there is nothing to grasp or obtain, that the thirst to "take, keep, and reject" must dry up in order to stop chasing after what does not exist. The human being does not see that the object does not exist by itself but only in dependence with his greed to grasp and possess. As long as one does not see, one is enslaved to craving.[44] Thus, the path of liberation is learning to see that the objects humans want to seize, grasp, and possess, do not exist as objects in and of themselves. Because thirst is so strong, so rooted in collective and individual human habit, this path is long and requires incremental progress. At the end, when a human being does not see this object as worthy of his craving, he sees correctly. This is liberation.[45]

The extinction of thirst makes possible the dissolution of the mental fabrications dividing everything in subject and object. Vision and knowledge of things as they are can now arise. In this operation, in this correct seeing, the fantasy world the human being creates dissolves. This is the mind's liberation and the assurance that there will be no new birth in the cycle of existences. This is deliverance (*vimukti*). As Dharmakirti's *Commentary on the "Compendium of Valid Cognition"* says: "The karma of one who has transcended craving for existence / Lacks the potency to project another birth / Because its cooperating conditions are gone. . . . Because the aggregates will arise again, if you have craving."[46]

In the earliest Buddhist traditions, the "Noble" who attains deliverance is called *Arhat*. The Tibetan translates this with *dgra bcom pa*—that is, destroyer, conqueror of enemies. Completely lacking thirst, this one is rendered incapable of producing divided mental fabrications anew. The *Arhat*, having attained the liberation from passions and ignorance, continues to live in a set of contaminated aggregates (*sāsravaskandha*) that have been produced from past actions and thus remain subject to sickness and suffering. But he is no longer in a state of appropriation (*upādānaskandha*), as are those beings who are yet marked by attachment.[47]

The Genesis Story Reconsidered

The second Truth of the Nobles and the teaching of dependent arising (*pratītyasamutpāda*) allow us to better understand how Genesis 2–3 also teaches a truth about the painful consequences of our greedy appetite for viewing and grasping objects. In applying this Buddhist lens to Genesis, however, we must keep in mind that every doctrine comes to its fullest meaning only in the tradition which gives it birth. This Buddhist teaching here acts as a lamp, helping us to see more clearly in Genesis that which has always been there. After having listened to the Buddhist teaching concerning craving-grasping-existence, we can describe anew the evil making process described in Genesis.

In Buddhist terms, we could say a thirst for grasping (*tṛṣna*) arose in the garden, in Eden. This thirst did not arise from itself but from an erroneous perception: an object, available as any other object in the garden, but viewed in isolation, as an object in and of itself generating a misunderstanding co-engendered with an irrepressible craving for it. This misperception arouses the craving to appropriate it, and leads to seizing and consuming it, to give it to another who will do the same. The confusion that leads to this appropriation is based on an illusory mental construction from which a greedy appetite to grasp is aroused. After an exchange with the compelling chatterer, the size and scope of the original gift—the whole garden, metaphor for the gift of life—is reduced to a ridiculously and excessively seductive object, good to grab and appropriate for oneself, through which it seems possible to succeed and dominate. Having seen it in this way, the human grasps after it. In this act, the human is self-reduced: He was the receiver-of-the-whole-garden; he is only now a prehensile eye and hand, a grasper-after-objects, implicating the second individual in the same confusion. Together, they represent humanity as a whole plunged into and immersed in the same error.

Building a seductive illusory world, the human becomes a grasper, a grabber. In grasping, he finds himself capable of destroying God's word, that which is the "in-between word." He is capable of destroying the relationship, and in consequence, of destroying himself. A new existence results. That which was "good" has been lost: the inter-said—the Word that bound the people and God in distinction. The "good" is lost through a complex alchemy process of non-listening, arrogance, ignorance, seduction, then craving, grasping, appropriation, and destruction. But even more, this loss is judged by the human himself as evil, and he experiences shame and fear.

This fear is also an illusory construction based on a simple and neutral fact: their nakedness, their vulnerability, their realized capacity of grasping and destroying the word, which separates and unites. The fear is based on an idea: "The Other will react badly against me; I am not worthy to receive his love." Paradoxically, because humans prefer to preserve their pride rather than undergo humiliation, they reject themselves before any possible rejection by their Creator. This is another consequence of their thirst: craving for domination over oneself, for mastery of one's own longings, for perfection. Refusing to accept their fallibility, they choose to stay in confusion. In hiding from God, they are choosing death for themselves instead of life. Not only do they destroy the living Word, thus creating their proper confusion, but they voluntarily cut the relationship with God. This flight testifies to the relationship they broke, and their inability to repair it.

New conditions of existence arise where the need for domination and control increase at the pace of longings for grasping, greedy appetites born from illusions, from mental constructs. The human enters into a world of divided thinking, which he generates himself with his confused activity: happiness and misery, good and evil. His internal and external divisions replicate themselves with each act arising from his confused longings. It is this craving after objects, this thirst for grasping, which harms relationships at all levels: with God, with oneself, with others, with nature. This is how human builds a painful world where pain and sorrow dominate.

Together with the destruction of the relationship, the breath of life weakens. Consequently, humans dwell in the shadow of death, i.e. as disunited forms of dust. But God commits himself again to lead them to life by expelling them from the garden, thus initiating the work of separation necessary to overcome the confusion and restore the in-between word for a life of communion. The cessation of craving and grasping in order to establish true relationship again is the ultimate goal.

Christic Kenosis and the Witness of Non-Grasping

By its insistence on what the Lam Rim calls the "motor of existences," the Buddhist tradition sheds some light on the process of committing evil, showing how humans confront their capability for craving and grasping. This is not a minor problem for one's happiness. In Buddhism, it is this activity that generates a cycle of unsatisfactory existences as long as it is not resolved, as long as it does not stop. In Christianity, it is the origin of our capacity to break relationships, and so also a key for being restored to the possibility of love and happiness. To free oneself from this grasping activity, then, is of central concern for the two traditions. In Buddhism, the practices of discipline, concentration, and reflection take aim at this craving. In Christianity, the redemptive, kenotic dimension of salvation accomplished in Jesus resonates with a renunciation of any grasping. As described by the Hymn to the Philippians:

> Let the same mind be in you that was in Christ Jesus, who, though he was in the form of God, did not regard equality with God as something to be exploited, but emptied himself, taking the form of a slave, being born in human likeness. And being found in human form, he humbled himself and became obedient to the point of death—even death on a cross. Therefore, God also highly exalted him and gave him the name that is above every name . . . (Philippians 2:5–9)

The Son's kenosis, by totally giving himself up to the Father and to human beings (in his humanity), allows the destruction of sin activity—the breaking of relationships with God and its consequences: "Kenosis evokes radical non-appropriation, abandonment of all self-will, in order to make oneself available to other than self."[48] The stopping of the sin process is achieved by the death and resurrection of Christ, thanks to his renunciation of all grasping. This work reveals the non-existence-in-itself of evil, the illusory existence that evil can possess for a time. Nevertheless, this appearance of evil has sufficient potential to make human existence painful since it has a measurable effect over time and space. With Christ's choice to love, a choice realized through his non-appropriation, the obstacle, expressed in the image of the horse's footsteps (the original meaning of *diabolos*) is without effect on him. Love and life can flow from their source and water, without obstacle, those dwelling in his own kenosis.

Conclusion

Beginning with Paul the Apostle in his first letter to the Corinthians, I pointed to the justification and reconciliation received through Christ's atonement, his obedience, in contrast to Adam and his disobedience. I highlighted how Christian salvation focuses on relationships. A dead relationship is transformed in a live one. In examining the trio of Buddhist notions—craving-grasping-existence—we saw the main cause of *duḥkha*—that is, longing/seizing—as being a key moment also for the Genesis myth: transforming given life into death. The misperception of humans makes them focus on a seductive illusory object leading to acts of appropriation whose consequences are disastrous. To reduce such an immense gift, the garden in Eden—i.e., the Life itself—to only an attractive and ridiculously small object to be grasped, held, and possessed is the starting point of the disrupting process of sin, the breaking of relationships leading to death. The need for salvation points here.

In contrast to the Genesis myth's Fall, the salvation accomplished in Jesus the Christ realizes a "renunciation" of any grasping, as the hymn to the Philippians sings. This is the atonement through Christ's blood, or his act of total obedience to the Father. The garden is once again accessible through him. All humanity acquires through the dead and resurrected Christ the capability of re-establishing any relationship. Being the propitiatory through which God is totally received by humanity, love and life coming from the Father are flowing through him for all.

We can thus find in the Buddhist perspective on greed and its cessation a light on Christ's exemplarity in his kenosis—which is his work of redemption. Though the two religious doctrines point each to a different doctrinal system, for both, the renunciation of craving-grasping seems to be an anthropological necessity for "living well."[49] In an age in which we are becoming more and more aware of the risks of destruction provoked through our human fantasies, Buddhist and Christian views concerning craving-grasping and their renunciation are of primary importance. Perhaps there is a common project for the two religious traditions: one in which learning to "live well" might offer a more righteous vision toward a better future for the world to which we belong and which we share.

Notes

1. Scripture quotations are from the New Revised Standard Version Catholic Edition (NRSVCE).
2. I use Sanskrit words for Buddhist concepts, even if they are used in another language, such as Tibetan.
3. Richard Longenecker, *The Epistle to the Romans: A Commentary on the Greek Text* (Grand Rapids, Mich.: Eerdmans, 2016), 566–74.
4. Longenecker, *The Epistle to the Romans*, 578.
5. Emmanuel Durand, *Jésus contemporain. Christologie brève et actuelle* (Paris: Cerf, 2018), 200. Author's translation.
6. Longenecker, *The Epistle to the Romans*, 582–83.
7. Longenecker, *The Epistle to the Romans*, 598. Douglas J. Moo, *The Letter to the Romans* (Grand Rapids, Mich.: Eerdmans, 2018), 343.
8. Ἐγένετο ὁ πρῶτος ἄνθρωπος Ἀδὰμ εἰς ψυχὴν ζῶσαν (1 Corinthians 15:45). Here, Paul uses the Septuagint's translation of Genesis 2 (καὶ ἐγένετο ὁ ἄνθρωπος εἰς ψυχὴν ζῶσαν; Genesis 2:7c) with two modifications: He adds "first" (πρῶτος) and Adam (Ἀδὰμ).
9. Ὁ ἔσχατος Ἀδὰμ.
10. I would translate: "Thus it is written: 'Come,' the first humanity, Adam 'in a living psyche'; the last, Adam in an alive-making spirit."
11. Ὁ πρῶτος ἄνθρωπος ἐκ γῆς, χοϊκός; ἄνθρωπος ἐξ οὐρανοῦ (1 Corinthians 15:47). On this passage, see Gordon Fee, *The First Epistle to the Corinthians* (Grand Rapids, Mich.: Eerdmans), 870–80; Anthony C. Thiselton, *The First Epistle to the Corinthians: A Commentary on the Greek Text* (Grand Rapids, Mich.: Eerdmans, 2000/2013), 1276–92.
12. See Claus Westermann, *Genesis 1–11: A Continental Commentary*, trans. J. J. Scullion (Minneapolis: Augsburg Fortress, 1990); Jean-Louis Ska, *Introduction à la lecture du Pentateuque: Clés pour l'interprétation des cinq premiers livres de la Bible* (Bruxelles: Lessius, 2000); David Cotter, *Genesis* (Collegeville, Minn.: Liturgical Press, 2003). On Genesis 2–3, see Walter Vogels, *Nos Origines. Genèse 1–11* (Montreal: Bellarmin, 1992/2000), 73–130; Jean-Louis Ska, "Genesis 2–3 Some Fundamental Questions," in *Beyond Eden: The Biblical Story of Paradise (Genesis 2–3) and Its Reception History*, ed. Konrad Schmid and Christoph Riedweg (Tubingen: Mohr Siebeck, 2008). 1–27; Tryggve Mettinger, *The Eden Narrative: A Literary and Religio-historical Study of Genesis 2–3* (Winona Lake, Ind.: Eisenbrauns, 2007); Ellen van Wolde, *A Semiotic Analysis of Genesis 2–3: A Semiotic Theory and Method of Analysis to the Story of the Garden of Eden* (Assen: Van Gorcum, Studia Semitica Neerlandica 25, 1989).
13. André-Marie Dubarle, *Le péché originel. Perspectives théologiques* (Paris: Cerf, 1983).
14. See Paul Ricœur, "Herméneutique des symboles et réflexion philosophique (1)," in *Le conflit des interprétations. Essais d'herméneutique I* (Paris: Seuil, 1969), 283–310; "Le 'péché originel': étude de signification," in *Le conflit des interprétations* (Paris: Seuil, 1969), 265–82; "Le mal: un défi à la philosophie et à la théologie," in *Lectures 3: Aux frontières de la philosophie* (Paris: Seuil, 1994), 211–33.
15. And not in Genesis 2:7, as Paul's citation in 1 Corinthians 15 could imply.
16. Longenecker, *The Epistle to the Romans*, 585. Moo, *The Letter to the Romans*, 347.

17. Vogels, *Nos Origines*; Stordalen, "Man, Soil, Garden: Garden Basic Plot in Genesis 2–3 Reconsidered," in *Journal for the Study of the Old Testament* 53 (1992), 3–26.

18. To be precise, Adam (*adam* אָדָם) is also used without the article in the Hebrew of Genesis 2:5 and 2:20 in a comparative context between the beginning of time and the current times, since the Fall. This implicitly refers to this moment of personalization, which comes in 3:17, when he is given a personal name: "there was no Adam to cultivate the soil"; and "for Adam, there was no help in accord with him." The two allusions to Adam are negative. At the beginning of time, there was no Adam, and there was no help in front of him. There was humanity alone, as a whole, not diversified, not individualized.

19. Ὁ πρῶτος ἄνθρωπος ἐκ γῆς, χοϊκός (1 Corinthians 15:47–49).

20. Καὶ ἔπλασεν ὁ θεὸς τὸν ἄνθρωπον χοῦν ἀπὸ τῆς γῆς (Genesis 2:7a).

21. Καὶ ἐνεφύσησεν εἰς τὸ πρόσωπον αὐτοῦ πνοὴν ζωῆς (Genesis 2:7b).

22. Gianfranco Ravasi, "Überschattet vom Baum der Erkenntnis: Hermeneutische Anmerkungen zu Genesis 2–3," in *Internationale katholische Zeitschrift: Communio* 20:4 (July 1991), 294–304.

23. Roberto Ouro, "The Garden of Eden Account: The Chiastic Structure of Genesis 2–3," in *Andrews University Seminary Studies (AUSS)* 40.2 (2002), 219–43.

24. Christophe Boureux, "Approche théologale du mensonge," in *Lumière et Vie* 218 (1994), 64.

25. I deliberately never use the word "desire" in this article, preferring to reserve it for man's fundamental orientation for life. Here, in this context, I use the words "longing," "craving," "greed," "appetite," "greedy appetite," to avoid confusion.

26. Dubarle, *Le péché originel*, 155–56.

27. The progressive path to enlightenment *Byang chub lam rim* (Lam Rim) is, strictly speaking, a doctrine and practice of the Gelugpa lineage of which Tsong kha pa (1357–1419) is the founder. He receives it from earlier Kadampa Tibetan lineages born in the eleventh century. He compiles them. His most important and famous text is the *Great [Treatise] on the Stages of the Path [to Enlightenment]*, whose abbreviation in Tibetan is *Lam Rim Chen Mo* (LRCM). This text has been known to Europeans for more than three centuries. The first "tibetologist," the Italian Jesuit Ippolito Desideri (1684–1733), translated it into Italian. He also left many reflections on Buddhist doctrine in Tibetan. See also David Seyfort Ruegg, Introduction, in Tsong-kha-pa, *Lam Rim Chen Mo. The Great Treatise on the Stages of the Path to Enlightenment*, ed. Joshua W. C. Cutler and Guy Newland (Ithaca, N.Y.: Snow Lion Publications, I. 2000, II. 2004, III. 2002), 376n36.

28. *The Lamp for the Path to Enlightenment, Bodhipathapradīpa, Byang Chub Lam gyi Sgron Ma*, abbreviated as Lam Sgron, is the foundation for the progressive way's lineage. It is attributed to the Indian master Dīpaṃkaraśrījñāna, also called Atīśa (982–1054), the main figure of the Dharma's later development in Tibet, commonly referred to as the second diffusion. A great scholar and practitioner of the *Mahāyāna* and *Vajrayāna*, he is said to have visited Tibet in 1042 after a long stay in Suvarṇadvīpa (Indonesia). His main disciple is the Kadampas's founder, 'Brom ston pa (1005–1064). More than 200 writings and translations are attributed to Atīśa in Tibetan canons. Cf. *Atisha. A Lamp for the Path and Commentary*, trans. R. Sherburne SJ, (London: George Allen & Unwin, 1983).; *Atisha's Lamp for the Path to Enlightenment: An Oral Teaching by Geshe Sonam Rinchen*, trans. Ruth Sonam (Ithaca, N.Y.: Snow Lion, 1997).

29. Tsong-kha-pa, *Lam Rim Chen Mo* I, Chapters XIII, "The General Characteristics of Karma" and XIV, "The Varieties of Karma," 209–46.

30. In Buddhist context, *karman* means any act, any activity or occupation, conscious, craved, decided, undertaken, and that has consequences. The "traces" left are part of a process of maturation, ripening, retribution, which, according to the causes and conditions, results in the production of an effect, a fruit, morally neutral.

31. Tsong-kha-pa, *Lam Rim Chen Mo* I, Chapters XVII, "The Eight Types of Suffering"; XVIII, "The Six Types of Suffering"; XIX, "Further Meditations on Suffering"; and XX, "The Origin of Suffering," 265–313.

32. Ibid., 282.

33. Details on this point in Tsong-kha-pa, *Lam Rim Chen Mo* I, Chapter XX, "The Origin of Suffering," 297–313.

34. I use this formula (and not Four Noble Truths) to express how reality is experienced by a Noble (*ārya*), a human being entered into the supra-mundane way by pure sight. Harvey proposes to use the expression "The Four True Realities for the Spiritually Ennobled." Peter Harvey, *Introduction to Buddhism* (New York: Cambridge University Press, 2013), 50ff.

35. Tsong-kha-pa, *Lam Rim Chen Mo* I, 270.

36. This is not the origin of the world, which is one of the four unthinkable concepts (*acintya*).

37. Tsong-kha-pa, *Lam Rim Chen Mo* I, Chapter XXI, "The Twelve Factors of Dependent-Arising," 315–25.

38. Carol Anderson, *Pain and Its Ending. The Four Noble Truths in the Theravāda Buddhist Canon*, Curzon Critical Studies in Buddhism (Richmond: Curzon, 1999), 105.

39. Tsong-kha-pa, *Lam Rim Chen Mo* I, 319.

40. "The *Compendium of Knowledge*: 'The actualizers and the actualized should be understood by way of three considerations: 1) What does the actualizing? It is done by grasping, which is caused by craving. 2) What is actualized? Birth and aging-and-death are actualized. 3) How does actualization occur? Actualization occurs by means of the empowerment of the latent karmic propensities that were infused in consciousness by compositional activity.... actualization should be understood as follows: non-virtuous compositional activity that is motivated by ignorance about karma and its effects deposits latent propensities of bad karma in the consciousness. This makes ready for actualization the group of factors of a miserable rebirth that begins with the resultant period consciousness and ends with feeling. Through repeated nurturing by craving and grasping, these latent propensities are empowered, and birth, aging, and so forth will be actualized in subsequent miserable rebirths.'" Tsong-kha-pa, *Lam Rim Chen Mo* I, 321.

41. Vasubandu, *Abhidharmakośa*, trans. Louis de La Vallée Poussin (Bruxelles: Institut belge des hautes études chinoises, 1980), Tome II, Chapter III, Str. 3, 3c-d. 7, Str. 27, 69.

42. Lam Rim Chen Mo describes these three members (out of twelve) as follows: "(8) Craving. This means both craving not to be separated from pleasant feelings and craving a separation from painful feelings. The statement in a sutra that "craving is caused by feeling" means that feelings accompanied by ignorance cause craving. Where there is no ignorance, craving does not occur, even if feelings are present. This being the case, contact is the experiencing of the object and feeling is the experiencing of birth or the fruition of karma. Hence, when these two are complete, experience is complete.

There are three types of craving, one for each of the three realms. (9) Grasping. Grasping refers to yearning after and attachment to four types of objects: (a) holding onto what you want . . . ; (b) holding onto views; (c) holding onto ethical discipline and conduct; and (d) holding onto assertions that there is a self. (10) Potential existence. In the past, compositional activity infused your consciousness with a latent propensity, that, when nurtured by craving and grasping, became empowered to bring forth a subsequent existence. The *Twelve Factors of Dependent-Arising*: "'Existence is a case of calling a cause [an activated propensity] by the name of its effect [the subsequent rebirth].'" Tsong-kha-pa, *Lam Rim Chen Mo* I, 318–19.

43. "The *Chapter of the Truth Speaker* says: 'The Conqueror feels great compassion when he sees beings whose minds are overwhelmed by attachment, who have great craving and always long for sensory objects, and who have fallen into the ocean of craving's attachment.'" Tsong-kha-pa, *Lam Rim Chen Mo* I, 183.

44. "You should be aware of the faults as described in *Engaging in the Bodhisattva Deeds*: 'Enemies such as hatred and craving have neither feet nor hands, and are neither brave nor intelligent. How, then, have they enslaved me? While they dwell within my mind, they are pleased to do me harm. They are not to be endured without anger. Tolerance of them is ridiculous!'" Tsong-kha-pa, *Lam Rim Chen Mo* I, 302.

45. The *Friendly Letter*: ". . . among all kinds of happiness, / The cessation of craving is the king of happinesses." Tsong-kha-pa, *Lam Rim Chen Mo* I, 168.

46. Tsong-kha-pa, *Lam Rim Chen Mo* I, 298.

47. Their passions and ignorance are extinct. This is "nirvāṇa with remainder" (*sopadhiśeṣanirvāṇa*). The final end of *duḥkha* and births takes place at the biological death. This is "*nirvāṇa* without substrate remainder" (*nirupadhiśeṣanirvāṇa*). Vasubandhu, *Abhidharmakośa*, Tome I, Str. 1, 8 a-b, 13. In Mahāyāna, *nirvāṇa* attained by seventh earth's *bodhisattvas* and above is dynamic, without dwelling, non-abiding (*apratiṣṭhitanirvāṇa*). At their biological death, they choose the best way to come back in the flow of existences for helping sentient beings on the way of liberation.

48. Pascal Ide, *Une théo-logique du don. Le don dans la trilogie de Hans Urs von Balthasar* (Leuven: Peeters, 2013), 33–34. Author's translation.

49. Cf. Pope Francis, *Laudato si'*.

How Q 5:75 Can Help Christians Conceptualize Atonement

Klaus von Stosch

Along with most other Christian theologians in Germany, I regard atonement as the restoration of the union in love between God and humans and the overcoming of all obstacles that prevent this loving union.[1] All obstacles that make it impossible for a human to be in union with God and that are a result of human responsibility are called "sin." Christian anthropology presupposes that all humans suffer in some sense from the condition that they are not in complete union with God. And the basic message of Christianity is that through Christ, and for many theologians through his suffering on the cross, a way to atonement has been opened to all humans.

I wish to show how difficult it is to establish a coherent theological theory of how the life, suffering, death, and resurrection of Jesus Christ enables atonement—both in the Western and in the Eastern traditions of Christianity. Then, I will turn to a particular verse in the Qur'an to show how it sheds light on these difficulties. Finally, I want to use this light to modify my own Christological model of atonement.

Some Problems in Western Debates on Atonement

In her recent book on atonement, Eleonore Stump distinguishes three different models of atonement in Christian tradition.[2] The most prominent ones among them are the Anselmian and the Thomistic models, both of which can be located in the Western tradition of Christianity.[3] As many probably know, the basic idea of the Anselmian model is that human sin makes it impossible for a just God to forgive humans for their sins without adequate satisfaction. Hence, the justice of God would be damaged if she forgave sins unconditionally. Moreover, in Anselm's point of view, her honor is threatened by human sin—an idea that was criticized by philosophers such as Nietzsche.[4] However, Gisbert Greshake makes clear that the *gloria Dei* in Anselm's thought has to be understood as the order of the world. If Peter hurts his sister, the order of the world is objectively disturbed.[5] There is a wound that has to be healed and that does not disappear through a divine decree. Something like an expiating deed from Peter is necessary. God cannot forgive because this would be against her justice and honor. With many theologians, Stump criticizes that, in this model, the obstacle for atonement lies in the loving God.[6] However, as Greshake makes clear, this kind of criticism is unfair because God's honor is the order of the world. Hence, the real problem is a problem within humankind.

That is why the Anselmian model is not as far away from the Thomistic model as many theologians and philosophers think. The advantage of the Thomistic model, for Stump, is the fact that the obstacle for atonement is not in God, but only in humankind. It is the sin of humans that makes atonement impossible. God stays always accessible and stays, in unchanged love, open to humans. For Anselmian theologians, however, God is not open for the sinner anymore because of respect for the victims. Hence, the Anselmian God needs satisfaction, but not for himself— as Stump and many others think. He needs satisfaction because he cannot bring humans to reconciliation without their help. And if humans do not agree with his reconciling will, and if they do not want to love their brother or sister, God will not undermine their free will because love will never destroy freedom. Thus, the problem within all Western models of atonement is located in human sin, in the human denial of love. The problem is that "human beings do not will what God wills, and the result is distance between human beings and God."[7]

In the Thomistic tradition, the solution to the problem is conceived like this: It is God who justifies humans as long as they do not resist God's good will. So, it is *grace alone* that makes justification happen. Humans have nothing to contribute here, but they can make it impossible for God to heal them by rejecting her love. The only thing that is necessary for humans to be justified is a surrender of their will—not submission but only surrender, as Stump points out repeatedly.[8] After this first justification, which is done by God alone, the process of sanctification can start, which needs cooperation between God and humans.[9] I do not want to go into details of this interesting model here, but I will quickly draw attention to its problem, a problem that is also seen by Stump herself.

Sanctification occurs through the cooperative grace of God together with the human, and God will help any human who simply asks for help here. Thus, Aquinas does not explain why this cooperation would need Christ. If justification does not need anything more than the surrender of human free will, it is not clear which role Christ can play here. Thus, the Thomistic tradition cannot explain why the suffering and death of Jesus are necessary for salvation.[10]

Stump tries to give her own interpretation to explain this need. She calls her own interpretation the "Marian interpretation of atonement" and summarizes it as follows: "On the Marian interpretation of the doctrine of the atonement, in his passion and death, Christ provides unilaterally one part of what is needed for union between God and human beings, namely the indwelling of human psyches in God; and he also provides the most promising means for the other part, namely, the surrender to God by human beings alienated from themselves and from God.... This return of estranged human persons *is* something that God would otherwise not have had; it *is* a gift given to God through Christ."[11]

Stump begins her reflections with the observation that persons who are divided with themselves cannot be unified with God because their will is destroying their own wholeness. Atonement becomes impossible because of human sin, even if God is ready to forgive.[12] What we need here is a power that integrates the divided human psyche and that helps this integrated psyche to surrender to God. Stump's idea for Christ's suffering on the cross is that Christ, through his divine knowledge, gets to know all human psyches of all times and brings them in all their dividedness toward God. For Stump "the human psyche of the person of Christ is opened on the cross to the psyches of all human beings. At one and the same time, Christ mind-reads the mental states found in all the evil human acts human beings have ever committed.... Flooded with such a horror, Christ might well lose entirely his ability to find the mind of God the Father."[13] This is why he really suffers from the distance from the Father and this is her explanation of the cry of dereliction. Christ suffers under all human sufferings by literally feeling their sorrows, pains, fragmentations, and alienations in his mind. He even feels the separation from God, which is caused by this alienation. When he hangs on the cross all human sufferings are hanging with him, his brain is literally taken over by the burden of all human brains, and his surrender is also the surrender of all those psyches that are brought together in this moment. According to Stump, "[t]hrough mind-reading, then, Christ can have all human sin within himself on the cross without himself being sinful."[14]

It is simply inconceivable in Stump's Christology (as in most traditional Christologies) that Jesus becomes sinful himself and is really distanced from God. Although, in Stump's account, Christ struggles psychologically because he does not feel how close God is, because Christ bears the sins of all humans, he is still without any sin and true alienation from God. At least he is not morally responsible for the alienation. Hence, he cannot feel how it is to be responsible for the alienation from God. If he were really distanced from God because of his own deeds and broke down under the burden of the cross and lost any confidence in God, he would not be the son of the Father and the hypostatic union would break. This is inconceivable for Stump's Thomistic account. That is why for her, as for Maximus Confessor, Jesus has no gnomic free will.[15] He is not able to run away from Jerusalem in the night of his betrayal, nor is he able to give in to the temptation of Satan. Hence, there is no logically possible world in which Jesus Christ, who has a divine and a human nature, really loses his path. Thus, the solution for the drama of humankind is a human who so differs ontologically from the rest of humankind that he does not objectively suffer from the greatest danger of humankind. He cannot get lost, nor can he lose his identity, his integrity, or his relation to God. As omniscient as the Father, he can mind-read as God, and is not only sinless but impeccable.

I am not sure whether this is really a good solution. The big problem of humankind is solved by a human who simply mind-reads other humans[16] who have a problem that he cannot have. Maybe we can find more convincing conceptions of atonement in the Eastern tradition.

Some Problems in Eastern Debates on Atonement

Eastern concepts of atonement are not so focused on the idea of human sin but on human development toward unification with God. The concept is based on the Greek idea of education (*paideia*). From a modern free will account, the Greek idea can be understood in a way that God or the divine Logos will try to help the human free will in a pedagogical process to grow and flourish and to gain more and more freedom through a relationship with God. The aim in this concept is human fulfillment and this is found in the imitation of God (*mimesis*) and in the participation (*methexis*) in divine life. Christ is the icon that will help humans in their process of reconciliation and fulfillment. Hence, the aim of atonement is the dynamic-ontological participation in God.[17]

Here, the concept of sin becomes decisive because it is usually sin that hinders humans in their development toward God. But as the metaphysics of a universal human sin has been challenged in modern times, more and more Christian theologians in Germany are trying to rethink the Eastern model in a way that is independent from the idea of sin, especially from the idea of original sin.[18] Let me focus on one interpretation of atonement in this line of thinking.

Thomas Pröpper, one of the most influential German theologians in the field of anthropology and atonement today, tries to understand salvation as the fulfillment of human freedom.[19] The basis of his theology is an analysis of human free will, which can be summarized as follows:[20] Libertarian free will only exists if it is really the free agent who is acting. Humans are, of course, influenced by their education, environment, biological nature, and so on. But if they were determined by all of this, their free will would be a mere illusion. Thus, if actions can really be understood as free (which cannot be proven), free will must be conceived as formally unconditional. Formal unconditionality of freedom points to the fact that in the perspective of a transcendental analysis of free will, it cannot be determined by anything but itself without being eliminated. Or, to put it differently, the idea of an ultimately (unconditionally) free subject is a necessary formal condition if the idea of moral responsibility is to have an assignable meaning.

At the same time, free will has to be exercised in the material world in a concrete way, which means that it is materially conditional. Hence, free agents cannot exercise what free will seems to be in its transcendental structure. This leads to a dilemma, which is expressed in the language of Thomas Pröpper as the dilemma of the mere conditional realization of the formal or transcendental unconditionality of free will. Let me try to translate this into more existential language with the help of Albert Camus. Camus emphasizes time and again the absurdity of human existence.[21] He sees this absurdity in the fact that human love always wants to be true and complete but will never succeed. Camus speaks of the quest for qualitative unity in human free will, and he tries to show in his novels, dramas, and essays that humans are only able to achieve moments of this unity and that longings for unconditional love are always in vain. He suggests that humans can be quite happy with this absurd structure of reality, but it is clear that from his perspective the most important desires of the human heart cannot be fulfilled. Humankind is not only an unfinished project, but it is impossible to come to fulfillment.

Pröpper tries to show, with the help of the transcendental analysis of free will of Hermann Krings, who argues in the tradition of Johann Gottlieb Fichte, that this existential longing for the unconditional is a necessary part of the development of free will.[22] But even if this cannot be proven, it is still compelling that every human is desperately searching for true and unconditional love, and philosophy has to reflect on what to do with this fact.

So, what is Pröpper's response to this existential desire, which seems to be at the very heart of human free will? Pröpper makes clear that humans can symbolically try to express unconditional love. Parents, for example, can love their children without preconditions, and, one hopes, many parents do this. They don't typically say before the birth of a child that it has to be beautiful and kind, but, rather, that they will love it no matter what. At least this should be the case as most will agree. Most parents will—again, one hopes—also not stop loving their children when they do not fulfill their expectations. Even if they do a lot of stupid and even evil things, parents will not stop loving them. That is why theologians such as Karl Barth and Wolfhart Pannenberg see in the love of parents the very best symbol or icon of divine love.[23] But still, this love is not unconditional: Parents will not always understand their children, will sometimes choose the wrong way to show their love, and will one day die. They might love without making claims and without insisting on certain conditions before or after love, but their love is not unconditional. It is a "real symbol," in the tradition of Karl Rahner, a symbol that already starts to realize what is still promised. But at the same time, this promise might be given in vain.

Only an unconditional being who is nothing other than unconditional free will can realize unconditional love completely. Hence the analysis of free will leads to the notion of God as absolute or unconditional free will. Free agents cannot know whether this God exists, but they can know that such a God who is freedom itself and who uses this unconditional free will for loving humans in an unconditional way will be the only solution for the existential problem of free will. However, this unconditional love can only reach humans in a human form. Therefore, the basic problem of humankind can only be changed by a human who embodies God's unconditional love. Only if God shows her love to me in an unconditional way through the means of a human will I know that I can be loved, that I am really loved unconditionally here in this world, and that my symbolic representation of unconditional love makes sense. And only if God enables me to love unconditionally will I be able to trust that it is I who can respond to this unconditional love adequately—a capacity that is given to humankind by the Holy Spirit.[24] For Pröpper, God reveals herself as the unconditional love in the life, death, and resurrection of Christ. He claims repeatedly: "Without the incarnation of Jesus and the way he was as a human being one could not conceive God as love. Without Jesus' willingness to die, the unconditional seriousness of this love could not be seen. And without his resurrection, God would not be revealed as its true origin."[25] Thus, the life of Jesus shows God's love for us, his death makes clear that God will only use the means of love to show her love, and the resurrection proves the unconditional nature of this love.

What does this theory mean for the question of sin, which is so central to Western theories of atonement? As the love of God is conceived as unconditional here, God's love will forgive every sin without imposing any form of condition. German theologians like to call this the categorical indicative of God's affirmation of humankind.[26] According to Pröpper "[i]n Jesus Christ the sinner is able to stand against himself with God by his side because God has already gone to stand by him."[27] Therefore, the power of sin is broken "because there is forgiveness for every person who only accepts it."[28] Even the difficulty of the distance to God has been abolished in the relationship of Jesus to his Father. In the end, the solution for the problem of sin is very similar to the Thomistic solution presented by Eleonore Stump. The difference is simply that Pröpper claims to be able to develop his theory without any reference to sin. For him, atonement is about human fulfillment, which is desperately needed by humans because of the structure of their free will, not because of their sins.

Let me summarize Pröpper's account of atonement with his own words: "The death and resurrection of Jesus ultimately shows what has already begun in the preaching of Jesus: God's self-revelation as unconditional love to the people. And this revelation is our redemption provided only that one understands revelation as the occurrence of freedom, in which God's self-determination becomes reality for the people through the respective freedom of Jesus."[29] This theory has become very influential in German theology today because it fits very well with a modern theory of revelation in which it can be said that the message, the sender, and the means of divine revelation are identical: God in her love is the sender, God's love the message, and divine love the means through which this love is revealed. This understanding of revelation makes clear that this revelation is our salvation and enables atonement. It is God's loving presence in Christ that helps us to encounter the fulfillment of our deepest desires.

Pröpper's theory of atonement has several problems, which I have discussed elsewhere[30] and which have been the subject of extensive studies.[31] Let me concentrate here on the Christological nucleus of Pröpper's theory of atonement. It consists in the claim that the human free will of Jesus is identical with God's self-determination in the logos. Pröpper's former student Georg Essen worked out this idea in his habilitation thesis, and he claims that the human free will of Jesus is numerically and formally identical with the free will of the divine Logos.[32] Essen is aware that a human free will cannot be materially identical with a divine free will, but he develops a Kenosis Christology, which says that the free will of the inner-trinitarian logos decides to become a human free will.[33] That is why the human free will is, from its very first moment of existence in the human life, numerically identical with the divine free will. At the same time, it has the same form as the divine will and is related to God and humans as the Logos relates to the Father and to humankind. The advantage of this theory, in comparison with Stump's Christology, is that it makes clear that Christ, as the kenotic Logos, has no omniscience in the sense of classical theism. He cannot mind-read and he has no other supernatural powers. Materially speaking, his free will is conditional as is everything human.[34]

But there is at least one serious problem with Essen's (and Pröpper's) Christology. If the free will of Jesus shares the formal unconditionality of all human free will, he must have the power to do otherwise. Thus, Jesus must have the option to run away from Jerusalem in the night of his betrayal and to give in to the temptation of Satan. As I will explain later in greater depth, this is a consequence that I like in Pröpper's theory. However, it becomes unacceptable in the framework of its application to the Trinity. As for Pröpper and Essen, the free will of the divine Logos and the free will of Jesus are formally and numerically identical;[35] the inner-trinitarian Son also seems to have the option to run away or to be tempted. Although this is a very nice idea, it is obviously polytheistic, and it should be unacceptable even for social trinitarianism.[36] Georg Essen also does not seem to be willing to accept this consequence. Hence, he needs something that ensures that the inner-trinitarian Son (who is formally identical with Jesus) will not run away. With Eleonore Stump, Maximus Confessor, and many others, he thinks that Christ has no gnomic free will and so is not able to sin.[37]

I have to admit that the question of whether Christ was only sinless or whether he was sinless and impeccable is not the first one that stood out to me in Christology and it is also not the first that will be relevant in the dialogue with Muslims. But it is interesting that the theories of atonement of Stump and Pröpper both seem to imply that Jesus is impeccable and therefore has no gnomic free will. Although this position is widespread in Western and Eastern theories of atonement, it has never been defined as a dogma by the magisterium—at least in my own reading of Constantinople III. So, there is some dogmatic space here and it makes sense to see whether we can learn something from the Qur'an.

The Qur'anic Intervention of Q 5:75

It is clear that the Qur'an emphasizes the humanity of Christ. There are many verses in the Qur'an that develop critical interventions against classical Trinitarian Christology, especially in surah al māʾida (= Q 5), but it would be another paper to deal with these criticisms.[38] What is less obvious is the question of how the Qur'an relates to the question of gnomic free will and of the impeccability or sinlessness of Christ. In scholastic Muslim theology, the doctrine of the ʿiṣma of the prophets is understood by many theologians in a way that it implies impeccability and infallibility. This also implies that Jesus, as prophet and messenger, has to be considered as impeccable. Before verifying whether this teaching is in coherence with the Qur'an, let us first of all have a closer look at the Christological teaching on this subject in the sixth and seventh centuries.

A quite popular teaching in Christology in that time was the idea of the incorruptibility of the body of Christ. This teaching was developed in the sixth century by Julian, bishop of Halicarnassus, who believed that Jesus had an uncorrupted human nature—as did Adam before the fall. In his understanding, this incorruptibility implied that Christ's human nature was not affected by the consequences of the fall—that is, it was not necessary for him to eat and drink or to suffer and die. This theory does not imply a docetist teaching,[39] though some adversaries tried to show that Julian was a docetist.[40] He simply wanted to say that it was not necessary for Jesus to eat and drink or to suffer and die in his human nature because this human nature was the nature before the fall. Hence, Jesus was only eating because he wanted to eat, not because it was a necessity.

Although Julianists were quite influential on the Arab Peninsula at the time of the formation of the Qur'an—which we know from acts of visitations of monasteries[41]—the theology of this sect alone would not justify its mention here; it did not survive very long. However, the basic idea of Julianism, the incorruptibility of the body of Christ, became official theology in the Byzantine Empire. In his last decree, in 565, Emperor Justinian made the incorruptibility of the body of Christ the official doctrine of the Empire, which everyone had to believe.[42] This imperial politics of religion was backed up by the theology of the most important theologian in Byzantium of that century, Leontios of Byzantium, who is well known still today as one of the most important defenders of the neo-Chalcedonian doctrine of enhypostasis. Leontios, as most theologians at that time, was convinced that the human nature of Christ was uncorrupted by original sin[43] and that this is why he did not need to eat and drink. We might still think that this is simply a weird idea of some sects and misled theologians. But even Maximus Confessor, the big defender of orthodox Christology at the time of the formation of the Qur'an and the last theologian who defended the human will of Jesus, believed that Jesus was only hungry because he wanted to be hungry, and he made clear that the fear and the hunger of Jesus was superior to our fear and hunger.[44] Moreover, he explicitly said that Jesus was without gnomic free will and that Jesus was impeccable.[45] In both respects, he agreed with his opponents in the debate on monotheletism. Both respects seem to belong together and to form one package in the Christology at the time of the formation of the Qur'an: Jesus did not need to eat and drink or to suffer and die, and had no problems resulting from a gnomic free will.

All of this became a question of power and politics. Justinian thought that the teaching of the incorruptibility of Christ's nature could help to reconcile the separation of the churches after Chalcedon. A main argument of miaphysite churches against Chalcedon was that it is inconceivable that a human and a divine nature can come together in one person. As the divine nature is immortal, this nature cannot be one with a human nature that is mortal, has a gnomic free will, and is needy of food and many other things. With the doctrine of the incorruptibility of Christ's body, this problem is overcome because an uncorrupted human nature is not in need of food, is not mortal, and has no gnomic free will.

How does the Qur'an react to this kind of Christology? If we are seeking a reaction of the Qur'an to the theology of the Byzantine Empire, we have to look at the very last period of the development of the Qur'an. Most scholars agree that *surāt al mā'ida* (= Q 5) is one of the very last surahs of the Qur'an, and in the perspective of traditional Islamic exegesis was revealed in the last two or three years of the life of the prophet Muhammad. Historically speaking, it makes sense that the Qur'an deals critically with the Byzantine Empire of this time. Byzantium defeated the Persian Empire after decades of struggles and wars in 628, and the Emperor Herakleios brought back what was believed to be the Holy Cross to Jerusalem in 630. Likely, there was a first battle between Muhammad's Arabs and the army of the Byzantine Empire at Mu'ta in 629,[46] and some classical Muslim commentators claim that Muhammad was afraid in 630/631 of an attack at Tabūk in the north of Syria.[47]

Surāt al mā'ida seems to reflect all these struggles and we have a lot of polemical debates with Christians in it. Sometimes it is very likely that these Christians are Byzantine Christians. I believe the following passage has such an anti-Byzantine connotation:

> They do blaspheme who say: "Allah is Christ the son of Mary." . . . They do blaspheme who say: "Allah is one of three in a Trinity" . . . Christ, the son of Mary, was no more than a messenger. . . . His mother was a woman of truth. They had both to eat their (daily) food. (Q 5:72f.75 in the translation of Yusuf Ali)

Let me provide a bit of historical explanation for some of the peculiar formulations of the passage. Why does the Qur'an claim that Christians say that God is Christ? It is true that some Christians like to say that Christ is God. Personally, I prefer Trinitarian speech here—that is, I prefer to say that Christ is the Son of God or the Logos of God—but many Christians would say that Christ is God. Nonetheless, I have never encountered anyone who put it the other way around. Christians might say that Christ is God, but they never say that God is Christ. So why is the Qur'an criticizing Christians for something they do not say?

Sidney Griffith argues that here the Qur'an is simply using polemical language. But a polemic that turns the word in your mouth is not very powerful. Hence, we should have a closer look at the question of whether such a Christology was defended in the sixth or seventh century. And interestingly enough we find this theology among the theologians who were promoted by Justinian. John Maxentios, the leader of the Scythian monks in the Theopaschite controversy in the 530s, insisted on the fact that we cannot only say that Jesus Christ is God, but also that God is Jesus Christ.[48] In the tradition of Philoxenos from Marbug, he insisted even on the idea that God himself suffered on the cross.[49] Justinian tried to use the theology of those monks to reconcile miaphysite and diphysite Christologies. He introduced their title for Christ *unus e trinitate* in the Empire, and he even convinced Rome to accept the title.[50] The Arabic formulation in Q 5:73, *thālithu thalāthatin*, which is usually understood as a critique of the trinity, is a loan word from the Syriac formulation and simply the transformation of the Syriac title into Arabic.[51] Hence, it is directed against Byzantine Christology. Those Christians are criticized who say, like Justinian's theologians, that God is Christ and that God is *thālithu thalāthatin*.

Q 5:75 argues that Jesus and Mary "had both to eat their (daily) food." This weird formulation is a very detailed response to the mainstream Christology of the Byzantine theologians who claimed that Jesus did not need to eat. That Mary is included here shows that, in Byzantine theology, not only was Jesus Christ the new Adam who did not suffer under the consequences of the fall, but also that Mary was the new Eve who likewise did not suffer under original sin. For Mary it is even clearer that the Qur'anic formulation can only be explained by imperial theology.[52] For theology at the time of the formation of the Qur'an, this meant that Jesus Christ did not need to eat and drink or to suffer and die. It is the very same Christology which said that Jesus was impeccable and that he had no gnomic free will. When the Qur'an says that Christ was no more than a messenger, this seems to imply that Jesus had a message to deliver and that he did not have any superhuman attributes or properties. Hence, the Qur'an says here that Jesus was like us. He had to eat and drink and to suffer and die. He was sinless but not impeccable, and he had the same gnomic free will as everybody. Why is this intervention so important for the Christian teaching of atonement?

How the Qur'an Helps My Understanding of Atonement

I have defined atonement as the restoration of the union in love between God and humans and the overcoming of all obstacles that prevent this loving union. Christians believe that through Christ, and for many theologians through his suffering on the cross, a way to atonement has been opened to all humans.

I agree with Eleonore Stump and scholars such as Hans Urs von Balthasar that, in the moment of the cross, Jesus Christ really suffers from the distance of the Father and that this is the explanation for his cry of dereliction. Christ suffered not only because of his own sufferings, but also because of the sufferings of the people he knew. He was affected by their sorrows, pains, fragmentations, and alienations in his mind and in his body. He might even have felt the separation from God, which is caused by this alienation. When he hung on the cross, those human sufferings were hanging with him. But I do not agree with Stump that this theological idea can be defended by his capacity to read the minds of all humans throughout all time periods. I do not agree with her that he was literally affected by all human beings of all times.

I rather share the Christology of the school of Karl Rahner, which sees in Jesus Christ the real symbol of God's love and care for humankind. Thus, the cross reveals who God really is. Through the death and suffering of Jesus, we can learn that God is affected by all the sufferings of her beloved creatures. The cross is the real symbol of God's love for humankind. Hence, it realizes already that which still has to be completed. With Wolfhart Pannenberg, I would say that Jesus is the eschatological prophet in whom the final destination of humankind is present in a proleptic way.[53] It is true that God suffers with all human beings in the Logos, that she shares all our needs and problems literally in the Logos, and this is revealed and already realized in Christ. But Christ is not a superhuman figure with superhuman properties. With Pannenberg and Essen, I would say that the Divinity of Christ is simply the unique intimacy of his relationship with the Father, which is identical to the inner-trinitarian relationship of Father and Son.[54] In this theology, Divinity is not a question of substance ontology but of relational ontology.[55] The basic idea is simply that we can share Christ's relationship to the Father through the power of God's Spirit and through the love of Jesus Christ. In this relational concept, atonement becomes possible because we can participate in the love of Christ toward God, and at the same time we can participate in God's love for us, which became reality in Christ. As God shares in Jesus our human condition with all its needs, sorrows, and pains, it becomes possible for humans to identify with this love and to overcome the ways we distance ourselves from God.

The old church always taught that what has not been shared by God cannot be saved.[56] The idea here is that God shares our problems, needs, and sorrows in Christ. We are not alone with them anymore and Christ heals them through his presence. In the logic of this theory of atonement, it is very important that Jesus Christ shares our human condition in all its ambiguity and that he also shares our libertarian free will. Only this makes it possible that my humanity, in all its ambiguity, is confronted with God's healing presence.

Our human problem is not that we are sometimes voluntarily hungry, but that we are hungry when we desperately want to eat. Our problem is not that we suffer when we want to suffer, but that there is suffering that alienates us and that destroys our identity. Our problem is not death in principle, but the early death of somebody who has so many unfulfilled hopes and dreams. Our problem is not a free will that always knows what is good and that knows how to realize the good, but the gnomic free will, which is sometimes torn back and forth. If we seek help in this situation through the healing presence of God in Jesus Christ, we cannot accept the incorruptibility of the body of Christ. We cannot accept a theory that conceives the human nature of Christ in such a way that he does not need to eat and drink or to suffer and die. If it is true that healing needs communion and that the only danger for this communion is my refusal to surrender, we simply cannot be healed by somebody who does not know what it is like to be endangered in one's identity through temptation. Only if Christ knows how much we are sometimes torn back and forth in our free will, only if Christ really has to fight in Gethsemane and on the cross, only if Christ is in real danger of losing his identity and betraying his mission, only then can he help me in my own struggles and distress, only then can he give hope to me in my weakness, only then can he convince me to surrender myself.

If all of this is true, Q 5:75 is an extremely helpful intervention for Christian theology. It encourages us to see the corruptibility of the body of Christ. It shows us how much Christ is with us in our despair and hopelessness, in our struggles and doubts. In some sense, it defends a crucial idea of Christianity—maybe one of the most important cornerstones for any coherent theory of atonement—against Christian mainstream theology of its time.

Notes

1. I am thankful for very helpful comments from Johannes Grössl and Aaron Langenfeld on earlier versions of this essay.
2. Cf. Eleonore Stump, *Atonement* (Oxford: Oxford University Press, 2018).

3. The third one is a model that she calls the Patristic model and that can be identified with the Eastern model, which will be our subject shortly.

4. Cf., for example, Friedrich Nietzsche, "Die fröhliche Wissenschaft," in *Kritische Studienausgabe vol. 3: Morgenröte. Idyllen aus Messina, Die fröhliche Wissenschaft*, ed. Giorgio Colli und Mazzino Montinari, 343–651 (München: dtv, 1999), 135: "Ob mit der Sünde sonst Schaden gestiftet wird, ob ein tiefes, wachsendes Unheil mit ihr gepflanzt ist, das einen Menschen nach dem andern wie eine Krankheit fasst und würgt—das lässt diesen ehrsüchtigen Orientalen im Himmel unbekümmert: Sünde ist ein Vergehen an ihm, nicht an der Menschheit!"

5. Cf. Gisbert Greshake, "Erlösung und Freiheit. Zur Neuinterpretation der Satisfaktionstheorie Anselms von Canterbury," in *Theologische Quartalsschrift* 153 (1973): 332–45.

6. Cf. Stump, *Atonement*, 115.

7. Stump, *Atonement*, 23. Stump's statement refers only to the Thomistic models. But I think that it is true for all Western models.

8. Stump, *Atonement*, 210, 369.

9. Stump, *Atonement*, 27, 202.

10. Some scholars might think that the Anselmian model is stronger here. But its strength is dependent on several premises that can be challenged today, such as medieval corporate order, platonic philosophy, and the Augustinian concept of original sin. As extensive critique of these premises cf. Aaron Langenfeld, *Das Schweigen brechen. Christliche Soteriologie im Kontext islamischer Theologie* (Paderborn: Ferdinand Schöningh, 2016), 68–154.

11. Stump, *Atonement*, 397.

12. Cf. Stump, *Atonement*, 127.

13. Stump, *Atonement*, 164–65.

14. Stump, *Atonement*, 169.

15. Cf. Karl-Heinz Uthemann, *Christus, Kosmos, Diatribe: Themen der frühen Kirche als Beiträge zu einer historischen Theologie* (Berlin: De Gruyter, 2005), 172: "Ein gnomischer Wille ist ein Wille, der zur Entscheidungs- und Willensfreiheit befähigt ist oder, richtiger gesagt, nicht befähigt ist, sondern mit dieser Wahlfreiheit belastet ist und nur in defizienter Weise frei sein kann." Thus, a person without gnomic free will has no alternatives in his or her free decisions, i.e., no libertarian free will.

16. It might be that Stump wants to say that Christ is not only reading the minds of other humans but that he takes over their first-person perspective. But as I think that it is logically spoken simply impossible to take over the first-person perspective of another person I cannot follow this idea.

17. Cf. Gisbert Greshake, "Der Wandel der Erlösungsvorstellungen in der Theologiegeschichte," in *Erlösung und Emanzipation*, ed. L. Scheffczyk, 69–101 (Freiburg-Basel-Wien: Herder, 1973).

18. Cf. the critique of the tradition of original sin in Thomas Pröpper, *Theologische Anthropologie*, Vol. II (Freiburg-Basel-Wien: Herder, 2011), 981–1091.

19. Cf. Pröpper, *Theologische Anthropologie*. Cf. Thomas Pröpper, *Erlösungsglaube und Freiheitsgeschichte: Eine Skizze zur Soteriologie*, 3rd ed. (München: Kösel, 1991).

20. Cf. Pröpper, *Erlösungsglaube und Freiheitsgeschichte*, 182–94.

21. Cf. Albert Camus, *Le mythe de Sisyphe*. *Essai sur l'absurde* (Paris: Edition Gallimars, 1942); Camus, *L'étranger* (Paris: Edition Gallimars, 1957); Langenfeld, *Das Schweigen brechen*, 158–81.

22. Cf. Hermann Krings, *System und Freiheit*. *Gesammelte Aufsätze* (Freiburg-München: Alber, 1980), 15–68, 161–84.

23. Cf. Klaus von Stosch, "Wunder Kinder. Was es bedeutet, Kinder zu haben," in Herder Korrespondenz Spezial: *Kinder, Kinder. Ethische Konflikte am Lebensanfang* (2017): 4–6.

24. This second aspect is not so much focused in Pröpper's school, and it is not my focus here too because I want primarily to discuss the Christological side of theories of atonement here. But I want to mention this very important aspect at least.

25. Pröpper, *Erlösungsglaube und Freiheitsgeschichte*, 197.

26. Cf. Pröpper, *Erlösungsglaube und Freiheitsgeschichte*, 202. Pröpper borrows this formulation from Gotthard Fuchs, "Glaubenserfahrung—Theologie—Religionsunterricht. Ein Versuch ihrer Zuordnung," in *Katechetische Blätter* 103 (1978): 199.

27. Pröpper, *Erlösungsglaube und Freiheitsgeschichte*, 203.

28. Pröpper, *Erlösungsglaube und Freiheitsgeschichte*, 207.

29. Pröpper, *Erlösungsglaube und Freiheitsgeschichte*, 59.

30. Cf. Klaus von Stosch, "Über Erlösung reden," in *Religionsunterricht an höheren Schulen*, Vol. 52 (2009): 80–87.

31. Cf., for example, Langenfeld *Das Schweigen brechen*.

32. Cf. Georg Essen, *Die Freiheit Jesu. Der neuchalkedonische Enhypostasiebegriff im Horizont neuzeitlicher Subjekt- und Personphilosophie* (Regensburg: Pustet, 2001), 291.

33. Cf. Essen, *Die Freiheit Jesu*, 312.

34. Cf. Essen, *Die Freiheit Jesu*, 310f.

35. Cf. Essen, *Die Freiheit Jesu*, 295.

36. Cf. Klaus von Stosch, *Trinität* (Paderborn: UTB/Ferdinand Schöningh, 2017), 112–36.

37. For a more extensive debate of Essen's Christology, cf. Magnus Lerch, *Selbstmitteilung Gottes: Herausforderungen einer freiheitstheoretischen Offenbarungstheologie* (Regensburg: Pustet, 2015).

38. For an extensive debate of these verses, see Mouhanad Khorchide and Klaus von Stosch, *Der andere Prophet. Jesus im Koran* (Freiburg-Basel-Wien: Herder, 2018).

39. Cf. René Draguet, *Julien d'Harnicasse et sa controverse avec Sévère d'Antioche sur l'incurrupitibilité du corps du Christ: Etude d'histoire littéraire et doctrinale suivie des fragments dogmatiques de Julien* (Texte syriaque et traduction grecque) (Louvain, 1924), 104.

40. In the polemical literature of late antiquity, Julianists were often supposed to claim that Jesus did not eat like us, nor did he use the bathroom. But this is a misunderstanding of his teaching. Cf. Ibid.

41. This is something I learned from Sidney Griffith.

42. Karl-Heinz Uthemann, "Kaiser Justinian als Kirchenpolitiker und Theologe," *Augustinianum* 33 (1999): 79; Alois Grillmeier, *Jesus der Christus im Glauben der Kirche*, Bd. 2/2: Die Kirche von Konstantinopel im 6. Jahrhundert, unter Mitarbeit von Theresia Hainthaler (Freiburg-Basel-Wien: Herder, 1989), 492. Some scholars challenge this opinion today. But at least everybody agrees that there was some activity in 565 that could be understood and was understood as Julianism. Cf., for example, the letter of the bishop Nicetius from Trier who accuses the emperor as heretic in summer 565 (Grillmeier, *Jesus der Christus im Glauben der Kirche*. Bd. 2/2, 494).

43. Cf. Uthemann, "Kaiser Justinian als Kirchenpolitiker und Theologe," 80.

44. Cf. Maximus Confessor, Disputatio cum Pyrrho, 297D, quotation from Guido Bausenhart, "In allem uns gleich außer der Sünde," in *Studien zum Beitrag Maximos' des Bekenners zur altkirchlichen Christologie* (Mainz: Matthias-Grünewald-Verl., 1992), 203: "[W]ie er auch wahrhaft hungerte und dürstete, hungerte und dürstete er doch nicht auf die Art und Weise wie wir, sondern auf eine uns überlegene Art und Weise, nämlich freiwillig; so fürchtete er sich auch, als er sich wahrhaft fürchtete, nicht wie wir, sondern auf eine uns überlegene Weise." I owe this hint to the dissertation of Cornelia Dockter.

45. Cf. Essen, *Die Freiheit Jesu*, 45f.

46. Cf. Walter E. Kaegi, *Heraclius: Emperor of Byzantium* (Cambridge: Cambridge University Press, 2003), 233.

47. Cf. Ġ. Sobhānī, *forūǧe abadīyyat* (Tehran: 1993), 385–410.

48. Cf. Uthemann, "Kaiser Justinian als Kirchenpolitiker und Theologe," 20–23.

49. Cf. Dana Viezure, "Philoxenus of Mabbug and the controversies over the 'Theopaschite' Trisagion." *Studia Patristica* 47 (2010): 137–46, 139: "Philoxenus argues that the strong formulations 'God the Word died,' 'God died,' 'the Immortal died,' 'One of the Trinity died' are needed in order to maintain the uniqueness of subject in Christ and to uphold orthodoxy."

50. Cf. Uthemann, "Kaiser Justinian als Kirchenpolitiker und Theologe," 34f.

51. Cf. Sydney Griffith, "Syriacisms in the 'Arabic Qur'an': Who Were 'Those Who Said Allāh Is the Third of Three' According to al-Mā'ida 73?" in *A Word Fitly Spoken: Studies in Medieval Exegesis of the Hebrew Bible and the Qur'ān*, ed. M. M. Bar-Asher et alia (Jerusalem, 2007), 100–8.

52. There is quite a lot of evidence for the fact that the Syriac fathers conceived Mary as a new Eve who is without sin—at least after the conception of Christ. Cf., for example, Jacob of Serug, *On the Mother of God*. Translation by Mary Hanbury. Introduction by Sebastian Brock (St. Vladimir Seminary Press: Crestwood, New York, 1998), Homily I, 36. However, we only have evidence for just a few Julianists talking of an incorruptibility of Mary's body; see, for example, the anti-Julianist references in Leontius of Byzantium, *Complete Works*, ed. Brian E. Daley (Oxford: Oxford University Press, 2017), 350–52; Sebastian Brock, "A letter from the orthodox monasteries of the orient sent to Alexandria, addressed to Severos," *Severos of Antioch, His life and times*, ed. John D'Alton/Youhanna Youssef (Leiden: Brill, 2016), 32–46, 39). This idea seems to have become popular in Byzantine imperial theology because of the incorruptibility of Mary's clothes, which protected the city at the siege of Constantinople in 619 (Antoine Wenger, "Les interventions de Marie dans l'église orthodoxe et l'histoire de Byzance," *De primordiis cultus Mariani*, ed. Ponteficia Academia Mariana Internationalis, Rome 1970, 423–31, 424).

53. Cf. Pannenberg, *Systematische Theologie*, Vol. 2, 336–64.

54. Cf. Pannenberg, *Systematische Theologie*, Vol. 2, 433; Essen, *Die Freiheit Jesu*, 290–97.

55. Cf. Klaus von Stosch, "Jesus als Gott der Sohn? Eine Auseinandersetzung mit der Christologie von Karl-Heinz Menke," in *Die Wahrheit ist Person: Brennpunkte einer christologisch gewendeten Dogmatik*, ed. Julia Knop, Magnus Lerch, and Bernd J. Claret, 129–49 (Regensburg: Pustet, 2015).

56. Cf. Gregory of Nazianz, ep. 101, 32: SC 208, 50.

Not for Myself Alone

ATONEMENT AND PENANCE
AFTER DAOISM

Bede Benjamin Bidlack

In *Creation and the Cross*, Elizabeth Johnson challenges Saint Anselm's satisfaction theology of atonement as he presents it in *Cur Deus Homo*.[1] Anselm argues that Christ had to suffer and die on the cross to make satisfaction to God on behalf of a sinful humanity so as to restore God's honor. Johnson writes that such a theology of atonement, while wildly successful in the Church for centuries, is no longer useful for contemporary Christian spirituality. She insists that the common interpretation of Anselm's satisfaction theology is difficult in light of a loving God who wants "mercy not sacrifice" (Matthew 9:13).[2] She acknowledges that the "wrath of God" understanding of Anselm's satisfaction theory took on a life of its own, even though there are other readings of Anselm's theology that are more amenable to the image of a loving God.[3]

The Catechism, hundreds of years of tradition, and millions of prayers and liturgies practiced with an understanding of a satisfaction theory of atonement stand in the way of abandoning this theology altogether. One implication is the loss of the satisfaction theology of penance held by the Church. Atonement and penance are interlocked and if Johnson wants to jettison the satisfaction theology of atonement, the satisfaction theology of penance goes with it.

The satisfaction theology of penance sees penance as a participation in Christ's suffering on the cross by a sinful humanity (Col 1:24; CCC §1460). By virtue of participation, the faithful are able to make sacrifices and turn away from comforts in order to make satisfaction for sin. Moreover, penance—the teaching goes—is needed for the sake of justice. Justice dictates that people are punished for their sins, not so much by a vengeful God, but as a logical result of sinfulness. Thus, the Church teaches that eternal and temporal suffering come about from sin (CCC §1472).

The grace of the Sacrament of Reconciliation can save one from eternal suffering, and according to satisfaction theory, penance can reduce the amount of temporal suffering the faithful must undergo either in this life or in purgatory before entering into eternal beatitude.

Johnson challenges this classical view, arguing that penance is not making satisfaction for sin because Jesus's passion and death were never for the sake of satisfaction. She interprets the cross as a theology of accompaniment, which sees the suffering of Christ as divine accompaniment with a suffering world, not satisfaction for a fallen world. It is clear that Johnson's approach presents certain pastoral and theological challenges. If she is right, then personal penance either needs a new theology or needs to be discontinued.

Before doing away with penance, one might consider whether other traditions can shed some new light on its meaning and practice. Here I will examine the place of penance and intercession in two Daoist liturgies and one private practice, all of which maintain an awareness of sin as contrary to the natural flow of the universe. The comparison yields a theology of penance that fills the void left by Johnson's accompaniment interpretation of the cross. I propose that penance is a necessary Christian response to sin that participates in the voluntary suffering of Christ. Penance is, in part, an act of accompaniment, as Johnson describes it; that is, it has a radically social dimension to it. As such, the focus shifts from the penitent's sinfulness to the social reality of suffering caused by individual and social sin. Yet the proposal here goes beyond a penance of accompaniment to assert that penance does participate in the atonement of the cosmos by virtue of Christ's atoning activity, namely his life, death, and resurrection.

Inspired by Daoist teachings, I define atonement as a return of the world—that is, the entire cosmos—to conformity with the Divine Will. Atonement has the sense of reconciliation, healing, and salvation; it is the fruit of penance. Moreover, penance implies bodily performance as a response to the sins of all humanity, not only to the guilt of personal sins. Because penance is loaded with satisfaction theology, I will occasionally use "voluntary suffering" in its place, especially with regards to Daoism.

Sin

The idea of sin, *zui*, appeared in China as early as pre-Han texts (Han Dynasty 206 BCE–221 CE) where the offended party is Heaven. Heaven is the infinite and impersonal reality of the universe, which presides above humanity and which has a will.[4] If humanity opposed Heaven, suffering in the form of disasters, wars, and illness would result. In order to placate Heaven, the emperor would make sacrifices or even repent. In the *Spring and Autumn Annals of Master Lü* and in the *Xunzi* (third century BCE), a story presents the Shang Dynasty (1600–1050 BCE) emperor approaching Heaven due to a drought:

> Tang himself entered the mulberry forest to pray. He said: "If I, the ruler, have sinned, then let the people not be blamed; but if the people have sinned, then let me, the ruler, take the blame! Let not the highest god and otherworldly spirits harm the destiny of the people for the personal incompetence of my single person!"
>
> Having said this, he cut off his hair and had his hands tied, making himself into a sacrificial victim. Thus he prayed to the highest god. The people greatly rejoiced at his actions, and a great rain fell.[5]

If one can resist reading this through a Christian lens and instead use a Daoist lens—the lens through which this comparative project is trying to examine satisfaction theory—one would see Heaven not punishing the people with a drought, but simply withholding rain due to their sin. Heaven does not cause bad weather; people do. The recognition and admission of sin along with self-sacrifice correct the incongruity and restores harmony between Heaven and humanity. What changes is not an anthropomorphized feeling of satisfaction on the part of Heaven, but the harmony between Heaven and humanity bound by the common thread of the universe: qi—variously translated as *vital energy, pneuma,* or *breath.* Qi is the ground of a monistic universe. When disharmony arises, there is an organic disruption of the cosmos that leads to suffering and even death. Thus, in Chinese religion, good is harmony and life, and evil is disharmony and death.

This is the sensibility that finds its way into early Daoist communities. Once Daoists begin to organize, they start codifying moral rules that more precisely identify the source of suffering as disharmony.[6] Disharmony leads to social unrest, personal suffering, and illness. In the second century, Celestial Master Daoism regarded its followers as protected by the Dao so long as they lived in harmony with the Dao with moral rules as their guide. Strictly speaking, those who lived this way would potentially never suffer the evil of illness and death.

People did get sick, of course, and illness was attributed to sin. Health could only be restored when the appropriate sin was recognized and treated. The ailing Daoist would sit in a quiet room and review his or her life to identify the suspect sins. These would be confessed to a priest who would treat the illness with a ritual, offer preaching for moral correction, and penance of some sort, usually in the form of public service.[7]

In addition to illness, the sins would cause a subtraction of days from the Daoist's life. The anthropology was one that viewed the faithful as having a star born along with them. When one sins, the once luminous star grows a bit dimmer. The cumulation of sins causes the star to expire, at which time the Daoist dies. For instance, the *Essential Precepts of Master Red Pine* (fourth century CE) states that all misdeeds are recorded and appropriately punished. Here, Heaven is not the supreme reality as it was in the Shang Dynasty; Heaven has been theologically surpassed by the Dao. Heaven is a bureaucracy of divinities in service to the Dao who mete out blessings and punishments while keeping an eye on humanity. The *Essential Precepts of Master Red Pine* explains:

> If the celestials subtract one year, the star [essence] above the person's head loses its luster and he or she runs into lots of difficulties. If they take off ten years, the star gradually fades and the person encounters disasters, decline, and various diseases. If they subtract twenty years, the star's radiance is reduced significantly and the person runs into legal trouble and is imprisoned. If they take off thirty years, the star dissolves and the person dies.[8]

The point is that the consequences of sin lead to both social suffering (for example, legal troubles) and personal suffering. Social and physical difficulties are caused not by mundane circumstances or natural causes, but from living contrary to the Dao. Consequently, the Dao rescinds its protection and leaves the culprit vulnerable to nefarious, supernatural forces. These forces include not only celestial punishment, but also illness caused by ghosts and demons. There is no indication that offenses could lead to any post-mortem punishment, like hell.

The idea of hell came in the creases of Buddhist scrolls from Central Asia. Buddhism arrived in China around the turn to the Common Era but did not have significant influence on Daoism for another three hundred years. When it did, the influence appeared in the texts of Numinous Treasure Daoism. This school is a rich combination of beliefs that have their origin in earlier Daoist schools, Confucianism, and especially, Buddhism. The style and doctrines of its texts so closely match Buddhist sutras that they have been accused of being plagiarized in medieval China.[9]

Buddhism was not embraced by the Chinese at first. For instance, the idea of leaving the family and living the celibate life of a monk or nun without leaving any progeny was deeply repugnant to Confucian sensibilities that focused on the family. Buddhism had to go through a process of becoming Chinese, or *Sinicized*, for it to be accepted.[10] One way the Chinese accomplished this was by drawing the Five Precepts that all Buddhists follow—do not kill, do not steal, do not engage in licentiousness, do not get intoxicated, do not lie—into the ancient system of the Five Phases.

Five Phases is part of a larger system of correlation or correspondence theory whereby the Chinese observe the cosmos and map those observations upon the human person and society. Conversely, the human person is seen as reflected in the cosmos. This theory was applied to every aspect of human life, from politics to food and medicine to religion. It has its origin in yin-yang cosmology that pre-dates Daoism and Confucianism.[11] In the third century BCE, the naturalist Zou Yan expanded the philosophical pair of yin-yang to the Five Phases: wood, fire, earth, metal, water. Five Phases are energetic moments within the cosmic flow of qi that, when understood, can be used to identify and correct interruptions and imbalances in this cosmic flow.[12] When mapped onto violations of the Five Precepts of Buddhism, they explain physical, social, and even environmental ailments.

In the *Precepts of the Highest Lord Lao*, one can see the close affinity between Daoism, Buddhism, and Five Phases cosmology. Composed sometime in the early Tang period (618–907), it is a conversation between Lord Lao and the guardian of the western pass, Yin Xi, mostly about explaining the Five Precepts:[13]

The precept to abstain from killing belongs to the east. It embodies the qi of Germinating Life and honors natural growth. People who harm and kill living beings will receive corresponding harm in their livers.

The precept to abstain from stealing belongs to the north. It embodies the essence of Great Yin and presides over the resting and storing of nature. People who steal will receive corresponding calamities in their kidneys.

The precept to abstain from licentiousness belongs to the west. It embodies the material power of lesser Yin and preserves the purity and strength of men and women. People who delight in licentiousness will receive corresponding foulness in their lungs.

The precept to abstain from intoxication belongs to the south and the phase fire. It embodies the qi of Great Yang and supports all beings in their full growth. People who indulge in drink will receive corresponding poison in their hearts.

The precept to abstain from lying belongs to the center and the phase earth; its virtue is faithfulness. People who lie will receive corresponding shame in their spleens.[14]

Violating a precept—that is sinning—thus results in bodily punishment by disrupting the flow of one's qi to vital organs. This is consistent with early Daoism that saw blessedness as life and punishment as death in this world, not in some otherworldly hell.

More important for this argument than the threat of hellfire and brimstone in Numinous Treasure texts is the Mahayana Buddhist notions of reincarnation, universal salvation, and the bodhisattva ideal. The faith surrounding these three doctrines permeates Daoist ritual to this day, even though Numinous Treasure as a school no longer exists.[15] Reincarnation in Numinous Treasure Daoism is the doctrine that, upon death, people do not dissolve into the Dao but continue to be reborn in different realms. Universal salvation is the notion that ritual behavior can relieve the suffering of other beings, and bodhisattvas are agents devoted to this end, that is, the salvation of all beings. For Daoists living out of a heavily Confucian-influenced society, working for the salvation of all beings really meant working for the salvation of one's own ancestors.[16]

Salvation, *du*, in this context means "to ferry across." In this case, it is to ferry across illusions, changes, and the distresses of this world and the next through which the souls of their ancestors are transmigrating.[17] Buddhist images of hell got married to the bureaucracy of imperial China in the religious imagination of the Chinese. Like a bureaucracy organized in a hierarchical order, hell has levels of the damned; each level has punishments appropriate to the sins people committed in their lifetimes. A person deep in the bowels of hell could, over time, be brought to the higher levels and maybe even rebirth on the earthly plane. If the person continued on this trajectory, he or she could be introduced to the heavenly bureaucracy. There, he or she would enjoy an eternal afterlife as a celestial bureaucrat.[18]

At the same time, the Daoists do believe in a this-worldly notion of salvation. Celestial Master Daoism in its early millenarianism saw the fulfillment of their movement as a world without death. Salvation can also mean "to ferry across" generations—that is, to not die.

It should be no surprise, then, that Daoists had an interest in longevity techniques that grew concurrently with Chinese medicine. These developed into external alchemy and later internal alchemy that sought to concoct an elixir of immortality that would bring the adept into union with the Dao and thereby bestow upon the adept characteristics of the Dao, such as eternal life. The dimensions that Numinous Treasure adds are the ideas that one continues to work out one's salvation even after the death of the body and ritual behaviors can help one through this.

Since everything is knitted together in one inseparable Dao, the word "atonement" in early Daoism means a healing of the relationship between the human community and a non-personal Dao. This sits in contrast to Christian theologies of atonement as being a reconciliation between a person and a personal God. The Daoist belief that everything moves together in a unified cosmos becomes, perhaps, clearer with the examination of Daoist solutions to the suffering caused by sin.

Solutions to Sin

Numinous Treasure Daoism provided solutions to sin and redemption that were largely liturgical. The following section will present two extremely important rituals and one solitary practice, all of which are interrelated: the recitation of the *Scripture of Salvation*, the Rite of Mud and Soot, and the practice of internal alchemy. To these, the *Scripture of Salvation* is foundational.

CHANTING THE SCRIPTURE OF SALVATION

A group of Numinous Treasure scriptures center around a deity named the Heavenly Worthy of Primordial Commencement (Yuanshi tianzun). In his compassion, he sends these texts to help the world along because it has wandered from the Dao. Among them is the *Wondrous Scripture of the Upper Chapters of Limitless Salvation*, or the *Scripture of Salvation*. The Chinese text itself is a translation, for the original utterance by the Heavenly Worthy of Primordial Commencement is incomprehensible in any human language. So powerful were these original words that they summoned deities from all over the cosmos. Thus the words themselves have tremendous power, even in their diluted, human form, and therefore are meant to be recited. They become accessible to humans through the translation offered by the August Heavenly Perfected, and the recitation of the *Scripture of Salvation* leads to the salvation of transmigrating people.

The convergence of Buddhist-inspired belief in transmigration, universal salvation, and the bodhisattva ideal led to the formation of liturgies for the salvation of those trapped in hell. Chief among them was the recitation of the *Scripture of Salvation* that is still recited in Daoist liturgies today.[19]

Daoists chant the scripture on behalf of all beings, but really for the sake of their own ancestors. Once in heaven, these ancestors can extend blessings downward to the living and future generations.[20] Unlike in Christianity, in this tradition, there is no single, savior figure who intercedes on behalf of all. Ancestors and the gods can help, but principally, humanity must participate in its own salvation.

After fasting, bathing, and prayers, Numinous Treasure Daoists proceeded to recite the *Scripture of Salvation* in solitude, not as a communal ritual. The liturgy only developed later, once the movement grew, owing much to the ritual master Lu Xiujing (406–477) who fashioned elaborate rituals that characterize Daoist liturgy to this day.[21] At the same time, the initial emphasis on individual chanting never entirely went away.

Much later, in 1226, Daoist savant, Xiao Yingsou describes the preparation for chanting in a commentary on the *Scripture of Salvation*:

All the people who recite passages (must) cleanse and fast. Entering the Chamber of Silence, arrange your ceremonial robes, clap your teeth, and burn incense.

Mentally bow to the east, south, west, and north—the four (cardinal) directions. Next bow to the northeast, then to the southeast, the southwest, the northwest, above and below. To each direction, bow once. When your bowing is finished, turn to the east and practice "Sitting Peacefully."

Next, clap your teeth. Recite an oral incantation for cleansing the mind and a cleaning the body incantation, and alert the body gods. Next clap your teeth, recite a cleansing Heaven and Earth incantation, and opening the *Scripture (of Salvation)*, a mystery containment incantation.

[Commentary]: When you have finished these incantations, then open the scroll and begin chanting.[22]

An additional point to return to is the connection between chanting for the sake of salvation and sitting peacefully (*pingzuo*). What's important at present is to notice that the chanting of the *Scripture of Salvation* is a *zhai*, variously translated as *ritual, rite, levée, fast*, or *retreat*, depending on the context. What Xiao suggests is a retreat when he writes for an individual entering his or her own Chamber of Silence. The expanded, liturgical version that Lu helped develop is *zhai* as a rite.

RITE OF MUD AND SOOT

One example of a penitential rite is the Rite of Mud and Soot (*tutan zhai*). It has its origins in Celestial Master Daoism, and so it predates Lu, but the earliest records of the rite are in the *Secret Essentials of the Most High* (*Wushang biyao*) an encyclopedia commissioned by Emperor Wu of the Northern Zhou Dynasty in 574 to contribute to religious stability in the kingdom after vitriolic court debates between Daoists and Buddhists.[23] There is some disagreement over exactly how Daoists performed the rite, but the general idea is that certain participants would undergo a harsh penance during which they would leave their hair undone, hands bound, and faces smeared with mud and ash. With a jade disc in their mouths, they would knock their foreheads to the ground. They repeated this mortification over three days.[24] In his *Texts of the Five Sentiments* (*Wugan wen*), Lu includes a later version of this rite he calls the Mud Rite of the Three Primes.[25] He consoles and encourages his followers by relating that he participated in the rite himself and is familiar with the physical demands of the penance. In order to rouse enthusiasm for the rite, he tells his readers that he performed the rite under the harsh conditions of winter.[26]

One interpretation of this rite sees the participants as penitents who feel the weight of guilt for their sins and therefore perform the harsh penance of the Rite of Mud and Soot on behalf of themselves and behalf of their ancestors.[27] This interpretation is quite common in Daoist studies. Some scholars see the ritual as being a communal penance where the wretched penitents are rolling about in the mud in a "frenzy"[28] or "lost in ecstasy."[29] The point of all of this is to elicit "sympathy" from the gods so that they can look forward to a more blessed future for themselves and heavenly ascent for their ancestors.[30]

There are two explanations for this widespread interpretation. First, many studies rely on Henri Maspero's 1950 presentation of the Rite of Mud and Soot, which was an early attempt at understanding the complex world of Daoism.[31] Second, modern scholars tend to start with Buddhist characterizations of the rite. In the *Disputing Deceptions* (*Biangan lun*) composed around 480, the Buddhist Xuanguang diminutively relates that the Rite of Mud and Soot began with the grandson of the founder of Celestial Master Daoism, Zhang Lu. He mocks the Rite of Mud and Soot: "One would roll in the mud like a donkey, smear the face with yellow soil, pluck off the head [covering?], hang [the hair?], from a willow, and mold [the body like?] clay until it was bruised . . . This is the height of stupidity and baseness!"[32] Indeed, the account leaves one imagining a frenzy.

A second reading of the rite refutes the interpretation of the disheveled appearance and knocking of heads as being suffering for the sake of eliciting a sympathetic response from the gods. Early Chinese religion denies any anthropomorphized Heaven that could be appealed to through empathy. Instead, the connection between early penitents and Heaven was more organic: the three realms of the cosmos—Heaven, earth, and humanity—are connected through the common bond of qi. With misbehavior, humanity is in disharmony with Heaven and earth, and disaster soon follows. This finds its way into the monastic Daoist view of the cosmos in the *Scripture of Great Peace*. In this text, the primordial qi of the universe extends through the human as the Three Treasures of Humanity: spirit (*shen*) associated with Heaven, essence (*jing*) associated with earth, and qi, associated with humanity.[33] Every person has the Three Treasures as bodily manifestations of qi, which unifies the cosmos. The result of sin is not the pang of guilt at dishonoring a god, but a cosmic response of illness or other calamity.[34]

The second interpretation of the Rite of Mud and Soot also agrees that the guilt of sin is not what is at play here, but the vicarious suffering with those in hell. The so-called penitents are not atoning for their sins nor are they overcome by guilt. Instead, they are taking upon themselves the suffering of those in hell, or *earth prisons*, and are willingly undergoing vicarious suffering. The evidence for this is their very appearance:

> Both the yellow earth smeared on the forehead and, most tellingly, the jade disk placed in the mouth mimic the condition of corpses in the grave. Ghosts appear in Chinese tales with their hair undone. The term "mud and soot" in Chinese literature commonly refers to the desperate state of the people in times of warfare and famine, but is also common in Daoist descriptions of unfortunates bound in earth prisons.[35]

Their suffering is not for themselves, but much more communal and intercessory in character.[36]

Moreover, some interpreters of this rite see not a group of supplicants, but a single Daoist priest undergoing the rite on behalf of his or her patron's family.[37] The rite would be another case of a priest interfacing with Heaven and hell for the sake of the people. The only benefit to those undergoing the rite could be the accumulation of merit, but that merit is transferred to their ancestors. In this case, one accrues merit not by preaching or doing works of charity, but by suffering. Lu Xiujing writes, "It creates merit though moral uprightness in suffering."[38]

Yet a third possibility is a middle way between the first two: They are penitents who seek to atone for their sins and those of their ancestors in hell, not out of the compulsion of guilt, but out of a communal responsibility that is peculiar to Chinese sensibilities in general, and Daoism in particular. The Rite of Mud and Soot does emerge out of an early Celestial Master—that is pre-Buddhist—understanding of evil and sin. People do need to take responsibility for their transgressions against the Dao. In an organic response, the person and the Dao fall into disharmony, and disaster and illness result. However, any sins not atoned for fall upon people's progeny and later generations in what is called *inherited evil* (*chengfu*).[39] The intention of the Rite of Mud and Soot is to work through this inherited evil for the supplicants' own sake and, later, in the Numinous Treasure version of this, for the sake of their ancestors suffering in hell. None of this is out of a personal sense of guilt. At the same time, the penitents appear disheveled and undignified, like those in earth prisons. The consequences of their sins are made public and take on a communal tone in the rite. What this reveals is not guilt, but shame.[40]

Guilt suggests a far more individualized sense of self that was deliberately avoided in ancient China despite tendencies toward its development.[41] Guilt is private and internalized, while shame is more public and shared in character. Shame acknowledges that one's sins and those of one's ancestors cause disharmony within the person, the community, and the cosmos. Thus, when the Rite of Mud and Soot was performed, it was out of a sense of renewing the world and restoring its harmonious flow with the Dao.[42]

Of interest here is the idea that people do bring harm upon themselves, the community, and ultimately the cosmos as a result of their sins. The damage from sin did not remain upon the individual alone. However, the burden of correcting the disharmony did not remain solely on the culprit either. The community—either as pious Daoists or as priestly Daoists—could intercede on behalf of all beings through ritual behavior such as chanting the *Scripture of Salvation* or performing the Rite of Mud and Soot. Even as this intercession was for all beings, it was practiced particularly on behalf of a local community or of one's ancestors. By the end of the Song Dynasty, a significant branch of Daoism took a turn to the individual with the meditation practice of internal alchemy. Even in this case, however, adepts did so for the benefit of others, at least in part.

INTERNAL ALCHEMY

Internal alchemy uses mental techniques to physically transform the body, to have it harmonize with the Dao such that it joins the Dao and shares its characteristics. Daoist immortals who have completed the process of alchemical transformation are reported to not only exist continually, but also to have powers such as bilocation, control over objects, and the ability to heal. They accomplish this by mentally guiding their qi along pathways in the body called *mai*, or vessels, and in so doing transform the so-called three treasures of humanity—essence, qi, and spirit—into qi of a more harmonious quality. From the outside, the adept appears to be in quiet, sitting mediation, but his or her qi is moving to bring about psychophysical change. The process is difficult and requires years of practice to complete. Daoists had more than a casual interest in Chinese medicine: The longer an adept lived, the more life there was to practice internal alchemy—the more internal alchemy, the longer the life. Provided the adept had built a sufficient foundation, even after the death of the body, he or she could continue the practice to achieve post-mortem immortality.[43]

On the surface, it would appear that the requirements of assiduous meditation would render internal alchemy a solitary, self-interested practice. Though it was the case for many, some saw it as an indispensable practice for saving the human community from the disharmony brought about by sin. As the alchemist cosmic-izes the body, the harmony with the Dao that he or she enjoys is not isolated but part of the act of sanctifying the cosmos.[44]

For many alchemists, bringing the cosmos to harmony with the Dao through one's body alone was not enough. This is clear in the example of Chen Zhixu (1290–1368?). Chen achieved enlightenment, but he felt his alchemical cultivation was incomplete and that he had to contribute to the salvation of others. In order to complete his cultivation, he authored the *Essentials of the Gold Elixir* (*Jindan dayao*).[45] In a likely apocryphal tale, the goddess, Mazu, saves Chen from death by drowning. This is why he expands the goal of his practice beyond his own immortality:

> The Lao people there sought his *dao* by force; unable to gain it, they got him drunk, placed him in a drum, and tossed it into the Pacific Ocean. The Consort of Heaven [Mazu] was startled into action, and ordered the sea spirits to guard him, and deliver him to the southern shore . . . Chen thought to himself, "My not having perished in that drum in the water, and being able to be alive today, is [because] Heaven will rely on me to transmit the *dao*."[46]

For Chen, writing and teaching were *spreading the Dao* (*bu* Dao). To share what he had learned was his duty, but it also had the beneficial effect of producing karmic merit and counted as a good deed on his heavenly record.[47] In addition to the *Essentials of the Gold Elixir*, he taught students and wrote a commentary on the *Scripture of Salvation* in which he compares the activity of the alchemist with the actions of the Heavenly Worthy of Primordial Commencement, who issued the *Scripture of Salvation* in order to move the age (*kalpa*) along with the Dao when, on its own, the age would fall quickly into calamity. Chen states that the alchemist acts similarly and is participating in the life and activity of the divine.[48] Internal alchemy involves participating in redeeming humanity when it falls into error. In Chen's approach to alchemy, there are three steps that reinforce one another. One pursues harmony with the Dao through internal alchemy. This practice gives one the necessary experience to teach with authority in the religious marketplace. Teaching redeems people from error and saves them from the disharmony of sin. In this way, teaching provides karmic merit that supports further development of one's alchemical practice.[49] Beyond himself and the living, the alchemist is generating salvific merit for his ancestors. In the *Essentials of the Gold Elixir* Chen writes:

> Now, one who has completed the *dao* unites his spirits with the Dao, and will be without decay for endless *kalpa*s. What is more, his merits will also reach to his nine generations of ancestors, and they will ascend together to [the heaven of] Upper Clarity in broad daylight.[50]

All of this is consistent with Numinous Treasure liturgical practice. Chanting the *Scripture of Salvation*—itself a solitary practice in its earliest stages—or participating in the Rite of Mud and Soot generates saving power for the sins of the ancestors and karmic merit for those participating in the rituals. Like these rituals, internal alchemy sends salvific qi into the cosmos to heal the transgressions of others.

The same emphasis on the cosmic and social efficacy of internal alchemy may be found in the writing of Xiao Yingsou (fl. 1226) who was a ritual master, advisor to the Song Dynasty emperor Song Lizong (r. 1225–1264), and author of one of the most influential commentaries on *Scripture of Salvation, The Inner Meaning of the Scripture of Salvation*.[51] Chen cites his commentary over a dozen times in his *Essentials of the Gold Elixir*.[52] Xiao links the *Scripture of Salvation* to the practice of internal alchemy, which he finds absolutely necessary for understanding the *Scripture of Salvation* and its salvific effects for oneself and others. Xiao states explicitly that practicing internal alchemy must be undertaken for the sake of others:

> Harken to the story of Li Guangxuan! In the past, Guangxuan assiduously and diligently sought the Dao over many years. One day on Mt. Shaoshi, he encountered an extraordinary being who told him: "Today, you seek the Dao, do you think you should only help and uplift others? or do you think you should only fulfill yourself? If you stop at making your own body spirit, then you are not worthy to be an immortal."[53]

Alchemists radiate salvific qi not only to their ancestors, but also forward in time to other people. Much like ancestors shower down blessings from Heaven to their progeny, alchemists radiate salvific qi to future generations in their alchemical practice. Xiao insists: "How could one body rise to salvation? It must be that blessings cascade to later generations."[54]

Alchemists emit a current that flows harmoniously with the Dao. Not only does it flow with the current, but the cosmos and humanity also get drawn along with it.

Comparative Turn

Thus far, I have traced the notion of sin and atonement from pre-Daoist China to the earliest Daoist communities. In ancient Shang theology, sin had cosmic repercussions in the form of natural calamities such as drought or flooding. Sins had to be acknowledged and people had to do penance for them. This returned the world toward its natural harmony between Heaven and earth. In Celestial Master Daoism, people needed to confess and atone for sin because the consequences of sin included cosmic retribution as well as causing the Dao to revoke its protection from the individual and his or her community.

The communal awareness grew in Numinous Treasure Daoism, which adopted this worldview and grafted onto it a Sinicized Buddhism. Sin was violating precepts and caused harm to the cosmos and society. Fortunately, Buddhism also inspired avenues to correct the problem: the ritual chanting of the *Scripture of Salvation*, the Rite of Mud and Soot, and internal alchemy. These solutions were concerned with personal sin, but also with the sins of the broader Daoist communities, including the ancestors.

In these Numinous Treasure traditions and later, atonement means bringing the cosmos, oneself, and the society into harmony with the Dao. Atonement is not suffering for the sake of rebalancing the scales of good and bad deeds to appease an offended god. Moreover, it is not the compulsion of personal guilt that inspires these rites and practices, but the duty to the gods, the ancestors, and even future humanity.

From this summary, let me suggest two points of comparative reflection. These points revolve around penance as participation in the cross and as an utterly social practice. Neither point depends upon a satisfaction theology of atonement or a satisfaction theology of penance.

First, the turn away from sin toward the divine is common to the two traditions. Both the Christian and the Daoist tradition acknowledge that the world is not as it should be and that people need to adjust it to fit the divine model of perfection. Divine intervention does help with the process, but at the same time there is a human desire to be like the divine and participate in divine life.[55] In the case of penance, people want to participate in saving action. Daoists want to perform voluntary suffering on behalf of their ancestors so as to cooperate with the Heavenly Worthy of Primordial Commencement. They participate by raising those trapped in hell through the chanting of the *Scripture of Salvation*, or in Chen Zhixu's case, by practicing alchemy and spreading the Dao. For Christians, participating in divine life is the invitation to be a follower of Christ. Penance can be in the form of working against suffering, such as caring for the sick or feeding the hungry. These are ways of participating in salvation, more commonly understood as building the Kingdom of God. These activities of love and justice may be called *penances of growth*. They are penances insofar as they involve self-sacrifice, and they contribute to growth because they work against suffering caused by sin while also building up the human community.

These works find their example in the ministry of Christ during his lifetime. Atonement is the fruit of penance. If atonement is understood as healing the suffering caused by sin, then one sees Christ already atoning well before the cross. Indeed, Christ's atoning action is constituted by not just his cross, but his life, death, and resurrection. These are three movements in one atoning activity of God; the cross is not the sole locus of atonement.[56] The implication for penance is similarly to recognize the penitential possibilities in serving others in a penance of growth.

In addition, voluntary suffering is a shared response to sin across these traditions. The Rite of Mud and Soot involves great sacrifice through its long hours of penance. The disciplines associated with internal alchemy and spreading the Dao—for example, through fasting and the hardship of travel—are another example of voluntary suffering and denial for the sake of bringing a lost world to harmony with the Dao.

Christians, of course, turn to the cross as the model of voluntary suffering. According to Johnson, the cross offers a theology of accompaniment. A theology of accompaniment interprets the cross as God's presence with the world "through its traumas and travail, even unto death."[57] God suffers with humanity and all of creation. With this explanation penance may be seen as accompaniment. Through penance, the comfortable imaginatively place themselves alongside the afflicted in a *penance of diminishment*.[58] Without the disciplines suggested by the Church such as almsgiving and fasting, the prayers of the comfortable lack a solidarity with the afflicted and may appear perfunctory. Penance of diminishment is voluntary suffering that diminishes the self in the sense that it reverses usual bodily processes.[59] Rather than eat, the penitent fasts; rather than sleep, the penitent holds vigil. In this way, the penitent experiences the suffering of others caused by sin, just as Christ did on the cross. That said, I see penance as more than this; it does lead to atonement, but it is atonement not just of the individual penitent but of the entire world. This is my second point: penance has a radically social dimension to it, the fruit of which is social atonement.

If penance were just accompaniment, Christianity and Daoism may not give it the importance they do. In the Daoist tradition, voluntary suffering is participation in divine, saving activity, not an act of solidarity with the poor. It releases qi that brings the cosmos toward harmony with the Dao. Christians can adopt this view, but carefully. I am not going so far as to say that human suffering on its own moves the cosmos toward fulfillment in Christ. We can draw only a correlation, not a cause.

Resurrection follows the cross, but the cross does not cause the resurrection (for example, Rom. 6:4–8). Suffering sanctified in the light of the resurrection transforms the sufferer and the cosmos by extension, because the human and the cosmos are continuous. Christ's life, death, and resurrection affect the entire cosmos.

Christ's death on the cross, and by extension Christian penance, makes sense only in light of the resurrection. What brings about atonement cannot be isolated to only his life (the incarnation as stressed in the Christian East) or his death (as stressed in the Christian West and satisfaction theology). The cross does bring about atonement, but not in isolation from the life and resurrection of Christ. Likewise, participation in the saving activity of God cannot be isolated to penance of diminishment but includes penance of growth. Moreover, because of the integral nature of the human person with other people and the cosmos, the atonement that results from penance does not remain with the individual, but always has a social and even cosmic dimension.

If one accepts the social dimension of penance—penance not for me alone, but for others—then there may be the risk of not changing anything, but returning to the abuses Johnson is trying to avoid. Christianity has been down the "penance for others" road before. Christian assistance with the burden of penance took hold very early in the Christian East and in a great variety of forms. For example, the relationship between a spiritual father and a penitent were described using economic metaphors and substitution language. The spiritual father, or in most cases the confessor priest or bishop, would offer himself for the sake of the penitent. A late fourth-century Syrian text, the *Apostolic Constitutions*, advises the bishop to be personally involved in the healing of those in his care. The idea was inspired by the example of Christ:

> If it is possible, the bishop should make the offense his own, and should say to the sinner: "just turn around, and I will bear death in your place, like the Lord has done for me and everyone."[60]

In addition, monks or anyone considered a spiritual father or mother could offer the abundance of their holiness for the sake of others. The holiness of a saint could be distributed to sinners.[61] In the West, as early as eighth-century Europe, one person doing penance on behalf of another was well established. It was called proxy penance: "Any of the faithful could, as an act of charity, pray, fast, or give alms on behalf of penitents. Such assistance was thought to speed up the process of atonement."[62]

It grew such that some were considered "professional penitents" among clerics, religious, and others who devoted themselves to the pursuit of holiness (*profesio santitatis*).[63] In time, it also led to abuse on both sides of the proxy transaction. On the one hand, the laity and priest-confessors could extort large fees, and on the other hand, the wealthy could hire large numbers of proxies for their personal benefit. Even in the early Middle Ages, there was both a promotion and a criticism of proxy penance. Although there were abuses, it did provide merciful relief to many who were sincere, but unable to complete their penance.[64]

Penance in the Christian East differs from proxy suffering in the medieval West by the intention of the penitent to suffer on behalf of others with or without their request and free of further obligation.[65] The caveat is that penance on behalf of others is a calling and best undertaken in consultation with the Christian community. For instance, in his Rule, Saint Benedict admonishes his monks during Lent that they should undertake a self-chosen penance only with the permission of the abbot (Rule of Benedict, Chapter 49).[66]

Perhaps the risk of abuse is not the social dimension of penance, but privileging the concern of personal salvation over the concern of the salvation of the community. A sense of doing penance for personal guilt is missing in Daoism. Similarly, a Daoist-influenced theology of Christian penance could place concern with the human community before concerns of personal sin. Suffering will come as a result of sin already. In imitation of Christ, Christians may take up penance, but not primarily to make amends for their own sins. An overemphasis on personal guilt may lead to a distorted and unhealthy spirituality of penance. Among other things, Johnson's observations are that a satisfaction theory of atonement has glorified suffering even to the point of justifying undeserved suffering and suggesting that suffering itself is the most reliable pathway to God.[67] Examples abound from the expectations that the poor accept unjust economic exploitation to self-flagellation to sleep deprivation. The Daoist tradition examined here de-emphasizes the self altogether. What is important is not one's own sins, but the sins of the community and what it does to the cosmos. Both Christianity and Daoism warn against turning on oneself in such a way that keeps the wounds of personal sin open rather than heal them, for example, the spiritual ailment of scruples. Instead, the greater concern is for others.[68]

"Others" includes the entire community of creation, the entire cosmos. The human community is not alone in the suffering caused by sin.

Innumerable entities suffer from diminishment, toxic invasion, over-harvesting, over-mining, and over-heating. Even the stars are dimmed by light pollution. Although the modern period began a process of separating the human from the cosmos, Daoism views the world monistically. They, the world, and the Dao are not separate, but exist in various phases of qi. Today, people are starting to rediscover their interconnection with the cosmos. Drawing from the Eastern Church and the Danish theologian Niels Gregersen, Johnson emphasizes the integral nature of the human person. Thus, the incarnation of Christ must be understood as "deep incarnation."[69] The body of Jesus is made from the same dust of all creation, like all human bodies. Deep incarnation recognizes that Christ takes up all of creation in his incarnation, death, and resurrection.[70]

To Daoists, the world is not just the human world or even the earth. It's the entire cosmos, including hell. When gazing at the magnificence of a clear night sky, placing the human at the front of the cosmos may appear too bold. Perhaps for this reason, many thinkers prefer to have earth in mind when they speak of the world. It's more manageable. Yet ancient peoples and contemporary Daoists have not lost their connection to the stars. These challenge Christians to undertake penance not just for the sake of the human or earth, but for the sake of the cosmos. Unlike Daoism, Christianity teaches that souls in hell are out of reach, but still Catholic Christianity retains the tradition of purgatory. Our penance is for not only the living and the earth, but also for the dead in purgatory who remain in the cosmos and within reach of the power of prayer.

This vision of the universe comes precisely because of, and not despite of, the body. The bodily suffering is a critical part of the Rite of Mud and Soot. In the alchemical tradition, the transformation of the body sanctifies the universe. For Christianity, resurrection comes about after Christ's bodily suffering. What happens to and through Christ's body is the means for communicating the good news of salvation. Christian spirituality traditionally sees the body as an obstacle to sanctification that must be beaten in service to the soul: the more it suffers, the better off the soul is. What is true of the body is true of the rest of creation. If the body is an obstacle fit for abuse, then so is creation. Such a hierarchical dualism has played a role in the exploitation of the vulnerable and the earth, and conventional Christian spirituality has largely played out in this way. Of course, this is not Catholic doctrine. To the contrary, sacramental theology insists that the body and creation are vehicles through which God's salvation works. With its bodily discipline, penances of diminishment have as their aim healing of oneself and the world through the body, not the abuse of it.

Conclusion

What I have done is put Elizabeth Johnson's *Creation and the Cross* in conversation with the Numinous Treasure Daoists and the traditions that flow from them. Johnson presents a persuasive argument grounded in scripture and developed out of an awareness of contemporary issues. She explains that we do not know how atonement works, but scriptures of both Testaments give ample reason to have faith that it does. She denies that Christ's suffering on the cross makes satisfaction for the wrong done to God by human disobedience. Instead, she offers an alternative interpretation of the cross in the form of a theology of accompaniment. The comparison with Daoism serves the purpose of preventing the reader of Johnson's work from too quickly losing important points she under-emphasizes as she discards Anselm's satisfaction theory of atonement, namely a theology of penance.

In summary, the comparison makes clear that a human response to sinfulness is necessary and that penance is often the mode of that response. Penance leads to atonement, which is a reconciliation, a healing, a re-conformity with the Divine Will. The comparison also argues that Christian penance is a participation in Christ's atoning activity which cannot be isolated to the cross—as satisfaction theology does—but is already at work in his life and fulfilled in his resurrection. Accordingly, penance is not limited to the cross (penance of diminishment) but includes participating in the atoning activities of Christ's ministry (penance of growth). The comparison also points to the radically social dimension of penance. Penance is not performed for the individual alone, but for the entire cosmos.

Notes

1. I thank Catherine Cornille for organizing the conference where this chapter was first delivered, for conceiving this volume, and for her helpful comments on earlier drafts of this chapter. I am also grateful to conference participants for their helpful comments, especially Ligita Ryliskyte, who gave a thoughtful response to my presentation.
2. An obvious example is Jesus's parable of the Prodigal Son who is never chastised by his father upon his return and never does penance as a condition of his restoration to his family (Luke 15:11–32).

3. Elizabeth Johnson, *Creation and the Cross: The Mercy of God for a Planet in Peril* (Mary-knoll, N.Y.: Orbis Books, 2018), 13. In contrast to this critique of Anselm is the view that he is arguing for Christ's sacrifice on the cross as a loving act of self-gift and obedience to the Father, not for the appeasement of a dishonored God. Nonetheless, I agree with Johnson that the common view of satisfaction theology has taken a life of its own. It is this lived theology as it appears in Johnson that is the focus of the present chapter. I thank Daniel Madigan and Leo Lefebure for pointing out the defense of Anselm to me.

4. Dainan Zhang, *Key Concepts in Chinese Philosophy*, trans. Edmund Ryden (New Haven: Yale University Press, 2002), 3–5.

5. Tsuchiya Masaaki, "Confession of Sins and Awareness of Self in the *Taiping jing*," in *Daoist Identity History, Lineage, and Ritual*, ed. Livia Kohn and Harold David Roth (Honolulu: University of Hawai'i Press, 2002), 48.

6. Livia Kohn, *Cosmos and Community: The Ethical Dimension of Daoism* (Cambridge, Mass.: Three Pines Press, 2004).

7. Terry F. Kleeman, *Celestial Masters: History and Ritual in Early Daoist Communities*, Harvard-Yenching Institute Monograph Series (Cambridge: Harvard University Asia Center, 2016), 60, 352.

8. Kohn, *Cosmos and Community*, 157.

9. Livia Kohn, *Hsiao Tao Lun: Laughing at the Tao Debates among Buddhists and Taoists in Medieval China* (Princeton, N.J.: Princeton University Press, 1995), 130.

10. For an exposition on this process, see Erik Zürcher, *The Buddhist Conquest of China: The Spread and Adaptation of Buddhism in Early Medieval China* (Leiden: Brill, 2007).

11. A. C. Graham, *Disputers of the Tao* (La Salle, Ill.: Open Court, 1989).

12. Livia Kohn, *Health and Long Life: The Chinese Way* (Cambridge, Mass.: Three Pines Press, 2005), 23–29.

13. This conversation between Lord Lao and Yin Xi closely resembles an interview with the Buddha by the devotees Trapusa and Bhallika in the appropriately named *Sutra of Trapusa and Bhallika*. See Kohn, *Cosmos and Community*, 145–46.

14. Kohn, *Health and Long Life*, 150.

15. Another school of Daoism, Highest Clarity, absorbed Numinous Treasure in the sixth century in a movement toward an integration of Daoist ideas and practice. Toshiaki Yamada, "The Lingbao School," in *Daoism Handbook*, ed. Livia Kohn (Leiden: Brill, 2000), 226.

16. Yamada, "The Lingbao School," 255.

17. Bede Benjamin Bidlack, *In Good Company: The Body and Divinization in Pierre Teilhard De Chardin, SJ and Daoist Xiao Yingsou*, East Asian Comparative Literature and Culture (Leiden: Brill, 2015), 94.

18. Stephen R. Bokenkamp, "Death and Ascent in Ling-pao Taoism," *Taoist Resources* 1, no. 2 (1989): 10–11.

19. Bokenkamp, "Death and Ascent in Ling-pao Taoism," 379.

20. Bokenkamp, "Death and Ascent in Ling-pao Taoism," 375.

21. Bokenkamp, "Death and Ascent in Ling-pao Taoism," 389.

22. Bidlack, *In Good Company*, 189–92.

23. John Lagerwey, *Wu-shang pi-yao: Somme Taoiste du VIe siècle*, Publications de L'ecole Française d'Extrême-Orient (Paris: Ecole française d'Extrême-Orient, 1981), 4–5. For

a brief history of the debates, see Bede Benjamin Bidlack, "What Child Is This? Jesus, Lord Lao, and Divine Identity," in *Comparing Faithfully: Insights for Systematic Theological Reflection*, ed. Michelle Voss Roberts (New York: Fordham University Press, 2016), 196–98.

24. For various accounts of this, see Charles Benn, "Daoist Ordination and Zhai Rituals," in *Daoism Handbook*, ed. Kohn Livia (Leiden: Brill, 2000), 311; Stephen Eskildsen, *Asceticism in Early Taoist Religion* (Albany: SUNY Press, 1998), 120–21; Livia Kohn, *The Taoist Experience* (Albany: SUNY Press, 1993), 106–7.

25. Pengzhi Lü, "Daoist Rituals," in *Early Chinese Religion*, ed. John Lagerwey and Marc Kalinowski (Leiden: Brill, 2009), 1310.

26. Lü, "Daoist Rituals," 1310; Benn, "Daoist Ordination and Zhai Rituals," 312.

27. These observations closely follow Stephen R. Bokenkamp, "Sackcloth and Ashes: Self and Family in the *Tutan Zhai*," in *Scriptures, Schools, and Forms of Practice: A Berlin Symposium*, ed. Poul Andersen and Florian Reiter (Wiesbaden: Harrassowitz Verlag, 2005), 33–48.

28. Benn, "Daoist Ordination and Zhai Rituals," 311; Eskildsen, *Asceticism in Early Taoist Religion*, 121.

29. Kohn, *Hsiao Tao Lun: Laughing at the Tao*, 107.

30. Benn, "Daoist Ordination and Zhai Rituals," 311–12; of a related ritual, Eskildsen, *Asceticism in Early Taoist Religion*, 119. This interpretation reads a lot like Anselm's satisfaction theory of atonement whereby penance is done to elicit mercy from an otherwise wrathful God. In other words, Elizabeth Johnson's observations regarding the impact of Anselm's satisfaction theory are too limited to Christianity. The theory appears to run so deep in the Western imagination so as to affect Daoist studies.

31. Henri Maspero, *Mélanges posthumes sur les religions et l'histoire de la Chine*, vol. 2, Publications Du Musée Guimet Bibliothèque de Diffusion, 3 vols. (Paris: Civilisations du Sud, S.A.E.P., 1950), 156–66; see Bokenkamp, "Sackcloth and Ashes: Self and Family in the *Tutan Zhai*," 36.

32. Bokenkamp, "Sackcloth and Ashes," 45.

33. Masaaki, "Confession of Sins and Awareness of Self in the *Taiping jing*," 44.

34. Masaaki, "Confession of Sins and Awareness of Self in the *Taiping jing*," 45.

35. Bokenkamp, "Sackcloth and Ashes," 38.

36. Bokenkamp, "Sackcloth and Ashes," 41–43.

37. Toshiaki Yamada, "*Tutan Zhai*: Mud and Soot Retreat," in *Encyclopedia of Taoism*, ed. Fabrizio Pregadio (London/New York: Routledge, 2008), 1001.

38. Bokenkamp, "Sackcloth and Ashes," 44.

39. This term first appears in the *Essential Precepts of Master Redpine* to explain why people who should be in perfect harmony with the Dao at birth often are not and are plagued with unfortunate situations they do not deserve—for example, birth defects. See Kohn, *Cosmos and Community*, 18.

40. Livia Kohn, "The Symbolism of Evil in Traditional China," in *Living with the Dao: Conceptual Issues in Daoist Practice*, ed. Liva Kohn (Cambridge, Mass.: Three Pines Press, 2006), 6–7. This piece was originally published as "Zur Symbolik des Bösen im alten China," in *Der Abbruch des Turmbaus: Studien zum Geist in China und im Abendland. Festschrift für Rolf Trauzettel*, ed. Ingrid Krüssmann, Hans-Georg Möller, Wolfgang

Kubin (St. Augustin: Academia Verlag, 1995), 113–34. It appeared at about the same time as her translation of the *Secret Essentials of the Most High*. She seems to be aware of the distinction between guilt, defilement, and shame about the same time that she is writing her very brief introduction to the translation. However, given space restrictions Kohn was unable to make a more nuanced introduction to her translation of this rite.

41. Kohn, "The Symbolism of Evil in Traditional China," 6–7. Kohn is benefiting from the work of Paul Ricoeur, Mary Douglas, and Ruth Benedict in her analysis.

42. Michael Saso and John Lagerwey have studied the current version of the Rite of Mud and Soot, which is a rite of cosmic renewal in Taiwan. See Michael R. Saso, *Taoism and the Rite of Cosmic Renewal* (Pullman: Washington State University Press, 1990), and Lagerwey, *Taoist Ritual in Chinese Society and History* (New York: Macmillan, 1987).

43. Anna Seidel, "Post-Mortem Immortality Or: The Taoist Resurrection of the Body," in *Gilgul: Essays on Transformation, Revelation, and Permanence in the History of Religions*, ed. Shaul Shaked, David Dean Shulman, and Gedaliahu A. G. Stroumsa (Leiden: Brill, 1987).

44. Wm. Clarke Hudson, "Spreading the Dao, Managing Mastership, and Performing Salvation: The Life and Alchemical Teachings of Chen Zhixu" (PhD diss., Indiana University, 2007), 35–37.

45. Hudson, "Spreading the Dao," 70.

46. Hudson, "Spreading the Dao," 78.

47. Hudson, "Spreading the Dao," 104.

48. Hudson, "Spreading the Dao," 35.

49. Hudson, "Spreading the Dao," 162–63.

50. Hudson, "Spreading the Dao," 531.

51. Bidlack, *In Good Company*, 90.

52. Hudson, "Spreading the Dao," 35n97.

53. Bidlack, *In Good Company*, 168.

54. Bidlack, *In Good Company*, 187.

55. Mircea Eliade, *The Sacred and the Profane: The Nature of Religion* (New York: Harcourt, Brace, 1959), 162–84.

56. Atonement occurs, then, as Christ's life-death-resurrection. Kenan B. Osborne, *Reconciliation and Justification: The Sacrament and Its Theology* (New York: Paulist Press, 1990), 16.

57. Johnson, *Creation and the Cross*, 106.

58. This typology of growth and diminishment I borrow from Teilhard de Chardin when he wrote of activities and passivities of growth and diminishment. Teilhard de Chardin, *The Divine Milieu*, trans. Siôn Cowell (Portland, Ore: Sussex Academic Press), 2004.

59. Gavin Flood, *The Ascetic Self, Subjectivity, Memory, and Tradition* (Cambridge: Cambridge University Press, 2004), 4.

60. *Apostolic Constitutions* II 20.6 as cited in Claudia Rapp, "Spiritual Guarantors at Penance, Baptism, and Ordination in the Late Antique East," in *A New History of Penance*, ed. Abigail Firey (Leiden: Brill, 2008), 125.

61. Rapp, "Spiritual Guarantors," 148.

62. Megan McLaughlin as quoted in Gavin Fort, "Penitents and Their Proxies: Penance for Others in Early Medieval Europe," *Church History* 86, no. 1 (March 2017): 2.

63. Kevin Uhalde, "Juridical Administration in the Church and Pastoral Care in Late Antiquity," in *A New History of Penance*, ed. Abigail Firey (Leiden: Brill, 2008), 100.

64. Fort, "Penitents and Their Proxies," 32.

65. Suffering without the request of another has a precedent in Christianity, such as the case of Saint Pachomius suffering on behalf of others. See Rapp, "Spiritual Guarantors," 139.

66. Even with the consultation with the Christian community, one may wonder how "voluntary" voluntary suffering is. For instance, some penitents in the sixteenth and seventeenth centuries were promoted like rock stars by their confessors. Did that play a role in their penance? (See Firey's introduction to *A New History of Penance*, 3.) Or even in the case of Daoism: in certain rites, only prescribed people can stand in for another, such as the son standing in for his deceased father in a funerary rite. I thank Michelle Voss Roberts and David Mozina for pointing this out to me.

67. Johnson, *Creation and the Cross*, 22–21.

68. This is not to reduce in any way the seriousness of personal sin. See Pope Saint John Paul II, *Reconciliatio et Paenitentia*, "Reconciliation and Penance," Liberia Editrice Vaticana, http://w2.vatican.va/content/john-paul-ii/en/apost_exhortations/documents/hf_jp-ii _exh_02121984_reconciliatio-et-paenitentia.html.

69. Johnson, *Creation and the Cross*, 184–85.

70. Johnson is aware of the work of the French Jesuit Pierre Teilhard de Chardin who made this observation nearly one hundred years ago, but he never used the term "deep incarnation."

Suffering and the Scandal of the Cross

God's Suffering in the Hindu-Christian Gaze

Francis X. Clooney, S.J.

In the following pages I consider some examples highlighting the exemplary and moral features of the crucifixion, and the aesthetic, contemplative power of gazing upon the crucified. Arguments in defense of the unique and saving atonement of Christ can be based on moral grounds (Christ as the exemplar of selflessness for the sake of others) or efficacious grounds (Christ's taking upon himself the sins of others free all from the penalties of sin); these arguments have generally fallen short of persuading Hindus to go beyond showing some respect for Christ's extraordinary love. Beyond the exemplary and efficacious, however, the aesthetic (visual, poetic) and contemplative gaze upon the crucified still more powerfully communicates what that death is about: *one ought to see* Christ crucified, *contemplate* him in his suffering.

This essay reflects on the Christian (Catholic, Jesuit) effort in India to explain and emphasize the importance of the atoning death of Christ. It does by considering certain historical and theological possibilities that have become evident in the past few centuries. In taking this path, I am seeking to learn from the history of Hindu-Christian relations, attentive now to the specific possibilities that come alive in the meeting of the great and complex traditions that can be grouped under the titles "Hinduism" and "Catholicism." Otherwise, we risk repeating ourselves, unaware of the longer arc of history of which our deliberations are a part.

Along the way, I will also have occasion to take note of some Hindu views on vicarious suffering, some of which challenge, and some of which resonate with, this fundamental Christian sentiment and commitment. We are, after all, never at the beginning of an interreligious relationship; we have some responsibility to understand what has happened in the past, to build on its strengths and avoid its flaws. In the end, a recognition of the power of the aesthetic and contemplative appropriation of Christ's death may also entail a certain mutuality, even a newly cultivated Christian ability to appreciate the suffering of a divine person in certain strands of Hinduism.

The Exemplary Death of Christ: The Moral Logic of Christ Crucified

The exemplary and efficacious models of atonement have both found a place in Catholic India, but we can assume more simply that many, if not most, missionaries simply announced, "Christ has died for our sins, and by his blood has saved us." Still, nuances occur often enough. For instance, certain Catholic writers in India in the sixteenth to nineteenth centuries seem to have downplayed the bloody aspects of the death of Christ, stressing rather the sheer fact of the Incarnation—God here, in the flesh—and the role of Jesus as the teacher who, in his own behavior, models the way to salvation. Roberto de Nobili (1577–1656), a famed Jesuit pioneer in south India, shows us in his Tamil writings his appreciation for the exemplary nature of the death of Jesus, yet without drawing great attention to the savior's bloody suffering.[1] In the twenty-fifth chapter of the third part of the *Ñānopadecam*—his great *Catechism*—he narrates the Passion in detail. There he also lists reasons for the sacrificial death of Christ, such as accentuate the exemplary nature of his death. Here is a list of topics, in my paraphrase:

> 1. That by reference to the suffering of the green wood (Luke 23.31), Jesus predicts the suffering of the dry wood; 2. The seriousness of God's opposition to sin; 3. The depth of God's grief at sin; 4. Jesus' setting of a good example for humans; 5. The importance of leaving behind all human goods; 6. The need to surrender body and soul both to God; 7. An exposition of how the good are to behave toward sinners; 8. The importance of not fleeing death; 9. The good qualities of true dharma; 10. Encouraging humans to have greater love for God; 11. The value of suffering for the sake of liberation; 12. Destroying the realm of the devil.[2]

For the most part, these reasons do not directly afford any atoning efficacy to the death of Christ, nor do they indicate that the crucifixion itself repairs alienation. Rather, they have to do with the exemplarity of Jesus's death and its effectiveness in instructing Christians in moral and religious values.

De Nobili devotes Chapter 11 of his late career *Tuṣaṇātikkāram (Refutation of Calumnies)* to answering the charge that the horrific death of Jesus proves that he is not God. In that context, too, he highlights exemplarity: The cross does not indicate that Jesus is a sinner or helpless victim, but only that by such a death he demonstrates the extremity of his love and limitless service. But we have little sense of the impact de Nobili's arguments might have made on Hindus more or less receptive to his moral and exemplary model of the efficacy of the death of Christ.

The Efficacious Death of Christ: Some Christian-Hindu Arguments

It was only in the nineteenth century that we know more surely about Hindu-Christian debates on atonement and the Christian doctrine about it. In that context the question of the efficacy of an atoning death and its relation to the teachings of Jesus (deemed by some Hindus to be quite sufficient, without the cross) came to the fore. The debates were not in a neutral space because most arguments were carried out in English, and in the context of a colonized India ruled over by foreign Christians. Hindus found horrific the idea of the death of the innocent person to please God and were repulsed by the emphasis on blood. The feeling seemed to be that there was no honest reason why one had to become a Christian to honor Christ's life, deeds, teachings, and moral conviction. Christians presented the atonement as a unique and necessary treasure of Christian tradition, such as was lacking to Hinduism but necessary for salvation. Hindus in turn resented the notion that such a death was a necessity they were obliged to accept, instead deeming the very scenario to be melodramatic and unnecessary if the goal was truly and simply the salvation of the human.

The great reformer Ram Mohun Roy (1772–1833), sometimes termed "a Hindu Unitarian," criticized the idea of atonement because he feared that it would distract from the excellent and more than sufficient teachings of Christ. His *Treatise on Christian Doctrine, Being the Second Appeal to the Christian Public in Defence of the "Precepts of Jesus,"* written as a second rejoinder to Christian attacks on his understanding of Christ, reports the Christian argument for the distinctiveness of the death of Christ:

In explaining the objects of Jesus's death on the cross, the (opposing) Editor confidently assumes, that "if we view Jesus Christ as atoning for the sins of men, we have everything perfectly in character: he became incarnate to accomplish that which could have been effected by neither men nor angels."

Roy rejects that suffering could be attributed to the *divine* person, and then insists that burdening an innocent *human* Jesus with all human suffering would be most unjust:

> That Jesus suffered death and pain in his human capacity as an atonement for the offences of others seems totally inconsistent with the justice ascribed to and even at variance with those principles of equity required of men; for it would be a piece of gross iniquity to afflict one innocent being, who had all the human feelings, and who had never transgressed the will of God, with the death of the cross, for the crimes committed [by others].[3]

An efficacious role for the suffering of Jesus as divine or human could not be defended. His alternative was rather to defend the *teachings* of Jesus as a quite sufficient contribution to mark the enduring importance of Christ.

In a sharp rejoinder to Roy, the missionary Joshua Marshman (1768–1837) wrote *A Defence of the Deity and Atonement of Jesus Christ, in Reply to Ram-Mohun Roy of Calcutta* (1822). In it he defends the importance to Christianity of the fact of atonement: The teachings of Jesus are efficacious only if they lead listeners to the realization that Jesus has died for them, and to the change of life that must follow upon this existential realization that Christ died for humanity. Near the end of his long and very thorough exegesis of atonement doctrine in the Bible he speaks more directly and passionately about Roy as a person who is admirable, but inadequately so. He appreciates what Roy has already risked—status, communal belonging, and so on—in campaigning for a more enlightened Hinduism. But by Marshman's estimate, Roy has not gone far enough because his conversion is intellectual but not affective. He relies on arguments but resists a complete, heartfelt dependence on Jesus, the loving savior.[4] He begs Roy to join the choir, though worrying about him: "In this song (of believers' praise and love) how can our author with his present views ever join? How can he unite in these adorations?"[5] But the necessary path was blocked for Roy, who did not see that a true recognition of the saving act of Jesus meant that in turn conversion would be required as the only adequate response to Jesus' saving death.

The nineteenth-century arguments were perhaps doomed to failure, or to the burden of only modest success. In a 2010 essay, Ankur Barua discusses Roy's view that the very idea of atonement—the death of the innocent for the sake of the guilty—is morally repugnant, implausible, and in any case, as Roy saw the matter, not rooted in the teachings of Jesus himself. Roy thinks that "through the intercession of Jesus, whom God has exalted above all the prophets, we can receive pardon for our sins, without believing in his vicarious sacrifice on the cross." Rather, "our sincere repentance is sufficient to 'make atonement' with the supremely merciful God."[6] Barua generalizes, holding that there was little wherewithal for a Hindu "to readily incorporate into their worldviews the notion that Christ died 'for us' in a providential divine plan. While the notion that suffering has a redemptive value is not entirely alien to their thought—for according to the theory of karma, each individual makes progress towards the divine by working out one's karmic merits and demerits—they have usually rejected the notion of one individual 'bearing the sins' of another."[7] Indeed, "While Roy himself does not refer to concepts such as karma, avatāra, and others . . . his rejection of the notion of the atonement sets the pattern for much of subsequent Hindu responses to the person and work of Christ."[8]

Even Swami Vivekananda (1863–1902), though largely sympathetic to Christ and his universal mission and a proponent of an open and inclusive Vedanta, was skeptical about the notion of atonement: "Human nature is selfish, and the vast majority of men and women weak; and to teach vicarious sacrifice makes us more and more weak. Every child is taught that he is nothing until the poor fellow becomes hypnotized into nothing. He goes in search of somebody to cling onto, and never thinks of clinging to himself . . ."[9] More pointedly, he also insists the "Eucharist is a survival of a very ancient custom of savage tribes" that gave great chiefs incentive to consume and imbibe the bravery and strength of captives. Jesus himself had nothing to do with blood sacrifice, but some Christians are eager to fit him into a sacrificial mentality, so that "the idea of human sacrifice, in the form of atonement or as a human scapegoat, had to come in." As a result, Christianity was tainted with "a spirit of persecution and bloodshed . . ."[10]

Interesting, too, are the views of Brahmobandhab Upadhyay (born Bhavani Charan Bandyopadhyay, 1861–1907) because he is a kind of bridge figure: a Hindu leader and intellectual who converted to Catholic Christianity and who, as a convert, retained deep respect for his Hindu roots, even to the extent that some wondered whether he really had converted. Atonement was a major point of disagreement between Upadhyay and Hindu reformers. This we see in debates appearing in a variety of English-language Hindu journals, such as the *Brahmavadin, The Awakened India, The Interpreter,* and the *Aryan Messenger.* Upadhyay defended atonement as necessary to Christian faith and valuable for Indian society as well; he was of the view that Advaita Vedāntins—including perhaps Vivekananda—were idealistic about self-perfection, but contemptuous of selfless love,[11] and thus blind to the mystery of divine love. In his view, the Brahmo Samaj reform community from Roy on was infatuated with the notion of self-salvation and self-divinization, and thus unwilling to recognize how humans love and help one another in important ways, and accordingly also unable to acknowledge the reconciliation God has brought about in Christ. In "Bear Ye One Another's Burdens,"[12] Upadhyay rebuts the *Arya Messenger*'s critique of vicarious atonement as the infliction on the innocent of the suffering of the guilty. Nor, he observes, is suffering for the benefit of others as unusual as sceptics charge. He quotes Bishop Joseph Butler and Cardinal John Henry Newman to show that this ideal is familiar in human life—as when parents willingly suffer for their children. In its extreme form, this love culminates in the death of Christ where in a "most wonderful manner" "infinite justice and infinite mercy" are united.

Near the essay's end, he elaborates on the fittingness of the death of Christ:

By a dispensation unthought by man, he has in the most wonderful manner united the ends both of infinite justice and infinite mercy. The Second Person of the Blessed Trinity took human nature, and in this moral nature showed to man the way of reconnection with God, his Maker. Bearing the ordinary difficulties and troubles of an earthly life, and the unjust hatred of the Pharisees, he preached the law of God, doing good to all, dazzling by his sanctity even the eyes of his enemies, and suffering the greatest humiliations, and an ignominious death on the cross in the fulfillment of his Messianic offices.

Jesus's death, though but that of a single man, was infinite in its effects:

> These acts had an infinite value, because he was a divine Person, though
> his human nature was finite. He offered them to God for the sins of men;
> and God having regard to his obedience, his zeal, his meekness, is labors,
> his sufferings and death, promised pardon to all men and the grace of
> adoption as his children, on condition that they believe in Christ the
> God-man, are sorry for their sins, and obey his law. Such is the meaning
> of the vicarious atonement of Christ, and no other.[13]

Upadhyay concludes the essay by observing that other religions too, and
particularly in India, knew the fact and value of vicarious suffering.[14]

But despite his deep understanding of both Hindu and Christian sen-
sitivities, Upadhyay too failed to win the day. Despite Upadhyay's cre-
dentials, his explanation of the atonement did not convince Hindus to
become Christians. The vast majority remained firmly set against the notion that God's own Son died on the cross in order to save them from
their own bad karma and from their own deities and own religious
traditions.

To assess where we are: theological arguments explain the efficacy and
centrality of that saving death for all humans; moral grounds highlight
the exemplary power of selfless love. But neither approach was sufficient
to persuade large numbers of Hindus to come to Christ. Neither side
seemed ready to budge. The crucified Christ was as it were starkly in the
middle, neither explained away nor recognized as the efficacious sacrament of the conversion of India.

But recognizing this impasse is not without its benefits. First, we learn
of and from the long history of Hindu-Christian reflection on this topic
and should be able to see that trying such arguments all over again, in
disregard for history, is of little benefit. Second, by learning from the re-
actions of Hindus, we may come to recognize the limits of moral exemplarity (Christ's selflessness) and even loving intervention (his suffering
all for the sake of humans), if such are perceived also as rebukes to the
traditions to which they have already belonged. Third, now informed by
a more precise historical and cultural awareness of what did not work in
the past, we are also encouraged to seek another route. Here then I turn
to the third strand of our consideration, the aesthetic appropriation of
the crucified by a contemplative gaze, which, I suggest, may have a force
greater than intellectual and moral arguments.

The Contemplative Turn:
Contemplating the Suffering Christ

Early on in the preparation of this essay for publication, in another context I happened upon a striking passage set in the court of the Mughal emperor Jahangir (1569–1627), and illustrative of the Jesuit way of acting in the presence of the crucified Christ. Fernão Guerreiro, S.J. (1550–1617) tells us:

> One evening, the King was looking through a portfolio containing the pictures of which we have already made mention, while the Fathers stood by him explaining their meaning. Presently he came upon one representing Jesus Christ crucified, which the Fathers, when he handed it to them, adored with great reverence, removing their caps and placing it on their heads.

The picture, and their behavior, leads to testimonies of some depth and piety, as the Jesuits impress upon Jahangir the contemplative power of the crucified:

> By keeping Him before our eyes in this form, we do Him the highest possible honor, because He suffered thus not for His fault, but for our sake, of His own free will giving up His life to expiate our sins and to teach us to give up our lives for Him. Whenever we think of this, *our hearts are filled with gratitude to Him, and we are never weary of gazing upon Him thus upon the cross.*[15]

The Jesuits in the imperial court are highlighting an instinctive, affective submission to this suffering Lord of love: "Are we not bound to love Him with all our hearts, and to be ready to lay down our lives for Him?"[16] Jahangir was impressed.[17] But from the Jesuit point of view the scene did not end well, since it was almost immediately sidetracked into a debate with the emperor's courtiers as to whether Jesus was divine or not, and whether a divine person could suffer. That debate led nowhere, whereas the contemplation, though short-lived, seems to have been more efficacious in bringing the mystery of Christ into the emperor's heart.

Contemplating the crucified Christ is, of course, a practice with venerable Christian roots, as old as the Gospel of John, which places the viewing of the crucified at the center of attention:

> Then the soldiers came and broke the legs of the first and of the other who had been crucified with him. But when they came to Jesus and saw that he was already dead, they did not break his legs. Instead, one of the

soldiers pierced his side with a spear, and at once blood and water came out. (He who saw this has testified so that you also may believe. His testimony is true, and he knows that he tells the truth.) These things occurred so that the scripture might be fulfilled, "None of his bones shall be broken." And again another passage of scripture says, "They will look on him whom they have pierced."[18]

Great power—by implication, life itself—lies simply in looking upon his suffering.

Though Jesus suffers, he is also in command, as this passage from John 18 reminds us:

> Jesus, knowing all that was to happen to him, came forward and asked them, "For whom are you looking?" They answered, "Jesus of Nazareth." Jesus replied, "I am he." Judas, who betrayed him, was standing with them. When Jesus said to them, "I am he," they stepped back and fell to the ground. Again he asked them, "For whom are you looking?" And they said, "Jesus of Nazareth." Jesus answered, "I told you that I am he. So if you are looking for me, let these men go." (John 18:3–8)

The sufferings of Jesus do not deprive him of his supreme freedom and even foreknowledge of all that will happen.[19]

A long Christian tradition recognizes the power of gazing upon the crucified. The *Spiritual Exercises* of Ignatius Loyola exhort the retreatant to stand before the suffering Christ, exposed to the great mystery. A number of passages point to the necessary encounter with the cross, before the crucified. Right at the start, in the first exercise of the First Week, we are instructed as follows:

> Imagining Christ our Lord present and placed on the Cross, let me make a Colloquy, how from Creator He is come to making Himself man, and from life eternal is come to temporal death, and so to die for my sins. Likewise, looking at myself, what I have done for Christ, what I am doing for Christ, what I ought to do for Christ. And so, seeing Him such, and so nailed on the Cross, to go over that which will present itself.[20]

In the second contemplation of the second week, we are again put on the spot:

> The third, to look and consider what they are doing, as going on a journey and laboring, that the Lord may be born in the greatest poverty; and as a termination of so many labors—of hunger, of thirst, of heat and of

cold, of injuries and affronts—that He may die on the Cross; and all this for me: then reflecting, to draw some spiritual profit.

It is not hard to imagine that the Jesuits with Jahangir were hoping that the Mughal's heart, too, might be smitten with compunction at so costly, so loving a death. We do not leave entirely behind the exemplary and efficacious levels of interpretation, but we do open up, beyond the moral and theological realms, a more direct moment and place of contemplative engagement with Christ in his sufferings.

The art historian Walter Melion has written an insightful essay on Ignatian contemplation as explained by the early Jesuit Jerónimo Nadal (1507–1580), in introducing his translation and edition of Nadal's *Annotations and Meditations on the [Liturgical] Gospels*. He says that Nadal's text helps us to go deeper into the Catholic and Jesuit way of approaching the suffering and death of Christ. Melion explains that the text is "an amplification of the Ignatian manual, which attempts to expand and codify its elements by the application of rhetorical and pictorial devices linking two registers of religious experience—private prayer and public liturgy."[21] The recommended practice is "free meditative practice" (*ex libera imaginatione*), by which Nadal uses images to intensify the meditations, and invites those meditating to apply the spiritual senses to each scene before them. The contemplation turns out to be constitutive of the significance of the cross, not in a merely subjective manner, but because the viewer is drawn into that greater and terrible reality. For example, Melion takes note of the passage in John 18 where Jesus, the accused and the victim, is entirely in charge. Melion observes:

> Nadal asserts that Christ himself licenses the use of rhetorical devices that convey truths by means of distinct and striking images. When he asks why Jesus went to meet his captors and identified himself to them, he receives the following response [from Jesus]: "I wanted to demonstrate to all men that I suffered voluntarily on their behalf, [and so] I advanced toward the soldiers and inquired: Whom do you seek? They said: Jesus of Nazareth. I replied: I am he. To which words I attached something of my virtue, thereby draining [those soldiers] of their powers, casting them down, and with them Judas, Satan, and all his satellites."

Melion catches nicely the power of the spectacle as read by Nadal:

> By using the term *demonstrare* to designate this exchange enacted purposefully to reveal the true nature of his sacrifice, Christ calls attention

to his mastery of ocular demonstration, a rhetorical figure possessing liveliness and distinction in the highest degree. By the power of the rhetor's words, such a demonstration makes the subject pass vividly before the eyes. Christ somewhat alters this technique: his simple words are accompanied by visibly forceful effects that demonstrate the divine virtue informing those very words.[22]

In turn, Jesus is showing "that his voluntary submission to his enemies, rather than simply signaling his weakness, further demonstrates his divine strength, proceeding as it does from a superhuman act of will ... Having first revealed, then constrained, his divinity, *Christ is like the performer who provokes his audience, but unlike the lyric poet, he is seen deliberately to have aroused the mob that inaugurates the Passion he embraces.*"[23] He creates a spectacle, transformative for those willing to receive the scene with contemplative openness.

Melion turns then to the Passion cycle and "the image of the sacrificial Christ." He draws attention to the scene where the cross to which Jesus has just been nailed is lifted up and inserted in the ground, a scene that "portrays the Crucifixion as an act of sacramental artifice made manifest by the Raising of the Cross."[24] Here, too, the point is that viewers are caught up in this scene of excruciating pain as the cross is lifted and Jesus hangs from his pierced hands and feet. Nadal contrasts the mere curiosity of the crowds with the pious empathy of Mary and her companions, whose spirits were transfixed by what they saw. As Melion puts it, "They imprint the image of Christ upon their hearts, dwelling by internal sense on a sight their eyes have found intolerable."[25]

Can this contemplative gaze improve our chances for interreligious understanding on a point so basic to Christian faith? Can a Christian draw Hindus into a simple and pure seeing of Jesus? For this to occur, there need to be prior dispositions, I suggest; and to understand these, we have to ask whether there is in Hinduism anything like the suffering of Christ.

The Suffering of Hindu Deities

But now we need to make a comparative move, considering for a moment what it means to suffer, for God to suffer, in Hindu traditions. We do not expect an exact parallel. But unless there is some resonance, the contemplation will fail. Here too we proceed best by examples. Chapter 4 of my

Hindu God, Christian God is focused largely on incarnation and *avatāra* (divine descents). There I showed how the suffering of an *avatāra* was often cast as a dramatic suffering enacted on a sacred stage, so to speak; properly contemplated, it promised, on the part of the audience, a salutary catharsis. In writing about the medieval Hindu theologian Vedānta Deśika's (1268–1369) theology of *avatāra*, and the reality of divine embodiment, I noted his interpretation of divine suffering as a kind of dramatic gesture: "In various texts it is mentioned that the Lord experienced suffering, grief, and fear during his divine descents. But due to the fact that he is not afflicted by sin, etc. . . . it must be understood that these [apparent sufferings] are simply *abhinaya*."[26] This term refers to theatrical or dramatic performance and the physical movements made by actors or dancers in the course of a performance. We know actors on a stage are playing parts, but the best actors are deeply engaged in their parts. We can be deeply moved by their joys and sorrows, triumphs and tragedies: "As a Vaiṣṇava Hindu theological term, *abhinaya* characterizes the Lord's real and free engagement in difficulty and suffering during his embodiment,"[27] even if that involvement is freely chosen and leaves him perfect and untainted. According to Deśika, the Lord's acts are similar to performance in a theater. As *abhinaya*, dramatic gestures, they were intended to produce feelings of horror and pity in the audience and draw them into the deeper truth of the narrative.

The twentieth-century commentator Vīrarāghavācārya (1897–1983), glossing Deśika's notion of dramatic suffering, asks pointedly whether it can be said that the Lord really suffers when on earth. In affirming the possibility, he draws on the popular Hindu epic, the *Rāmāyaṇa*, which in large part portrays the trials and tribulations of prince Rāma; his wife, Sītā; and Rāma's brother, Lakṣmaṇa, in years of forest exile, and then most acutely through the kidnapping of Sītā and the long war fought to set her free. Rāma and Sītā suffer together and in separation, physically and psychologically. Rāma is vindicated in the end, even if his relationship with Sītā is scarred by what has happened. Their struggle is so great and all-consuming that at its end Rāma has to be reminded by the gods that he is indeed God on earth, deep down untouched by all that has happened. Vīrarāghavācārya highlights the exemplarity of this suffering, since the lord suffers due to the suffering of others. "Devotees see him suffering in ways that are unlimited and without precedent, etc. Then they cry out, 'How could this little one suffer in this way?'"[28] They cry out because they cannot believe that it is all just a display by the eternal, impassible Lord of all. All contemplate what happens; because they love the lord, they suffer with him. It is a show, a spectacle, that transforms those who see it. The suffering of an *avatāra* is in a certain way as real as the most effective performances on stage. Though a kind of fiction, such action has for centuries really affected audiences of receptive and alert believers, as God most compellingly demonstrates his commitment to his people on earth.[29]

We can return for a moment to Nadal, who constantly encourages readers to look more closely and thereby to get involved, enthralled by what they contemplate. Indeed, Jesus himself is managing the scenes that viewers are invited to contemplate since, according to Nadal, manifestation is a necessary step on the pathway into experiencing, being purified, and being transformed by the vicarious suffering and atoning death that Jesus Christ suffers. Some Hindus similarly thought that Rāma truly suffered, and that contemplating his suffering was an efficacious practice. In different ways these dramas show us the spectacle of God's costly involvement in the world, and sensitivity to the one can foster rather than preclude sensitivity to the other.

Some theologians may, of course, rise in protest at the notion of "theatrical suffering" in order to insist that such a display is nothing like the real suffering of Jesus. More can be said on that topic in another context; certainly, we have here a different view of the human and divine and what experience here on earth means. But my more limited point here is that Hindus are not unfamiliar with the power of the spectacle of divine suffering. We may share a contemplation of the dying of Christ that does not reduce to theological or moral versions of atonement.

A Matter of the Heart

Hindus in modern times, too, appreciated the contemplative, experiential turn and, apologetics aside, were able to think more deeply about the suffering Christ, albeit in Hindu terms. Some nineteenth-century reformers revered the spectacle of the suffering Christ, as they worked out their own interpretations of the Atonement. Keshab Chunder Sen (1838–1884), for instance, stepped around the missionary debates we reviewed earlier, instead seeking to attend to matters of the heart. He embraced atonement as the work of reunion, but saw that it proceeded along an affective and not merely rational path. In his famed lecture, "Asia's Message to Europe," he put it this way:

Christ actually saw himself, an undivided Christ with his seamless raiment, dwelling and breathing in every human heart. And so he offered
himself before God as an atonement for all mankind.[30]

He plays upon the presumed dismay of his audience:

Atonement did I say? What a startling announcement you would think
I have made before this great assembly! Yes, I would have you believe in
Christ's atonement. All India must believe that Christ is the Son of God.
Nay, more than this, I will make myself bold enough to prophesy, all
India will one day acknowledge Jesus Christ as the atonement, the
Universal Atonement for all mankind.[31]

But the way to this realization lies in a deeply personal approach: "Seated
at the feet of Jesus, I wonder at the philosophical depth of his doctrine;
I wonder at the immeasurable breadth of his heart." It seems that for Sen
atonement is a kind of reconciliation, an at-one-ment. But what is striking is that this now is a matter of heart, an extravagant contemplation of
the blood of Christ:

His atoning blood overflowed the little embankments of his Jewish humanity and burst like a universal deluge upon all humanity, swallowing
the remotest parts of the globe, east, west, north and south, in its shore-
less immensity . . . Humanity has sunk deep in the sea of Christ's atonement and there is no getting out of it. They do him grave injustice who
believe that his atonement embraced only the small body of his disciples,
or that it applies only to one sect in the world, namely those who call
themselves Christians.[32]

Sen's cry is direct: "Jesus, thou art atonement incarnate."[33] The truth, he
sees, is a general one: God with us, manifest in Jesus, atoning for the entirety of the world. The appeal is affective: The flow of blood washes
clean the entire world, as if sweeping away the complications and arguments encumbering the doctrinal truth of atonement.

On the Suffering of Sri Ramakrishna

The suffering of the famous Hindu mystic Ramakrishna (1836–1886) becomes a locus where Hindu and Christian insights can begin to cohere
in contemplation of the holy person who suffers. As Ramakrishna's disciples pondered his last months, they wondered how it could be that he

suffered so terribly. Was he not God on earth, and free of any karma meriting suffering? Could he not by focused meditation free himself from the cancer? Did he choose to suffer for the sake of humans? Christianity was very present in nineteenth-century Bengal (as we saw earlier, regarding debates over atonement), and it seems likely that Christian notions affected even the insiders' interpretation of Ramakrishna's suffering and death.[34]

A reminiscence from Swami Abhedananda, a direct disciple of Ramakrishna, directly evokes the Christian spectacle of the death of Christ:

It may be asked why the Master had cancer. It is really difficult to answer this question. Once while staying at the Shyampukur house the Master said, "The Divine Mother has shown me that people are getting rid of their sins by touching my feet. I am absorbing the results of their sinful actions, so I am suffering from this terrible cancer." This is called "vicarious atonement." Jesus Christ suffered this way in his life.[35]

That the Master suffers so greatly in the flesh and does not seek to evade the suffering compels onlookers to think differently about him and about themselves.

Other disciples too recognized the efficacy of the master's suffering. Years later, Baburam Ghosh, become Swami Premananda, recalled how in his final illness Ramakrishna extended his compassion very widely, to the whole human community:

In spite of being criticized, the Master helped people. When he was suffering from the excruciating pain of cancer, every day he would wait for seekers of God to come. Sometimes he would look out at the street and say: "What has happened? Nobody has come today." Once Hazra said to the Master: "Why are you so anxious to see Naren? Put your mind in God. There is no reason to think about those boys." Like a simple child the Master believed what Hazra said, and he went to the Panchavati, where he had most of his visions. There the Divine Mother told him: "What a fool you are! Have you come to this world for your own enjoyment? Shame!" Then the Master said: "Mother, if for the good of humanity I am to suffer a million times, I shall bear it gladly."[36]

He suffers as did Jesus: "Day and night he felt a burning sensation all over his body. In spite of all this terrible suffering, he never desisted from showering grace on people and helping them realize God. This went on for a year and a half. If this is not crucifixion, I don't know what it is."[37] The passage does not say that Ramakrishna's suffering was entirely for the sake of others, but that even while suffering he cared for others. For that reason, Ghosh was deeply moved.

In Swami Saradananda's *Ramakrishna and His Divine Play*,[38] his very early account of the life of Ramakrishna, the parallel to Christ is again made explicit. Ramakrishna suffers due to the sins of those around him, as he took on those sins in his suffering:

> At Dakshineswar the Master had sometimes told us that he would not hesitate to be born millions of times and suffer for the good of humanity. So it is not surprising that instead of being perturbed by this vision, he narrated it to us joyfully . . . Narendra and a few others heard of the Master's vision and found it in the truth of vicarious atonement (in which one voluntarily takes upon oneself the suffering caused by the sins of others], a fundamental doctrine of Christianity, Vaishnavism, and other faiths.[39]

Although Saradananda does not make explicit where the doctrine is to be found in Vaiṣṇavism, we can infer that the notion of atonement as vicarious suffering was familiar in the circle of Ramakrishna's disciples, and deemed a positive resource in making sense of his cancer.[40]

Earlier I quoted Swami Vivekananda, noting his skepticism regarding atonement. It is telling though that in his famous "Christ the Messenger," he recognizes atonement as a manifestation of divine love:

> Let us, therefore, find God not only in Jesus of Nazareth, but in all the great Ones that have preceded him, in all that came after him, and all that are yet to come. Our worship is unbounded and free. They are all manifestations of the same Infinite God. They are all pure and unselfish; they struggled and gave up their lives for us, poor human beings. They each and all suffer vicarious atonement for every one of us, and also for all that are to come hereafter.[41]

Why does Vivekananda feel so strongly in this regard? An intriguing 1894 American newspaper report gives a biographical clue to his sentiments when outside the apologetic context: "Mr. Vivecananda [sic] told me that his father was a great believer in the Lord Jesus, as he called Him, and that when a boy he had read in the Gospel of St. John the thrilling description of the crucifixion of the Savior and wept over it."[42] But most importantly, he is moved because he is thinking also of Sri Ramakrishna, his own master, who suffered terribly from cancer in his last days, and yet even in his suffering would not turn away those who came to see him. Vivekananda affirms at every turn that Ramakrishna chose his suffering and bore it for others.

I have lingered at length on the case of Ramakrishna because his suffering and death occurred in a context where Christians knew of Hindu deities, and some Hindus were quite familiar with the story of Jesus. The intersecting gaze of Hindus and Christians on Ramakrishna, on Christ, opened a powerful interfaith space: in facing up to the suffering of the beloved, one gains the ability to see and be moved by the suffering of another who has suffered for love's sake.

Telling the Story of the Suffering Christ, in an Artful Fashion

Early Jesuits were adept at reimagining and retelling the story of Jesus. I referred earlier to Jerome Xavier, who told the Gospel story in a straightforward but rhetorically effective manner in the *Mirror of Holiness* (*Mir'at Al-Quds*) that he composed and had illustrated for the emperor and the Mughal court. Written in Persian and in prose, it tells the familiar scenes simply:

> In all the things Jesus suffered, Blessed Mary was standing in front of him and watching. She was patient and said nothing, but in her heart she knew what was happening to him. Of the twelve Apostles, John was present and near her. Then Jesus looked at his mother and said, "Woman, this is your child." He did not say "mother," lest her heart break. Then he looked at John and said, "Behold, your mother." This is the third word he spoke on the cross, and what he meant by these two words was that the Blessed Lady would see all Christ's followers as her sons, and they would all consider her their mother, as Jesus stated afterwards. From that time on, John took the Lady as the source of his happiness, and all Christians take her as their mother in all their actions.[43]

In the same period, Thomas Stephens, S.J. (1549–1619) was composing his *Kristapurāṇa* (*History of the Christ*) in the genre of Marathi poetry, telling the full life of Christ after a lengthy overview of Old Testament stories. Without hesitation he recounts Christ's suffering and death in simple, stark terms:

> In his pain and agony, the Son of God did not forget his Mother, and the Mother did not forget her Son.
>
> At that time she stood near the cross. Mary Cleopas, her relative, and Magdalene Mary were there near the cross with our Lady.
>
> Jesus' Mother was grieved because of separation from him. She wanted to look up at her Son but her eyes welled up with swirling tears.
>
> Time and again she wiped her eyes and looked at his face for a moment, and then she gazed at his feet and hands.
>
> Close up, his body seemed ruined, as that of a leper. On his head she saw the crown of sharp thorns. She saw the blood flowing from the wounds of the nails and whip lashes.
>
> With that a sword of sorrow pierced in the heart of the gentle Mother.[44]

Such piety, familiar in the Europe of his time, found a new life in India, as Stephens employed it to pierce the hearts of his listeners as well, that they might be touched and so begin to transform their lives.

More than a century after Xavier and Stephens, in his epic Tamil-language poem *Tempāvani* (*The Unfading Garland*), Constantine Beschi, S.J. (1680–1747) told eloquently and with passion the drama of the Incarnation. This epic of almost 4,000 verses is a beautifully rendered retelling of many key Biblical scenes from Adam and Eve up to, but not including, the public ministry of Jesus, recounted by St. Joseph and others as occasions prompted. Christ's cross is neither the center nor climax of this epic, yet Beschi does not neglect to bring the cross into his epic. During the return of the Holy Family from Egypt recounted in the thirtieth chapter of the poem, they pass Mount Moriah. It was there, the young Jesus explains to his parents, that Abraham nearly sacrificed Isaac. He then goes on to speak of his own death, a similar offering that will actually occur, on another mountain. Joseph is horrified, and weeping, protests that such suffering is hardly necessary:

> Seeing this compassion ending all bounds, disturbed, aggrieved,
> The master of asceticism wept and said,
> "If the help of Abraham and Isaac were enough to end sin that time,
> Why must you die to protect sinful humans who have ended good order,
> When you are already able to offer grace that ends the very ocean?"
> (30.115)

Jesus's response displays his own intense longing for the cross:

"If you compare red coral to a hot fire, will the coral burn?
Are the real thing and its type exactly the same?
As with Isaac, this is a sacrifice that protects the whole erring world."
With compassion the holy son continued, (30.116)

"But until that day arrives, can there be joy for me here?
Even until now I've not seen that tall tree where I shall die, and
So there is no end to my distress."
Jesus was like a great ocean of compassion, unequaled even in all times
   to come. (30.117)

To assuage his impatient grief, angels manifest the glory and power of
the cross:

So as to end the grief of the holy son who was like the sun illumining
   the whole world,
The heaven-dwellers combined the lights illumining the sky,
And manifest on high a cross brighter than day itself.
With sweet melodious words, distress gone, rejoicing within, he spoke:
   (30.118)

Jesus cries out,

"It is my love, a beautiful adornment, for my love this is the vehicle;
My excellent adornment, the way to re-open the celestial house;
It's a lovely garland giving joy scepter of my rule,
Adornment greater than all, life of my very life—may it flourish
   forever!" (30.119)

He is then lifted up:

That very moment he rose up in the body bearing the force of his love.
He drew that cross to his chest like an ornament, there he rested,
Immersed in an ocean of ambrosia, he lacked nothing of bliss.
He shone in all directions, and light itself suffered by comparison. (30.120)

Like the sun's rays rising above the ocean waves,
The son ascended there, as if his life's breath was gone.
Below, as if corpses, unspeaking, unmoving,
The ascetic Joseph stood there with his flowering staff, and the mother too,
Weeping, their faces as if scorched in a fiery furnace. (30.121)

Jesus relents, for it is not yet time:

> Seeing their sorrow, their tears, that ocean of grace once more
> descended to earth.
> That his parents might rejoice, he smiled, "Let's go."
> They worshipped, sang, and gave praise;
> They traveled a long distance through a wild place as dark as the hearts
> of sinners
> And to a mountain came. (30.122)[45]

Beschi manages to tell the story movingly as an event of exquisite beauty and deep poignancy, without ever mentioning blood or actual crucifixion. Perhaps he assumes that his readers will know of the cross already; more likely, contemplation of the cross as a site of intense, tearful love is in his mind more productive. It is also characteristic of Beschi's Jesuit tradition that the wrenching sadness and blinding luminosity of the scene concludes abruptly in a return to mission, as Mary and Joseph get up and continue on their way. The reader is invited to imagine this prediction of the cross, to suffer accordingly, and to walk on with that holy family.

As we have seen, de Nobili did not emphasize the cross and the efficacy of the bloody death of Christ because he recognized that the very idea of vicarious blood sacrifice would be so alien and distasteful to Hindus. Some missionaries were determined to argue the details of atonement theology. At issue for certain Jesuit missionaries, however, was the best way of presenting the faith, neither denying the cross nor accentuating the horror of it, nor in so heavily apologetic manner that the presentation would drive away interested Hindus. Xavier, Stephens, and Beschi saw the matter differently, and therefore put the spectacle right in the center of their teaching of the faith, that everyone might encounter it.

Seeing-Together the Suffering Lord

Such insight into suffering can work the other way as well, as Christians learn to re-envision the suffering of Christ in light of Hindu models. The compassion and vulnerability of Mohandas Gandhi even unto death comes to mind, and it is no surprise that Dorothy Day, upon hearing the news of his assassination, could speak of Gandhi's witness as in perfect harmony with the loving dying of Christ:

"Greater love than this no man hath, that a man lay down his life for his friends." There is no public figure who has more conformed his life to the life of Jesus Christ than Gandhi, there is no man who has carried about him more consistently the aura of divinized humanity, who has added his sacrifice to the sacrifice of Christ, whose life has had a more fitting end than that of Gandhi. "A prophet is not without honor save in his own country . . . he came into his own and his own did not receive him." The folly of Gandhi's life, the failure of Gandhi's life—it is the folly and failure of the Cross. The failure of the supernatural in the world. The failure of those who would teach love and non-violence in a world which has apostatized, which accepts no absolutes, has no standards other than utilitarian, is devoid of hope, persecutes the prophets, murders the saints, exhibits God to the people–torn, bleeding, dead."[46]

My suggestion then is that figures as diverse as Sen, Ramakrishna and his disciples, and admirers of Gandhi intuitively related to the image of the suffering lord who dies for love of his disciples. Even if not always literally so, this verges on the contemplative gaze I have been stressing as a way around the tougher theological and moral considerations that have made the death of Christ a sticking point in Hindu-Christian understanding.

To contemplate the suffering Christ is in itself efficacious. If appreciation of Jesus's death on the cross is not immediately recast as an argument about the difference between Hinduism and Christianity, it can constructively open a space for a Hindu-Christian contemplative practice, beyond the ordinary words and ideas of dialogue.

Nor is this my intuition alone. Elsewhere in this volume, Michelle Voss Roberts has recognized that a focus on iconic visualizations of suffering, the blood of suffering not hidden but in plain view, can find a certain place in Indian contemplative practice: "Viewing the cross as a *maṇḍala* encourages evolution in one's understanding of its salvific mystery over time . . . The cross is like a *maṇḍala* because, as [Sthaneshwar] Timalsina aptly puts it, *maṇḍala*s have an "extra-semantic power" that is powerfully rooted in the senses and imagination." Speaking personally, Voss Roberts finds that tantric visualization practice encourages her "to wrestle with the cross as a paradoxical symbol of love" rather than looking away; calm and the restoration of confidence may later return, but only by and after direct attention to the blood.

My proposal on the superior power of a contemplation of the suffering Christ as resonant even in an interreligious context resonates nicely with Voss Roberts's appreciation of the visualization of suffering. Here the contemplation becomes specifically comparative. There is power in *seeing* the crucified Christ alongside the dying Ramakrishna, or even while recollecting the sufferings of Rāma and Sītā. This opens a way to see again the meaning of the suffering of *any* sentient being, the power of the spectacle of the death of the good person, and even, by faith, the suffering of a divine person manifest on earth. In turn, this opens a way to see anew, more vulnerably, the suffering of Christ, now intensified by Hindu visions of divine suffering rather than in competition with them. In evoking the Jesuit tradition of gazing upon the cross of Christ, I have made a personal intimation similar to that of Voss Roberts. To contemplate Christ crucified is at the essence of Jesuit spirituality throughout history and now too. But by now we have learned, I think, that living by this vision and taking it to heart need not obscure other visions of intense suffering that arises in compassion and as love's ultimate expression. This is something some Jesuits learned in India, and shared with pious Hindus looking for a way to love Christ. Simple contemplation of the crucified is something we can appeal to even today in the enactment of an interreligious piety of vicarious suffering.

In the final estimate, we need not include that all such exemplary suffering is the same, but only that intense human suffering in its various forms may be deemed sacred, received with the deepest reverence interreligiously, and allowed to intensify our reverence for all such instances of suffering love. What we learn from history is how such contemplation works when it is not reduced to rational and moral arguments about atonement that, while of value, do not even satisfy the believer in Christ as far as we might hope and desire.

Notes

1. See Francis X. Clooney, "Roberto de Nobili's Dialogue on Eternal Life and an Early Jesuit Evaluation of Religion in South India," in *Western Jesuit Scholars in India: Tracing Their Paths, Reassessing Their Goals* (Leiden: Brill, 2020), 82–96.

2. Summarized from the *Ñāṇōpatēcam* (*Catechism*), edited by Savarimuthu Rajamanickam, S.J., 4 volumes. Thotthukudi: Tamil Illakiya Kalakkam, 1966–1973, Vol. 3, 418–28.

3. Rammuhun Roy, *A Treatise on Christian Doctrine, Being the Second Appeal to the Christian Public, in Defence of "Precepts of Jesus,"* The British and Foreign Unitarian Association, 1834 (second edition), 59–60.

4. Joshua Marshman, *A Defence of the Deity and Atonement of Jesus Christ, in Reply to Ram-Mohun Roy of Calcutta* (Kingsbury, Parbury, and Allen, 1822), 253–54.

5. Marshman, *A Defence of the Deity*, 256.

6. Ankur Barua, "'I am the Living Bread:' Ram Mohan Roy's Critique of the Doctrine of the Atonement," *Journal of Hindu-Christian Studies* 30 (2017): 66–67.

7. Barua, "'I am the Living Bread,'" 69. See Barua for details on his imbedded references. Tsoukalas reviews many of these arguments, and favors rejecting any easy comparisons: since *avatāra* and incarnation differ, then of course the views of atonement cannot be the same.

8. Barua, "'I am the Living Bread,'" 69.

9. Swami Vivekananda, "History of the Aryan Race," *The Complete Works of Swami Vivekananda* (Calcutta: Vedanta Press & Bookshop, 1947).

10. Swami Vivekananda, "Lecture on the Kathopanishad," Saturday, July 27, 1895, *The Complete Works of Swami Vivekananda*, Vol. 7, https://en.wikisource.org/wiki/The _Complete_Works_of_Swami_Vivekananda/Volume_7/Inspired_Talks/Saturday, _July_27. This is Vivekananda, the orator, not hesitant to add a strong dose of polemic to his speeches; but later, we will see another side of him.

11. Brahmabandhab Upadhyay, *The Writings of Brahmabandhab Upadhyay*, Vol. II (English writings), ed. Julius Lipner and George Gispert-Sauch (Bangalore: United Theological College, 2002), n289.

12. Upadhyay, *The Writings of Brahmabandhab Upadhyay*, Vol. I (1991), n92.

13. Upadhyay, *The Writings of Brahmabandhab Upadhyay*, Vol. I, n92.

14. Upadhyay, *The Writings of Brahmabandhab Upadhyay*, Vol. I, notes 95, 96, 98. In other essays, Upadhyay argues against the notion that vicarious suffering would lead to a loss of responsibility in society for one's own action. Quite the opposite: a refusal to respect the value and fact of vicarious suffering would make "society an unfeeling machine, a mere aggregate of units without any more tie to bind them into an organic whole. It is tantamount to saying that nobody is his brother's keeper."

15. Fernão Guerreiro, *Jahangir and the Jesuits, with an Account of the Travels of Benedict Goes and the Mission to Pegu, from the Relations of Father Fernão Guerreiro, S.J.*, trans. Charles H. Payne (London: G. Routledge and Sons, 1930), 58; my emphasis.

16. Guerreiro, *Jahangir and the Jesuits*, 59

17. An earlier encounter shows Jahangir's father, Akbar, in a sign of deep respect, placing on his head an image of the Virgin given him by the Jesuits. Akbar, too, had not converted, but he showed sincere appreciation for the Jesuits' gift. See Pierre Du Jarric, *Akbar and the Jesuits: An Account of the Jesuit Missions to the Court of Akbar by Father Pierre du Jarric, S.J.*, trans. Charles H. Payne (New York: Harper and Brothers, 1926), 111.

18. John 19.32–37, with the embedded quote, Zechariah 12.10. All biblical translations are from the NRSV.

19. On the contemplative gaze as an efficacious spiritual act in the early Society of Jesus and hence in comparative studies, see Francis X. Clooney, "Finding God in All Things: Some Catholic and Hindu Insights," *Western Jesuit Scholars in India: Tracing Their Paths, Reassessing Their Goals*. Leiden: Brill, 2020, 260–74.

20. Ignatius Loyola, *The Spiritual Exercises*, trans. Elder Mullan, S.J. (PJ Kennedy and Sons, 1914).

21. Walter S. Melion, note on 94, in Jeronimo Nadal, S.J., *Annotations and Meditations on the [Liturgical] Gospels*. On the usefulness of Melion's work interreligiously, see Francis X. Clooney, "Finding God in All Things: Some Catholic and Hindu Insights," *Western Jesuit Scholars in India: Tracing Their Paths, Reassessing Their Goals* (Leiden: Brill, 2020), 260–74.

22. Walter S. Melion, note on 106, in Nadal.

23. Walter S. Melion, note on 107, in Nadal. My emphasis.

24. Walter S. Melion, note on 95, in Nadal.

25. Walter S. Melion, note on 100, in Nadal.

26. Francis X. Clooney, *Hindu God, Christian God: How Reason Helps Break Down the Boundaries between Religions* (New York: Oxford University Press, 2001), 116.

27. Clooney, *Hindu God, Christian God*, 116.

28. Clooney, *Hindu God, Christian God*, 116.

29. On the distinctive suffering of Rāma and akin to the suffering of Christ, see the hints given in this regard in Daniel H. Ingalls's introduction (pp. ix–xiv) in Frank Whaling, *The Rise of the Religious Significance of Rama* (Motilal Banarsidass, 1980). Although space does not allow elaboration here, one might turn also to the *Bhagavad Gītā*, Chapters 2–4, to see a portrayal of human suffering as parallel to the suffering of an *avatāra*: Bodies definitely suffer, but the detached and wise person looks with tranquility upon that suffering.

30. Keshab Chunder Sen, *Asia's Message to Europe. A Lecture Delivered on the Occasion of the Fifty-Third Anniversary of the Brahmo Somaj at the Town Hall, Calcutta, on Saturday the 20th January, 1883* (Calcutta: R. S. Bhatta, 1883), 24.

31. Sen, *Asia's Message to Europe*, 24–25.

32. Sen, *Asia's Message to Europe*, 26.

33. Sen, *Asia's Message to Europe*, 25.

34. See also Francis X. Clooney, "Renewing the Study of Ramakrishna: A Proposal," *Prabuddha Bharata* 116.1 (2011): 203–8.

35. Swami Chetanananda, *Ramakrishna as We Saw Him* (Vedanta Society of St. Louis, 1990), 222.

36. Swami Chetanananda, *Ramakrishna as We Saw Him*, 110.

37. Swami Chetanananda, *Ramakrishna as We Saw Him*, 110.

38. More familiarly known, in an earlier translation, as *The Great Master*.

39. Swami Saradananda, *Ramakrishna and His Divine Play* V.12.3.1 (The Great Master), trans. Swami Chetanananda (Vedanta Society of St. Louis, 2003), 900.

40. Elsewhere in the *Ramakrishna and His Divine Play*—too long to quote here—we find an account of Ramakrishna's discussion between Ramakrishna and pandit Shashadhar Tarkachudamani, who had asked him why he was suffering. After all, as a great soul, he might simply meditate on the diseased part of his throat and thus cure it. Ramakrishna replies that he no longer cared for his body; his suffering is nothing but the divine Mother's will and is bountiful for the sake of others. If he can no longer eat, it is because by her will, it is rather many disciples who are fed on his behalf (III.2.41–42, 431–32).

41. Swami Vivekananda, *Christ the Messenger*, Boston: Vedanta Centre, 1900, 25.

42. A newspaper report in the *Baltimore Sunday Herald*, October 14, 1894, quoting the Rev. Hiram Vrooman.

43. *Mir'āt al-quds (Mirror of Holiness): A Commentary on Fr. Jerome Xavier's Text and the Miniatures of Cleveland Art Museum, Acc. No. 2005.145.* Commentary by Pedro Moura Carvalho, with translation of the *Mir'āt al-quds* by Wheeler M. Thackston, Jr. (Leiden: Brill, 2011), 230.

44. Thomas Stephens, *Kristapurāṇa*, ed. and trans. Nelson Falcao, SDB (Kristu Jyoti Publications, 2012), chapters 48/49, 106b–112. Adapted from Falcão's translation, in Stephens.

45. My translations from *Tempāvaṇi*, though I am indebted to Sister Margaret Bastin, FSJ, for her help in reading these verses in August 2018, and also to M. Dominic Raj, whose *Tēmpāvaṇi: A Garland of Unfading Honey-Sweet Verses*, Amazon, Inc., 2019, appeared only after I had done my translation. For the text of *Tempāvaṇi*, see Raj, or *Tēmpāvaṇi: Mūlamum Uraiyum*, commentary by Sister Margaret Bastin, FSJ (Tirucci: Uyir Eḻuttu Patippakam, 2014).

46. Dorothy Day, "We Mourn Death of Gandhi Non Violent Revolutionary," *The Catholic Worker* (February 1948; accessed online at https://www.catholicworker.org/dorothyday /articles/463.pdf).

More Than Meets the Eye

THE CROSS AS MAṆḌALA

Michelle Voss Roberts

The diverse worship styles in the chapel services at an ecumenical School of Divinity in the southeastern United States were a highlight of teaching there. Community worship was a sort of laboratory. There, theological options discussed in the classroom took flesh through the sensitive crafting of space, language, and gesture. The chapel committee exercised great care to employ images of the divine and models of atonement that were inclusive. Favorite communion songs included "One Bread, One Body," "For Everyone Born, A Place at the Table," and "Come to the Table of Grace." These songs do not rely exclusively on the bloody language of substitutionary atonement but interpret the rite through themes of unity, hospitality, and healing.

One scene played out enough times there to give me pause. It is Thursday morning, we have gathered for worship, and the time has come to celebrate communion. A committee of diverse members of the community has selected the music and liturgy. And then someone—often the preacher of the day or the person at the keyboard—changes course and, unbidden, decides that we're going to sing about The Blood. Like a primordial collective cry, the music swells and voices invoke Jesus's powerful blood, shed for humanity, which flows to the heights and the depths, and which strengthens and comforts the faithful.[1]

I have grappled long and hard with possible reasons for this irruption of The Blood. Perhaps it is habit, a kind of muscle memory, that when we come to the table, we should sing about it. Hymns like this shaped my early theology deeply. But in the context of the coursework that takes place in that building, another dynamic is at work. I *know* the students are aware of how the logic of "blood shed for me" can reinforce unhealthy ideals of sacrifice and suffering for women and racialized persons. I also know that they have been exposed to alternative views of the salvific work of Christ and of the significance of the table. I know this because I've taught them. They've read (or at least they were assigned) Delores Williams's womanist rejection of surrogacy, as well as Valerie Saiving's feminist critique of self-sacrificial love.[2] The recurrent takeover of the worship service feels like a rebuke, a rude gesture directed at faculty like me.

I struggle with my response to this tug-of-war over our shared worship space. Many—though not all—of the students who stand up and shout "Hallelujah" for The Blood are African American students from charismatic traditions. The element of student resistance is salient. With this song and its theology, they claim the worship space as their own, an island in a predominantly white institution. I want to celebrate this and honor their contribution. I wonder how, if at all, this glorification of The Blood squares with their critical theological studies. I try to understand this cross-cultural interaction, but I will always be an outsider to the experiences of these students.

Meanwhile, I also struggle to make my peace with The Blood. Although in my denomination's liturgies, one may share "the cup of peace" and "the bread of life," it's pretty hard to avoid The Blood in scripture and liturgy. Many Christians claim to drink it on a regular basis. I admit that the cross is a scandal and a stumbling block for me. I do not stumble as the apostle Paul imagines in 1 Corinthians 1:18–25, where the cross exemplifies a power in weakness that seems "foolish" to those who associate divinity only with power and exaltation. No, I'm fine with that. I worship the God who tents among us as a helpless infant and as a working-class teacher who troubles empires. It's the calculus related to divine wrath and need for appeasement that gives me pause. I have a hard time worshiping the God who can find no other solution to human sin and limitation than to require someone to be executed—or even who, as the scholastics put it, would find this a "fitting" solution to a predicament.

My encounter with Hindu traditions has shaped my understanding of the violent event at the center of the Christian story. The Bhagavad Gita accepts three basic religious paths (*mārgas*): right action (*karma*), liberating knowledge (*jñāna*), and loving devotion (*bhakti*). Though the polemics between sects are often quite vigorous, this generous inclusion of different salvific paths (reminiscent of the Vedic teaching that the wise call truth by many names) helped me to appreciate that Christians, too, have interpreted salvation differently. Christ's death as payment for my sins is not the only Christian *mārga*. For some Christian theologians, the resurrection saves humanity by breaking the hold of death on all mortals. For others, Christ's life and ministry show confused humanity how to live. For still others, the incarnation—God becoming human—effects the divinizing work of salvation that brings humanity into union with God. Because each soteriology interprets the human condition and the saving work of Christ differently, one could respond to the chapel experience simply by trying to understand the variety of theological choices communities make.

The role of music and embodied response in the chapel service indicate that, beyond the problem-solution, cause-and-effect logic of the different paths to salvation, powerful affective and imaginative resonances are at play in when the students invoke The Blood. As womanist theologian JoAnne Terrell testifies in her important book on the atonement, these aesthetic triggers do not disappear when one's soteriology changes. She wrote the book because she found herself unable to relinquish the pull of the crucifixion on her religious imagination, even long after she rejected the passivity, uncritical enemy love, and surrogacy she associated with it. Terrell employs an aesthetic practice of contemplation in order to find a way through the dissonance. She muses of the crucifixion, "Perhaps in contemplating this mandala I can effect some relief from my sense of alienation, and find in it . . . spiritual principles that bring meaning, purpose and direction to my life."[3] Her reference to the cross as *maṇḍala* prompts me to probe her metaphor comparatively. What can be learned about the atonement when embodied contemplative practice intersects with theological critique? How can Hindu practices shed light on the importance of difficult religious symbols and their interpretation?

Because several comparative thinkers, including Graham Schweig and Jyoti Sahi, have also gravitated toward the *maṇḍala* as a helpful point of comparison with the cross, I begin by surveying the theological work that *maṇḍalas* perform in their work and in Terrell's. I then turn to my own comparative reading of two theologians who contemplate a shocking image as a theologically illuminating practice: Julian of Norwich's meditation on her vision of an extremely bloody crucifixion scene, alongside the tantric *maṇḍala* practices of the non-dual Śaivism of Kashmir. Hindu traditions, other comparativists, and this comparison in particular help me discern a theological response to those Thursday mornings in chapel. I will offer an interpretation of the cross as *maṇḍala* that is less focused on sacrifice or payment for sin than the "at-one-ment" of divinization. The diversity of *mārgas* in the two traditions permits this interpretation to enter into conversation with others to discern, through the same *maṇḍala*, the solidarity of Christ with suffering humanity.

The Cross and the Maṇḍala

Terrell confesses to a certain revulsion at the crucifixion, which she associated at a young age with the brutalities of plantation farming. However, her experiences of the Black church and of her own mother's murder make her unable to part completely with the idea that sacrifice can be efficacious. A hologram in her childhood home exemplifies this tension. From one angle, this "*maṇḍala*" displays a bloody crucifixion scene, and from another, Christ glorified. Her imagination ricochets between these juxtaposed images and the deathly and life-giving forces in her family's experience.[4]

Terrell does not enlarge on her use of the term "*maṇḍala*" other than to explain in a footnote that it originates in "Asian cosmologies" and that "in Jungian psychoanalytic theory, a *maṇḍala* is a symbol representing the goal of psychic wholeness, a process of centering or producing a new center of personality."[5] Graham Schweig elaborates. *Maṇḍala*, meaning "circle" or "round," comes from a Sanskrit root meaning to adorn or decorate. *Maṇḍala* patterns representing the cosmos date back to the ancient Vedic altars. They also serve as aids to meditation in a variety of yogic traditions.[6] Similarly referencing Jung, Schweig describes the *maṇḍala* as "an archetypal image whose occurrence is attested throughout the ages," which "signifies the wholeness of the self" and "serves as a threshold into the spiritual."[7] He reads the circle dance (the *rāsa līlā* or *rāsa maṇḍala*), which culminates the love story between Krishna and the cowmaidens (*gopīs*), in this framework. The circle denotes eternity, even as the dance pervades this world. It is all-inclusive and yet conveys a sense of closed intimacy, so that the dance honors both the community and the individual.[8]

Contemplating this symbol alongside the central symbol of Christianity, Schweig ponders the resonance between the corresponding scriptural narratives. As the epitome of divine love, the symbol of the *rāsa maṇḍala* evokes the eight phases of the love story in the tenth book of the *Bhāgavata Purāṇa*: awakening, anticipation, meeting, conflict, separation, loss, reunion, and rejoicing in the triumph of love.[9] Schweig argues that, although different religious traditions may focus on different moments, all of the phases belong to the love relationship between God and humanity: "For example, the phase of 'loss' symbolized in the Cross, representing the crucifixion of Christ, has become the ultimate focal point of worship for Christians. This symbol, however, does not preclude the highly celebrated phase of rejoicing in the triumph of love, found in the resurrection of Christ."[10]

Within these phases, Schweig focuses on the centrality of sacrifice in the crucifixion and the *rāsa maṇḍala*: "Each vision of divine love contains the powerful elements of sacrifice in love, suffering in love, and salvation in love" though "very differently and distinctively."[11] For both the *gopīs* and Jesus Christ, the "expressions of sacrifice are ultimate, total, and necessitate death as a means to a salvific end"; but in the Vaiṣṇava context, human souls reach union with Krishna through their sacrifice, whereas for Christians, God's sacrifice accomplishes salvation.[12]

Terrell and Schweig both deploy a hermeneutic of sacrifice in their contemplations of the cross. Christ's death—his blood—saves humanity. However, recalling the plurality of *mārgas*, other legitimate hermeneutics can be applied to the Christ story. When the perspective shifts—when the focus falls instead on the incarnation, the resurrection, or the life and ministry of Jesus—the symbol resonates with different soteriologies. Schweig does not question the redemptive power of Christ's sacrificial death. Terrell shifts the meaning of sacrifice from substitutionary atonement to Abelard's subjective theory of moral influence.[13] Jyoti Sahi presents an opening for yet another interpretation of atonement.

Sahi has wrestled with the Indian *maṇḍala* tradition over the long arc of his career as an artist and lay theologian. Although he painted *maṇḍalas* as a young man, criticisms from other Indian Christian artists such as Sr. Genevieve, who explicitly excluded them from her oeuvre in the 1980s, intensified his ambivalence toward the *maṇḍala* form.[14] At stake for him was the connection between form and content. How could a "gnostic path of yoga whereby an individual centers himself, and passes beyond the temporal cycle of suffering to an inner spiritual repose" square with the cruciform realities of historical suffering?[15]

Sahi has reconciled with the *maṇḍala* after studying the myths of tribal peoples on the margins of the dominant Indian tradition. In an important 2008 essay, "Yoga and the Wounded Heart," he returns to a meditation of the cross as a *maṇḍala* via a synthesis of India's wisdom traditions, including diverse Hindu paths as well as Christianity.[16] This time, he begins with the cross. He discerns that he must approach it through a "yoga of the heart . . . a way of understanding that works through images and intuition rather than through rational or discursive thought. It is a way of being hospitable and of meeting God, not through a direct vision but through a friendship that unfolds slowly by traveling together with Christ on the journey of life."[17] Along this dreamlike path, Sahi encounters numerous images. From one angle, he contemplates the tree from which the cross was built, which has mythical connections to the Garden of Eden, the Ark of the Covenant, the Temple, and other items in the history of salvation. From another angle, the cross becomes a living body—the vine of which believers are the branches.[18]

This *maṇḍala* holds the painful dimensions of life that Sahi earlier worried it would exclude. Its purpose is not perfection and symmetry but the act of orienting everything around a focal point:

> The center is the place where the image of the Lord is found. Around this center we find the space of "creation" with its four cardinal directions and its outer circumference, which comprises the outer limits of our consciousness . . . irrational, chaotic images that seem to lurk in the shadows of our search for unity and order but still need to be recognized and included in the wholeness that comprises our self-awareness.[19]

In this periphery, other archetypes emerge: the healing serpent in the tree, the seed-like shape of the wound in Christ's side, Christ's "karma yoga" as a maker of yokes, and the positions of the yogic sun salutation as Stations of the Cross.[20]

Searching for aesthetic traditions that do not eschew "images of suffering and death" in the quest for wholeness, Sahi finds that "in folk art, and even the art that is to be found in the Tantric (esoteric) traditions of India, the terrible and dark images of destructive energies have been represented often in connection with the feminine principle."[21] In comparison with tantric visual practices, the soteriological emphasis shifts away from a logic of sacrifice. Alongside tantric *maṇḍalas*, the cross becomes the focal point for bodily practices that awaken awareness that humanity is at-one with God.

To see how this is the case, let us turn to specific examples from the two traditions: Kṣemarāja's tantric visualization of the ferocious form of Śiva known as Bhairava, and Julian of Norwich's contemplation of her vision of crucifixion. For both theologians, the practice of visualizing a violent image leads to saving knowledge of their union with the divine.

Tantric Visualization Practices

Maṇḍalas are unavoidable in the study of the nondual Śaivism of Kash-mir. Indeed, maṇḍala patterns appear throughout India in the construc-tion of Vedic altars, temples, and cities; in rituals that designate rulers as lords of their realms; in mantras and arrangements of the letters of the alphabet; and so forth. However, the frequent reference Abhinavagupta and his students make to the ritual use of maṇḍalas indicates a level of significance not accorded them in other schools.[22]

In the nondual Śaivism of Kashmir, practitioners first access a maṇḍala in rituals of initiation and then begin a daily practice of visualizing it in-ternally. In this tradition's cosmology, Parama Śiva emanates thirty-six tattvas of the cosmos, which are his body. Practitioners mentally install these tattvas, and their corresponding deities, on the points of the maṇḍala, using corresponding phonemes and mantras. They then install the deities within their own bodies. The practitioner realizes the non-dual teaching that one's limited consciousness is identical with absolute consciousness. Everything is related to everything else. Using Christian terminology, one might understand this meditation (bhāvanā) as a di-vinizing practice: According to a frequently cited tantric maxim, one must become the deity to worship the deity.[23]

Among the maṇḍala-like figures that appear with regularity in the nondual Śaiva traditions are the śrīcakra and the triśūlābjamaṇḍala.[24] The śrīcakra (or śrīyantra) is a concentric geometric pattern of intersect-ing triangles, circles, and lotus petals, inscribed within the four cardinal points of a square. For those who employ it ritually, it is "not a mere out-line, nor a mere consecrated area, but a cosmic event and reality":

> through the practice of bhāvanā . . . that is, by creative identifying
> meditation . . . the cosmic event, the expansion and unfolding power of
> the cakrāvatāra is to be so intensely visualized, imagined, and felt to un-
> fold in the cosmos as well as in the adept's mind and body, that he [sic]
> identifies with it.[25]

Abhinavagupta's writings feature the triśūlābjamaṇḍala, the form of Śiva's trident, which maps the hierarchy of the tattvas onto the central energy channel of the practitioner's body. Beginning with the "impure" creation (the elements obscured by māyā), the practitioner visualizes the shaft of the trident rising through the body. Starting with the earth princi-ple at the base of the spine, the meditation practice moves through the elements and then the principles of sensation, action, and cognition, up to the cosmic principle of *māyā*. The plinth of the trident, located within the head, represents the transition to the "pure" creation. Here, one imagines that the corpse form of Sadāśiva gazes upward to the point above the skull that transcends perception and duality. The trident culminates in three lotuses, which enthrone the three goddesses Parā, Parāparā, and Aparā. These three symbolize the identity of undifferentiated bliss, the divine impulse to self-differentiate, and the manifest world as modes of the same divine consciousness.[26]

Sthaneshwar Timalsina's translation of the eleventh-century *Hymns in Imitation of Bhairava* (*Bhairavānukaraṇastava*, henceforth BAS), attributed to Abhinavagupta's pupil Kṣemarāja, may serve as a textual exemplar of this process.[27] Timalsina's work on tantric visual culture demonstrates a functional continuum between *maṇḍalas* and anthropomorphic visualizations of deities. Not only is Bhairava the deity who resides at the center of the *maṇḍala*, but the practice of visualizing his form has a similar function as meditation on *maṇḍalas* more generally.

The BAS hymns focus on the form, adornments, and activities of Bhairava, who is the predominant embodiment of Śiva for the Kaula branch of non-dual Śaivism. Bhairava's appearance reflects Kāpālika origins: He is a renunciant who lives in the cremation ground, carries a skull as a cup, and is accompanied by a dog. His wide eyes "depict him as immanent, oriented toward the world," and his various names associate him with furious emotions and destructive characteristics.[28] In this tradition, he is "the supreme reality, embracing all that exists, and is identical to the self."[29]

To facilitate visualization, Kṣemarāja's hymn systematically describes Bhairava's appearance. Bhairava wears fire and water, a "rosary of hands and heads," entrails, and a blood-stained elephant hide (BAS 12–15, 34–35). He holds a sword, shield, rope, hook, bow and arrow, trident, stick, hammer, axe, lotus, and citron fruit (BAS 17–20, 26–33). He makes gestures of granting boons and removing fear (BAS 21–22). He clutches a severed head and a staff and cup made of skulls (BAS 23–24, 31). He plays the lute, bell, and drum (BAS 25). The third eye on his forehead incinerates desire (BAS 36). He wears the "sky as raiment" and has a dark hue (BAS 38–39). He is surrounded by goblins in the cremation ground (BAS 41). Each verse not only names one of Bhairava's weapons or adornments but also explains the meaning the singer attributes to it. For instance, the three musical instruments denote that he can listen to the three states of consciousness: waking, dreaming, and dreamless sleep (BAS 25). His hammer and axe denote his ability to shatter difference (BAS 29), while his nakedness signifies the self's freedom from illusion (BAS 38).

Despite Bhairava's fearsome appearance, these visualization practices lead to knowledge that he is the essence of reality, the unity that threads through the diversity of selves: "Lord! As you are of the nature of supreme Brahman but still assume the form of Bhairava, you demonstrate that one who knows the reality is liberated even where there is difference" (BAS 40). He is consciousness itself, both manifesting and dissolving the world of senses and their objects (BAS 1–11). Meditation on him reveals that the self consists of the same essence of consciousness. As Kṣemarāja reflects,

> By carrying fire and water, or [by] the flow of nectar and poison, you in-struct that, although the world is [comprised of] conflicting [natures], this world (etat) does not conflict in me, [being] of the nature of being and consciousness [alone]. (BAS 12)

Ultimately, meditation on Bhairava, the deity at the heart of the maṇḍala, culminates "in the state of highest absorption (samāveśa) wherein the yogin experiences himself as Bhairava."[30]

Timalsina argues that the "process of deciphering meaning" in Kṣemarāja's hymn is inherent to the tantric visualization process.[31] When one sees and reflects upon this image, one understands not only the vis-ible features but the very nature of reality. As he emphasizes, this pro-cess is not a mere reception of an image, but an active and imaginative interaction, which draws upon the practitioner's memories—both the community's inherited symbolism as well as "previous experiences, either gleaned through sensory modalities or constituted through imagina-tion."[32] As Gavin Flood describes the effect of this practice of remem-bering (smaraṇa), "The tantric practitioner lives within the maṇḍala . . . lives within the vision of divinity such that the symbolic world of the text becomes the lived world of the body. Representation in text, icon, and rite coalesce in the experience of the lived body."[33] Maṇḍala visualiza-tion practices actively and intentionally construct the reality the practi-tioner comes to inhabit.

Meditation on the Cross as Divinizing Practice

Julian of Norwich experienced a series of sixteen physical and spiritual visions ("shewings") in 1373, when she was thirty years old. She spent the rest of her life contemplating their meaning. The showings alternate between corporeal manifestations of the crucifixion—focusing especially on the head of Christ and the copious amounts of blood that flowed from it—and "ghostly" or interior revelations of God's care for the world. The short text (ST) is a fairly straightforward narration of her experiences. The long text (LT), revised after some fifteen to twenty years of contemplation on the visions, works out its theological implications.[34]

Earlier, Julian reports, she had prayed for three "graces" from God. "Knowledge of the passion" was the first. The second was that, as a preparation for this understanding, she would become so sick that she would believe she were dying and would receive last rites. Her third request was for three "wounds": contrition, compassion, and increased longing for God (ST i).

Her first request reflects the popularity of devotions to the passion of Christ during the fourteenth century.[35] At the beginning of the short text, she reminds her readers of paintings that "resemble Christ's passion," in order to frame a desire for a "truer recollection" of it (ST i, 125–26). Such images were part of the visual culture of the time. Accordingly, in the second chapter, she reports that when she became seriously ill, "the parson, my curate" arrived with a crucifix and these instructions: "Daughter, I have brought you the image of your savior. Look at it and take comfort from it, in reverence of him who died for you and me" (ST i, 128). She takes these instructions very seriously. Though tempted at several points to look elsewhere, she remains resolved to keep her eyes fixed upon it (ST i, 128).

Julian's original request indicates her understanding of *why* recollection of the passion would be beneficial. She applies a condition—only if it was God's will—to the requests for knowledge of the passion and for sickness, but she asks for the three wounds without condition (ST i, 127). She considers contrition, compassion, and increased longing for God appropriate requests for any Christian. She harbors no doubt that God wills these for her as well. These three dispositions are the very reason, and the desired result, of her first two requests. Mortal illness and knowledge of the passion, she suspects, will lead most directly to the character she seeks. She is not interested in suffering for its own sake but wants a direct path to the place within each soul where divine love unites with humanity.

Furthermore, though the corporeal revelations are a great and unusual gift, what matters most is the intimate knowledge of the passion and her repeated "recollection" of it, especially insofar as she could share its meaning with others.[36] She would have been content "that our Lord . . . would fill my body full with recollection and feeling of his blessed Passion," and even at the point of her illness, she reiterates, "I never wanted any bodily vision or any kind of revelation from God, but only the compassion which I thought a loving soul could have for our Lord Jesus" (ST iii, 129). Nevertheless, she does experience a physical vision of Christ on the cross—most particularly, of the changing complexion of his face as it copiously bleeds, dries and withers in death, and speaks to her. More vivid than any painting, this experience stays with her for her continued meditation for years to come: the "bodily vision ceased, and the spiritual vision persisted in my understanding" (ST v, 133). She directs attention away from herself as the recipient of a private revelation. God did not intend it for her alone: "Everything I say about myself I mean to apply to all my fellow Christians" (ST vi, 133).

And what should her fellow Christians learn? After fifteen years or more of contemplation, she would write at the end of the long text, "Know it well, love was his meaning. Who reveals it to you? Love. What did he reveal to you? Love. Why does he reveal it to you? For love" (LT 86, 342). Even in the short text, the reader can discern the comfort Julian derives from witnessing Christ and his blood. Immediately following her first corporeal vision of the bleeding head of Christ, she has a spiritual vision of a small thing, "no bigger than a hazelnut," in her hand. She is astonished that such a small thing should be made, loved, and preserved by God, and she realizes that God similarly treasures her. The soul, a created thing, would be nothing without its creator. She explains that the fragile boundary of her creaturely lifespan keeps her from being "substantially united to him . . . so attached to him that there can be no created thing between my God and me" (ST iv, 131), whereas at death, "when the soul has become nothing for love, so as to have him who is all that is good, then it is able to receive spiritual rest" (ST iv, 132). The second bodily vision of the passion yields a similar comfort: the flowing blood on the cross reminds her of the living waters of creation. She understands it as a spiritual vision that God "is present in all things" (ST viii). These theological reflections on The Blood offer a model of atonement, not as punishment for sin, but as union with God in love.

The long text, the result of years of contemplative practices, amplifies and clarifies this basic meaning. It describes Christ's passion in greater detail (and with more blood). The longer version is keen to emphasize conformity with the teachings of "Holy Church." To clarify the nature of union with God, Julian distinguishes between the substance and sensuality of the human being (LT 45). She specifies that her teaching of God's all-encompassing love pertains to "those who will be saved" (LT 9, 192), for she did not see anyone else. Most memorably, she adds the parable of the Lord and Servant, a narrative answer to her puzzlement over why Christ's death was necessary (LT 51). The meaning of at-one-ment emerges not only from gazing upon the cross in a physical vision, but also from the prolonged practice of recollecting the passion and searching out its meaning.

Comparison

Reading Julian of Norwich alongside Kṣemarāja can influence Christian theologies of the atonement by helping to clarify two things: divinization (at-one-ment) as a possible meaning of the crucifixion, and visualization as a practice that leads to recognition of union with God.

How is at-one-ment with God revealed in the *maṇḍala* of the crucifixion? The visualization ritual in the BAS maps the divine body onto the body of the practitioner, who aims to carry into the ordinary world of perception and difference a realization of *identity* with absolute consciousness. By contrast, Julian never completely dissolves the duality entailed in the relationship between herself and the Lord, but her vision strongly affirms the immanence of divinity in all things. God's being is the being of all that is. In the long text, she explains the difference: the soul's substance differs from God's only because it is created, whereas God is uncreated (LT 54).

For Julian, then, salvation as union differs from the ontological identification of the self with absolute consciousness in Kṣemarāja's tradition. In her embodied practices of union, she looks not to the soul's *created* union but to the *incarnation*, where humanity and divinity unite in Jesus Christ (cf. ST xi, 144). Rather than transcend pleasure and pain, as non-dual teaching would have it, the incarnation provides the grounds for identifying with Christ's physical pain. Julian perhaps comes closest to "mapping" Christ's body onto her own when she claims, "In all this time that Christ was present to me, I felt no pain except for Christ's pain" (ST x, 142). In accordance with her request to recollect the passion of Christ, during the course of this vision she experiences not the pain of her own illness, but *his* pain.

She further clarifies that embodied beings are both substance and sensuality. Our "substance" is always united with God. By contrast, although

"God is in our sensuality," human sensuality can become disoriented. In Christ, the union between substance and sensuality was complete. Seeking and contemplating Christ can help to heal the rift that creatures experience in this life. As Grace Jantzen explains Julian's Christological logic of at-one-ment, "The task of spirituality, made possible by the incarnation in which Christ fully united sensuality and substance, is to follow him and find in him the reunification of our own sensuality with our substance and become whole again in God."[37] Prayerful meditation on the unity of substance and sensuality in the crucifixion has the effect of transforming the will, thereby removing the obstacle of sin that stands in the way of one's at-one-ment with God (ST xix, 158).

Over the years, Julian comes to affirm a second kind of union, the union of love. The unity of neighbor love participates in the unity of love between God and creation:

> For it is in this unity of love that the life consists of all . . . who will be saved. For God is everything that is good, and God has made everything that is made, and God loves everything that he has made. . . . And thus will I love, and thus do I love, and thus I am safe. (ST vi, 134)

Julian's mandalic practice instills the knowledge that she is safe (saved) because she participates in the bond of divine love that is the very life of creation and can be experienced in the love of human community.

The realization of at-one-ment takes time, for both Kṣemarāja and Julian. This comparison highlights how counterintuitive the visual foci for these of these divinizing soteriologies are. The terrible, ferocious Bhairava lives in impure cremation grounds and wears emblems of gruesome destruction: entrails, skulls, blood, and an armory of weapons. The image shocks the uninitiated Christian viewer, who may have become accustomed to the horror of the crucifixion. Julian disciplines herself not to turn away from her vision, in which the piteous, annihilated Christ hangs from nails driven through his hands and feet, head bleeding profusely, his visage desiccated in the most agonizing of deaths. As these images evoke the utter limits of what a body can bear, they implicate God: deity as destroyer, deity destroyed. The practitioner reaches insight only by continuing to gaze on the paradoxical image over time.

Kṣemarāja and Julian must make meaning of what they see. There is more than meets the eye. The deity at the center of the *maṇḍala* requires interpretation. Kṣemarāja knows that the Lord's terrible, off-putting aspects can pose obstacles for potential practitioners. His hymn explains the esoteric meaning of each attribute. Bhairava's weapons exist for the cutting of ignorance, the slicing of duality, the smashing of everything that keeps his devotees from liberation. Devotees overcome their revulsion and fear not by avoiding them but by going straight through them, into the recognition of the unity of reality.

For her part, too, as much as Julian had craved sympathetic knowledge of Christ's suffering, something still bothers her about it. Over the span of a lifetime, she struggles with what the cross communicates about God. She cannot quite square the means of salvation with the overwhelming assurance of love that it brings her. Her vision becomes a text for her to exegete over the years, so that her experience and her powers of reason work together to discern the image's meaning. Sin stands in the way of humanity living out the image and likeness of God. Why does God not prevent it? What can Jesus mean when he tells her "sin is necessary"— including the crucifixion (ST xiii, 148)? Surely less masochistic means could accomplish salvation.

The deity at the heart of Julian's *maṇḍala* requires interpretation as well. Already in Chapter xix of the short text, Julian uses her astute psychological powers to explain how existential friction is necessary to turn human beings toward God. Though God's love is always available, it only occurs to us that we need to pray when we are in trouble. Prayer makes us "supple" to the love and will of God. God first grants awareness of our sinful condition, which causes us to "[believe] that God may be angry." In contrition and confession, we attempt "to appease God's anger," which eases our conscience. Only then can the soul receive God's assurance, and it hears God saying, "I am glad that you have found rest, for I have always loved you and I love you now, and you love me." This is how, "with prayers . . . and with other good works that Holy Church teaches us to practice, the soul is united to God" (ST xix, 159).

But is God actually angry? Does God need to be appeased, as many have claimed in their teachings that the cross satisfies God's righteousness or justly punishes human sin? For Julian, this kind of logic cannot rightly be called love. The revelations do not show her any anger in God (LT 45). The long text labors to explain that God was, in fact, never angry with humanity. Human beings, however, excel at producing blame (LT 50). In the parable of the Lord and Servant, the servant (humanity) runs forth, full of desire to do the Lord's will. When he falls into a ditch, he is full of self-loathing and believes the Lord must be angry with him. He is unable to see that, all this time, the Lord has been looking upon him with tender compassion. The Lord's loving solution is the incarnation: Jesus takes on humanity and gets down into the ditch. He is with us in our pain (LT 51).

The crucifixion does not appease a wrathful deity, though that would certainly make sense from our side of the equation (LT 48) and from the perspective of Church teaching, which "can best help us toward integration by holding us responsible and attaching blame," as Jantzen charitably puts it.[38] Rather, in the cross we most clearly see God uniting with us in a terrible moment of estrangement. Julian's teaching of the motherhood of Christ makes sense of this unglamorous union. Like a mother recollecting labor pains, Christ affirms, "If I could suffer more, I would suffer more" (ST xii, 145). Far from suffering as punishment or for its own sake, the passion makes visible the depths of divine love that does not abandon humanity in suffering.

Placed beside tantric visualization practices, one can also notice in Julian the active, creative role of the practitioner. Timalsina demonstrates that tantric visualization practices are not meant to be a mere passive reception of a tradition.

> Visualization . . . constitutes the processes of both memory and imagination. Texts and traditions are called into play in the process of memory formation and retrieval, when the subject enlivens the past experiences by calling them to mind. As an act of imagination, the subject's gaze is not passive and directed only towards the past, but creative and engaged with what is being viewed.[39]

Similarly, Julian's constructive theological mind wrestles with an inherited practice. Instructed to gaze upon the crucifix, she does, and she receives great comfort. However, her inquisitive mind engages the image to wrest a meaning congruent with her understanding of God's nature. She mobilizes the practice of seeing, not to look obsessively at her own faults, but to gaze upon the compassionate heart of God. This practice of gazing upon the cross awakens a sense of what is most real about humanity: that it is preciously "knit and oned" to God.

Conclusion

Viewing the cross as a *maṇḍala* encourages evolution in a Christian's understanding of its salvific mystery over time. There is more than meets the eye. The diverse interpretations of the Christian community reflect more than logic—more, certainly, than a simple calculus of divine satisfaction through the punishment of the perfect victim. Deeply embodied, sensed, and remembered, these interpretations bear relevance for individual and community experiences. The cross is like a *maṇḍala* because, as Timalsina aptly puts it, *maṇḍalas* have an "extra-semantic power" that is powerfully rooted in the senses and imagination.[40]

As Francis X. Clooney's contribution to this volume highlights, affective and aesthetic approaches to the atonement have a long history in Hindu-Christian mutual understanding. Recognizing that "the very idea of vicarious blood sacrifice would be . . . alien and distasteful to Hindus," early Jesuit missionaries in India "thought that Indians must be enabled and allowed to see the crucified in a simple and direct fashion, rather than just hearing moral and theological arguments in support of a doctrine of vicarious atonement." They drew on local categories as well as the Ignatian method of spiritual formation. Jerónimo Nadal, for example, appealed to *abhinaya*, dramatic action, to describe how Christ's actions arouse affective responses in the gospel and its hearers. A contemplative approach has long facilitated interreligious understanding of the cross in India; and now, in a circuitous manner, Hindu-Christian comparative theology can shed light on an intercultural, intra-religious situation. The practice of contemplating the cross as *maṇḍala* helps to illuminate diverse apprehensions of atonement close to home in North America.

JoAnne Terrell observes that slavery gave African Americans a lens through which they "fixed their gaze on the cross of Jesus, deriving from it a way to understand and cope with their own painful experiences of proscribed existence."[41] She affirms both the "scriptural warrants" and "psychological benefit" of identifying the unjust sufferings of one's own community with the cross of Christ.[42] However, by fixing her own gaze on the crucifixion/resurrection images as a *maṇḍala*, other meanings come into view. She contemplates Martin Luther King, Jr.'s notion of at-*one*-ment that entails not only individual reconciliation with God but also the "redemption of the community."[43] She chooses not to glorify suffering, but to redefine sacrifice as surrendering something valuable for a higher good, "a potentially salvific notion with communal dimensions that got lost in the rhetorical impetus of the language of surrogacy."[44] She appropriates Abelard's soteriology of moral influence, concluding "that anyone's death has salvific significance if we learn continuously from the life that preceded it."[45]

The project of "learning continuously" points to the agency Christians exercise in interpreting the cross. African American spirituals, hymns, confessional utterances, and the shout—all experienced in Thursday morning's chapel services—witness to experiences of divine presence amid hardship.[46] The students who sing about The Blood exercise agency when they connect their present situation with communal and individual memories of God's help in times of trouble. This article's comparative conversation prods me toward agency and toward deeper conversation with my fellow Christians. When my own memories cause me to want to look away from The Blood, I can choose to remain. If Christ entered into a productive solidarity with suffering, as Terrell affirms of her crucifixion-resurrection-*maṇḍala*, then I can enter into solidarity with my neighbors. I can worship with them and work alongside them to resist and transform oppressive powers. Solidarity and resistance might entail suffering—even blood.

As a *maṇḍala*, the cross has an aesthetic function. It assists in a spiritual transformation that comes through long contemplation. Kṣemarāja's interpretation of the terrifying Bhairava encourages me to wrestle with the cross as a paradoxical symbol of love—even when I would rather look away. I discover in Julian a faithful companion who will not avert her gaze, who will stay with the passion until she has banished its associations with punishment and divine anger—until it "soothe[s her] doubts and calm[s her] fears."[47] Something shifts when I remain with the people in my community who are so moved by the power of The Blood. Like the worship of the struggling early church, their worship presents a kind of "resistance art" that demands creative reception and an aesthetic eye.[48] Perhaps I can sing their song after all, though likely in a different soteriological key. In this key, The Blood "will never lose its power" because God's love never changes. It can "give me strength from day to day" because it unites me with the love that made me, loves me, and preserves me. This lifeblood "reaches to the highest mountain, and it flows to the lowest valley," connecting me to God and to all creation.[49] I may not reach a full understanding of what the *maṇḍala* means in the context of my fellow Christians' experiences, but we can continue to contemplate it together.

Notes

1. See, for example, the lyrics of Andrae Crouch, "The Blood Will Never Lose Its Power," at https://www.azlyrics.com/lyrics/selah/thebloodwillneverloseitspower.html.

2. Valerie Saiving, "The Human Situation: A Feminine View," in *Womanspirit Rising: A Feminist Reader in Religion*, ed. Carol P. Christ and Judith Plaskow (New York: Harper & Row, 1979), 25–42; Delores S. Williams, "Black Women's Surrogacy Experience and the

Christian Notion of Redemption," in *Cross Examinations: Readings on the Meaning of the Cross*, ed. Marit Trelstad (Minneapolis: Fortress Press, 2006), 19–32.

3. JoAnne Marie Terrell, *Power in the Blood? The Cross in the African American Experience* (Maryknoll, N.Y.: Orbis, 1998), 131.

4. Ibid., 131, 142.

5. Ibid., 145n2.

6. Graham M. Schweig, *Dance of Divine Love: The Rāsa Līlā of Krishna from the Bhāgavata Purāṇa, India's Classic Sacred Love Story* (Delhi: Motilal Banarsidass, 2007 [2005]), 174.

7. Ibid., 175.

8. Graham M. Schweig, "The Crucifixion and the Rāsa Maṇḍala: A Comparative Sketch of Two Great Symbols of Divine Love," *Journal of Vaishnava Studies* 21, no. 2 (2012): 178, 180; cf. Graham M. Schweig, *Dance of Divine Love*, 175–80.

9. Schweig, *Dance of Divine Love*, 173.

10. Ibid., 173–74.

11. Schweig, "The Crucifixion and the Rāsa Maṇḍala," 171.

12. Ibid., 182.

13. Terrell's survey of traditional soteriologies, which leads to her reclamation of Abelard's subjective theory, omits the divinization tradition (Terrell, *Power in the Blood?* 105–6).

14. For images and an analysis of her work, see Anand Amaladass and Gudrun Löwner, *Christian Themes in India Art from Mughal Times to the Present* (New Delhi: Manohar, 2011).

15. Jyoti Sahi, *Stepping Stones: Reflections on the Theology of Indian Christian Culture* (Bangalore: Asian Trading Corporation, 1986), 2.

16. Jyoti Sahi, "Yoga and the Wounded Heart," *Religion and the Arts* 12 (2008).

17. Ibid., 46.

18. Ibid.

19. Ibid., 47.

20. Ibid., 46–59.

21. Ibid., 74.

22. See, by contrast, Hélène Brunner, "Maṇḍala and Yantra in the Siddhānta School of Śaivism: Definitions, Description, and Ritual Use," trans. Raynalt Prévèreau, in *Maṇḍalas and Yantras in the Hindu Traditions*, ed. Gudrun Bühnemann et al. (Leiden: Brill, 2003), 174–76.

23. *nādevo devam arcayet*: none but a god may worship a god. André Padoux, "Maṇḍalas in Abhinavagupta's Tantrāloka," in *Maṇḍalas and Yantras in the Hindu Traditions*, 233.

24. For the finer distinctions between different types of diagrams, see Gudrun Bühnemann, "Maṇḍala, Yantra, and Cakra: Some Observations," in *Maṇḍalas and Yantras in the Hindu Traditions*.

25. Padoux, "The Śrīcakra According to the First Chapter of the Yoginīhṛdaya," in *Maṇḍalas and Yantras in the Hindu Traditions*, 240.

26. Alexis Sanderson, "Maṇḍala and Āgamic Identity in the Trika of Kashmir," in *Mantras et Diagrammes Rituels Dans L'Hindouisme*, ed. André Padoux (Paris: Centre National de la Recherche Scientifique, 1986), 176–80. This article describes the *triśūlābjamaṇḍala* ritual in detail, as found in Abhinavagupta's writings.

27. Kṣemarāja, *Bhairavānukaraṇastava*, trans. Sthaneshwar Timalsina, in Sthaneshwar Timalsina, *Language of Images: Visualization and Meaning in Tantras* (New York: Peter Lang, 2015), 145–57.

28. Timalsina, *Language of Images: Visualization and Meaning in Tantras*, 113–14.

29. Ibid., 115.

30. Ibid., 116.

31. Ibid., 117.

32. Ibid., 28.

33. Gavin Flood, *The Tantric Body: The Secret Tradition of Hindu Religion* (London: I. B. Taurus, 2006), 173.

34. Citations are from Julian of Norwich, *Showings*, trans. from the critical text by Edmund Colledge and James Walsh (Mahwah, N.J.: Paulist Press, 1978). I indicate whether the citations are from the short text (ST) or long text (LT), the chapter number and, when necessary, the page number in that volume. I have also consulted the newer critical edition: Julian of Norwich, *The Writings of Julian of Norwich: A Vision Showed to a Devout Woman and a Revelation of Love*, ed. Nicholas Watson and Jacqueline Jenkins (University Park: Pennsylvania State University Press, 2006).

35. For an overview of how Christians of this period engaged with images of the crucifixion, see Chapter 2 of David S. Areford, *The Viewer and the Printed Image in Late Medieval Europe* (Surrey and Burlington, Vt.: Ashgate, 2010).

36. See Catherine Willits, "The Obfuscation of Bodily Sight in the *Showings* of Julian of Norwich," *Journal of Literary and Cultural Disability Studies* 8, no. 1 (2014).

37. Grace Jantzen, *Julian of Norwich: Mystic and Theologian*, 2nd ed. (London: SPCK, 2000), [1987]), 148.

38. Ibid., 198.

39. Timalsina, *Language of Images*, 142. Though Timalsina focuses elsewhere on "mystical" experiences or alternate states of consciousness, I would specify that "experience" includes sensory, personal, familial, institutional, and historical experiences as well— any input from the sensing and remembering capacities. Cf. Timalsina, "A Cognitive Approach to Tantric Language."

40. Sthaneshwar Timalsina, "A Cognitive Approach to Tantric Language," *Religions* 7, no. 12 (2016): 139.

41. Terrell, *Power in the Blood?*, 11.

42. Ibid., 139.

43. Ibid., 80, 124.

44. Ibid., 142.

45. Ibid., 127.

46. Ibid., 49.

47. Crouch, "The Blood Will Never Lose Its Power."

48. Terrell, *Power in the Blood?* 53.

49. Crouch, "The Blood Will Never Lose Its Power."

Divine Suffering and Covenantal Belonging

CONSIDERING THE ATONEMENT
WITH HESCHEL AND MOLTMANN

Daniel Joslyn-Siemiatkoski

Post-supersessionist theologies identify soteriology as a primary site for the articulation of supersessionist Christian theology. R. Kendall Soulen describes the standard Christian theological narrative as a supersessionist one in which the story of Israel and its covenanted life with God conveys meaning only in so far as it prepares for the saving activity of Jesus Christ. Such a reading distorts the witness of the Scriptures of Israel and the Church. As such, any attempt to develop a non-supersessionist Christian theology requires a re-articulation of soteriological narratives and claims.[1] In this chapter, I engage in a comparative reading of Abraham Joshua Heschel and Jürgen Moltmann on divine suffering to argue that understanding covenantal belonging is necessary for articulating a non-supersessionist Christian theology of the atonement.

I have chosen to use Heschel's *Heavenly Torah* in favor of some of his more prominent works because of its focus on the nature of Torah, which is necessary for any Christian who theologically engages with the Jewish tradition. The category of Torah illustrates the concept of Israel's covenanted relationship with God that traditional Christian theology often obscures. The use of Moltmann is apt given his demonstrated engagement with Heschel's work and their shared concerns for making sense of the human condition in light of the realities of modernity.

I emphasize the concept of covenantal belonging because it may suggest a form of mutuality that avoids the standard narratives that Soulen describes. It helps to resolve some of the key questions that a Christian reading of Heschel on divine suffering may generate. While Heschel (and the broader rabbinic tradition) recognize suffering as a possible mark of righteousness, such suffering does not have a vicarious role, or bring about the salvation or redemption of others. As Marianne Moyaert shows in her chapter in this volume, vicarious suffering has been a hallmark of Christian thinking about atonement. Although suffering in itself is not meaningless in the Jewish tradition, public hanging, which would include the crucifixion of Jesus, is interpreted in light of the Deuteronomistic tradition as a curse. Though Heschel's theology includes the notion of divine affliction, it plays a different role in the Christian Trinitarian understanding of God. The work of Moltmann illustrates both the continuities and the discontinuities between the Jewish and Christian understanding of the cross. It also opens up the possibility for a concept of covenantal belonging that includes the mutual belonging of both Israel and the Church. This would allow for nuanced understandings of the suffering of Christ in light of God's suffering with Israel that disrupts supersessionist narratives of salvation history.

Heschel and Divine Suffering

In *Heavenly Torah as Refracted Through the Generations*, Heschel investigates a hermeneutic for interpreting God's revelation of the Torah at Mount Sinai. He sets forth paradigmatic figures for two broad hermeneutical approaches—Rabbi Ishmael and Rabbi Akiva from the second century CE.[2] Ishmael stands for a minimalist approach to interpreting Torah, emphasizing the primacy of plain readings of the literal meaning of Torah. Rabbi Akiva represents a maximalist school of reading Torah, holding that each letter of Torah contains layers of meaning that are potentially endless. The dynamics between the Akivan and Ishamelite approaches contribute to the genius of rabbinic Judaism and its use of dialectical debate as a means of generating interpretive and theological insights.

DIVINITY AND HUMAN SUFFERING

Heschel introduces his understanding of divine suffering in *Heavenly Torah* through his discussion of the tabernacle where the Israelites worshiped in the period from the giving of Torah at Sinai to the construction of the temple in Jerusalem by King Solomon. The tabernacle was significant for the Israelites not only because it was the place where sacrifices to God were offered but because the divine presence, or the Shekinah, dwelt there upon the ark of the covenant. Ideas about this divine presence led to a debate that Heschel elucidates between the schools of Ishmael and Akiva over divine participation in human suffering and redemption. The school of Akiva argued that through the divine presence of the Shekinah, God identifies with the suffering of Israel to such a degree that it can be said that God goes into exile with Israel and requires redemption as much as Israel does. This is more than just divine compassion or empathy. In Akiva's view "the afflictions of the nation [of Israel] inflict wounds on God." Indeed, Akiva argues from 2 Samuel 7:23 that the phrase "whom you have redeemed for yourself from Egypt" refers not only to the redemption of Israel but of God's own self in the Exodus event. In contrast, Ishmael argues that God's chief focus was not on God's own redemption but Israel's.

This debate over the nature of Israel's suffering led Heschel's translator and annotator Gordon Tucker to observe an analogue to Christian debates over the suffering of Jesus Christ: "How can the person of God be humanized, to facilitate empathic identification, without either jeopardizing divine omnipotence or, worse, inviting a sense of human moral weakness to enter the divine description?"[3] Recognizing that the Jewish tradition also has a concept of divine co-suffering with humanity helps reframe the standard Christian theological narrative. Following Soulen, Christian theology is enriched by recognizing in Heschel's work that there is a prior history of God's suffering with humanity that is focused upon the people of Israel.[4]

AFFLICTIONS OF LOVE

Heschel utilizes the school of Akiva to articulate his understanding of divine participation in human suffering. As he reads it, Akiva held that God was intimately bound to Israel in love, epitomized by participation in Israel's suffering and its redemption. A midrash on the burning bush in Exodus 2 exemplifies this view: "It says: 'In all their affliction He was afflicted' (Is. 63:9), God said to Moses: 'Do you not realize that I live in trouble just as Israel lives in trouble? Know from the place whence I speak unto you—from a thorn-bush—that I am, as it were, a partner in their trouble.'"[5] In this teaching, Heschel sees a call for Jews to participate in the sufferings of God given the degree to which God suffered on behalf of Israel. He argues that God is a partner in Israel's sufferings. Indeed, God is "wounded by their sufferings and redeemed by their liberation."[6] Heschel acknowledges the seeming paradox of this position. He observes that such a claim seems contradictory. How could the one who saves be in need in salvation? To resolve this, he suggests that "just as the Creator, whose glory fills the universe, contracted His Shekinah between the two staves of the Ark in order to reveal His words to Moses, so did God compress His Shekinah into the history of Israel so that He might be revealed to His chosen nation as they went into exile together."[7] Israel is called to follow God in suffering. This involves the paradoxical path of divine contraction. The Creator of the universe experienced a form of self-limitation when he contracted himself as the Shekinah to dwell above the ark of the covenant. The people of Israel themselves are also called to such a path.

Part of the condition of being in the world is the experience of suffering that Heschel calls afflictions. When considering afflictions that fall upon a person, the Akivan perspective held that there are two forms. One form is afflictions for the purpose of punishing transgressions that are part of the moral designs of God. The other form is afflictions that one takes on to avoid violating God's will. Akiva describes this second form as "afflictions of love" that express either a person's love for God or God's love for a person. Here, Heschel focuses on how afflictions of love convey human identification with God's own sufferings. In Jewish thought this form of righteous suffering is often understood to increase merit in the world to come.[8] Rabbi Akiva's martyrdom exemplifies this view. In the context of the Bar Kokhba rebellion in the 130s CE, Akiva violated the Roman decree against teaching Torah publicly. As punishment, he was wrapped in a Torah scroll and burned alive while reciting the *Shema*, the Jewish declaration of faith in God. Heschel argues that Akiva sought martyrdom as part of the path of the affliction of love that the righteous seek. To not teach Torah would have been to violate the will of God and so diminish God's glory. To pursue God's glory then includes "human participation in the afflictions of heaven." The embrace of such suffering shows the truest love of God.[9]

The esoteric hermeneutics of the school of Akiva is necessary for understanding this interpretation of the meaning of human suffering. Just as every letter and word of Torah can be mined for its deeper spiritual significance, so can all experiences that pass between the people of Israel and God. Tucker observes that the Akivan notion of martyrdom as a kind of co-participation with divine suffering "is reflected in the Fourth Gospel's celebrated statement that 'There is no greater love than this, that a man should lay down his life for his friends' (John 15:13). For one who speaks of afflictions that generate love for God and the world, the 'friend' is God."[10] Here Tucker lays bare what is both implicit and audacious in Heschel's reflections on divine immanence, suffering, and the relationship between God and the people of Israel. Furthermore, this signals to the Christian reader that Christian understandings of Jesus's self-sacrifice reflects co-emergent elements of Jewish belief.[11]

Yet Akiva's example also raises the question of on whose behalf one takes on divine afflictions and forgiveness. Heschel reiterates Akiva's teaching that God can grant pardon for transgressions between human beings and God, but not between people. Only one person can forgive another. Thus, Akiva could forgive his Roman persecutors, but God could not. When this extends to communal suffering, the question of granting pardon gets more complicated. As one recent interpreter of Heschel explains, this means that "the individual can accept her sufferings with love, and the community can similarly accept its, but the individual must be extremely careful when she seeks—individually—to accept the sufferings of the community as a whole." To accept sufferings means to forgive those who inflict them, but individuals cannot do this for a community or a people.[12]

Heschel indicates the perils of accepting divine afflictions as he develops this theme. He employs the story of four sages who had a vision of the heavenly realms. Of the four, one died, one became a heretic, one went mad, and only one, Akiva, returned unscathed. Heschel observes, "They dared to look, and in so doing, they found that the pains of the nation were indeed paralleled by the pains of the Creator. Thus, instead of bearing their own afflictions, they began instead to share in the afflictions of Heaven."[13] To reflect and articulate the meaning of suffering, whether human or divine, places one at great risk. Indeed, it can lead to personal destruction or to incomprehension. And yet, if successful, taking on the afflictions of heaven can lead to self-transcendence. It can make one a blasphemer or a teacher of Israel.

HUMANITY IN THE IMAGE OF GOD

The issue of righteousness and public discourse about God appears in Heschel's reflections on the creation of humanity in God's image. Heschel observes that "the doctrine of the image of God has a powerful appeal, for it compares the likeness of the created to its Creator, the image of mortal human to the One who brought the world into being. This likeness is not only the secret of a human being's creation but is part of the very essence of the human's existence. In his very existence a human being is a reflection of the Holy and Blessed One."[14] While this is an uplifting view of human nature, and one that resonates with strands of the Christian theological tradition, Heschel quickly observes that this view of human nature is potentially dangerous since it suggests humans have the potential to become like God.

Heschel illustrates the riskiness of articulating the doctrine of *imago dei* by considering a biblical instruction on how to handle an executed body. Deuteronomy 21:22–23 teaches that "If a man is found guilty of a capital offense and is put to death and you impale him on a stake, you must not let his corpse remain on the stake overnight, but you must bury him the same day. For an impaled body is an affront to God." Citing the rabbinic commentary *Sifre on Deuteronomy*, Heschel considers the possibility that people will inquire about the cause for the impalement of this person. The response would be, "Because he blasphemed God's name." But as the passage from Deuteronomy indicates, even stating this would be an affront to God's name.[15] The issue at hand in this passage is the concern over blasphemy, which in rabbinic thinking falls into the categorical concept of the desecration of the divine name, or God's very identity. By definition desecrating God's name is blasphemy. One executed for blasphemy must have his corpse removed immediately, lest bystanders be told the blasphemy uttered and God's name be further desecrated. We can associate this view with the school of Rabbi Ishmael, which lays emphasis on the distance between humanity and divinity and the necessity of maintaining divine honor.

Heschel expands upon the problem of displaying an executed body by citing a parable from Rabbi Meir, a member of the school of Akiva: "There were twin brothers who were alike in appearance. One became a ruler over the entire world, the other a highway robber. When the latter was impaled on a cross, every passerby would exclaim, 'It appears that the king had been impaled.' That is why the Torah teaches us that 'an impaled body is an affront to God.'" This parable reflects the perils of the close resemblance between humanity and divinity. To potentially confuse the human for the divine could lead to inadvertent blasphemy. Such a risk is revealed in this prohibition against leaving an impaled body hanging overnight. The unrighteous one might be mistaken for the king.[16] If we examine the Babylonian Talmud's commentary on this parable, it shows that Rabbi Meir argued that God feels anguish over the death of a blasphemer who is executed. Even for such a person, a blasphemer and desecrator of God's name, the Shekinah, God's presence on earth, grieves.[17] In this need to distinguish between the human and the divine and the hanging of a blasphemer we can anticipate Christian discourses in which Jesus is identified as the one who hangs upon a tree. To this we will return.

From Heschel, we can see the tight link between suffering and covenant. The self-limitation and sufferings of the Shekinah comprise part of a larger plan of redemption. Redemptive suffering then comprises a significant, but not entire, portion of how Judaism conceptualizes salvation and redemption.[18]

Moltmann and Divine Suffering

The work of Jürgen Moltmann is a fertile place for comparative theologizing with Heschel's thought on divine suffering. In *The Crucified God*, Moltmann makes explicit use of Heschel's idea of the pathos of God and draws upon other rabbinic concepts that Heschel expresses in both *The Prophets* and *Heavenly Torah*. Both theologians present a focused critique of the concept of divine impassibility, especially in light of theology after the Shoah.[19]

Moltmann makes clear that his work on divine suffering is driven by his own experiences as a member of the German army during World War II and his experiences as a prisoner of war. As a post-Shoah Christian theologian, Moltmann intentionally engaged with the Jewish concept of divine suffering both as an act of repentance and repair and as a vital aspect of his own articulation of the meaning of human suffering. Explicating Heschel's views in *The Prophets*, Moltmann writes, "In the *pathos* of God, man is filled with the spirit of God. He becomes the friend of God, feels sympathy with God and for God. He does not enter into a mystical union but into a sympathetic union with God. He is angry with God's wrath. He suffers with God's suffering. He loves with God's love."[20] Moltmann also expresses the rabbinic view that God suffers with Israel and redeems himself with Israel from Egypt.[21] With Heschel and rabbinic sources, Moltmann too is convinced that a core aspect of God's revealed identity is a willing participation in the suffering of humanity.

Yet Moltmann posits a fundamental distinction between a Jewish view of the suffering of God and his Christian articulation of it. He argues that the Christian claim that God suffered on the cross makes sense only from a trinitarian perspective. Ultimately, Moltmann holds that Heschel and the rabbis express a view of an externally oriented pathos by the God of Israel directed toward sympathy with the people of Israel. In contrast, God in Christ suffers within his own trinitarian self at the crucifixion.[22] While both Heschel and Moltmann affirm that the suffering of humanity is part of the divine life, the focus differs, and so does its meaning. In what follows, I will note some key differences between Heschel and Moltmann: monotheism and trinitarianism; covenantal election and universalism; and the death of Jesus in relation to the Law (or Torah). Exploring these differences helps us see the usefulness of recovering the link between divine suffering and covenantal belonging in Christian theology.

MONOTHEISM AND TRINITARIANISM

Moltmann argues that a trinitarian theology of the cross is the only approach that makes sense of the meaning of the death of Jesus Christ. When speaking of the crucifixion, it must be that of the Incarnate Son of God, the Second Person of the Trinity, and not only the crucifixion of the human person Jesus. The death of Jesus on the cross is inseparable from his coexistence as God the Son with God the Father. Thus, "Jesus' death cannot be understood 'as the death of God,' but only as death in God."[23] The crucifixion of Jesus is, for Moltmann, the suffering of the Father in relationship to the Son: "The Son suffers death, the Father suffers the death of the Son. The Fatherlessness of the Son is matched by the Sonlessness of the Father, and if God has constituted himself as the Father of Jesus Christ, then he also suffers the death of his Fatherhood in the death of the Son."[24] Moltmann distinguishes himself from Heschel on the question of divine suffering despite their similarities. This is due to a monotheistic versus a trinitarian orientation that differentiates Jewish and Christian theological traditions.

If Heschel's theology of divine suffering involves the outward orientation of God toward Israel, then Moltmann's theology of divine suffering begins with the relationship of the Father to the Son. In turn, the Son, revealed in history as Jesus Christ, is the key for the redemption of humanity. Moltmann argues that the Incarnation of the Son is most fully expressed in the event of the crucifixion: "When the crucified Jesus is called the 'image of the invisible God,' the meaning is that *this* is God, God is like *this*. God is not greater than he is in this humiliation . . . God is not more divine than he is in this humanity."[25] For Moltmann, the Trinity is at the core of Christian identity because the Trinity is present at the cross. We know God the Father through what happens to God the Son on the cross.[26]

Moltmann identifies this expression of God's identity in terms of the concept of kenosis, the self-emptying of God. As the Jewish tradition understood God to self-limit when dwelling with Israel as the Shekinah, so the Christian tradition understands that God the Son emptied himself out and took on human nature. The ultimate expression of this kenosis is found in the death of Jesus Christ on the cross (Philippians 2:5–8). Drawing from Romans 8:32, Moltmann understands the death of Jesus Christ as a mutual act of the Father giving up his Son to death, resulting in Jesus becoming god-forsaken at that moment. "In the forsakenness of the Son the Father also forsakes himself. In the surrender of the Son the Father also surrenders himself, though not in the same way . . . But the Father who abandons him and delivers him up suffers the death of the Son in the infinite grief of love."[27] My interest in this position is not the patripassianism of which some have accused Moltmann but rather the relational dynamics he highlights when reflecting upon Jesus' experience of being forsaken. This reciprocal suffering of loss and forsakenness is the suffering of the inner trinitarian life. The Father does not suffer and die as the Son does, and yet the rupture and loss of the Son in the crucifixion is a suffering for the Father. Using Heschel's language regarding the dwelling of the Shekinah above the ark of the covenant, this might even be a kind of self-limitation of God. We can also reflect here on Moyaert's discussion of Levinas on kenosis in this volume and see in the kenosis of the cross the subjectivity of humanity intersecting with divine subjectivity.

For Moltmann, Galatians 2:20 is key to understanding the significance of this trinitarian event—those with faith in the Son of God live because he lovingly died for them. This verse makes sense if one utilizes the Christological doctrine of the communication of idioms. Here Moltmann follows Luther in using this concept to speak of the inner relationships between Christ's human and divine natures, especially in relationship to the passion. This concept "made it possible to conceive of God himself in the god-forsakenness of Christ and to ascribe suffering and death on the cross to the divine-human person of Christ. If this divine nature in the person of the eternal Son of God is the center which creates a person in Christ, then it too suffered and died."[28] The trinitarian suffering of Christ experienced as god-forsakenness is an expression of love for the purpose of liberating humanity from its own experience of being god-forsaken:

"In the cross, Father and Son are most deeply separated in forsakenness and at the same time are most inwardly one in their surrender. What proceeds from the event between Father and Son is the Spirit which justifies the godless, fills the forsaken with love and even brings the dead alive, since even the fact that they are dead cannot exclude them from this event of the cross; the death in God also includes them."[29] The death of the god-forsaken crucified Jesus liberates others and releases them from their own condition of being god-forsaken.[30]

COVENANTAL ELECTION AND UNIVERSALISM

Although both the Jewish and Christian traditions have strands that speak of the suffering of God, they differ with regard to the question of for whom God suffers. From Heschel's perspective, God's suffering is aimed toward the people of Israel with which God has entered into a covenant. Members of the people of Israel are called into a loving relationship with God and even sublimate their own suffering into divine suffering, taking on divine afflictions as Akiva did. In contrast, Moltmann articulates a universal orientation in the divine suffering expressed in the event of the death of the Son of God that results in loving liberation for all humanity.[31] Moltmann sees the Jewish theology of divine suffering as a necessary prelude, yet he views it as insufficient for the problem of the universal human condition: "the pathetic theology of Judaism must begin from the covenant of God with the people and from membership of the people of God." Here there can only be "a dipolar theology which speaks of God's passion and the drive of the spirit in the suffering and hopes of man."[32] For Moltmann, the covenantal election of Israel must be opened up to include a trinitarian relationality ground in the suffering of Jesus. It is not enough for the external suffering of God to be present to Israel. It now must be experienced within the trinitarian life of God for divine suffering to effect universal redemption.[33]

Moltmann situates the kenotic movement of the Son of God as a new chapter in the redemptive work of God that moves beyond the covenantal life with Israel: "[God] does not merely become the covenant partner of an elect people so that men must belong to this people through circumcision and obedience to the covenant in order to enter into his fellowship. He lowers himself and accepts the whole of mankind without limits and conditions, so that each man may participate in him with the whole of his life." This means that the god-forsaken condition of Jesus Christ on the cross is a movement beyond the covenantal relationship expressed through obedience to Torah: "God does not become a law so that man participates in him through obedience to a law. God does not become an ideal, so that man achieves community with him through constant striving. He humbles himself and takes upon himself the eternal death of the godless and the godforsaken, so that all the godless and the godforsaken can experience communion with him."[34] It is important to understand that Moltmann does not hold that this death in some way abrogates God's covenant with Israel. On the contrary, he affirms an ongoing covenantal life with God for the Jewish people.

THE DEATH OF JESUS AND THE LAW

Moltmann's elevation of universalism over Israel's covenantal election encapsulates the essential tension in the meaning of the death of Jesus if read from within the Jewish matrix. While Moltmann is careful throughout his work to emphasize a fundamental solidarity between the Church and Israel, he also frames the trial and death of Jesus to be, among other things, about the conflict between his radical opening of the Torah and the closed readings of the traditions of the Law held by the chief priests and Pharisees. This is clear when he states:

> Thus when we have spoken of the conflict into which Jesus came with the "law," this does not refer to the Old Testament *Torah* as instruction in the covenant of promise . . . For a Christian there can be no question of any guilt on the part of the Jews for the crucifixion of Jesus . . . there can only be a question of an offer of God's law of grace, and therefore only a question of hope for Israel.[35]

The conflict that leads to the death of Jesus for Moltmann does involve misinterpretation of Torah by Jewish religious leaders in Jerusalem, but this is only a symptom of the human condition of forsakenness.[36] While the effort to avoid the deicide charge in his writings is laudable, this stance does raise the question of whether Moltmann views Torah itself as a vehicle of grace.[37]

In Moltmann's argument, Paul's framing of Jesus as an accursed one who is hung upon a tree for blasphemy is important. Paul writes "Cursed is everyone who hangs upon a tree" (Deut. 21:23; Gal. 3:13). In the Jewish tradition, the means of Jesus's death by crucifixion conveyed that he was considered accursed. Yet in the Christian tradition, his death by crucifixion is understood as necessary since all other people experience the condition of being accursed, or god-forsaken. If, for Moltmann, the death of Jesus is not for the sake of Torah obedience, as it was for Akiva, but rather a death that liberates in order to expand God's covenantal bonds, then several issues arise. First, what is the status of Israel's covenantal relationship with God, especially as expressed through the keeping of the mitzvot? Second is the more complicated question of the righteousness of Jesus. While Paul emphasizes that Jesus became unrighteous so that others might be made righteous, this very mode of looking at the death of Jesus becomes a stumbling block when viewed from within the Jewish tradition. This is the comparative moment that this essay has been building toward: If in Pauline terms Jesus dies as one under a curse from the Law (Gal. 3:13), can he ever be regarded as a righteous figure within a Jewish framework that would reflect the historical self-understanding of Jesus? Put another way, could Jesus as a Jew be righteous according to the prevailing Jewish definitions of his era if the mode of his death signifies unrighteousness?

Any attempt to address these questions illustrates the incommensurability between Jewish and Christian perspectives on Jesus, crystallized in the manner of his death. By "incommensurability," I mean fundamental claims that Jews and Christians each make that the other cannot fully embrace. One example of incommensurability between Jewish and Christian views is Moltmann's vision of Jesus Christ as the Incarnate Son of God who becomes godforsaken for a godforsaken humanity. For Moltmann, this is epitomized in Galatians 3:10–14:

> For all who rely on the works of the law are under a curse; for it is written, "Cursed is everyone who does not observe and obey all the things written in the book of the law" (Deut. 27:36). Now it is evident that no one is justified before God by the law; for "The one who is righteous will live by faith" (Hab. 2:4). But the law does not rest on faith; on the contrary, "Whoever does the works of the law will live by them" (Lev. 18:5). Christ redeemed us from the curse of the law by becoming a curse for us—for it is written, "Cursed is everyone who hangs on a tree" (Deut. 21:23)—in order that in Christ Jesus the blessing of Abraham might come to the Gentiles, so that we might receive the promise of the Spirit through faith.

A traditional reading of this passage portrays the Torah, which Paul in Greek renders as Law (nomos), as an instrument that curses humanity, Jews and Gentiles alike. Jews are cursed because they are unable to keep all of Torah; Gentiles because they do not even have the possibility of living by Torah since they are not in covenant with God. Any penalty that humanity suffers under this curse can only be lifted by God. For Paul, the removal of the curse upon humanity is lifted when Jesus becomes the accursed one who hangs upon the tree, that is, crucified. Yet Jesus is not himself guilty. The very act of being crucified conveys that the curse is reversed. Embodying the curse of the Law in his death, Jesus lifts the curse all suffer under. This is for Paul the meaning of atonement.[38]

Reading Galatians in light of Heschel, this passage describes Jesus taking up divine affliction for the sake of the love of God. Jesus suffers to the point of becoming a curse so that others might be liberated from a curse. Further, affirming the creedal confessions of Jesus's identity as the incarnate Son of God, we could say that this was indeed the king from Rabbi Meir's parable who actually was hung on the tree and confused for a robber. Yet these assertions would find great resistance from within the Jewish tradition. From a rabbinic reading, one suffers the penalty of hanging from a tree for a severe sin, including blasphemy. In Galatians, Paul is toying with the implication that Jesus himself was a violator of Torah by applying this verse from Deuteronomy to interpret the meaning of his death. Indeed, the passion narratives state that Jesus was handed over for execution because of charges of blasphemy against him (Mark 14:63–64; Matt. 26:65–66; Luke 22:70–71). The death of Jesus by crucifixion (hanging on a tree) was used as a Jewish objection to his righteousness and Messiahship as early as the middle of the second century.[39] Later rabbinic narratives about the death of Jesus use the fact of his crucifixion as evidence for his status as a blasphemer and one who fell outside the observance of Torah. This rhetorical move both firmly places Jesus within his Jewish context while simultaneously denying all Christian claims about his Messiahship and divinity.[40]

If, from a traditional Pauline perspective, the Torah offers only curses, then the death of Jesus as an embodiment of the curse and the elimination of it through the power of God manifested in his resurrection has a strong internal logic. The difficulty of this approach is that readers of Paul have missed other aspects of his theology which affirms the place of Israel in God's divine plan. Instead, Paul's writings have been utilized to denigrate the role of the Law and de-Judaize Jesus. Following N. T. Wright, a corrective might begin with recognizing that Galatians 3:1–14 assumes a reading of Deuteronomy in which it is assumed that Israel (the Jewish people) will consistently fail at keeping Torah. In light of this, only

God can redeem Israel, which is accomplished through cycles of exile and restoration. Paul understood the death of Jesus on the cross at the height of Roman occupation of the land of Israel as one of those moments of exilic experience. The resurrection of Jesus after hanging as one cursed under the Law is the definitive moment of divine restoration of Israel that also has universal significance so that the Abrahamic covenant is also opened to the Gentiles.[41]

Considering Moltmann in light of Heschel, we can affirm that in the crucifixion of Jesus we see one who takes on divine afflictions as an expression of God's love. This love is oriented toward both a suffering Israel that moves in and out of covenantal fidelity and humanity in general (the Gentiles) that experiences itself as forsaken by God. Yet, the application of the concept of divine afflictions requires a Christian theology that articulates a positive theology of Torah itself. If the Torah is only a vehicle of cursing, then from within a Jewish theological matrix Jesus is only ever one outside of Torah. But if we consider the keeping of Torah as a manifestation of a covenantal relationship between God and Israel, then taking on the status of one cursed under the conditions of Torah might be interpreted as an extreme case of taking on divine afflictions, of suffering on the behalf of others the penalties of not keeping Torah. Such suffering is for Israel part of striving to fulfill the covenant of the Torah given at Sinai. But for Gentiles, their suffering is in part because they cannot fulfill the covenant made at Sinai. The work of Jesus is to suffer so they too might enter into the covenant through Abraham. The ignominy of Jesus's death resonates with Heschel's discussion of the four sages who dared to look into the heavenly mysteries and "instead of bearing their own afflictions, they began instead to share in the afflictions of Heaven."[42] Jesus's intense suffering as one under the curse of the Law can be read from a Deuteronomistic perspective as a form of sharing in the pains of the Creator looking upon the sufferings of Israel.

Affirming this articulation of the work of Jesus Christ illuminates an essential difference between Jewish and Christian notions of divine suffering. While Judaism states that God suffers alongside humanity and that humans might transcend themselves by taking on these sufferings, human endurance of divine afflictions does not serve as a vehicle for the redemption of others. Akiva might heighten his righteousness in his martyrdom, but he does not convey righteousness to others. Other Jews would need to do that for themselves and this path exists in the form of keeping Torah and covenant with God. At times, the Jewish tradition does speak of a vicarious death on behalf of others, notably in the story of the mother and seven sons in 2 Maccabees 7 and 4 Maccabees. Elsewhere, there is a notion of the "merit of the fathers," specifically the merit of the patriarchs that intercedes on the behalf of Israel in calamity. But these are minor strands in a tradition that overwhelmingly emphasizes redemption through the vehicles of Torah and covenant.[43]

Moyaert's treatment of Levinas on the death of Jesus highlights the ethical impossibility of suffering for others from a Jewish perspective. This incommensurability impels us toward viewing the death of Jesus and its redemptive meaning in the symbolic forms that Moyaert suggests. Jesus's death illustrates his own righteousness before God at the very moment when he seems to be outside the Law. And yet, in this vindication of his righteousness, he gains righteousness for others, whether Jews who affirm Torah as the basis for covenant with God or Gentiles who are not bound by Torah but claim the Abrahamic covenant.

Conclusion

The retrieval of the category of covenantal belonging through an engagement with Jewish traditions illustrates the benefits of comparative theology for the broader discipline of theology here in regard to Christian soteriology. Interpreting the death of Jesus in conversation with Jewish texts creates a space in Christian theology to simultaneously affirm the salvific nature of God's covenantal relationship with Israel expressed through keeping Torah and the covenantal belonging of Gentiles in the Abrahamic covenant through the death of Jesus. Along with Moyaert, I would offer a comparative theology reading of the death of Jesus in light of Jewish sources that does not require redemption and restoration of believers in Jesus Christ to also include the exclusion and replacement of the Jewish people.

Divine suffering occurs in the context of covenantal sharing between God and humanity. We can observe a continuity between Jewish and Christian traditions as seen in the works of Heschel and Moltmann. Through them we see how comparative theology is a vital method for the development of a non-supersessionist Christian theological understanding of Judaism. It has the benefit of both affirming Christian emergence out of a Jewish context while not using Judaism as representative of a negative set of categories against which to positively define Christianity. Rather, it utilizes an open and inquisitive approach toward Jewish texts on their own terms that provides an opportunity to more fully understand Christianity itself without therefore making a positive view of Judaism dependent on Christian categories.

Notes

1. R. Kendall Soulen, *The God of Israel and Christian Theology* (Minneapolis: Augsburg Fortress, 1996), 25–56.
2. Abraham Joshua Heschel, *Heavenly Torah as Refracted Through the Generations*, ed. and trans. Gordon Tucker (New York: Continuum, 2005).
3. Heschel, *Heavenly Torah*, 106; Jerusalem Talmud Sukkah 4:3 (54c). This theme of divine pathos is a long-standing one in Heschel's writing, first appearing in *The Prophets* and treated elsewhere in his writings.
4. On Heschel's concept of divine pathos, see John C. Merkle, "Heschel's Theology of Divine Pathos," in *Abraham Joshua Heschel: Exploring His Life and Thought*, ed. John C. Merkle (New York: Macmillan, 1985), 66–83; Shai Held, *Abraham Joshua Heschel: The Call of Transcendence* (Bloomington: Indiana University Press, 2013), 135–73.
5. *Midrash Rabbah Exodus*, trans. S. M. Lehrman (London & New York: Soncino Press, 1983), II.5, 52–53.
6. Heschel, *Heavenly Torah*, 119.
7. Heschel, *Heavenly Torah*, 121.
8. Heschel, *Heavenly Torah*, 134; cf. Babylonian Talmud Berachot 5a.
9. Heschel, *Heavenly Torah*, 135.
10. Heschel, *Heavenly Torah*, 129.
11. Here it is important to note that there is a chronological discrepancy. Akiva suffered martyrdom roughly a century after the death of Jesus. The point is not to argue for chronological priority or make claims for influence but rather to show how Christianity and Judaism reflect shared beliefs and worldviews because of their common scriptural heritage.
12. Heschel, *Heavenly Torah*, 134; Held, *Abraham Joshua Heschel*, 171.
13. Heschel, *Heavenly Torah*, 121.
14. Heschel, *Heavenly Torah*, 263.
15. Heschel, *Heavenly Torah*, 263. Citing *Sifre on Deuteronomy*, Ki Tetzei, 221; Mishnah Sanhedrin 6:4.
16. Heschel, *Heavenly Torah*; Tosefta Sanhedrin 9:6.
17. Babylonian Talmud Sanhedrin 46b.
18. This essay has not addressed the ritual sacrifice system in Israelite religion and its continued significance in rabbinic Judaism. A fuller investigation on the theme of atonement in Judaism would also include this.
19. Jürgen Moltmann, *The Crucified God: The Cross of Christ as the Foundation and Criticism of Christian Theology*, trans. R. A. Wilson and John Bowden (New York: Harper & Row, 1974), 270–74; Jürgen Moltmann, *History and the Triune God: Contributions to Trinitarian Theology*, trans. John Bowden (New York: Crossroads, 1992), 27–29. On the influence of Heschel on Moltmann's thought, see John Jaeger, "Abraham Heschel and the Theology of Jurgen Moltmann," *Perspectives in Religious Studies* 24, no. 2 (1997): 167–79.

20. Moltmann, *Crucified God*, 272.

21. Moltmann, *Crucified God*, note 165. Heschel is not the source for this but rather Peter Kuhn, *Gottes Selbsterniedrigung in der Theologie der Rabbinen* (Munich: Kösel-Verlag, 1968).

22. Moltmann, *Crucified God*, 274.

23. Moltmann, *Crucified God*, 207.

24. Moltmann, *Crucified God*, 243.

25. Moltmann, *Crucified God*, 205.

26. See Joy Ann McDougall, *The Pilgrimage of Love: Moltmann on the Trinity and Christian Life* (Oxford: Oxford University Press, 2005).

27. Moltmann, *Crucified God*, 243.

28. Moltmann, *Crucified God*, 234.

29. Moltmann, *Crucified God*, 244.

30. Moltmann's insight is generated from his reflections on the pain of both Jewish victims of the Shoah and German perpetrators. Moltmann's autobiography reveals that it is his own experience of god-forsakenness as a German prisoner of war and his guilt of about his unwilling participation in German Nazism as a conscripted soldier that informs his writing of *The Crucified God*. Likewise, he turns to Jewish sources, such as Elie Wiesel's *Night*, to articulate the god-forsaken experience of Jews in the Shoah. See Jürgen Moltmann, *A Broad Place*, trans. Margaret Kohl (Minneapolis: Fortress, 2008), 30, 190, 266; idem, *Crucified God*, 273–74.

31. This does not exhaust the possible forms of covenantal belonging within Christian and Jewish theologies. The category of the Noachide covenant, for instance, is a means for Judaism to locate gentiles within the pattern of redemption. Likewise, the reception of *Nostra Aetate* since the Second Vatican Council indicates ways in which Christians can conceive of salvation outside the visible church. See Jonathan Sacks, *The Dignity of Difference* (New York: Continuum, 2003); and Leo D. Lefebure, *True and Holy: Christian Scripture and Other Religions* (Maryknoll, N.Y.: Orbis, 2014).

32. Moltmann, *Crucified God*, 275.

33. Moltmann, *Crucified God*, 275–76.

34. Moltmann, *Crucified God*, 276.

35. Moltmann, *Crucified God*, 135.

36. Moltmann, *Crucified God*, 128–35; Moltmann, *The Way of Jesus Christ: Christology in Messianic Dimensions*, trans. Margaret Kohl (New York: HarperCollins, 1990), 160–68.

37. Elsewhere I argue that seeing Torah as an on-going source of revelation and a vehicle of grace for the Jewish community is necessary for developing a fully non-supersessionist Christian theology. See Daniel Joslyn-Siemiatkoski, *The More Torah, The More Life: A Christian Commentary on Mishnah Avot* (Leuven: Peeters Publishers, 2018).

38. N. T. Wright, *The Climax of the Covenant: Christ and the Law in Pauline Theology* (Minneapolis: Fortress Press, 1991), 153; J. Louis Martyn, *Galatians: A New Translation with Introduction and Commentary*, The Anchor Bible, vol. 33A (New York: Doubleday, 1997), 318.

39. Justin Martyr, *Dialogue with Trypho* 89.1.

40. Babylonian Talmud Sanhedrin 43a; Peter Schäfer, *Jesus in the Talmud* (Princeton: Princeton University Press, 2007), 68–74.

41. Wright, *Climax of the Covenant*, 137–56.

42. Heschel, *Heavenly Torah*, 121.

43. Daniel Joslyn-Siemiatkoski, *Christian Memories of the Maccabean Martyrs* (New York: Palgrave Macmillan, 2009); idem, "The Mother and Seven Sons in Late Antique and Medieval Ashkenazi Judaism: Narrative Transformations and Communal Identity," in *Dying for the Faith, Killing for the Faith: Old Testament Faith-Warriors (1 and 2 Maccabees) in Historical Perspective*, ed. Gabriela Signori (Leiden: Brill, 2012), 127–46.

The Clash and Continuity of Interpretation of Redemptive Suffering Between African Religions and Christianity

Elochukwu Uzukwu, C.S.Sp.

In marked contrast with the history of colonial perceptions of Christianity and of African traditional religions, African theologians have come to regard Christianity as an indigenous African religion of salvation. Many of the highly revered Church Fathers and Mothers such as Tertullian, Cyprian, Vibia Perpetua and Felicitas, Clement of Alexandria, and Origen were African. The salvific power of Christianity was also part of the experience of Ethiopian orthodox Christianity, of the elite Kongo Catholicism (especially of Nzinga Mvemba, Afonso I, reigned 1509–43), and, later, of the experience of the "slaves of the church," slaves of the Capuchins in the Kongo (seventeenth to nineteenth century).[1] Christianity was also a "saving" experience even during the colonial and postcolonial era, which saw the emergence of numerous prophetic movements that affirmed the religion as indigenous to Africa because Christ is Healer and Savior. Theologians such as John S. Mbiti and Kwame Bediako constructed their theology from the premise that Christianity is not a "Western religion"—the saving Gospel differing from its Western translation crystallized in its dominant form of Christendom.[2] Their fundamental assumption, which I share, is that missionaries neither brought God nor Jesus Christ to Africa. Rather, missionaries were sent by God, the One originally at home in African religion and cultures.[3]

These views of Mbiti and Bediako are still a major and dominant theme of African theology. They affirm continuity between African Traditional Religions (ATR) and Christianity, whether evaluated with the inculturational or the evangelistic template. This opens the door to exploring how traditional African understanding of humans, ancestors, deities and God, and the complex traditions and histories of African peoples can contribute to a renewed interpretation of the suffering of Jesus Christ as having a healing and reconciling or redeeming effect for Africans and the world.

My approach to redemptive suffering, or the Christian theory of atonement, will take on board the creative developments in indigenous African Christianity: the merging of the Christological title "Christus Victor" (dear to patristic atonement theory) with the more popular Christ-Healer, the Life Giver.[4] Bediako and Sanneh argue that African Christians not only translate linguistically the texts of the Hebrew scriptures and the Christian New Testament, but also express it concretely in everyday life, through their faith-practice, the communities becoming an axis of the ongoing revelation of God in Christ for healing, liberation, and salvation or renewal of life.

My reflection will take two pathways. First, I draw attention to figures of "redemptive suffering" in African Traditional Religions. These are persons endowed with, possessing or being possessed by, "spirit" that empowers them to function for the good or health of the society in general and for the benefit of individuals. The area covered by my brief survey is the extensive Niger-Congo linguistic family (from Nigeria, Benin Republic, Togo and Ghana in West Africa, to the Kongo kingdom, i.e., Congo and Angola, in West Central Africa). Second, I highlight the way in which spiritual and religious power is used in African Christian communities and the conflicting interpretations and evaluations of this reality. My argument is that the meshing of indigenous with Christian elements enables African Christians to reinvent the discourse on redemptive suffering in contemporary Christianity.

Spiritual Power and the Health of the Community in African Traditional Religions

Nganga, experts in the Bantu world (central and eastern Africa), are "traditional medical practitioners."[5] Eric de Rosny prefers this Bantu term, *nganga*, to "healers," because healers operating in rural Europe do not have the extensive reach that *nganga* have in Cameroon and other parts of the Bantu world.[6] De Rosny, himself initiated as seer, *ngambi*, testifies that his clients know "in one way or another that a *nganga*, that is, an heir to the traditional practice of medicine, 'opened my eyes.'"[7] Similar to the Bantu *nganga*, the West African *babalawo* (Yoruba), *bokono* (Adja-Fon), or *dibia* (Igbo) are defined as purveyors of divination and esoteric knowledge. Not only do they have knowledge of herbs and of healing, but they are also visionaries who enter with ease into the problems of clients; they warn, predict, and interpret events.[8] They also function as priests. These empowered persons are always intimately connected with a revealing "spirit," such as the *vodun* of land and health *Sakpata* (Adja-Fon), *Orunmila* (Yoruba), or *Agwu* (Igbo) who takes possession of the minister and/or the devotee.

In the Kongo kingdom (West Central Africa) the *nganga* and the *kitomi* (also called *nganga kitomi*) are endowed with spiritual-religious power and are closely connected to the local or territorial *Bisimbi* or *Nkita* spirits. They supervise the investiture of kings and princes, assure rainfall, and take care of health-related needs of members of the community. In Kongo, Catholic priests and the Catholic church ferociously contested the power of *nganga* and *kitomi*. They denounced the shrines dedicated to powerful deities or spirits that controlled territories or lands. However, curiously, the same Catholic priests took over the spiritual-religious power as exercised by *nganga* and *kitomi*. They were understood by Kongo people to exercise such powers *for good or for ill*. They were named and acknowledged as *nganga*, as Thornton points out:

> In Christian Kongo, however, the merging of the functions of shrines and churches complicated the situation. . . . priests called *kitomi*, mentioned regularly in seventeenth century reports of Kongo, related to territorial deities, called *nkita*, that were honored in shrines in other places. *Nkita* were territorial, organized along the local divisions of the country, and were responsible for natural events, public morality, and political order.[9]

It is vital to note that beside the beneficial exercise of spiritual-religious power (*kindoki* in Kikongo lexicon), there lies the ever-threatening possibility of the abuse of the power for personal or selfish gains, *ndoki* (witchcraft or sorcery). Faced with the devastating effects of abuse, the Kongo religious association of *kimpasi* (initiates) devoted and consecrated themselves to the eradication of the selfish use of spiritual power. "In Kongo, at least," Thornton notes, "the *kimpasi* congregation sought to regulate and control problems related to an overabundance of hatred and its cognate witchcraft in a region. The purpose of the congregation, which propitiated the territorial deities, was to create a new generation of people who had been cleansed of this and were now prepared to live better lives."[10]

The cross played an important role in *kimpasi* initiation. Cécile Fromont appears to support the missionary claim that *kimpasi* congregation borrowed the symbol from Catholicism. Thornton reports evidence of the fused indigenous and Catholic sense of the cross in *kimpasi* initiation sites. First of all, *kimpasi* in Kikongo lexicon means "suffering." In the initiation enclosure, an altar is built on a prominent mound. On the altar is positioned a cross: "which was simultaneously an invocation of Christianity and a marker symbolizing the junction of This World and the Other World common to the Kikongo-speaking world, both Christian and non-Christian."[11] Deschi-Obi follows Thompson insisting on the originality of Kongo *Cross*, based on the Kongo cosmogram. In this cosmology key moments of life of the initiates moved *counterclockwise* (following the motions of the Sun: East-North-West-South) peaking in *Kalunga* (sea, river, ancestral world, God). Consequently, "The Kongo *yowa* cross does not signify the crucifixion of Jesus for the salvation of mankind: it signifies the equally compelling vision of the circular motion of human souls about the circumference of its intersecting lines."[12] Both, in fact, may be seen to transmit theological ideas of "redemptive suffering": Contact with Kalunga (point of death-regeneration) and Jesus's redeeming death on the Cross generates redemption and healing.[13] The overflow of this redemptive spiritual empowerment (*nganga* and *kimpasi*) and the overflow of the desire to resist evil for the common good would mobilize popular Catholicism in the Kongo to revivalism (the Antonine movement), which came to be opposed by clerical orthodoxy.

The call or vocation to the ministry of mediating spiritual power (*nganga, kitomi, kimpasi, bokono, babalawo, dibia*) is generally destabilizing. It is accompanied by severe and at times incurable illnesses (cured only by initiation). At times, the "call" takes forms of madness or even death (initiates into *Sakpata* and *kimpasi* die to rise into new life).[14] Lovell describes graphically the destabilizing manifestation of *vodun* (deity/ spirit), requiring candidates to be initiated into the therapeutic ministry. Signs of *vodun* appearance include sudden trance, bulging eyes, contorted mouth, flailing limbs, and foaming.[15] These and other violent signs lead to the negative description of the possessing spirit/deity as *evil spirit* of madness. However, initiates such as John Anenechukwu Umeh, who is a university professor, argue that it is wrong to think that *Agwu*, the deity of divination, healing, and health ministry, is a spirit of madness. Rather, other spirits at the service of *Agwu* use illness, loss of memory, and temporary loss of consciousness to awaken the destined and chosen candidates to their responsibility: "The person being shaken up is merely being reminded by the appropriate servant of Agwu that he or she is called upon to the high and divine service as a Dibia; and as soon as compliance is achieved all the troubles would disappear."[16] This extreme "stretching" of the candidates (and their families) assures their *availability* for redemptive work in the spirit. Their readiness to go through the rigors of initiation confirms the operationality of redemptive suffering in ATR.

Finally, possession has the effect of transforming the initiate into a channel or "container" for the health-generating operation of the god/deity/spirit. The border between person and spirit, generally porous for all persons in the African world, is permanently bridged. This is evident in the rites of initiation. In some *vodun* initiation (as in the *kimpasi*), there is a narrative of the real or symbolic death, funeral, and "resurrection" of candidates. Consequently, calling the initiates back to life from the great beyond assures existence for the sole purpose of the common good, mediating healing within the community. This is a ministry in a religion that is dominated by a therapeutic economy. In *vodun* possession, Lovell notes, there is a "merging of identities of the possessed and the spirit that possesses." "Container and contained become fused."[17] This is why the language of marriage (*iya-orisa* in Yoruba, or *vodhunsi* in Fon: wife of the spirit, whether the possessed is male or female) is used to describe the fusion.

Fusion of Indigenous and Christian Revelatory Economy

From a Christian perspective, the endowment with spiritual-religious power for the common good, displayed in the therapeutic experience of "spirit" for the benefit of community and individuals, but not for the selfish benefit of the stretched channel, is interpreted as part of ongoing revelation of God's spirit. ("To each is given *the manifestation of the Spirit for the common good*," 1 Cor. 12:7). There is no dissociation of "Spirit" in Christianity from Jesus the Christ. The spiritually stretched (initiated/ordained) candidates for prophetic ministry in the community are interpreted as "experiencing" the spiritual power of the Christ event—that is, Jesus's unparalleled self-giving on the cross. Their experience is ongoing revelation: In their performance one has a reinvention of the narrative of the Christ-experience.

In the African reception and translation of Christianity, the fusion or the elimination of borders between the possessed and the "possessing" spirits, to achieve therapeutic effectiveness,[18] has been creatively meshed into the prophetic ministry of those empowered in Jesus Christ. This explains the popularity of the language of endowment with "Spirit" and the recognition of prophetic ministry. At conversion to Christianity, ATR diviners, healers, seers-visionaries, Africa's "traditional medical practitioners" (WHO), are transformed into the practitioners of ministries now deriving from or intimately connected with the prophetic power of Jesus Christ for the good of the community.[19] An illustration of this within African Christianity is the *Celestial Church of Christ* of Benin Republic, West Africa. Redemption from evils threatening human life and human flourishing is materialized in and mediated by Christian prophets, ministering as visionaries to the community. Another example of extreme stretching of people endowed with spiritual-religious power to reveal the ongoing effectiveness of the redemptive suffering of Jesus Christ in Kongo Catholicism is the contested Antonine movement of eighteenth- and nineteenth-century Kongo.

Redemption in the Celestial Church of Christ

My intention here is to highlight the power of liturgical performance as portal that mediates the flow of the spiritual-religious power effortlessly into chosen candidates for the ongoing manifestation and revelation of the healing God in the Christian community. As Monica Wilson points out, communities "express in ritual what moves them most, and since the form of expression is conventionalized and obligatory, it is the values of the group which are revealed."[20] This could not be better illustrated than by the Celestial Church of Christ. Their ritual points to the effectiveness of the redeeming work of God in Christ, in the Spirit, displayed in prophetic ministry.

The Celestial Church of Christ was founded in 1947 by Samuel Oschoffa in Benin Republic (West Africa), following a vision-revelation from God, and displays in the call of the Prophet the theological imagination dominant in African Initiated Churches. The prophet-founder was addressed by God,

> Samuel, Samuel, Samuel the Blessed has confided a mission in you on the part of Jesus Christ—because many Christians die without having seen the presence of Christ, because illness drives them towards fetish and diabolic things—and they are thus marked for death and hell. I give you the power to make miracles of healing through the power of the Holy Spirit.[21]

This initiatory revelation configures the flow of spiritual-religious power in this Church. It also characterizes the experience of similar churches founded by prophetic personalities, such as Simon Kimbangu (1887–1951) of Congo, Simão Toko (1918–1984) of Angola, and William Wade Harris (c. 1860–1929) of Liberia and Cote d'Ivoire. The founders are truly African Christian reinventions of leading Hebrew prophets, Elijah and Elisha.[22] The ordained ministers share the charisma of Hebrew prophets. The persistence of ongoing revelation characteristic of African religions is fully reproduced in the ministry of newly ordained/appointed ministers of the Celestial Church of Christ, who make predictions for healing and health, for liberation from the evil that causes illnesses, and for the good of the church. The liberation from evil or from satanic power is liberation from all that threatens or diminishes life in the community. Liberation or healing embodies the foundational African expression of integral health and wholeness, including prosperity, peace, and wellbeing, or "the desirable state of life in a comprehensive sense."[23]

The ordination liturgy of the Celestial Church of Christ proclaims the need for integral health and pleads with God to bestow on the candidates the gift of vision for the "accurate predictions" or discernment of evil (illnesses):

> Vision is the most important thing in your Church. Vision is the basis of her glory. Put it into your Church [Response of the assembly—*Nishé* or *atché*—"so be it"!].
>
> You spoke and said that vision gives weight to your Church. You said that a Church that has no vision is lost. This is why we put into your hands your laborers who provide accurate predictions.[24]

If the church founders, such as Oschoffa, carry, thanks to the Holy Spirit, the mantle of Elijah and Elisha, the visionaries are carved in the image of other great Hebrew prophets:

> This is why we put into your hands your laborers who provide accurate predictions. Come and watch over them.
> Put Ezekiel into them [*Nishé* or *atché*—"so be it"]!
> Put Jeremiah into them [*Nishé* or *atché*]!
> Put Isaiah into them [*Nishé* or *atché*]!
> Put Amos into them [*Nishé* or *atché*]!
> Put Obadiah into them [Nishé or *atché*]!

God of glory [Assembly response—*wiwe*—"holy one"], come down
and penetrate/remain for our sake in our Church.[25]

The language of the rite is irrepressible in its intentionality. It achieves
in performance what it intends—the production of women and men
(prophetic-visionaries) whose persons are porous and open to the revelatory operation of the Holy Spirit (of Christ) that drives the Prophets.
Fernandez's study of this church confirms Thornton's and Bediako's view
of an African reinvention of Christianity: It is the recapture, in the extremely stretched candidates, of the suffering and generosity of the prophets of old, an ongoing revelation that confirms the truth and universality
of Christianity.[26] The predictions of the prophets-visionaries are carefully
recorded, documented and preserved like the Bible which is considered
the repository of "all previous visions of the Holy Spirit."[27]

The redemptive suffering of Christ that liberates from sin-illness is
carved in the persons of the elect, prophets who are totally open to the
in-and-out of the Holy Spirit, driving the human spirit to transcendence
to effect the work of the Spirit. The language of "enter into them," "put
into them," is the language of *vodun* invasive possession. We see here
again the reinvention of "redemptive suffering" in the extreme stretching of the candidates, through the descent of the Holy Spirit of Christ, to
make them visionaries for the good of the community:

> God, save us for we are your children. Save us from evil spirits. Save us
> from evil people. And help us to worship you, as we should unto our
> death . . . you that spoil the works of Satan, come and show your labor-
> ers (those who through suitable intercessions contribute to the extension
> of the kingdom of God) the plan to be followed. Come and stay with your
> laborers. Your servants (the visionaries) are prostrate on the floor in your
> name. Descend and enter into them. . . .[28]

Initiates are born into a new life: "the life of initiation and the penetra-
tion of the world of spirits," for the good of the community.[29] The language and the rite embody what Bediako argues is foundational African
"primal imagination," ontologically embedded within ATR-African culture and carried into the reception or translation of the gospel of Jesus
Christ.[30]

There is, however, a problem in the ministerial (prophetic) display of
the redeeming work of Jesus Christ. The stress on Spirit does not always
allow for a developed Christology. However, one might argue that a Spirit-

Christology that views the incarnate Son of God, suffused with humanity and divinity thanks to the Holy Spirit, creates in the extremely stretched prophets a Christ-availability at an unparalleled level. Their prophetic performance can correctly be described with the language of redemptive suffering. As Tillich suggests, from the unambiguous, unparalleled prophetic availability of Jesus of Nazareth, Spirit-Christology responds to the question "as to how the divine Spirit could find a vessel in which to pour itself so fully." The response is the Incarnation of the Word, "the embodiment of the New Being," in Jesus as the Christ, "for historical mankind."[31] This language of the vessel available to the divine Spirit helps not only to appreciate the limitless Christ-availability carved in the "flesh of the church" ("local" or "particular" in legitimately diverse contexts).[32] The Christ-availability (passion-death-resurrection) is cause of the health-generating performance of ordained ministers. It is thanks to the spiritual power of the Spirit of Christ that redemptive healing is mediated to the community. Salvation and healing of humanity are thus anchored in the Christ, the origin/pioneer and finisher of salvation (cf. Heb. 12:2).

Redemptive Protest in Kongo Catholicism and the Antonine Movement

The Church of the Kongo demonstrates, in a different but related idiom, the prolongation into Christianity of the indigenous revelatory pattern of the manifestation of spiritual-religious power (*kindoki*). The experience of *nganga kitomi*, *nganga marinda*, and especially the unparalleled availability of initiates of the *kimpasi* congregation, whose members operate/suffer for the benefit of the community, impacted the Church and the entire society. In the Kongo experience of indigenous African religion, spiritual-religious power is available to any human.

The Kongo kingdom, perhaps from its foundation, was characterized by conflicts, bloody purges, alliances, and wars in the struggle for power. The resolution of the power struggle in the emergent Catholic kingdom of the Kongo was effected in the battle Royale of July 25, 1506. The extraordinary victory of Nzinga Mvemba, Afonso I (reigned 1509–43), gave him control as the Mani Kongo (King of the Kongo). His long reign displayed a kingdom under the redeeming guidance of Santa Cruz and "Santiago," annually commemorated—making July 25 a national holiday, "Afonso's day."[33] The victory was secured thanks to the assistance of the

Jesuits and the Portuguese. However, the liturgical-theological interpretation of the victory is not dissimilar from the theological interpretation of the experience of Roman emperor Constantine and his vision of the Chi-Rho sign (embossed on his standard) responsible for his victory over Maxentius at the battle of the Milvian bridge (312 CE). The outnumbered Catholic army of Nzinga Mvemba called upon Santiago. According to the written report of Nzinga Mvemba himself, when their adversaries were questioned, they responded that "when we [Catholics] called upon the Apostle Santiago, they [adversaries] all saw a white cross in the sky and a great number of armored horsemen which so frightened them that they could think of nothing else but to flee."[34]

Santa Cruz and the horsemen led by Santiago effortlessly meshed into Kongo Catholic theological imagination as the interpretation of the revelatory divine intervention in favor of Nzinga Mvemba to solidify Catholic Kongo. Christus Victor, the victorious Christ that led Mvemba to victory, was the dominant motif. But the rejection by capuchin missionaries of the Kongo cosmogram (used by *kimpasi* and initiates into military service) was exclusivism at its best—the Devil at work. This cross, used in Kongo initiation and martial arts captures some of the original Kongolese cosmology:

> The Kongo *yowa* cross does not signify the crucifixion of Jesus for the salvation of mankind: it signifies the equally compelling vision of the circular motion of human souls about the circumference of its intersecting lines . . . The four disks at the points of the cross stand for the four moments of the sun, and the circumference of the cross the certainty of reincarnation: especially the righteous Kongo person will never be destroyed but will come back in the name or body of progeny.[35]

By dismissing the commonality of "ideas of death and regeneration," Catholicism missed the opportunity for dialogue. Capuchin missionary Cavazzi claimed, "The devil taught [the *kimpasi* initiates] that to entice new Christians . . . they should paint on their idols the venerable sign of the cross . . . so as to hide their pernicious sentiments and their sacrilegious impiety."[36] However, I believe that the commonality reveals at a deep level the drama of the inscrutable divine performance regenerating and redeeming community through initiates and in Christ; God originally at home in African religion and cultures.

Another twist was introduced into the interpretation of Santa Cruz (Christus Victor) over a century and half after the reign of Afonso I (who was being transformed into the originator of Christianity). This came in the wake of the disasters that tore apart the Kongo kingdom and Kongo Catholicism after the Battle of Ambuila (1665), where the Portuguese and their mercenaries emerged victorious. Not only was there then a surge in the experience of political, economic, and social evils, but there was the fairly permanent transition into the reign of confusion in the Kongo kingdom that ultimately led to its demise.[37] In the midst of this, Kimpa Vita and the Antonine movement popularized a novel foundation narrative suffused with Kongolese saints and Kongolese reinterpretation of Catholicism and spiritual empowerment. Jesus was born in Mbanza Kongo (São Salvador, the Kongo capital, referred to as Bethlehem in the catechism). He was baptized in Nazareth (a disguise for the northern province of Nsundi where Afonso was governor). Jesus and Mary were actually Kongolese, and St. Francis belonged to the clan, *kanda*, of the Marquis of Vunda, original settlers of the Kongo capital. This "truer version of church history" was revealed to Kimpa Vita by God through Saint Anthony of Padua who possessed her (entered her head).[38]

Kimpa Vita, or Dona Beatriz, was a former *nganga marinda*, or expert endowed with spiritual religious power "to address social problems as well as individual ones."[39] She was also a former initiate of *kimpasi* (consecrated to the reduction and eradication of suffering in Kongo society whose symbol is the Kongo cosmogram). Ongoing revelations and prophetic utterances by Kimpa Vita called for change, typical of the African revelatory economy, which was deeply enmeshed within the popular Catholic piety of the time focused on devotion to Saint Anthony, the "second God."[40] The narrative of the possession of Kimpa Vita by Saint Anthony included real or symbolic death and resurrection to become the visible embodiment of Saint Anthony who made prophetic utterances through her. The visions declared that Kongo, besieged by a host of evils, must be liberated from disunity, from endless civil wars that depopulated the capital Mbanza Kongo, from exploitation of the commoners by the nobility, from the evil of slavery, and from the evil of the selfish use of spiritual-religious power that led to the increase in *ndoki* or witchcraft.[41]

The nationwide cleansing (healing) crusade driven by the itinerant medium Kimpa Vita and the Antonines was radical: All fetish (*nkisi)* had to be destroyed; only the *right intention* counted. Instead of Christus Victor, a revisionist or purist interpretation of redemptive suffering for the common good emerged. Only through ethical performance ("intention only") of the human energized agent and the entire community would

God's redemptive presence be displayed. This diminished the potency of the sacraments, the Cross, and other sacramentals.

The conflict of interpretation turned into deadly confrontation. Capuchin missionaries, the embodiment of Catholic orthodoxy, understood "right intention" as subject to their interpretation. While it was acceptable to exclude indigenous religious symbols (*nkisi*), it was not allowed to attack the Catholic symbols (*nkisi*). In the typical inquisitorial trial of Kimpa Vita, Italian Capuchin Father Bernado da Gallo questioned her about Santa Cruz (the emblem of Christus Victor) in the following words: "In the Mbidizi valley . . . did she [Kimpa Vita] not burn crosses along with objects of witchcraft? Did she not try to get rid of the cross in the royal square, if the king had allowed it?" She responded, "It is true. But the crosses of the valley also had superstitions attached to them."[42] The focus on "intention" that sufficed for the "redemption" of Kongo diminished the power of Santa Cruz central to Kongo Catholic identity, the visible symbol of the ransom paid for sins. "Kongo Christianity," says Adrian Hastings, "never had its village priest or eucharist, but it had its Santa Cruz, the Christian symbol standing in the middle of the village in place of the fetish which had been torn down . . ."[43]

Kimpa Vita and the Antonine "resistance" or "liberation" theology was anchored in ethical performance suffused with Catholic and Kongo symbolism. In touching base with *Kalunga* (the point of death-regeneration in the Kongo cosmogram) to be renewed with ancestral and divine energy, they touch base with Jesus the Savior fused into Saint Anthony. Through revelations from Saint Anthony, they claim power to transform their world. Their commentary on Salve Regina (transformed into Salve Antoniana) summarizes the priority of the ethical for the transformation of the Kongo to rid it of all evils:

> *Salve* you say and you do not know why. *Salve* you recite and you do not know why. Salve you beat and you do not know why. God wants the intention, it is the intention that God takes. Baptism serves nothing, it is the intention that God takes. Confession serves nothing, it is the intention that God takes. Prayer serves nothing, it is the intention that God wants. Good works serves nothing, it is the intention that God wants. The Mother with her Son on her knees. If there had not been St. Anthony what would they have done? St. Anthony is the merciful one. St. Anthony is our remedy. St. Anthony is the restorer of the kingdom of Kongo. St. Anthony is the comforter of the kingdom of Heaven. St. Anthony is

the door to Heaven. St. Anthony holds the keys to Heaven. St. Anthony is above the Angels and the Virgin Mary. St. Anthony is the second God.[44]

The preferred ethical performance set aside other devotional practices/ symbols that were interpreted as superstitious. This theology had no chance in the face of the regnant capuchin orthodoxy. They made bonfire of Kimpa Vita and her consort. She was a deviant Catholic declared a heretic, an agent of the Devil. She was burned on the pyre on July 2, 1706.

On the other hand, ambiguity and ambivalence surround the Christological question with regard to the Antonine movement. Kimpa Vita's extraordinary step to "burn crosses" along with objects of witchcraft was controversial. It was the major symbol of redemptive suffering that sufferers look upon, carry in their hands or wear around their necks for safety and protection. No symbol was as powerful as the Cross in Kongo Catholicism, dramatized in the victory of Mvemba Nzinga (Afonso I). Kimpa Vita responded that there were superstitions attached to the Cross. This demarcated the Antonines as radical reformers of the Catholic faith. Their theological insight was inspired by the fusion of Kongo ethical imperative, best embodied in *kimpasi* initiates (the Kongo cosmogram), and the reception of Catholicism (symbolized in Santa Cruz). In the Kongo cosmogram, the journey, counterclockwise, of the extremely stretched *kimpasi* initiates peaks at Kalunga—symbolizing permeation with ancestral and divine saving power for the common good. Fused with Catholicism, the Antonines claim that the operationality of spiritual-religious power in the community must be for the common good. This is a revision of the dominant elite local narrative theology of the conversion of Kongo kings that inaugurated Catholicism as indigenous religion. In place of Christus Victor, who paid ransom for sins, one is given lessons on the prophetic redemptive suffering that expands the transformational idiom of atonement. Christ's victory (symbolized in Santa Cruz) is worth nothing unless there were a radical transformation of society to ensure the priority of the common good. In other words, the social health of community trumps over and against greed, over and against the selfish deployment of spiritual-religious power that is *ndoki* (witchcraft).

Kimpa Vita, former holder of the office of *nganga marinda*, which was socially oriented to serve the common good, commanded respect. Other *nganga*, catering only to individual needs, leave the door open for abuse: All forms of "individualism" are often "likely to be accompanied by greed,

the prime ingredient in motivating *ndokis.*"[45] *Ndoki* should not be cyni-
cally dismissed as magical thinking in a comparative theology of atonement. For as Buakasa and Bujo (Congolese sociologist and theologian)
insist, behind the language of *ndoki* lies "something not put into words,"
namely that "every individual has the potential to become a sorcerer."[46]
Bujo believes that the combat against all forces of evil and the redemption of society from witchcraft/sorcery are the urgent or supreme concern of religion: "The fundamental intention of [the idiom of witchcraft]/
sorcery is to draw attention to evil, which can totally destroy human
relationships, and hence the entire community . . ."[47]

Kimpa Vita and the Antonines took the matter a step further by radi-
calizing, against dominant Catholic orthodoxy, the ethic of the common
good that must be transparently displayed in the exercise of spiritual-
religious power. They attacked the use of *nkisi* or symbolic religious objects deployed against the common good (whether indigenous *nkisi* or
the Catholic Santa Crux), despite the lack of the political power to sustain the reform.

The clash of interpretations, or perhaps the clash of ideologies between
the Antonine movement and official Catholicism, was predictable in
Kongo Church where the orthodox Capuchin theological rationality
dominated. The dominant Catholic orthodoxy, supported by royalty,
crushed the free flowing "non-orthodox," non-policing ongoing revelatory economy characteristic of the African indigenous religious imagination. The socioreligious impact of "spirit," which became manifest as
Saint Anthony within the free-flowing Kongo Catholicism, did not disappear with the defeat of the reformers. The evils denounced by Kimpa
Vita and the Antonine movement continued to reign unabated: interne-
cine wars, war prisoners sold into slavery, and the Kongo kingdom destroyed. Some of the prisoners of war sold into slavery continued their
Kongo Catholic movement with passion in the Atlantic world—Haiti,
South Carolina, Mexico—with attendant revelations and predictable inquisitorial condemnations by Catholic orthodoxy.[48] But they never lacked
followers acclaiming the effectiveness of their mediation, channeling
healing and wholeness into the society.

Conclusion

The Kongo experience displays a revolutionary or reformist Catholic
revivalism led by laypeople extremely stretched spiritually to become

channels of integral healing. Bearing the imprint of African revelatory and mystical experience fused into Catholicism, they focused on reversing the path of the disorienting socioreligious, sociopolitical and economic evils of Kongo society. Groomed as *nganga marinda*, divinely inspired and consumed by the desire to achieve the common good and also raised in a *kimpasi* congregation, Kimpa Vita sought to reduce evil in the society by projecting the ethical as trumping the external rituals of orthodox Catholicism. The health-generating death-resurrection of Jesus, enmeshed with the community regenerating ethics of the Kongo cosmogram, is preferred to the Santa Cruz that can be misused. Curiously, the ethical imperative was drummed through another devotional Catholic symbol, Saint Anthony, who possessed the devotee and guided the ethical rhetoric.[49]

The contribution of Kimpa Vita to the conversation on redemptive suffering could be styled "moral transformation," appealing to divine intervention carved in human performance to transform human affections and ultimately to transform Kongo society. This is characteristic of the African mysticism of "descent." Rather than the uplift or "ascent" of individual souls (mystics) to the divine mansions, the mysticism of "descent," dramatized in "possession," brings the deity down to the level of the human, to the messiness of human earthly existence, to transform the world. The experience could be provoked socially (i.e., under social pressure) to assuage the social (human) lament for healing.[50] How else could one interpret the display of an array of Prophets (Ezekiel, Obadiah) in the Celestial Church of Christ whose legendary ministry in the Name of Yahweh is replicated, or "put into them," the possessed, in the Spirit of Jesus, to challenge a plethora of evils (illnesses, witchcraft, broken families, and societies)? Similarly, embodying Saint Anthony, the divine is brought down to the habitation of the human, thanks to Kimpa Vita, for a clear social intent, to change Kongo society. Suffused with the experience of spiritual-religious power, under the popular spiritual guide, Saint Anthony, the Antonines confronted evil so that the society could be renewed. But they tragically perished in the effort to reduce evil and suffering.[51]

What is challenging in the deployment of the Christian imagination enmeshed with Kongo or West African earth-concerned religious polity clamoring for integral health and wholeness is the subtle, though unclearly stated, role of Jesus the Christ. In West African therapeutic Christianity, the enunciation of Christology is in the power of the Holy

Spirit (the Spirit of Christ), carved in the bodies of the visionaries, possessed by the Spirit. Expressing the dominance of the pneumatological in African Initiated Churches, Olayiwola states:

> The fact that the *elemi* [possessed mediums] attribute their "power" to the Holy Spirit suggests that they believe in the Trinity. None of them mentioned explicitly the name of Jesus Christ. This, however, does not imply that Jesus is unimportant to them, but that in their calling the Spirit predominates.[52]

Mediating healing for the common good, driven or "stretched" by the Holy Spirit, they make available the fruits of the passion-death-resurrection.

The focus on the therapeutic and the rejection of symbols that do not transparently contribute to the common good—including the Cross, embraced only by Kongo reformers—make healing the dominant trope of redemptive suffering. The moral transformational option of the revivalist movement of seventeenth- and eighteenth-century Kongo Catholicism (Kimpa Vita and Antonines) is not opposed to the insights of liberation hermeneutics by its rejection of or ambivalent attitude toward the Cross. One must note that not all crosses are redemptive as Cone points out in *The Cross and the Lynching Tree*.[53] One must note that in the Rwandan genocide (1994) crosses in churches did not save Christians from being butchered by fellow humans/Christians. So the claim that "intention alone counts" (Kimpa Vita) introduces a prophetic challenge (hermeneutic of suspicion) to any interpretation of redemptive suffering. Atonement does not simply focus on the "ransom" but embraces "healing" (*mhola*)[54] of human communities mediated by initiated and extremely stretched men and women who touch base with ancestral energy that, for Christians, crystallizes in the energy of the death-resurrection of Jesus the Christ.

The tendency to individualism and every selfish religious practice that undermines the common good is believed to increase the threat of the destruction of the entire community through violence and war. This prevented human flourishing in Catholic Kongo and continues to prevent human flourishing in the Democratic Republic of the Congo, Africa, and more than two-thirds of the contemporary world. The combination of a prophetic theology of atonement or redemptive suffering and integral healing of the society creatively realizes in stretched ministers and in the entire Church community the Christ-availability for the transformation of the world.

Notes

1. See the hesitation and discussion of this category of Christians in Kabolo Iko Kabwita, *Le Royaume Kongo et la Mission Catholique (1750-1838). Du Déclin à L'extinction*, Mémoire D'églises, ed. Paul Coulon (Paris: Karthala, 2004), Chapter 4. See also the missionary experience of Spiritans in the nineteenth century, Charles Duparquet and Gérard Vieira, *Le Père Duparquet. Tome iii, Lettres et Écrits, 1870-1876: De L'exil à Bagamoyo Au Succès De Landana*. Mémoire D'églises (Paris: Karthala, 2014), 575.

2. John S. Mbiti, *Bible and Theology in African Christianity* (Nairobi: Oxford University Press, 1986). Kwame Bediako, *Christianity in Africa: The Renewal of a non-Western Religion* (Edinburgh & New York: University of Edinburgh Press and Orbis Press, 1995); and *Theology and Identity: The Impact of Culture upon Christian Thought in the Second Century and in Modern Africa* (Costa Mesa, Calif.: Regnum Books, 1992).

3. Mbiti, *Bible and Theology in African Christianity*, 11.

4. Stinton studied these Christological titles and gives pride of place to Christ-Healer: Diane B. Stinton, *Jesus of Africa—Voices of Contemporary African Christology* (Maryknoll, N.Y.: Orbis, 2004). See also Robert J. Schreiter, ed. *Faces of Jesus in Africa*, Faith and Cultures Series (Maryknoll, N.Y.: Orbis Books, 1991). Moral transformation, more than satisfaction, could also be adaptable to the African experience.

5. The definition is that of the World Health Organization.

6. Eric de Rosny, *Les Yeux de ma Chèvre: Sur les pas des maîtres de la nuit en pays Douala* (Paris: Plon, 1981). Note the corollary of "opening the eyes" in the title of the book. De Rosny is a Jesuit priest and initiate into indigenous medical practice as *ngambi* (seer). English translation: *Healers in the Night*, trans. Robert R. Barr (New York: Orbis, 1985).

7. "For a Mission of Vision—a Testimony," in *Africa: Towards Priorities of Mission—Acts of the Inter-continental Congress of the Spiritan International School of Theology (SIST), Attakwu, Enugu, Nigeria, November 11-17, 1996*, ed. P. Ikechukwu Odozor, Chinedu Amadi-Azuogu, and Elochukwu Uzukwu (Enugu: SIST Publications, 2000), 95.

8. Elochukwu E. Uzukwu, *God, Spirit, and Human Wholeness: Appropriating Faith and Culture in West African Style* (Eugene, Ore.: Pickwick Publications, 2012), 184.

9. "Religious and Ceremonial Life in the Kongo and Mbundu Areas, 1500-1700," in *Central Africans and Cultural Transformations in the American Diaspora*, ed. Linda M. Heywood (New York: Cambridge University Press, 2002), 78.

10. Ibid., 82. Was there fusion of Kimpasi symbols and those of Kongo Catholicism? Fromont is undecided as to whether there is commonality of symbols or fusion of the "ideas of death and regeneration" captured by the cross and indigenous symbolism of the crossroads (meeting point with/of spirits and symbol of regeneration) common across Africa. Cécile Fromont, *The Art of Conversion: Christian Visual Culture in the Kingdom of Kongo* (Virginia: Omohundro Institute of Early American History and Culture, and University of North Carolina Press, 2014), 78-79.

11. John K. Thornton, *The Kongolese Saint Anthony: Dona Beatriz Kimpa Vita and the Antonian Movement, 1684-1706* (New York: Cambridge University Press, 1998), 56.

12. T. J. Desch-Obi, "Combat and the Crossing of the Kalunga," in *Central Africans and Cultural Transformations in the American Diaspora*, ed. Linda M. Heywood (New York: Cambridge University Press, 2002), 355. Desch-Obi cites from Robert Farris

Thompson, *Flash of the Spirit: African and Afro-American Art and Philosophy* (New York: Random House, 1983), 108–9.

13. Fromont, *The Art of Conversion*, 78. Capuchin missionaries, Girolamo da Montesarchio, and Giovanni Antonio Cavazzi (mid-seventeenth century) blame the similarity and interpretive fusion on the Devil. One almost hears echoes of Tertullian, third century, revolted by the commonality between Mithraic rituals and Christian sacraments in the reaction of the capuchin missionaries. For Tertullian, the demon perverts the truth. And "by the mystic rites of his idols, vies even with the essential portions of the sacraments of God." Tertullian, *On Prescription Against Heretics*, 40. See http://www.newadvent.org/fathers/0311.htm

14. This is the claim of A. Serpos Tidjani, dependent on his ethnographic data "Rituels," *Présence Africaine* 8–9, no. spécial, Le Monde Noir, dirigé par Théodore Monod (1950). Kimpasi also die and rise with initiation. Before being carried into the kimpasi enclosure for initiation, initiates were tied and retied with thin strings by *nganga*; as tying redoubled around the body they lost consciousness, "fell into a deep trance— a catatonic state that people believed was death" (Thornton, *The Kongolese Saint Anthony*, 37).

15. Nadia Lovell, *Cord of Blood—Possession and the Making of Voodoo* (Sterling, Va.: Pluto Press, 2002), 49–53.

16. Umeh was initiated as *Dibia* and later became a university professor. John Anenechukwu Umeh, *After God Is Dibia*, Vol. I: Igbo Cosmology, Divination and Sacred Science in Nigeria (Lawrenceville, N.J.: Karnak House; US distributors, Red Sea Press, 1997), 107. Summarized in Elochukwu E. Uzukwu, *God, Spirit, and Human Wholeness: Appropriating Faith and Culture in West African Style* (Eugene, Ore.: Pickwick Publications, 2012), 91–93.

17. Lovell, *Cord of Blood*, 97.

18. The therapeutic effectiveness, the axis of the mediation of redemptive healing, explains the facility with which Christians move from the church to the *nganga* with little difficulty. See Frans Jozef Servaas Wijsen, *There Is Only One God—A Socio-Scientific and Theological Study of Popular Religion and Evangelization in Sukumaland, Northwest Tanzania* (Nijmegen: Uitgeverij Kok-Kampen, 1993), 201.

19. Rosny, *Les Yeux de ma Chèvre*, 48–49. Frans Wijsen had also argued that the *nganga* (traditional medical practitioners) at conversion to Christianity could easily transition into Christian prophets. Wijsen, *There Is Only One God*, 201; 217.

20. Monica Wilson, "Nyakyusa Ritual and Symbolism," *American Anthropologist* 56, no. 2 (1954). 240.

21. James W. Fernandez, "The Cultural Status of a West African Cult Group on the Creation of Culture," in *African Religious Groups and Beliefs—Papers in Honour of William R. Bascom*, ed. Simon Ottenberg (Meerut, India: Archana Publications, 1982), 245.

22. This group and its followers are so influential that evangelical theologian Kä Mana called them "galaxy of prophets and founders." Kä Mana, *La Nouvelle Évangélisation En Afrique* Chrétiens En Liberté (Paris; Yaoundé: Karthala; Clé, 2000), 122ff.

23. David Westerlund, "Spiritual Beings as Agents of Illness," in *African Spirituality: Forms, Meanings, and Expressions*, ed. Jacob Obafemi Kehinde Olupona, World Spirituality (New York: Crossroad, 2000), 168.

24. Albert de Surgy, *L'Église du Christianisme Céleste—un exemple d'Église prophétique au Bénin* (Paris: Karthala, 2001), 205.

25. Ibid., 205–6.

26. John K. Thornton, *Africa and Africans in the Making of the Atlantic world, 1400–1680*, Studies in Comparative World History (New York: Cambridge University Press, 1992), 246; Kwame Bediako, *Christianity in Africa: The Renewal of a Non-Western Religion* (Edinburgh and New York: University of Edinburgh Press and Orbis Press, 1995), 123; for Bediako, translatability is revelatory.

27. James W. Fernandez, "The Cultural Status of a West African Cult Group on the Creation of Culture," in *African Religious Groups and Beliefs—Papers in Honour of William R. Bascom*, ed. Simon Ottenberg (Meerut, India: Archana Publications, 1982), 250.

28. Surgy, *L'Église du Christianisme Céleste*, 205.

29. See the extraordinary narrative of Tidjani: Tidjani, "Rituels," 305. Summarized in Uzukwu, *God, Spirit, and Human Wholeness: Appropriating Faith and Culture in West African Style*, 181–86.

30. Kwame Bediako, *Theology and Identity: The Impact of Culture upon Christian Thought in the Second Century and in Modern Africa* (Costa Mesa, Calif.: Regnum Books, 1992), 4; see also his *Christianity in Africa: The Renewal of a Non-Western Religion*, 258. A new book on Bediako (in press) by Tim Hartman draws attention to this stress on the continuity between the ontological past of Africans and the present translation of the Gospel of Jesus Christ.

31. Tillich, *Systematic Theology*, vol. 3 (Chicago: University of Chicago Press, 1967), 144–45.

32. Ecclesiological reality studied by Jean-Marie-Roger Tillard, *L'Église locale—Ecclésiologie de Communion et Catholicité* (Paris: Cerf, 1995).

33. John K. Thornton, "Religious and Ceremonial Life in the Kongo and Mbundu Areas, 1500–1700," in *Central Africans and Cultural Transformations in the American Diaspora*, ed. Linda M. Heywood (New York: Cambridge University Press, 2002), 85. Thornton addressed this in detail in *The Kongolese Saint Anthony: Dona Beatriz Kimpa Vita and the Antonian Movement, 1684–1706*, 31–35.

34. Thornton, *The Kongolese Saint Anthony*, 33.

35. Desch-Obi, "Combat and the Crossing of the Kalunga," 354–55.

36. Fromont, *The Art of Conversion*, 78.

37. This is the ~dominant theme of Kabwita's study. Kabolo Iko Kabwita, *Le Royaume Kongo et la Mission Catholique (1750–1838): Du Déclin a L'extinction*, Mémoire D'églises, ed. Paul Coulon (Paris: Karthala, 2004).

38. Details of this revision of history are found in Thornton, *The Kongolese Saint Anthony: Dona Beatriz Kimpa Vita and the Antonian movement, 1684–1706*, 110–14. The mother of Mary was Kongolese, "a slave of the Marquis Nzimba Mpangi" (114).

39. According to Thornton, because the office of *nganga marinda* was "socially oriented and served the common good," it was highly respected; "whereas those offices that dealt more with personal problems were inclined to be suspect. Individualism was likely to be accompanied by greed, the prime ingredient in motivating ndokis." Ibid., 54.

40. This is explicit in the transformation of the popular Salve Regina into Salve Antoniana. Ibid., 216.

41. See Thornton, *The Kongolese Saint Anthony: Dona Beatriz Kimpa Vita and the Anto-nian movement, 1684–1706*. For the study of Kongo religion, see also Wyatt MacGaffey, *Religion and society in central Africa: the BaKongo of lower Zaire* (Chicago: University of Chicago Press, 1986).

42. Thornton, *The Kongolese Saint Anthony*, 123.

43. Adrian Hastings, *The Church in Africa 1450–1950* (Oxford: Clarendon Press, 1994), 92.

44. Thornton, *The Kongolese Saint Anthony*, 216. The original Kikongo version is lost; Thornton translates the Italian rendering of Bernado da Gallo.

45. Uzukwu, *God, Spirit, and Human Wholeness*, 54.

46. T. K. M. Buakasa, *L'Impensé du discours. "Kindoki" et "nkisi" en pays kongo du Zaïre*, 2nd ed. (Kinshasa: Facultés Catholiques de Kinshasa, 1980), 283ff; Bénézet Bujo, *Foundations of an African Ethic: Beyond the Universal Claims of Western Morality*, trans. Brian McNeil (New York: Crossroad, 2001), 134.

47. Bujo, *Foundations of an African Ethic*, 128; 140.

48. See Jason R. Young, Rituals of Resistance: African Atlantic Religion in Kongo and the Lowcountry South in the Era of Slavery (Baton Rouge: Louisiana State University Press, 2007).

49. In the African indigenous religious theology of mystical experience, the Supreme Being never possesses the devotee nor the initiate (*nganga* or other). For example, the Supreme Being (Emitai) of the Diola of Senegambia communicated frequently through a female prophet *Alinesitoue*, and other prophets, for the good of Diola people. While *Emitai* never possessed, the minor deities/spirits possessed and are worshipped in their chosen shrines. This is the genre of the manifestation of Saint Anthony in the story of Kimpa Vita. For the study of the Diola see, Robert M. Baum, *West Africa's Women of God: Alinesitoué and the Diola Prophetic Tradition*. Bloomington: Indiana University Press, 2016.

50. The dominance of the sociological in African mysticism was patently raised and discussed by Edward Geoffrey Parrinder and Roger Bastide in "Le Mysticisme des Médiums en Afrique occidentale," in *Réincarnation et Vie Mystique en Afrique Noire*, ed. Dominique Zahan and Roger Bastide (Paris: Presses Universitaires de France, 1965), 138–42. I discussed this in "Mysticism with a social agenda" in Uzukwu, *God, Spirit, and Human Wholeness: Appropriating Faith and Culture in West African Style*, 205–10.

51. Consonant with *kimpasi* mysticism, Kimpa Vita was reputed to resurrect periodically.

52. David O. Olayiwola, "Aladura Christianity in Dialogue with African Traditional Religion (the Yoruba Example)," *Studia Missionalia* 43 (1994): 354.

53. James H. Cone, *The Cross and the Lynching Tree* (Maryknoll, N.Y.: Orbis Books, 2011).

54. The term used by Sukuma of Tanzania to express well-being in a comprehensive way. David Westerlund, "Spiritual Beings as Agents of Illness," in *African Spirituality: Forms, Meanings, and Expressions*, ed. Jacob Obafemi Kehinde Olupona (New York: Crossroad, 2000), 168.

Rethinking Redemption

Redemptive Suffering After the Shoah

GOING BACK AND FORTH BETWEEN JEWISH AND CHRISTIAN TRADITIONS

Marianne Moyaert

When I was a child, whenever I entered a church with my father and looked up to the crucified Christ, he would hush me and say, "Be quiet and pray for he died so that you may be free." I did not understand a word he was saying (my father did not believe in the value of over-explaining religion), but in my recollection these moments were comforting. In the quiet moment of prayer, directed to God in Christ, I did not feel alone, and I felt I could admit to all my little and more grave faults. Never did I forget to also pray for my loved ones and those that had gone before me. While I did not understand much, I did understand that what Christ did was supposed to free us, to return us back to a life in communion with God and our fellow human beings, both the living and the dead. I also understood that in this life we were called to *imitatio Christi*—that is, to do as he did, and atone on behalf of others.

Years later, when I entered university to study theology in Leuven, I returned to the figure of Christ and the cross, now not as a comforting figure, but rather as a figure that stands between two communities and their traditions—Jewish and Christian—and connects them while also radically dividing them. I wanted to better understand the so-called "Jewish No" to Jesus. This question introduced me to the domain of Christology, Jewish-Christian relations, and post-Shoah theology with its complex questions about suffering, forgiveness, and reconciliation. Long before I knew anything about comparative theology, I listened to Johann Baptist Metz according to whom after the Shoah responsible Christian theologians must write their theology both in dialogue with Jewish partners and in comparing Christian and Jewish sources.[1]

In this chapter, I revisit the Christian doctrine of vicarious or substitutionary at-one-ment, according to which an innocent one—Christ Jesus—intervenes and takes the burden of the sins of the world on himself and thus brings about redemption. *That* reconciliation between God and humans would be made possible because Christ offers himself up is one of the most difficult teachings to explain to contemporary hearers. I see two main reasons for this difficulty. First of all, the idea of *stellvertretung* is at odds with "our" modern sense of autonomy, moral responsibility, and justice. Kant especially argued that

> [Moral evil] is no transmissible liability which can be made over to another like a financial indebtedness (where it is all one to the creditor whether the debtor himself pays the debt or whether someone else pays it for him); rather it is the most personal of all debts, namely a debt of sins, which only the culprit can bear and which no innocent person can assume even though he be magnanimous enough to wish to take it upon himself for the sake of another."[2]

There is no escaping responsibility and it makes no sense to speak about *shifting the burden of guilt* for one's own faults. The weight of guilt may not be carried by anyone but the moral subject.

Secondarily, since the Shoah, the idea that *suffering may somehow be redemptive* has come under tremendous pressure.[3] The reality that the murder of six million Jews happened in the heart of Europe and that most Nazis were baptized has destroyed "Christian" innocence. Any claim Christians seek to make regarding the redemptive nature of Christ's suffering must be confronted with the reality that the cross brought anything but redemption for the Jewish people, who suffered at the hands of people who prayed to God in Christ.[4] Inspired by Ricoeur, I would say that after the Shoah, Christians have to pass through the dark night of losing their precritical (naïve) faith in order to reach a more mature faith.[5] Reorientation requires accepting disorientation. My question is if the doctrine of vicarious atonement, which has spoken to so many Christians throughout history and brought so much consolation, has indeed become meaningless or whether it is possible to retrieve some of its comforting appeal without being "out of step with the Jewish victims of Hitler's inferno."[6]

In this chapter, I approach the doctrine of vicarious atonement through figure of the suffering servant. I probe how this figure has been used both by Christian and Jewish scholars throughout the centuries to better understand the role of Christians and Jews respectively in God's plan of salvation and to make sense of their respective historico-cultural experiences of suffering in light thereof. The leitmotiv in my going back and forth between Christian and Jewish traditions is a sense that something did go terribly wrong in Christian-Jewish relations and that Christians have to bear the burden of this history and critically examine what role its understanding of the Christ figure played in the emergence of anti-Judaism. Moving back and forth between Christian and Jewish thinkers, I will seek to surface the meanings created and reflected in different theologies of redemptive suffering, and show how Jewish interpretations of the suffering servant hold a painful mirror to Christians. I will end by suggesting that from a Christian perspective precisely in the long process of reconciliation between Jewish and Christian communities, the doctrine of vicarious atonement may still have an important role to play. I suggest that we should turn to the realm of symbols (instead of the ethical realm) to understand the redemptive power of Christ's vicarious atonement.

Christ's Vicarious Atonement

The theology of vicarious atonement starts from the finding that something has gone wrong between God and human and between human beings. Human beings are sinful and, as a consequence, relations have been harmed, trust has been broken, and the question is *how can we restore what was once "one."* How can we bridge the gap between God and human beings? Key to a theology of vicarious atonement is the idea that Christ Jesus functions as the unique mediator between God and humans and that his death, which is sacrificial in nature, initiates a new covenant in which those who follow him may participate. This theology draws on the power of sacrifice (the root of the Hebrew Korban Sacrifice means "to be close") to overcome the distance between humans and God.

CHRIST, THE LAMB OF GOD WHO TAKES AWAY OUR SINS

One of the most powerful Biblical images in support of Christ's atoning sacrificial suffering and death may be found in the Gospel of John 1:29, "Behold the Lamb of God, who takes away the sins of the world!" Most Johannine scholars recognize two different passages from the Hebrew Scriptures as background for this unique Johannine title, namely "the paschal lamb (πρόβατον), whose blood saves the Hebrews in Egypt and whose flesh becomes their Passover communion meal (Exod 12:1–14); the

Suffering Servant, who is compared to a silent lamb (πρόβατον and αμνός) led to slaughter (Isa. 53:7–8)."[7]

First, Jesus's sacrificial death is understood in light of the redemption of Pesach and the evangelist identifies Jesus with the Paschal lamb, the blood of which was used to mark the doorposts of their houses as a sign that Israelites lived there (Ex 12:21–23). Upon seeing the mark, the angel of death would pass over these homes and the firstborns of the Israelites would be protected, while the first-born of the Egyptians would be slayed that night.[8] During the time of the Second Temple, this sacrifice was made annually on the eve of Pesach. The sacrificial lamb (for example, Lev. 1:10) was supposed to be male, without blemish and not a limb was to be broken. Thus, we may understand why John makes explicit that none of Christ's bones were broken (John 19:31–34). He wants the reader to make the connection and understand that Christ, the sacrificial lamb, has been offered so that we may be free.[9]

However, within Jewish traditions, the Passover lamb was not *a sin offering*. It seems that John creatively reinterpreted the image of the paschal lamb through the figure of the suffering servant from Isaiah 53, who silently is led to the slaughter and bears the sins of the many (53:4–6). By reading the metaphor of the sacrificial lamb, which brings redemption, through the lens of the figure of the suffering servant, who carries the burden of our sins, Christ Jesus becomes "the Lamb of God, who takes away the sin of the world." Through his obedience unto death, Jesus assumed the role of the suffering servant, who was rejected during his lifetime and gave his life as an atoning sacrifice.[10] This would become one of the key images to project Christ's redemptive suffering.

In the next centuries, the questions the first followers of Jesus had to deal with after the crucifixion and the non-arrival of their expected Kingdom of God would continue to be raised both by Jews and "gentiles." The early Church fathers were often challenged to apologetically explain how the cross while deeply scandalous was paradoxically glorious. The figure of the Lord's servant who as a lamb was silently led to the slaughter would continue to inspire apologists like Justin Martyr, Ambrose, and Irenaeus. Commenting on Isaiah 53:7, Ambrose (Letter 69) also explicitly makes the connection with John 1:29:

> It is the price of our freedom, as Peter says, "You were redeemed with the precious blood," not of a lamb but of him who came in meekness and humility like a lamb and freed the whole world with the single offering

of his body, as he himself said, "I was led like a lamb to be sacrificed," and John also said, "Behold, the lamb of God, behold the one who takes away the sins of the world."[11]

Eusebius refers to the suffering servant in an effort to refute Jewish objections against Christ Jesus. To his mind Isaiah 53 is a prophecy about Jesus's own humility unto death so that we may be reconciled with God, and he adds that those who call themselves followers of Christ should follow his example: because this "is the pattern that hath been given unto us; for, if the Lord was thus lowly of mind, what should we do, who through Him have been brought under the yoke of His grace?"[12] It may be that following Jesus's example also includes accepting a life of suffering. Justin Martyr also takes recourse to the figure of the suffering servant to argue that Jesus is the one this prophecy speaks about and that his death fits in God's plan of salvation. According to him, Isaiah 53 means "to demonstrate that Christ, "having become man for our sakes . . . endured to suffer and to be dishonored, and that He shall come again with glory."[13] In his apologetics, *Contra Celsum*, Origen deals with the objection that Christ cannot have been divine, because "Jesus' body was no different from any other, but, as they (sic. the Christians) say, was little and ugly and undistinguished." This is where Origen draws heavily on the prophecy on the figure of the suffering servant, of whom it was said that he "had no form nor beauty." When an objection follows regarding Christ Jesus's passivity during his suffering, Origen again refers to Isaiah, where it is said that God's servant is led to slaughter like a sheep. However, Origen adds, this does not mean Jesus was not in control of his own destiny: "He underwent that (*sic.* his suffering) of his own free will." Central to this Christology is the idea that Jesus must be seen as a voluntary sacrifice for the salvation of those who believe he is the Savior sent from God. God's will and that of Christ Jesus are one. From this perspective, Christ's self-sacrifice is also God's sacrifice.

PRELIMINARY CONCERNS IN LIGHT OF THE
HISTORY OF CHRISTIAN-JEWISH RELATIONS

The doctrine of Christ's vicarious atonement has figured prominently in anti-Jewish supersessionist theologies with its stereotypical binaries of old and new; rejected and embraced; blind and enlightened; prophecy and fulfillment, and so on. Placed in an anti-Jewish polemical theological framework, *substitutionary atonement* feeds *substitution theology*: Christ takes our place and those who claim to follow him take the place of those who did not recognize him. Replacement follows after replacement, substitution after substitution, vicariousness after vicariousness. The prophecy about the suffering servant actually reinforced this anti-Jewish pattern of thinking.

While Christian scholars identified Christ Jesus as the suffering servant, they came to associate the Jewish people with those who rejected, persecuted, and killed him because they did not recognize Christ's true nature. The Jews supposedly mocked him, laughed at him, tortured him, and even killed him without realizing he was God's beloved one. This typological pattern of thinking is grist to the mill of those who would later coin the deicide charge (cf. Melito of Sardis), which turned Jews into Christ-killers and murderers of God.

Second, *Christ, the Lamb of God who takes away our Sins*, came to be seen as the ultimate sacrifice that ended all sacrifices (Heb 9:26). Within the theology of vicarious atonement, the Jewish cultic system that revolved around animal offerings came to be seen as hollow and powerless. A theology emerged according to which these offerings were only able to bring "provisional" relief and expiation and, in fact, trapped Israel in an endless pattern of sacrifices that served no real salvific purpose and only continued to remind them of their own sinfulness without any hope to break free (Heb 10:1–4). Christian scholars would start to consider Christ's sacrificial death as at long last having ended this negative spiral. This also meant, however, that Jewish sacrificial cult lost its meaning and purpose in God's plan of salvation. The destruction of the Temple (in 70 BC) and the end of cultic practice came to be regarded by Christians as an affirmation of this line of thinking. From an anti-Jewish Christian mindset, this also meant that Judaism became an anachronism.

Third, within the Christian tradition an ambivalent approach to suffering developed. On the one hand, Jewish misfortunes came to be regarded as divine punishment (for the fact that they did not recognize the true nature of Jesus and turned their back to him) and as an affirmation that they no longer had any role to play in God's plan for salvation. Whatever misfortunes befell them, they were all deserved. On the other hand, Christian suffering, while not regarded in itself as intrinsically good, would often be seen as providing an opportunity to take on the cross as Jesus had done. It provided Christians with an opportunity to partake in Christ's suffering. As Alice Eckhardt puts it: "The church celebrated the suffering of God's new people as a faithful witness to God's truth as embodied in Christ and his church, and as a faithful witness to Christ's power to save, . . . it perceived the suffering of the unfaithful ones—the people of the 'old' covenant—as nothing less than deserved punishment for their 'hardheartedness and unbelief.' Their suffering verified for Christians that God had indeed rejected his former people."[14]

In sum, the doctrine of vicarious atonement when framed in a supersessionist theology, has had devastating consequences for Christian-Jewish relations and the prophecy of the suffering servant served to reinforce the us-them binary. This prophetic song, which appeared on the scene at the end of the Babylonian Exile (586–539 BC) in response to a situation of marginalization and oppression by a mighty ruler and was meant to console, turned into a text that helped to justify symbolic and real violence against Christian adversaries and against the Jews first.

In the next section of this comparative theological chapter, I want to explore the way Jewish scholars, speaking again from a perspective of suffering now at the hands of Christian rather than Babylonian rulers, reappropriated the figure of the suffering servant and his atoning suffering and applied it to refute Christ's sacrificial death and project a perspective of hope. As I will show, this process of reclaiming the Lord's servant started around the time of Anselm's project, which is also the time of the crusades.

Jewish Commentaries on the Suffering Servant

The history of the relations between Jewish and Christian communities is complex and far from straightforward. Times of relative peace alternated with more violent episodes, periods of economic exchange with marginalization and exclusion, disinterested tolerance with aggressive persecution and forced conversions. While the patristic period gave rise to rather harsh anti-Jewish rhetoric, the centuries that followed were dominated by the expansion agenda of Western Christianity, including the dissemination of the gospel and the education of "pagans." The Jews and their rejection of Christ Jesus were not an immediate priority. This changed around the millennium and, during the late Middle Ages, Jewish-Christian relations deteriorated and rather than viewing the Jews as "unwitting witness to the truth of Christianity,"[15] as suggested by Augustine, fierce missionary activities targeting the Jews arose. This was the time of semi-orchestrated pogroms, staged polemical debates, forced conversions, marginalization, and expulsions. This was the time of the Rhineland massacres, when entire Jewish communities were wiped out as crusaders made their way to "liberate" Jerusalem for the Saracens. It was also the time of the blood libels and the burning of books.

RASHI'S COMMENTARY OF ISAIAH

In response to this situation of increasing violence, Jewish scholars did what they always had done, they turned to their scriptures in an effort to reconcile their current situation with their covenanted status. If Christians struggled with the question of how to make sense of Christ's suffering in light of his messianic claims, Jewish people struggled to align their suffering with their election and their claim that the covenant remains unbroken.[16] Conscious of and deeply affected by Christian theological interpretations, some revisited Isaiah 53. In doing so they re-appropriated this figure that was "taken from them." Characteristic of this medieval development is a collective interpretation of the suffering servant in Jewish interpretations at the cost of the messianic interpretations, which seems to have prevailed among earlier rabbinic commentators.[17]

The first major Jewish commentator to develop this collective interpretation was Rashi (1040–1105),[18] who, according to Avraham Grossman, "linked the prophecies about the suffering servant with the fate of the Jewish people in Christian (Edom's) lands."[19] His collective interpretation is not only addressed to the Jewish people, which he sought to comfort, but also targets Christianity, whose key doctrine, namely that of vicarious atonement, he wanted to refute.[20] Yitzak Baer argues that Rashi's commentary has to be read against the background of 1096 attacks against the Jewish communities, which occurred during the first crusade. I will highlight only the most important comments:

Is. 52:13 Behold My servant shall prosper; he shall be exalted and lifted up, and he shall be very high.
    Rashi: **Behold My servant shall prosper**: *Behold, at the end of days, My servant, Jacob, [i.e.,] the righteous among him, shall prosper.*
    . . .

Is. 53:3 Despised and rejected by men, a man of pains and accustomed to illness, and as one who hides his face from us, despised and we held him of no account.

Rashi: ***Despised and rejected by men:*** *was he. So is the custom of this prophet: he mentions all Israel as one man, e.g., (44:2), "Fear not, My servant Jacob"; (44:1) "And now, hearken, Jacob, My servant." Here too (52:13), "Behold My servant shall prosper," he said concerning the house of Jacob.* יַשְׂכִּיל *is an expression of prosperity . . .*

Is. 53:4 Indeed, he bore our illnesses, and our pains-he carried them, yet we accounted him as plagued, smitten by God and oppressed.

Rashi: ***Indeed, he bore our illnesses:*** *Heb.* אָכֵן, *an expression of "but" in all places. But now we see that this came to him not because of his low state, but that he was chastised with pains so that all the nations be atoned for with Israel's suffering. The illness that should rightfully have come upon us, he bore.*

yet we accounted him: *We thought that he was hated by the Omnipresent, but he was not so, but he was pained because of our transgressions and crushed because of our iniquities.*

Is. 53:12 Therefore, I will allot him a portion in public, and with the strong he shall share plunder, because he poured out his soul to death, and with transgressors he was counted; and he bore the sin of many, and interceded for the transgressors.

Therefore: *Because he did this, I will allot him an inheritance and a lot in public with the Patriarchs.*

and with transgressors he was counted: *He suffered torments as if he had sinned and transgressed, and this is because of others; he bore the sin of the many.*

and interceded for the transgressors: *through his sufferings, for good came to the world through him.*

Rashi's interpretation seems to have served several purposes. First, identifying the suffering servant with Jacob/Israel helped to make a stronger case against Christian messianic interpretations of Isaiah and to block aggressive Christian attempts to proselytize: "By polemicizing against Christian theology—against the identification of Christ with the 'suffering servant'—Rashi absorbed one of its cardinal tenets—namely the dogma of vicarious suffering as a means of salvation; Israel takes here the role of Christ."[21] Second, and more important, it enabled Jews to interpret their own suffering as a form of exilic martyrdom and not, as some Christian theologians suggested, as a punishment for the murder of Christ. Contrary to the picture that was deeply ingrained in the Christian culture surrounding them, they were not abandoned by God and their plight was not a divine punishment.[22] The Jewish people are, and continue to be, God's beloved people and they "maintained [their] guiltless qualities in the face of great pain."[23] Third, this reading provided them with a hopeful perspective and placed their present plight in a future perspective. They are suffering and dying for the sanctification of the Name of God and doing so would guarantee them a place in the World to Come. It gave consolation and hope. They "would be rewarded for accepting God's death decree."[24] Fourth, this eschatological hope not only projected a day when they would be "high and exalted" again, but also when the nations of the world and their kings would finally come to see not only the greatness of Israel, but would also realize their own mistakes and would realize that Israel's suffering was not a divine punishment, but rather that they carried the burden of the sins of others.

Around the same time, the Spanish medievalist philosopher Judah Halevi (1074–1141) wrote a dialogue between the king of Khazar, a Christian, a Muslim, and a Jew. The latter is provoked to defend Judaism and especially the degraded status of the Jewish people and he does so by referring to Isaiah 53. In his interpretation, Halevi, who convinced the King of his right, links Israel's elected status with its deprivation, thereby strongly objecting against the often-heard claim that Jews would suffer because of their sins. In a beautiful commentary of the suffering servant, Halevi writes:

> Israel amongst the nations is like a heart amongst its organs—[the heart is a very sensitive organ, in that] it becomes considerably ill from the influence of the other organs and also considerably healthy from their influence . . . The Divinity in relation to us is like the soul in relation to the heart [just as the soul first connects to the heart and then spreads to the rest of the body, so does God's influence in the world connect first to Israel and then spread to the rest of the world. . . . Just as the heart's inherent equilibrium and pure makeup allows the soul to attach to it, so, too, does the Divinity attach Itself to Israel because of their inherent nature. But [despite the heart's inherent purity,] it still becomes tainted at times because of other organs. . . . Similarly, Israel becomes tainted from their assimilation with the other nations, as it says, "And they assimilated with the nations and they learned from their ways." (Psalms 106:35)[25]

According to Halevi, Israel is the link between God and the nations. On the one hand, without the heart (Israel) the body (the nations) has no connection to the soul (God). Israel is responsible for spreading the influence of God in the world and God has chosen Israel because of its inherent nature, its purity. When Israel keeps the commandments, they reflect God's light, which then flows into the world so as to inspire the nations. On the other hand, being the link between God and the nations, Israel is also susceptible to what happens in the world and the extent to which the nations draw nearer to God or rather turn away from God, affects the health of the heart. If the nations refute what Israel offers them, the heart becomes sick. Thus, Israel suffers for the sake of others. Halevi's passage, however, adds another line of thought with strong biblical roots, that even the beloved one, if she goes astray, may undergo punishment or chastisement. The nature of this disciplining is never such that God would cut off Israel, its purpose is rather that Israel would repent and return. God is always forgiving. Thus, Halevi states that if Israel would come under the influence of the nations and become assimilated, Israel will become tainted. As the prophetic tradition shows, that is when disciplining will follow.

THE SHOAH, JEWISH SUFFERING
AND THE SUFFERING SERVANT

Following Rashi and Halevi, in the next centuries several Jewish scholars would continue to read the fate of Israel through the figure of the suffering servant. Doing so they rejected the idea that their suffering was *punishment for their sins*. They were able to uphold their status of righteousness in a world that saw them as Christ-killers who were abandoned by God. This interpretation gave them a special place in God's plan for the world and reaffirmed their elected status as a small people serving a greater purpose. Most importantly, it helped them to refute Christian culture by reverting the story at the heart of the Christian tradition and it gave them a hopeful perspective—one day everything will be set straight and those who claimed to have replaced Israel would finally have to recognize just how wrong they had been.

After the Shoah, however, there was, generally speaking, little "patience with a theology of suffering," certainly not with any attempt to somehow attribute any kind of meaning or intrinsic value to it.[26] Jewish responses to the Shoah have varied from loss of faith to *chutzpah*, from pantheism to ethics. Nevertheless, I have found that the figure of the suffering servant is referenced quite often, both by reform and orthodox

Jewish scholars who continue a long tradition. Let me just name three of them.

The first is Ignaz Maybaum. He turns to Isaiah 52–53 to make sense of the Shoah within a "classical theological framework" in which God acts through Israel to bring redemption to the world and urge Israel's oppressors to repent and turn back (Teshuvah). He argues that the Shoah is in keeping with a number of other dramatic events, like the destruction of the first and second temple, and he even adds that from this perspective the Shoah is not unique (except if we take the scale into consideration). Each of these events (which he calls Churbans, i.e. a catastrophe with messianic power) functioned as a catalyst to bring progress: the destruction of the first temple that initiated the diaspora of Israel spread God's law over the world; the destruction of the second temple ended the cultic system and strengthened the focus on Torah study and synagogue; the Shoah finally means the end of the anti-Jewish Middle Ages and the beginning of modernity: "The innocent who died in Auschwitz, not for the sake of their own sins but because of the sins of others, atone for evil; they are the sacrifice which is brought to the altar and which God acknowledges favorably. The six million, the dead of Auschwitz and of other places of horror, are Jews whom our modern civilization has to canonize as holy martyrs; they died as sacrificial lambs because of the sins inherent in western civilization. Their death purged western civilization so that it can again become a place where men can live, do justly, love mercy, and walk humbly with God."[27]

Eliezer Berkovits, an orthodox rabbi, references the suffering servant in a polemical charge against Christianity. His writings are an accusation without any mercy. Christianity and its claim about Christ's redemptive suffering have become hollow, empty of meaning.

> The Christian attempt to rob Israel of its dignity of Isaiah's suffering servant of God has been one of the saddest spiritual embezzlements in human history. At the same time, the way Christianity treated Israel through the ages only made Isaiah's description fit Israel all the more tragically and truly. Generation after generation Christians poured out their inequities and inhumanity over the head of Israel, yet they "esteemed him, stricken, smitten of God, and afflicted." At the same time, they misunderstood the true metaphysical dignity of the suffering of God's servant. What is the weight of one sacrifice compared to the myriad of sacrifices of Israel? What is one crucifixion beside a whole people

crucified through centuries? But, it is maintained, the one crucified was a god, whereas the untold millions of Jewish men, women, and children were only human beings. Human beings, only! As if the murder of an innocent human being were a lesser crime than the killing of a god. A god after all does not have to die. If he is killed, it is because he offers himself freely as a sacrifice. A god chooses to be killed; he knows what he is doing and why he is doing it. And when he dies, he does not suffer as a god. But the little boy who at the door of the gas chamber says to his mother: "But, Mama, I was a good boy!" that is something quite different. That is crucifixion. . . . Such is crucifixion. And it has been suffered not by gods, but by human beings, endured again and again on innumerable occasions all through Jewish history in Christian lands. That deicide is the greatest of human crimes is among the most dangerous fallacies ever taught to man. . . . Unfortunately, the teaching of deicide became an excuse, and often a license, for homicide. Pity any god thus caricatured by his devotees.[28]

As Christian supersessionist theology once used this prophetic image against the Jewish people, Berkovits holds up a mirror to Christians and surfaces the shallowness of claims about redemptive suffering coming from people who have brought harm to others while being spared from tragedy. In this reading, when Isaiah speaks about the Lord's servant who was despised, and rejected, he is speaking about the Jewish people, who were stripped from their humanity, denigrated, starved to death, gassed and burnt. When Isaiah describes the Servant being led like a lamb to the slaughter he is speaking about Jewish parents, spouses, and children, "who filed so silently to the gas chambers, not daring to open their mouths."[29] When Isaiah speaks about those who hid their faces from the servant's ugly face, he is talking about us, the Christians, pretending to not know and not to see and he forces us to recall all those times when Jewish people knocked on our doors, looking for shelter, and we turned away. Berkovits not only surfaces Christianity's triumphalism but also questions the redemptive nature of the cross, which has brought nothing but harm for the Jews, and makes a mockery of the crucifixion of Christ—a "god" who chose to die—with the death of Jewish children, who were truly innocent and links the anti-Jewish deicide charge with the gas chambers.

A third scholar who deals with the suffering servant from a Jewish perspective is Levinas. His interpretation is twofold. He first connects this figure with the persecutions and suffering that the Jews underwent during the Nazi regime: "Chapter 53 was drained of all meaning for them. Their suffering common to them as to all the victims of the war, received its unique meaning from racial persecution which is absolute, since it paralyses by virtue of its intention, any flight . . ."[30] He continues saying that the situation of the Jews under the Nazi regime was "an experience of Passion" because of the radicality of the persecution from which no escape was possible. Hitlerism nailed humanity to the fatality of its race.[31] People were unable to see Jews as people; they saw only Jews, who were viewed as inferior; they remained blind and deaf to the ethical command *You shall not kill.*[32] Levinas also connects this first reading of Isaiah 53 with a critique of Christianity by noting that the Christian sacrifice, the cross, had not changed the world—on the contrary. Christianity is too much focused on the relation of faith with God and the concern with getting to heaven and too little with the concern about the other: "The true eucharist lies more in the encounter with the other than in the bread or the wine, in other words, the personal presence of God lies in the encounter."[33] The idea that someone else died for our sins is, according to Levinas, a dangerous idea, for it minimalizes personal responsibility. Levinas's religion is one without promise. God, he claims, is not in heaven.[34]

Levinas's second interpretation of the suffering servant is, in fact, a reflection on the radical form of humanism that he advocates in response to racist tribalism. For him, the figure of the suffering servant embodies the responsibility to which all are called, without, however, having consciously chosen that responsibility.[35] In Levinas's interpretation, this song is about responsible subjectivity that, "persecuted by men and nevertheless incapable of shirking his task[,] is described in terms close to this chapter from Isaiah."[36] The position in which the "I" finds itself, Levinas argues, is entirely that of responsibility or service, as in Isaiah 53. At issue is a calling that is not based on a free choice or a duty that we decide to take upon ourselves. Rather, the figure of the suffering servant points in the direction of a human being who in passivity bears the burden of the other and who is fully available. For Levinas, bearing the suffering of others is not just the task of Israel, but each human being is called to pour out its life for others. This is what each is called to when faced with another who claims our attention: to not remain indifferent, to carry the burden of the other; to bear the weight of his existence, while sacrificing one's egotistical interests and complacency. This is what it may still mean, to suffer for others. Levinas connects this with kenosis: emptying one's being for the sake of others. In his words: "the suffering of suffering, the suffering for the useless suffering of the other person, the just suffering for the unjustifiable suffering of the Other, opens upon suffering the ethical perspective of the inter-human."[37] This is not the same as self-effacement, but instead this is where any subject finds the fulfillment of his/her subjectivity.

Levinas, moreover, refutes any kind of final eschatological redemption, in which the Messiah will come to liberate all of us and establish the End of Times. Such an eschatological perspective leads nowhere except to reduced vigilance and diminished responsibility. Such a perspective will put us to sleep. According to Levinas, "Messianism is therefore not the certainty of the coming of a man who stops History. It is my power to bear the suffering of all. It is the moment when I recognize this power and my universal responsibility."[38] There is no hiding, no sleeping, no relief.

Theological Hermeneutics and the Process of Cross-Reading

I deliberately chose to give various Jewish scholars the floor, not only to avoid the risk of reifying "Judaism," but also because I wanted to foreground how Jews, not unlike Christians after the death of Christ, struggled with the question of how to reconcile their suffering with their covenanted status. Furthermore, I also wanted to really hear the Jewish critique of one of the key Christian doctrines (and have it sink in) because I am in agreement with Ricoeur when he states that Christians have to pass through the dark night of loss of faith if we want to retrieve a more mature post-Shoah faith.[39]

In the final section of this chapter, I seek to make explicit how reading the doctrine of vicarious atonement through Jewish eyes and going back and forth between Christian and Jewish traditions challenges me to revisit the central Christian idea that Christ died for us.

PRELIMINARY REFLECTIONS

My going back and forth between Christian and Jewish readings of the suffering servant have, first of all, reaffirmed my sense that both Jews and Christians, when faced with pain, grief, and suffering, look for consolation in some form, hope that this is not all there is. They seek to make sense of senseless suffering. Important for both Jewish and Christian communities is to affirm that their suffering is not a punishment from God, but that they are and remain beloved. The song about the suffering servant, whether read through Jewish or Christian eyes, implies a fierce criticism of the retributive view of suffering. Suffering does not deny election, whether Jewish or Christian, but rather affirms it (cf. also Proverbs 3:12).

However, the human desire to make sense of senseless suffering should not be confused with a theological effort to develop a theodicy that justifies God's (non-)agency in the face of great human suffering. Not only do efforts to develop a theodicy often speak over the heads of those who are in pain, it also not infrequently results in a dubious picture of God. The songs about the suffering servant are poetry; they are not systematic theology and I am not sure it is a wise idea to further develop them into a full-blown theodicy. Reading Ignaz Maybaum has made me aware of the limits of what one may do with the figure of the suffering servant. Poetry consoles and comforts; theodicy seeks to explain what is beyond explanation. Arguing how the murder of six million Jews is part of God's design and how it was but one more expression of Israel's atoning role in God's plan for salvation is, in my view, repulsive. Also, this line of reasoning "seems to cast Nazi murderers as servants of God."[40] What I am left with is the picture of an immoral God who is willing to sacrifice his own beloved people to advance history without taking into consideration that this is too much for their shoulders to carry and without asking them if they were willing to carry this burden. Here I am with Levinas when he argues for the end of theodicy and when he claims that suffering is useless.

The process of cross-reading highlights that it is important to take asymmetrical power relations into account when developing a theological hermeneutics of biblical figures. A story that offers comfort and relief in one context (i.e., for people who find themselves in a situation of marginalization and even persecution) easily turns into a text of terror that justifies violence when read from a perspective of political power. While both Christian and Jewish communities turned to the figure of the suffering servant and both found meaning in the idea of vicarious atonement—suffering for the sake of others—Constantine Christians have rarely suffered for others at the hands of non-Christians, while "Jews, alas, have been martyred at a disturbing rate throughout the centuries, most often at the hands of others, and especially at the hands of Christians."[41] To speak of redemptive suffering when one is not affected by suffering or even afflicts suffering on others is not only cheap and hollow, but also potentially oppressive.

Furthermore, wrestling with the suffering servant made me realize that this song is susceptible to binary patterns of thinking, pitting us versus them. However, consoling it may be that God is on your side and that the others are completely misjudging what is actually happening, it is, in all likelihood, not going to advance the process of restoring the relations between communities who understand their role in God's plan for salvation differently. Both Jewish and Christian commentaries on the suffering servant claim that there is only one beloved people, that the claim projected by the other is fraudulent, and that this will be revealed in the eschaton. This is relevant in view of Christian-Jewish relations and the violent history of Christian anti-Judaism, which at least to a certain degree can be traced back to a supersessionist and exclusionary interpretation of Christ's redemptive suffering, an interpretation in which substitution followed after substitution. Rethinking the Christian doctrine of vicarious atonement in a non-supersessionist way will have to include a rethinking of how Christ's new covenant relates to the first covenant never revoked.[42] Rather than falling for a story line in which in the end of times God will prove one of these people right and the other wrong, the challenge is to develop a theology in which both Church and Israel are called to sanctify God's name and heal the world (*Tikkun olam*) and to work for the Kingdom of God now until the fullness of the redemption comes on a day known only to God.[43]

TOWARD AN ETHICIZATION OF THE DOCTRINE OF ATONEMENT?

The obvious starting place for such a collaborative theology would be to take seriously the self-understanding and self-definition of our Jewish conversation partners and steer away from old patterns of othering. Israel is called to be a light for the nations, making God present in this earthly realm through its faithfulness to the Torah. Jewish scholars teach that "in his infinite mercy God waits for man's return to him, and when this happens, God forgives all his sins. The rabbis taught that not only are the sins of a repentant sinner forgiven, but they are turned into virtuous deeds. So great is the power of repentance."[44] The sense of "being enveloped by the eternal of God for Israel [has] never really [left] the awareness of the people."[45] Israel, therefore, has no need for Christ's sacrificial death to be reconciled with God. The Torah suffices to show them the way and to repent and return whenever they falter. They know God will always receive them back. God's love is unconditional and while God's anger lasts a moment, his mercy is forever (Ps. 30:6). From this perspective, Israel asks what may be the meaning and significance of Christ's atoning death?

One possible trajectory is opened by the fierce Jewish criticism that the classical Christian doctrine of vicarious atonement leads to a forgetfulness of human responsibility. Think of Berkovits's lashing out at the hypocrisy of Christians who talk a lot about taking up the cross, but know not what suffering is and consider his anger at Christians who are so preoccupied about the deicide charge that they forget to care about homicide. Levinas, too, charges that "all those who participated in the Shoah had received Catholic or Protestant baptism in their infancy." Christians have been so preoccupied with the restoration of vertical relations between God and humans, they have been so concerned about satisfying God's honor, that they have lost sight of their horizontal (i.e., interpersonal relations) and Jewish people have paid the price. Redemption has become something that God does in Christ and this focus on God's agency has come at the cost of human agency in this world. Christianity read through Jewish eyes focuses too much on heaven and too little on this-worldliness and the restoration of inter-personal relations. At this stage, I can imagine that some would suggest to further explore Levinas's ethical re-interpretation of the doctrine of vicarious atonement. The latter no doubt would bring us far along in the direction of shifting our gaze from heaven to this world and from expecting redemption as a divine gift to taking responsibility for the suffering of the other and realizing that God reveals himself in the face of the other who needs us. There are various reasons—and in fact the literature affirms this—why Christian theologians would find this Levinasian turn quite appealing.

First, such a turn is appealing because Levinas's ethics enables a move from particular (Christian responsibility and failure) to a universal calling—we are all infinitely responsible for the other. We are all indebted to the Other, we are all in the service of the Other. Once we have established that, we can perhaps talk less about Christian guilt with regard to the history of Jewish suffering and more about how every human being is singled out. Second, however radical Levinas may be, he speaks to the mind of the modern human being—for whom the old religious notions such as sin and sacrifice make little sense but who may still find meaning in religion if it presents itself under the guise of ethics (cf. Kant).[46] Third, modern man prefers to ask *what can we do* rather than reflect on where we fail, where we fall short, where we need help.

However, appealing this ethical reinterpretation of the suffering servant may be, speaking from a Catholic point of view, I hesitate to fully embrace Levinas's ethics of radical responsibility. The reason for this is that Levinas's reinterpretation of substitutionary atonement doesn't reckon with the problem of the burden of sin and how it can crush human beings even to the extent of distorting their relation with God and with their fellow human beings. Interestingly enough, it is precisely this exercise in cross-reading that reawakened my theological awareness of the heavy weight of sin and the human desire for redemption.

Reading Rashi, Berkovits, and Levinas is like taking "a guilt bath," to use the words of Catholic post-Shoah theologian John Pawlikowski. It is cruel and hard, even to the extent that one feels like crumbling. As a post-Shoah comparative theologian, I am painfully aware of the burden of history, which has not only deeply wounded Christians' relationship with the Jewish people, but has also negatively affected our relation with God, in whose name we have claimed to act. It is as if one hears God call out and ask, "What have you done?"[47] Reading these Jewish scholars makes me realize (and sense) what it may mean to be crushed by the burden of guilt, what it may mean to suffer under the weight of sin and to see no way to set things straight to restore what one has destroyed.

Repentance and conversion are the hardest thing because they entail that we have to admit to ourselves, to others, and to God that we have failed and wronged. We have to face the consequences of our actions. However, if this burden is too heavy, if what one has broken seems unrepairable, there is no hope: People get stuck and their hearts harden.[48] Rather than trying to confess, repent, and restore, people might deny their part in this history, cover up their tracks, continue as if nothing has happened or at the first chance they get blame and shame the victim and resort to old habits. The ethicization of the figure of the suffering servant as a moral example may show too little sensitivity to this powerful human reality of being crushed. On the contrary, Levinas's ethics of radical responsibility seems to only add to this burden—our responsibility is infinite and there is no escape, no one lifting the burden *for us*, no one to turn to, no perspective of relief.

It is true that *ethically* speaking, it also makes little sense to say that sins can be carried like a burden and may be lifted from the shoulders of one being to be transferred to the shoulders of another being. Ethically speaking, substitution is an impossible idea. Ethically speaking, we are our brother's keeper and when we fall short we should work toward restoration and reconciliation. No one can do the work of repentance and reconciliation in our place. However, to my mind, religion cannot be reduced to ethics nor should the doctrine of vicarious suffering be understood solely within an ethical framework.

Starting from the crushing sense of the burden of responsibility and the human desire for this burden to be lifted from our shoulders, in the final part of this chapter, I want to suggest leaving the ethical realm and moving into the realm of the symbolic. I want to suggest understanding Christ's vicarious atonement—i.e., the idea that he did something for us in our place so that we might be free—as a symbolic act. Before making this point, I bring this point closer to home by explaining the substitutionary power of symbols.

CHRIST'S VICARIOUS ATONEMENT AS A SYMBOLIC ACT

Symbols are often regarded as evocative expressions of those dimensions of life that may not be captured. They make perceptible that which is intrinsically invisible, ideal, or transcendent.[49] Here, the emphasis is on the capacity of symbols to refer beyond themselves to deep human feelings, experiences, and desires. Symbols mediate and direct our attention to that which is real. Sometimes, however, symbols do more than express; sometimes they function as substitutions—that is, they take the place of something/someone else. Here several examples come to mind. First, when overwhelmed by anger directed at a person who has deeply hurt us and whom we would love to hit, we will throw something against the wall, hit a tree, or smash a plate. We may cut up the picture of a beloved one that has betrayed us, while we would really like to hurt him. Here, the symbol replaces the person, and in doing so it channels and diverts anger and slows this emotion down until we can get on with life without actually having to hurt another person.

Second, when a loved one dies, we may cherish as a kind of relic the pillow from her bed or her favorite T-shirt. These material objects do more than remind us of our deceased love one. The T-shirt or pillow rather make present in an intimate way that which is absent—we will smell and touch the pillow, rub our face into it, wear the T-shirt when we go to bed, or wrap our body into it. The symbol in its capacity of substitution both bridges a distance and a gap that would otherwise be unbearable and channels our pain and grief in such a way that we are not overwhelmed by it. It helps contain what may otherwise crush us—anger, grief, love, fear. It brings order in the chaos of the overwhelmingly dark night of grief.

As substitutions, symbols may not only take the place of something/someone else; they may even *do* something *in our* place, thereby at once (temporarily) discharging us from responsibility. By taking over and relieving us from doing this or that, symbols liberate. Three examples come to mind. During the exams of my children, which last about two weeks, I feel like I have to think of them while they take their tests. I feel like I have to be with them in spirit. Just like my grandmother did before me, I light a candle in front of Mary. I do so because it frees my mind from having to think of them; I can rest assured that Mary will do so in my place.

A second example. Grieving the death of a beloved one is heart-wrenching and the sense of loss may be all-consuming. There is always a risk that the person left behind will find it impossible to return to life and to find joy again. Both in Jewish and Christian traditions various symbolic practices exist, which discharge a person from having to decide for herself when it is appropriate to end the period of mourning and to put her life back on track again. Different rituals exist to bring back structure and rhythm to life so that the grieving person does not succumb. One such symbolic act is the erection of a tombstone. As a symbol, the tombstone has an important task: It remembers, grieves, mourns in the place of those who are left behind, so that they may temporally forget. This symbolic substitution liberates them and enables them to continue their life.

The third example that comes to mind is that of the Benedictine Sisters of Perpetual Adoration (*Ordo Sancti Benedicti Adorationis Perpetuae*). In this order, the sisters worship God as God is present in the consecrated Eucharist without interruption. The goal of this never-ending prayer is to restore the relationship of humankind with God, which is harmed by the unbelief, indifference, and sins of human beings. These sisters pray without cessation to repent for what others have done. They pray not only for us, but in our place (substitution) and in so doing they follow the example of Christ.

Building on these examples, highlighting the substitutionary and liberating power of symbols, I suggest Christ's self-sacrifice belongs to this

symbolic order (rather than to the realm of ethics). His vicarious atonement may be understood as a symbolic act in line with what I have just
explained. Even though Christ Jesus himself is without sin, he repents
in our place; even though he is innocent, he undergoes our penalty; even
though he is without fault, he offers himself up so as to bridge the gap
between God and humans. None of this is necessary from God's perspective, as if God would need to be appeased; rather, Christ enables atonement because humans are unable to do so on their own. Like a scapegoat,
Christ carries the sins away and lifts the burden of guilt. This symbolic
act functions like a form of ex-oneration, a lifting (ex) of the burden (onus)
of guilt. What is more, as a symbolic mediator, Christ intercedes for us
sinners; he represents us (takes our place) before God and thus helps
bridge the distance between God and us and meets the human longing
to be freed.

Interestingly enough, this symbolic pattern is continued in the liturgy
of the Eucharist, which reenacts the now-ness of the sacrifice of Christ
once and for all. In the gift of Communion, Christ comes to us again
and again. When bread and wine (called *oblata*—things offered) are
transformed in Christ's body and offered for our sins, table and altar are
inextricably related, and by imbibing bread and wine, our sins are ex-
onerated and we partake in the new covenant established by Christ.[50]
This ritual is life-giving, liberating, and redemptive and for that we express our gratitude and give thanks. In doing so, we also recognize that
Christ's self-sacrifice was an act of grace, which we, as sinners, did not
deserve. When we recognize during the Eucharist how Christ reconciled
us with God even though we do not merit this, the appropriate response
is that of gratitude and imitation.[51] By eating the wafer and drinking the
wine, we partake in Christ's sacrificial death and undergo the exonerat-
ing power of this ritual so that we can start anew, go out into the world
and follow Christ's example. *Imitatio Christi* becomes possible thanks to
the cross. That call to imitation includes following the prophetic example Christ set in his earthly mission as well as the way he made amends
on behalf of others.

While the prophetic criticism from the Jewish side that the doctrine
of vicarious atonement as well as its liturgical reenactments "can too
easily become a religious substitute for turning away from evil and living a life of righteousness" should be taken seriously, I think we should
not forget the power of symbolic substitution, which might speak to a
deep human desire for *salvation*. What is more, exoneration and resto-

ration, relief and repentance, replacement and responsibility do not necessarily exclude one another. Once our burden has been lifted, and following the example of Christ, we may begin to restore our relations with our fellow human beings because that is something no one can do in our place. Looking back, I think this is also what my father was trying to convey to me.

Notes

1. Johannes Baptist Metz, "Facing the Jews: Christian Theology After Auschwitz," in *The Holocaust as Interruption, Concilium* 175, ed. Elisabeth Schüssler Fiorenza and David Tracy (Edinburgh: T. & T. Clark, 1984), 43–52.

2. Immanuel Kant, *Religion Within the Limits of Reason Alone*, trans. Theodore M. Greene and Hoyt H. Hudson (New York: Harper & Row, 1794/1960), 66.

3. Michael Wyschogrod, *Abraham's Promise: Judaism and Jewish-Christian Relations* (Grand Rapids: Eerdmans, 2004), 53.

4. See Irving Greenberg, "Cloud of Smoke, Pillar of Fire: Judaism, Christianity, and Modernity After the Holocaust," in *Auschwitz: Beginning of a New Era?, Reflections on the Holocaust*, ed. *Eva Fleischner* (New York: KTAV Publishing, 1977).

5. Paul Ricoeur, *The Conflict of Interpretations: Essays in Hermeneutics* (Evanston: Northwestern University Press, 2007), 448.

6. Quotation: Zev Garber, Foreword to Henry F. Knight, *Confessing Christ in a Post-Holocaust World: A Midrashic Experiment* (Greenwood Press, 2000), xvi.

7. Some also refer to the Sacrifice of Isaac. Sandra Schneiders explains that "is invoked by a few scholars but regarded by most as the weakest background and by a few as irrelevant." See Sandra Schneiders, "The Lamb of God and the Forgiveness of Sin(s) in the Fourth Gospel," *The Catholic Biblical Quarterly* 73 (2011): 1–29.

8. There is a lot of discussion among the sages why G-d would need such an external sign, considering the fact that God knows everything.

9. For a list of Christological readings of Isaiah 53 from the New Testament through the twelfth century, see David Berger, ed., *The Jewish-Christian Debate in the High Middle Ages: A Critical Edition of the Nizzahon Vetus with an Introduction, Translation, and Commentary* (Philadelphia: Jewish Publication Society of America, 1979), 283.

10. See, for example, Matt. 8:17, 12:18–21; Acts 8:30–33; Mark 15:28; Luke 22:37, 24:26, 24:46.

11. Ambrose, Letter 69, quoted in Mark W. Elliott, ed. *Ancient Christian Commentary on Scripture, Old Testament XI (Isaiah 40–66)* (Downers Grove: Intervarsity Press, 2014), 166.

12. Cyril C. Richardson, *Early Christian Fathers*, trans. Cyril C. Richardson (New York: Touchstone, 1996), 17.

13. Roberts et.al. *The Anti-Nicene Fathers: The Writings of the Fathers Down to A.D. 325 Volume I, The Apostolic Fathers with Justin Martyr and Irenaeus*, Vol. 1 (New York: Cosimo Classics, 2007), 179.

14. Alice L. Eckhardt, "Suffering: Challenge to Faith, Challenge to God" (1994) http://preserve.lehigh.edu/cas-religion-faculty-publications/12.

15. Eckhardt, "Suffering: Challenge to Faith, Challenge to God."

16. Leora Batnizky, "On the Suffering of God's Chosen: Christian Views in Jewish Terms," in *Christianity in Jewish Terms*, ed. Tikva Frymer-Kensky, David Novak, Peter Ochs, David Fox Samuel, Michael Singer (Boulder: Westview Press, 2000), 206.

17. This collective interpretation is not a medievalist development but rather a retrieval of an interpretation that with certainty already existed in the third century, something we know because Origen (248 CE) in his apologetic rebuttal of Jewish objections against Christ mentions and rejects the Jewish collective interpretation of the suffering servant.

18. The whole of the Jewish community in medieval Europe was familiar both with the writings and also with the reputation of Rashi. In times of peace, they looked to him for wisdom and instruction. In times of distress they looked to him for answers and comfort. Rashi's influence helped to mold Jewish thought from medieval times into the present. Charles E. McLain, "A Comparison of Ancient and Medieval Jewish Interpretations of the Suffering Servant in Isaiah," *Calvary Baptist Theological Journal* 6 (1990).

19. Avraham Grossman, "The Commentary of Rashi on Isaiah and the Jewish-Christian Debate," in *Studies in Medieval Jewish Intellectual and Social History: Festschrift in Honor of Robert Chazan*, ed. David Engel, Lawrence H. Schiffman, and Elliot R. Wolfson (Leiden: Brill, 2012), 59.

20. Funkenstein suggests that in this period both Christians and Jews inverted and subverted each other's biblical narratives in an effort to deliberately distort each other's self-understanding and collective memories. See Ibn Ezra (1089–ca.1164) and Radak (1160–1235 CE), who also wrote in the eleventh to twelfth centuries, likewise appropriated the figure of the suffering servant as referring to Israel, which found itself in a state of dispersion and suffering.

21. Amos Funkenstein, "The Dialectics of Assimilation," *Jewish Social Studies* 1/2 (1995): 1–14), 9.

22. Marc A. Krell, "Comparative Philosophical Approaches to Salvation: An Examination of a Particular Instance of an Interreligious Experience," *Shofar: An Interdisciplinary Journal of Jewish Studies* 16 (1998): 82.

23. Joel Rembaum, "The Development of a Jewish Exegetical Tradition Regarding Isaiah 53," *The Harvard Theological Review* 75/3 (1982): 298.

24. Rembaum, "The Development of a Jewish Exegetical Tradition Regarding Isaiah 53," 298.

25. *The Kuzari: In Defense of the Despised Faith*, trans. N. Daniel Korobkin, 2:35, 90–92, quoted in Leora Batnizky, "On the Suffering of God's Chosen," 211.

26. Robert Gibbs, "Suspicions of Suffering," in *Christianity in Jewish Terms*, ed. Tikva Frymer-Kensky, David Novak, Peter Ochs, David Fox Samuel, and Michael S. Singer (Oxford: Westview Press, 2000), 221.

27. Nicholas de Lange. *Ignaz Maybaum: A Reader* (New York: Berghahn Books, 2001), 168.

28. Eliezer Berkovits, *Faith after the Holocaust* (New York: KTAV, 1973), 125–26.

29. Joel Marcus, *Jesus and the Holocaust. Reflections on Suffering and Hope* (Grand Rapids, Mich.: Eerdmans, 2017), 28.

30. Emmanuel Levinas, *Difficult Freedom: Essays on Judaism* (London: Athlone, 1990), 12.

31. Emmanuel Levinas, "L'inspiration religieuse de l'alliance," *Paix et droit* 8 (1935): 4.

32. There is a whole program behind that command, *You shall not kill*. After all, Levinas argues, there are various ways of killing a person. It does not necessarily have to be, he argues, by pulling a trigger. Indifference, underappreciation, and exclusion kill as

well. All these forms of violence, Levinas states, are characterized by the fact that they do not look those whom they do violence to in the eyes.

33. France Guwy, ed., *De ander in ons: Emmanuel Levinas in gesprek: een inleiding in zijn denken* (Amsterdam: Sun, 2008), 45.

34. Michael de Saint Cheron, *Conversations with Emmanuel Levinas, 1983–1994*, trans. Gary D. Mole (Pittsburgh: Duquesne University Press, 2010), 16.

35. Renée van Riessen, *Man as a Place of God: Levinas' Hermeneutics of Kenosis* (Dordrecht: Springer, 2007),119.

36. Catherine Chalier, "Le serviteur souffrant: Isaïe 52, 13–15; 53, 1–12," in *Mythe et philosophie: Les traditions bibliques*, ed. Christian Berner (Paris: Presses Universitaires de France, 2002), 154.

37. Emmanuel Levinas, "Useless Suffering," in *The Provocation of Levinas: Re-Thinking the* Other, ed. Robert Bernasconi and David Wood (London: Routledge, 1988), 159.

38. Levinas, *Difficult Freedom*, 89–90.

39. Ricoeur, *Conflict of Interpretations*, 442.

40. Adam Gregerman, "Interpreting the Pain of Others: John Paul II and Benedict XVI on Jewish Suffering in the Shoah," *Journal of Ecumenical Studies* 48 (2013): 459.

41. Robert Gibbs, "Suspicions of Suffering," in *Christianity in Jewish Terms*, ed. Tikva Frymer-Kensky et al. (Oxford: Westview Press, 2000), 228.

42. See Marianne Moyaert, "Comparative Theology after the Shoah: Risks, Pivots and Opportunities of Comparing Traditions," in *How to Do Comparative Theology: European and American Perspectives in* Dialogue, ed. Francis Clooney and Klaus von Stosch (New York: Fordham University Press, 2018), 174–87.

43. Orthodox Rabbinic Statement on Christianity, *To do the will of our Father in Heaven: Toward a Partnership between Jews and Christians*, 3 December 2015; http://cjcuc.com /site/2015/12/03/orthodox-rabbinic-statement-on-christianity/.

44. David Berger and Michael Wyschogrod, *Jews and Jewish Christianity: A Jewish Response to the Missionary Challenge* (Hoboken, N.J.: KTAV, 1978), 29.

45. Wyshogrond, *Abraham's Promise*, 68.

46. I am quite aware of the fact that I am not doing justice to the complexity and nuances of Levinas's ethics.

47. Cf. God's question directed at Cain in Genesis 4:10.

48. The experience of being overwhelmed by one's iniquities and being burdened by a too heavy weight is very biblical (Ezra 9:6, Ps. 40:12; Ps. 65:10).

49. Paul Tillich, "The Religious Symbol," *Daedalus* 87 (1958): 3.

50. In this light we may consider the eucharistic prayers said by the priest following Christ's words when breaking the bread: "'Take this, all of you, and eat it. This is My Body which will be given up for you'" and when taking the cup of wine: "Take this, all of you, and drink from it. This is the cup of My Blood, the Blood of the new and everlasting covenant. It will be shed for you and for all so that sins may be forgiven. Do this in memory of me," (cf. 1 Cor. 11:24–25).

51. Lawrence A. Hoffman, "Jewish and Christian Liturgy," in *Christianity in Jewish Terms*, ed. Tikva Frymer-Kensky et.al. (Oxford: Westview Press, 2000), 186.

Judgment on the Cross

RESURRECTION AS DIVINE VINDICATION

Joshua Ralston

"Among the strangest things which you people bring forward is your statement that (Jesus) gave his blood for the salvation of men."[1] So claims Abū l-Walīd al-Bājī, an eleventh-century Andalusian Muslim, in response to a missionary treatise written by an unknown monk from France. Al-Bājī's critique of Christian understandings of Jesus's death is one succinct expression that captures centuries of Islamic discourse on the cross. From the earliest discussions of Jesus Christ's death in the Qur'ān through medieval polemics to contemporary Muslim fatwas, the cross remains one of the "outstanding neuralgic issues" in Christian-Muslim debate.[2] Muslims across the centuries have challenged the historicity of Jesus's death, rejected its salvific meaning, mocked its metaphysical implications, and questioned the propriety of its ubiquitous presence in churches, liturgy, and ritual. Even in her sympathetic and moving meditation on the cross, Mona Siddiqui still finds the Christian redemptive logic unnecessary. She writes, "Its mystery is moving, but I cannot incline towards what it says about a God in form, a God who undergoes this inexplicable agony for an inexplicable act of mercy. It is not the language of redemption that I cannot understand, it is the necessity of God's self-revelation for this act of redemption."[3] As Mark Swanson cleverly writes, the cross is foolishness to the *Ḥunafā'*.[4] It is also a stumbling block to anyone foolish enough to write a Christian account of the atonement in comparative dialogue with Muslims and the Islamic tradition.

Given the seeming Qur'ānic rejection of not only the theological import of Jesus's death but also its very historical fact, a Christian-Muslim comparative theology of the atonement is a seeming im-possibility.[5] How could it be otherwise given the fundamental place of the cross in Christian theology, worship, preaching, piety, and liturgy? A comparative approach between Christianity and Islam—and we could add Judaism—walks into a delicate and historically fraught terrain. These traditions' history of overlapping scriptures and shared yet diverging views of God raise serious questions about how far comparative theology might go in addressing areas of acute theological disagreement. While this is certainly the case with debates around the Trinity, the incarnation, the prophethood of Muḥammad, and the divine origins of the Qur'ān, it is all the more so when discussing the atonement. The Iranian-American Shiʻa thinker Seyyed Hossein Nasr argues that while "doctrines such as the nature of Christ or the Trinity can be understood metaphysically in such a way as to harmonize" the Christian and Islamic accounts, the crucifixion will still remain a wedge. This is not simply because of the Qur'ān, but also because "the meaning of the crucifixion and the idea of redemption it signifies are perhaps the most difficult of all aspects of Christianity for an ordinary Muslim to grasp."[6] It is not possible, at least given my own Christian theological commitments, to turn away from the concrete question of Jesus's saving significance and move instead to a general study of redemption, sacrifice, or divine mercy in the two traditions.[7] Whatever broader resonances and divergences might be found through a comparative study of thinkers will inevitably have to address the question of Jesus, who remains today—as he was in the famous story of the King of Axum—the line in the sand that divides Christians from Muslims.[8] To write a Christian theology of the atonement in conversation with the Islamic tradition is to engage a history of judgments against the cross and its meaning. The method and approaches of comparative theology, then, must be leveraged to re-evaluate polemics, exploring how and to what extent long-standing debates might be carried out in a different tone and method—even if the original judgments stand.

Muslim Judgment on the Cross

SCRIPTURE

At first glance, the most challenging aspect of writing a Christian theology of the atonement in conversation with Islam is the apparent Qur'ānic rejection of the crucifixion itself. The well-known verses from Sūra al-Nisā' read as follows:

> And for their boast, "Behold, we have slain the Christ Jesus, son of Mary, (who claimed to be) a messenger of God!" However, they did not kill him,

and neither did they crucify him [*mā qatalūhu wa mā ṣalabūhu*], but it only seemed to them so [*shubbiha lahum*]. And truly, those who hold conflicting views are indeed confused, having no knowledge of it, and following mere conjecture. For it is certain, they did not slay him. Rather God raised him to Himself. God is the exalted in might, the Wise. (4:157–58)

The plain meaning of the text appears to suggest an outright rejection of the crucifixion of Jesus and a polemic against both Jews and Christians. The most common Muslim reading has been that the Jewish authorities were tricked into killing a substitute often depicted as either Judas or a willing volunteer. Within the Qur'ānic context of Sūra al-Nisā', which is generally agreed by both the classical Islamic tradition and contemporary Western scholarship to be a late Medinan revelation, the verses carry inter-religious implications. They are located within a longer discussion of the rejection of prophets by the Jewish people and are part of a growing Qur'ānic interest in distinguishing the emerging Muslim community in Medina from Jews and Christians. In this context the focus is less on Christian claims about Jesus, although these are present throughout the sūra, and more on Jewish rejection of divine prophets—and by extension Muḥammad.[9] Beyond the text's internal discourse around Jews, other scholars have noted docetic influences from early Christian writings such as *Acts of John*, as well as resonance with canonical texts such as Philippians 2:5–11 and Peter's sermons in Acts 2 and 5.[10] Even more fascinating is Todd Lawson's claim in *The Crucifixion and the Qur'ān* that John of Damascus's (in)famous account of the Ishmaelite heresy offers the first textual argument—Muslim or Christian—that the verse's meaning entails an explicit rejection of the historicity of the crucifixion.[11] It might be that the Damascene is simply relaying the settled interpretation a century after the death of the prophet, or it could be that Christian readings of the text encouraged Muslim interpreters toward a position of rejection.

The text itself also presents two complex linguistic and interpretative questions. The first is what the relationship between the boast of having killed Jesus and the retort *mā qatalūhu wa mā ṣalabūhu* (they did not kill him, and neither did they crucify him) means. Is this retort and the later restatement that *wa-mā qatalūhu yaqīnan* (they did not slay him) to be read as clear denial of Jesus's death? Or is it better understood as a divine critique of the earlier boast and claim to have defeated Jesus's pro-

phetic mission? Under this later reading, God's vindication and exaltation of Jesus is not necessarily a denial of the historicity of the cross but
is a recognition of the divine origin of Jesus's message. Second is the
meaning of the term *shubbiha lahum*, what Lawson calls a "textbook example of a multivocal phrase."[12] The most literal reading of the words
would be that it was made to appear to them that Jesus was killed; however, a long tradition of exegesis has preferred to render the phrase to imply that there was a substitute for or likeness of Jesus that was crucified.
Debates about its meaning are a regular feature in classical and contemporary *tafsīr*, with the dominant exegesis being an outright denial of
Jesus death and the affirmation of a human replacement.[13] A classical example of this can be found in the *tafsīr* of the fourteenth-century Athari
Ibn Kathīr of Damascus, when he tells a story of 'Isa (Jesus) asking for
a volunteer to take his place and God making the young man to look
like Jesus.[14]

There have been a number of other readings that offer more nuanced
interpretations of the words *mā qatalūhu wa mā ṣalabūhu* and *shubbiha
lahum*, including the great Ash'ari thinker Fakhr din al-Razi's rejection
of the substitutionary theory. In his *al-Tafsīr al-Kabīr*, he argues that the
substitutionary theory would call into question the justice of God and
also create epistemic uncertainty for all humans as it defies *al-qanūn
kulli*, or the universal law of rationality.[15] While he does not go on to affirm Jesus's death directly, Isma'ali exegetes and philosophical interpretations have tended to accept Jesus's death and read the verses as affirming
his mission as being a sign of God's exaltation of Jesus. More recently,
Mahmoud Ayoub's has offered a considerate reading of the verses with
attention to both historical criticism and Christian-Muslim relations arguing that they are not concerned with the physical fact of Jesus's death
but are an affirmation of the persistence and power of God's message even
in the face of rejection. Ayoub contends that the "denial of the killing of
Jesus is a denial of the power of human being to vanquish and destroy
the divine Word, which is forever victorious."[16] While the primary focus
of this paper is not on the scriptural issues dividing Muslims and Christians, these examples all indicate the complexity of Qur'ānic interpretation, opening up ways for Muslims to affirm the Qur'ān without denying
the crucifixion, and meriting further exploration for both Christian-
Muslim dialogue and comparative theology.

In fact, 4:157–58 is not the only mention of Jesus's death in the Qur'ān.
For instance, 5:75 states that that "the Messiah, son of Mary, was only a

messenger, messengers before him have also died" and in 19:33 the infant Jesus says, "Peace be upon me the day I was born, the day I die, and the day that I am resurrected." While these and other verses might create the space for affirming Jesus's death and possibly even a deeper theological or mystical interpretation of 4:157, the dominant interpretation of the Qur'ān as a whole has been that Jesus was neither killed nor crucified. Instead, Jesus is understood to have either died a natural death later or is alive with God, awaiting the day of judgment when he will return to earth.[17] Without denying the dominant reading of Jesus's death, its mere historicity is not the biggest challenge that Muslims present to Christian theologies of atonement. As Lawson notes, "It would seem that a simple crucifixion, which did not carry with it such un-Islamic concepts as vicarious atonement, could easily be accepted."[18] Muslims present much stronger judgments on Christian ideas about the meaning of the cross than its bare historical fact. Even if a persuasive reading of Sūra al-Nisā' could be made that affirms Jesus's death, this is far from an affirmation of its saving significance.

The most pressing challenges that the Islamic tradition presents to Christian theologies of the atonement revolve around the morality and necessity of a death to secure divine mercy and how this impacts human redemption and moral action in the world. Two critiques from texts over a millennium apart will be outlined, one focused on Christian accounts of the atonement that prioritize the incarnation and the other that primarily critiques cross-oriented models of redemption. In both, key ideas from the Islamic traditions around God's free mercy, the individual's responsibility for their own sins and moral actions, and the eschatological nature of salvation are leveraged against Christian claims that redemption has been accomplished in and through Jesus.

'ALĪ AL-ṬABARĪ: THE INCOHERENCE OF INCARNATION AND SALVATION

One of the most wide-ranging early critiques of Christian theologies of atonement comes from the pen of 'Alī al-Ṭabarī, a Persian polymath who converted to Islam from the Church of the East (Nestorian in the common Arabic parlance) around 850 CE. In al-Radd 'alā al-Naṣārā (The Refutation of the Nazarenes), he challenges the logic of the incarnation and questions the necessity and fittingness of Christ's descent for salvation.[19] He is less focused on a critique of the cross as such and more interested in deploying Jesus's death as a rhetorical tool to push Christians onto the horns of a Christological dilemma. According to him, the cross is the supreme example of the incoherence of Christology, be it Melkite/ Chalcedonian, Jacobite, or Nestorian. Jesus's death presents a metaphysical impossibility for Christian talk of God's nature and Christ's person. If there is a unity of divinity and humanity in Jesus, as all three major Eastern traditions affirm in some fashion, Muslims argue that it becomes necessary to say that the eternal God dies. This is an anathema to classical Christian and Muslim theologians alike. On the other hand, if this is not the case, then there must be a separation within Jesus where only the human nature dies and not the divine nature, but then al-Ṭabarī claims that it is thus transparently obvious that Jesus is not fully God and thus Christian ideas are disproven.[20]

Hidden within this Christologically focused critique of Christian theology, al-Ṭabarī also challenges the soteriological necessity of the incarnation and death of Jesus. Referencing both the creeds and liturgy, he notes how all three Christian traditions affirm that the incarnation was a means of salvation from sin; "they have said that the reason for his descent was expressly to free people from the bonds of sin."[21] Two major issues arise from this claim. The first is why it is necessary or appropriate for God to act in this way in order to offer mercy and free human beings from sin. With models of atonement theory often described as *Christus Victor* in mind, he asks why Christians believe this narrative of descent, imprisonment, and freedom is needed. Why does forgiveness and freedom demand an exchange with Satan? For instance, al-Ṭabarī challenges Christian configurations of atonement by illustrating the absurdity of Satan holding power over God: "It is the most amazing thing that the eternal Creator should be forced to send down his eternal Son from heaven, and then hand him over to Satan through his holy victorious Spirit so that Satan could tempt him and humiliate him. Who is it that forced him to do this? What was the achievement for him or his creation in it?"[22] He goes on to argue that far from reinforcing the justice and mercy of God, the Christian narrative of salvation through incarnation, death, and resurrection unwittingly empowers Satan and evil, providing it purchase over the divine life and attributes. Al-Ṭabarī maintains that Satan and evil are given such cosmological power in this schema that there is inevitably a dualism that challenges divine power and mercy. Rather than exalting the mercy and humility of God's love in Christ, Christian theology imagines a cosmic war between two equal parties, an idea abhorrent to his theological and scriptural understanding of divine power.

This relates to the second key issue that al-Ṭabarī raises around an incarnational and *Christus Victor* model of salvation, namely its effectiveness. He notes how Christians claim that salvation is only possible through God's own Son, and not via prophets, messengers, and books as the Muslims claim. The Christian scripture and creeds profess that in Jesus Christ's life, death, and resurrection, reconciliation has been wrought (Romans 4) and death defeated (1 Cor 15:55–57).[23] Again al-Ṭabarī turns his attention to the Christian creeds that he once confessed, noting how the aim of the eternal Word's descent was to "subdue Satan and deliver humankind from his grip."[24] And yet, a mere glance at history and humanity contests this claim. Death still stalks every creature; sin has not been overcome; Satan and evil seem as powerful over the world as they were before the incarnation. The very goal that God the Father sent the Son to accomplish in the incarnation is unfinished: "According to what they claim, his Son returned without doing any of this, not destroying sin or death, even though he had descended for it."[25] Al-Ṭabarī presses this point by asking why an incarnational atonement would be necessary if it proves to be just as constrained and limited as Christians claim the prophets are. Why did God send his only Son to save human beings if the result would be the same rejection given to prophets? If salvation has truly been accomplished in Jesus Christ, why does history testify against this?

For al-Ṭabarī, this is further proof that the Christian account of atonement and redemption is misguided. The Christian vision of salvation is neither necessary nor fitting.[26] It is unnecessary because Satan does not have as tight a grip over either divine power or human beings that the *Christus Victor* schema assumes; it is unfitting because it is no more effective than God's revelation through prophets and Books. Why develop a convoluted metaphysical and ontological argument about a God-Man and his incarnation and death when an appeal to God's power and mercy is more effective, simple, and rational? Al-Ṭabarī testifies that it is God's power and mercy alone that saves—and "when God wills a thing there is no resistance to it."[27]

ISMAʾIL RAGI AL-FARUQI: DIVINE MERCY AND HUMAN MORALITY

In his probing and polemic work *Christian Ethics*, published in 1967, the Palestinian Ismaʾil al-Faruqi critiques the morality of Christian visions of redemption. While the earlier portions of the book cover issues in philosophy of religion and comparative methodology, offering an Islamic reading of Jewish and Christian law, the second half is focused explicitly on the problems latent in Christian ideas of "peccatism" (original sin) and "saviorism" (soteriology). While Madigan's chapter in this book focuses more on al-Faruqi's critique of Christian sin talk, this chapter will focus more on his ethical critique of Christian atonement theology. The dominant tradition under al-Faruqi's critical gaze is Western Christianity and especially Protestantism, as indicated by his engagement with figures such as John Calvin, Martin Luther, Reinhold Niebhur, Paul Tillich, and Karl Barth. At the heart of al-Faruqi's critique is a critical concern about the morality of Christian claims about redemption, both these theologians' depiction of God and their vision of the ongoing moral and sociopolitical life of human beings.

According to al-Faruqi, Christianity is unique amongst all the global religious traditions in being a religion of redemption. He alleges that Christianity—and here he clearly has certain expressions of Protestantism in mind—loudly proclaims itself unique because it alone offers a theology of redemptive mercy unbound to human works. This is not to say that other traditions, such as al-Faruqi's Sunni Islam, do not speak of a human or cosmic predicament that demands addressing. All religions conceive of a set of problems facing human beings and then present a solution or way forward. However, "Christianity is unique in that it has made redemption its be-all and end-all; it has woven a divine scheme of redemption into the very nature of the Godhead" by asserting that salvation has been secured in a "single, unique, and final redemptive event."[28] To expand on this distinctive element of Christianity, he compares his Islamic understanding of redemption with Protestant Christianity. For instance, both Christianity and Islam have a conception of God engaging with humanity and history in a unique and definitive way—for Christians in the revelation of Jesus and for Muslims in the prophethood of Muḥammad and the revelation of the Qur'ān. On closer inspection these similarities conceal greater differences. Muslims do assert that the revelation of the Qur'ān is "the most perfect and complete" but it is not distinct from God's prior revelations to humanity through books and prophets.[29] What God sends down in Mecca and Medina is the same message that God has spoken to Abraham, Moses, Jesus, and the other prophets. God's will and demands were truly given and are knowable prior to the revelation of the Qur'ān. In contrast, the Christian claims about Jesus are wholly unique. As indicated in the opening of the Epistle to the Hebrews, God has altered God's mode of communication, moving from prophets to God's Son. Prior to Jesus, there was thus no full knowledge of God or God's salvific intent. After the advent of Jesus, there is no genuine knowledge of God or God's salvific intent apart from the Christian message. This vision of revelation as a unique event of redemption creates strict divides between those who are in God's fold—because of knowledge alone and not moral action—and those who are outside God's community.

In addition to separating off God's revelation in Jesus from all previous claims of divine engagement with humanity, Christianity differs from Islamic ideas about how redemption relates to the importance of human action in history. The central problem in Christian talk of redemption is its already completedness. Christianity, unlike Islam, proclaims that atonement has already occurred, that the most important thing has already been done. What remains for humanity is to accept God's action on their behalf. However, al-Faruqi avers that if redemption is accomplished once and for all in Jesus, apart from any human effort or action, it leaves human beings largely unchanged and offers little impetus for moral transformation. All that separates the Christian from the non-Christian is faith, belief, or knowledge of the Christian message. Christian claims of God's unique revelation and redemption in Jesus Christ robs history and life in this world of its true significance and creates moral paradoxes. On the one hand, Christianity implores people to follow the way and teaching of Jesus. On the other hand, Christian theology loudly proclaims a freedom from the law and offers assurance that salvation has already been secured. The social and theo-political import of Christian views of salvation are also abhorrent, leading to a strange combination of personal moral laxity and arrogance. The Christian awaits moral transformation in the after-life, overlooking their own shortcomings and sins as both already forgiven and somehow inevitable. At the same time, the Christian is possessed by a self-righteousness that they alone have the true message of redemption and salvation, one that places them spiritually and morally above others. The very saviorism that Christianity proclaims as having been accomplished already by Jesus ironically lends itself to the creation of Christian attitudes of saviorism toward others. al-Faruqi even goes so far as to connect this vision of redemption to the cultural superiority of the West and its colonial endeavors: "What European Christendom had allowed itself to do vis-à-vis the non-Christian world during the last five centuries . . . is an effect of that self-righteousness which saviourism breeds and nourishes."[30]

In addition to these searing ethical concerns regarding human action, both individual and social, al-Faruqi also finds the Christian account of redemption to present a morally truncated vision of God. The primary focus of his critique revolves around theologies of the atonement that place their central weight on Jesus Christ's death on the cross, highlighting the limitation of models of exchange, sacrifice, and substitution. He begins his critique by focusing on the relationship between divine mercy and justice, the very issues that animate both Anselmian theories of ransom and Calvinist accounts of penal substitution. Al-Faruqi recognizes that the various Christian metaphors of atonement are seeking to affirm both God's mercy and the need for justice, but there is an inherent inconsistency built into these schemas. Christianity insists that it alone is a religion of grace and love, where salvation is grounded in the "sheer mercy of God."[31] And yet at the very same time, Christian theologies of the atonement also maintain the justice behind Jesus's death, some going as far as saying that the death was necessary: "The act of Jesus is a sacrifice; the act of God the Father who sent Jesus is mercy, and the act of God who demanded that the Father do something in expiation, is justice."[32] For al-Faruqi, the claim of a wonderful exchange is actually a horrible conflict built within God's nature that divides the divine will between mercy and justice. Islam, too, faces the tension between mercy and justice; however, it differs fundamentally by not "resolving" it through an act in history, most specifically the death of an innocent man. Instead, Islam "teaches the mercy of God and proclaims His merciful acts from every lip" but this does not "run counter to justice" because God is "merciful and just."[33] How this is the case is not worked out in detail by al-Faruqi, other than to affirm that God's order upholds creation and that God's mercy and justice have an eschatological character. In contrast, Christianity seeks to resolve this mystery too early and does so through a cruel injustice.

How is a death justice? How does pain secure mercy? How can one death, or even one life, atone for the sins of the world? These questions, which have long engaged Christian theologians, are the central injustice of Christian soteriology according to al-Faruqi. Three interrelated issues animate his critique. The first relates to the claim of the necessity or fittingness of the cross: "To claim that God *had* to die because God is merciful, is too shallow a self-contradiction to stand."[34] In much the same way as in al-Ṭabarī's critique of the *Christus Victor* model, al-Faruqi claims that substitutionary models of atonement end up giving something, in this case retributive justice, purchase over God and therefore constraining divine freedom. Rather than affirming God's mercy, God is made to need payment, justice, or blood in order to forgive. This leads to the second critique, namely that physical, emotional, and psychological pain are not redemptive and can never be "retribution for moral evil."[35] In general, physical abuse is an inappropriate response to atone for moral evil because it more likely destroys the victim and morally hardens the perpetrators. Al-Faruqi also perceptively notes how this runs afoul of Jesus's own teaching. How can it be that God's own self requires physical pain and death in order to forgive when that same God has sent Jesus to the earth, teaching people to turn the other cheek and not repay evil for evil? Finally, al-Faruqi challenges the vicarious and representative nature of Christian redemption. In large part this is unnecessary because of the Muslim rejection of original sin, exemplified in the Qur'ānic notion that each individual carries their own burdens and are judged on their own actions (cf. 35:18, 2:286). Moral evil, then, concerns the individual and God alone and is not transmitted or shared across humanity. As such, "nobody can atone for anyone else" in the Islamic tradition.[36] This final critique of Christian theologies of atonement returns us to the original critique of the moral impact of Christian ethics. Christian salvation proclaims a unique and complete atonement for humanity, even as it leaves human beings unchanged in this world: "Whereas the Muslim comes out from his encounter with God conscious mainly of the fact that the greatest task lies ahead and that it is to be fulfilled in his ethical conduct, the Christian comes out of from his encounter with God pleased, satisfied, proud, and relieved that the greatest task was done and is behind him."[37]

THE CONTOURS OF MUSLIM JUDGMENTS

Having paid significant attention to the questions and critiques raised by the Qur'ān and two different Muslim thinkers, I want to provide a list of the central contours of Muslim judgments on Christian theologies of the atonement before turning to my sketch of a Christian framework carried out in a comparative mode.

1. The Qur'ān challenges the historicity of Jesus's death and instead emphasizes God's victory over those that challenge the divine message.

2. The logic of redemption through incarnation and crucifixion is puzzling at best and appears to constrain the freedom and mercy of God.[38]

3. Atonement is not accomplished through a substitution or representative but depends on God and each individual.[39]

4. Salvation is not an event of the past but is oriented toward a future judgment.

5. The atonement, particularly in Protestant accounts, renders moral action and history largely meaningless.

Muslims present in stark and clear terms the challenge of why, what for, and what does this matter for life. Before I move on, I want to make sure that I avoid too quick of a juxtaposition between Christianity and Islam, making the first a religion of grace and love and the second of works and the law. The Islamic tradition also understands God to be both merciful and just, gracious and fair. This is expressed theologically and doxologically in a number of ways, for instance in the ninety-nine names of God, which include the Merciful (*al-Rahman*) and Compassionate (*al-Rahīm*) as well as the judge or arbitrator (*al-Hakīm*) and the just (*al-'Adl*). Moreover, while human action, belief, and merit are important in Islamic views of salvation, more so than in Christianity, it is not the case that Muslims simply earn their salvation. God and God's mercy remains the final agent of salvation. The largest difference, then, lies in whether or not there is an agent or act that elicits, merits, or establishes God's mercy. If what is meant by this question is akin to certain rendering of Jesus's death that view it as a propitiation or sacrifice to God, then the answer is an unequivocal no. For Sunni Ash'arī thought, God's mercy is a divine prerogative.

Resurrection and Redemption as Divine Vindication
COMPARATIVE THEOLOGICAL ROADS NOT TAKEN

In light of the breadth and depth of Muslim judgments against Christian theologies of salvation, be they focused on the incarnation or the cross, it would appear judicious to shift the theological and dialogical focus away from the incarnation or the cross and toward more productive sites for comparative exchange. One route would be to forgo discussion of Christ's representative or substitutionary merit and instead develop a comparative theology through the traditions of *imatio Christi* or exemplar models of atonement, particularly drawing on prophetology and those insights from Christian theology in the last century that connect with the aforementioned Muslim critiques. Such a move can be seen in a recent opinion piece in the *New York Times* on the *Islamic Jesus* by Mustafa Akyol, which argues that Muslims have much to learn from the life and teaching of Jesus, particularly the synoptic Gospels and the epistle of James.[40] While there is wisdom and theological fruit to be found in such an approach—and it would surely be a chief component of a broader Christian Christology written with Islam—on their own these theologies fail to offer a coherent and rich enough account of the Christian tradition, scripture, or confessions. For one, even two figures often thought of as representatives of the exemplar model, Abelard and Schleiermacher, do not themselves offer an account of Jesus's saving significance only through the model and teaching of his life. To take Schleiermacher only, he explicitly rejects the "empirical view" of redemption, which limits Christ's saving power to only his teaching and example. For Schleiermacher, it is not that Jesus saves by teaching; Christ saves by communicating and incorporating human beings into his God-consciousness and blessedness through the community of faith.[41] For the great Berliner, Enlightenment views, and we might say by extension Islamic ones, are insufficient in that they do not address the real need of human beings for redemption. Al-Faruqi also recognizes the overlap between theologies that view Jesus as perfect exemplar, what he terms the "didactic" view, and the Islamic tradition. While al-Faruqi thinks that this account is "unquestionably true," he also queries how Christian theology would be wholly distinct from Islamic accounts of Jesus if that is all the Christian tradition had to say about Jesus. If the didactic view is all that is involved in Christian theologies of redemption, then "there would be no need for any mystery in redemption; certainly not for Jesus to be anything more than the saint, the genius, the inspired man—in short the Prophet he was."[42] Al-Faruqi seems to be suggesting that a Christology and soteriology of exemplum alone accedes the argument to Muslims. Moreover, they still do not account for how didactic or exemplum models of atonement have to account for the cross. In fact, the exemplum models often culminate in the claim that the cross is the ultimate model of sacrifice, obedience, or commitment to God that is to be emulated, thus running aground on many of the same questions and challenges that other atonement theories do.

Is the atonement only a stumbling block that makes comparative theology and Christian-Muslim dialogue impossible? If what is meant by

dialogue and comparison is a move toward agreement, then yes. However, I take the invitation of comparative theology to be not primarily
concerned with agreement but probing difference, to carry out theological debate through a model of mutual exchange and witness in a posture
of humble particularity.[43] We might note that the critiques that have been
laid out thus far are not foreign to internal Christian disputes. Many of
them resonate with and even foreshadow internal Christian arguments
against classical models of substitution, ransom, or exchange, particularly those raised in the last two centuries by the liberal theological tradition, feminist and womanist theologians, and liberation theologians.
Questions of how substitutionary atonement displaces moral action was
a concern of many Enlightenment thinkers, such as John Locke in his
Reasonableness of Christian Religion and Immanuel Kant in *Religion
within the Boundaries of Mere Reason.* The problematic valorization of
death and sacrifice have also been increasingly critiqued by Christian
theologians. One of the most powerful comes from Delores Williams who
argues that Jesus's saving power is not found in the cross but in his life,
challenging the ramifications of a Christian theology of surrogacy that
negatively controls Black women's bodies and lives. For her, the cross is
"an image of defilement, a gross manifestation of collective human sin.
Jesus, then does not conquer sin through death on the cross."[44] Including Muslim interlocutors and voices in this ongoing reflection on Christian claims might both challenge too neat divisions between religious
traditions, showing unlikely allies and conversation partners, even as it
alters existing theological categories and assumptions.

The rest of the chapter, then, will consider how shifting the theological focus of the import of the atonement to the resurrection—and not
placing the primary explanatory power of salvation on first and foremost
on the incarnation, the crucifixion, or the imitation of Jesus provides a
framework from within which Muslim concerns around propitiation,
morality, and eschatology might be re-thought. What it will not do, however, is negate the scandalous particularity of Christian proclamation
that God has acted decisively for the sake of the world in and through
Jesus. I make this claim not as a bald assertion of fact, immune to Muslim critique and challenge, but as recognition of how Christian theology
is shaped and determined by Jesus Christ just as Islamic theology remains
framed and bound by the Qur'ān as the *furqān,* or final standard of
judgment.

RESURRECTION, ASCENSION, AND SCRIPTURAL RESONANCE

One of the most important methodological commitments developed in recent Christian-Muslim theological exchange is to search for resonances or comparisons that do not initially appear obvious or straightforward. For instance, Daniel Madigan's brilliant essay on reading John with Muslims explores how Muslims and Christians alike grapple with understanding how a transcendent God communicates the Divine Word through creaturely medium, be it Jewish flesh or Arabic script.[45] His move to note structural and theological resonances, even as these are understood in distinct ways, opens up new avenues for discourse and debate. The Word as Jesus and the Word as Qur'ān are the more productive comparative links than what seems the natural comparison between the Bible and the Qur'ān, Jesus and Muḥammad. In his essay, Madigan shows how the logic of Christian claims about the incarnation of the Word are not wholly alien, even if they remain questionable, to Islamic thought because Sunni Islam, too, must grapple with an eternal Word made present through the creaturely medium of texts, language, book, and pen. These reframings have been carried out further by other more recent engagements, such as Jerusha Lamptey's study of Muḥammad and Mary as bearers of the Word.[46] While it seems unlikely that such a productive shift around debates on the incarnation is possible when turning to the crucifixion, there may be constructive possibilities if we attend to the equally central Christian confession of the resurrection of Jesus and its resonance with Muslim views of the ascension.

It is worth stating the obvious; the most primal and important Christian confession is not that Jesus died, but that God has raised Jesus to new life. It is this confession—given first by the women at the tomb—that turns a cruel and unjust death into a matter for theological reflection and soteriological proclamation. The resurrection of the Crucified One, not the cross in and of itself, is what saves. The primacy of the resurrection is evident throughout the early preaching in the Book of Acts. In 2:22–24, 3:14–16, 4:8–12, and 5:30–32, Peter continually emphasizes the divine reversal of human judgment against Jesus. Human beings stand in judgment against Jesus and his message, rejecting and killing him, but God through the Spirit overturns these human judgments. In this preaching, it is the resurrection, which is intimately connected to both the exaltation and vindication of Jesus, that serves as good news. We might say that for Luke's Peter, the resurrection and ascension of Jesus is an act of divine vindication of Jesus and his mission. This divine vindication of Jesus, which is also the exaltation of him as Lord, forms the ground of proper Christian talk of salvation. Following Paul—later in the letter to the Church in Corinth that opened this chapter—it is only because of the resurrection that we rightly and foolishly call the cross "saving." Without this act of divine vindication, we Christians are fools but to be pitied.

In turning briefly back to the text from Sūra al-Nisā', it is fascinating to notice how ascension and rescue are nearly as crucial to interpreting the text as the more controversial ideas around Jesus's death and crucifixion. The critical turn in the text is to be found in verse 158 and its assertion that "but God raised (*rafaʻa*) him up unto Himself, and God is mighty and wise." The resonance with Peter's early preaching as depicted in Acts, particularly the move from the claims of the crowd to have killed Jesus to God's vindication of Jesus, are noteworthy. In his recently published biblical commentary on the Qurʾān, Gabriel Said Reynolds argues that the text and broader context is "comparable to those passages in the Acts of Apostles where the Crucifixion is presented as the climax of a long history of Israelite infidelity."[47] The central transition in both texts is not principally to be found in the cross—as vital as this is for both traditions and their diverging understandings of God's acts of salvation—but in God's vindication of Jesus. The resurrection or ascension is God's counterjudgment against human judgments. For the Christian tradition, this occurs in the surprising and unique eschatological act of God's Spirit resurrecting Jesus after an unjust death on the cross. For Muslims, this vindication is seen in the mysterious act of God raising (more closely akin to an ascension) Jesus to God and sparing him an unjust death. The differences are obvious, but the central concern that God has vindicated Jesus might provide at least some opportunity for Christian theologians to begin to think atonement with Muslims as an act of divine vindication over against false human judgments.

RESURRECTION AS AN ESCHATOLOGICAL
EVENT OF DIVINE VINDICATION

In turning to the resurrection as the central frame for interpreting the saving power of Jesus, it is vital to clearly define the meaning of the resurrection. The resurrection is not merely the resuscitation of the man Jesus or a promise of life after death for those who believe; it is the vindication of Jesus and his ministry by the one he calls Father in the power of the

Spirit. Ingolf Dalferth writes, "The resurrection of Jesus by God is thus not a historical fact, however incomparable its uniqueness . . . The resurrection of the crucified one does not mean that he came back to the life in this world that he had left on the cross: what God did for the crucified Jesus resulted in new life, not in a new version of the old life."[48] The resurrection is the first fruits, or promised down payment, on God's ultimate triumph over all that impedes and inhibits the flourishing of creatures. Placing the primary weight of a theology of the atonement on the resurrection of Jesus of Nazareth from the dead should be understood as both a vindication of Jesus's life and mission and also as an eschatological promise of divine triumph. The resurrection both vindicates the before of Jesus's ministry and promises ahead to the future consummation of all creation through the judge Jesus.

Prioritizing the resurrection as central to salvation resists the valorization of suffering that Muslims rightly challenge. The cross and resurrection are not the eternal elevation of death into the Godhead, as can be seen in the speculative tendencies of Balthasar or Moltmann and their readings of Revelation 13:8, but the promise of suffering's cessation. Jesus's death is caused by opposition to his ministry and his proclamation of God's rule and the enactment of the kingdom through healings, table fellowship, and solidarity with women, the sick, sinners, and tax collectors. Jesus dies because of his persistence in and commitment to the kingdom of God, not in order to appease God's wrath or render a ransom back to God. The death of Jesus—like the resistance to the message of prophets in both the Hebrew and Islamic texts—is not caused by God but by human obstinance. The critiques of al-Faruqi, al-Bājī, Ibn Taymiyya, and Mona Siddiqui are vital to affirm. Whatever the saving meaning of Jesus's incarnation and death it should not be understood as something necessary for God. As Kathryn Tanner notes, "God is not changing God's relation to us in Christ but changing our relation to God."[49] Additionally, there is no power—be it sin, evil, justice, or human beings—that constrains or compels God to act. While the tendency to offer a metaphysical or moral account of either the necessity or fittingness of Jesus' death is understandable, particularly in the face of explicit challenges raised by non-Christians to its theo-logic, it runs the risk of turning from the concreteness of the Gospel accounts to speculative theologies of justice, mercy, and punishment. In answering questions, it often creates new problems. For Christians, the question is not why did Jesus die but that he did. Put otherwise, we might rein in the speculative tendencies of theology with a more constrained exegetical consideration of how the texts construe the surprise of the crucified and resurrected One.

Turning to the Scriptural account, particularly those in the Synoptic Gospels and the Acts of Apostles that narrate Jesus's ministry, death, and resurrection, we find less interest in broader metaphysical views of exchange.[50] In fact, attending closely to Scriptures' notion of the cross might reframe the dominant juridical readings of the cross and resurrection that are a common feature in theological accounts of Christ's saving work, particularly within my own Reformed Protestant tradition. The typical configuration of these penal models of the atonement place a justly tried and condemned humanity before the righteous judgment of God. By God's grace, Jesus stands in our stead and endures the punishment of God that we sinners rightly deserve. While there is some logic in this metaphor of exchange, particularly as it attempts to name the seriousness of sin and the demands of justice, its limitations outweigh its benefits in so far as it places conditions on God's grace and divides the will of God into two, one of justice and one of mercy. For my purpose, the more interesting fact—given the Reformed insistence on theology guided by scripture—is that it overlooks the place of human judgment and public law in the scriptural narrative. In all three synoptics and the Gospel of John, it is not God that stands in judgment against Jesus but human beings: the political authorities, religious teachers, and even Jesus's own disciples. Public law and human beings condemn Jesus and his ministry movement and Kingdom proclamation. It is not God the Father that judges humanity and Jesus on the cross; human beings do. The resurrection, then, is God's supreme verdict overruling human judgments of what counts as proper power and piety. Human judgment and law and our claims to wisdom are reversed, while the death dealing potential of law and politics exposed. The revelation of God's atoning work in judgment against human injustice should not, then, create morally or politically arrogant subjects per al-Faruqi's concern. Instead, the divine verdict against claims to power and justice through the law calls into question all those who equate their judgments with God's.

This altered reading of the judgment of God on the cross and resurrection has potentially liberative theo-political implications. As thinkers such as James Cone and Jon Sobrino note, the vindication of Jesus and his innocence is good news to all of those throughout history who have been falsely condemned, judged, and tried by the powers and principalities. The resurrection is the promise that the courts, police, judges, and systems of this world do not have the final verdict on human worth or value. Jesus's vindication is a promise that those both then, now, and in the future who were lynched, shot without trial, disappeared by Bashar al-Assad, left stuck at borders, or whose cases are thrown out on technicalities or rejected because of a lack of financial access to courts will too be vindicated by God. The divine vindication of Jesus is a "dangerous memory" that places God's power and priority alongside the "crucified people" of this world, spurring resistance and action. This, however, remains an eschatological promise. In fact, Jürgen Moltmann borrows from the classical account of *Christus Victor* by describing salvation as a "conquest of the deadliness of death." And yet, he updates this classical vision by attending more closely to the reality and ongoing power of death in this world and refusing to focus the primary message of the Gospel as concerning a post-mortem life: "Jesus' resurrection was not seen as a private Easter for his private Good Friday but as the beginning and source of the abolition of the universal Good Friday, of that god-forsakenness of the world which comes to light in the deadliness of the death of the cross."[51] Reading atonement as the divine vindication of the innocent Jesus is an affirmation of God's solidarity with and commitment to a justice not of this world's making. The exposure of injustice on the cross, and the vindication of those crushed by unjust power, remains, however, an eschatological hope. The alreadyness of the atonement as divine vindication is a promise, one that sends human beings outward by the same Spirit who raised Jesus into acts of mercy and justice.

If this is a faithful reading of the New Testament witness, namely that the resurrection is an act of divine vindication and the verdict of God proclaiming Jesus's innocence, and by extension showing solidarity with the victims of injustice—this still does not account for how Jesus's life, death, and resurrection prove saving to sinners. This is, of course, a central confession of scripture and the Christian faith: Jesus saves sinners. Here we should follow Schleiermacher's interpretation and note that it is not the cross and resurrection in abstraction that is saving, but these events in relation to the totality of Jesus's life and ministry. The resurrection is not a minimization of the theological import of the incarnation, ministry, and death of Jesus, but the very act by which God identifies God's own life with Jesus's. Schleiermacher insists that we not primarily locate Christ's redemption on the cross, but attribute it to the "total activity of Christ," including "his ongoing effect on the church."[52] In turning toward Jesus's ministry, we see that it is marked throughout by the proclamation of the Kingdom, meal practices that incorporate sinners, the healing of the sick, engagement with those in need—be they rich or poor, Jew or even Gentile, male or female. Moreover, Jesus is given what only God rightly has: the power to forgive. Jesus is the one who declares sinners to be righteous. The resurrection is not simply a vindication of Jesus's innocence in the face of the accusations levied by some Jewish authorities and the Roman powers, but also God's vindication of the entirety of his ministry including his proclamation of forgiveness and his claim that he came to seek and save the sick and lost. The resurrection is a divine assurance that the forgiveness offered and given by Jesus to all is, in fact, the very grace of God.

THE EXALTATION OF JESUS AS JUDGE

Through the resurrection, not only are Jesus and his ministry vindicated, but Jesus is also exalted and raised to the right hand of the one he calls Father.[53] Through God's judgment rendered on Jesus through the Spirit's raising, it is also revealed that Jesus is the One who renders proper judgment. The judge that is judged in our place by us is now the one who is exalted to judge us creating equity and justice amongst the nation. As John 5 notes, there is a connection between resurrection and judgment: "Indeed, just as the Father raises the dead and gives them life, so also the Son gives life to whomever he wishes. The Father judges no one but has given all judgment to the Son" (John 5:21–22). However, far from using this judgment as a means of retribution, Jesus is the same one who comes to Peter in John 21 in an act of reversal and forgiveness, turning Peter's three denials into three affirmations of love. Peter's sins are not ignored, but neither do they remain the final verdict. While individuals are certainly held to account for their actions, as indicated in Romans 2, human worth before God ultimately does not depend on a weighing up of the scales between good deeds and bad ones. Human worth depends alone on the divine verdict already enacted and given in God's vindication of Jesus and the exaltation of Jesus as judge of the world. Jesus is the one on the cross who prays for the forgiveness even of those who perpetrated the crime against him. Jesus also begins his ministry by announcing the need for repentance, healing sickness, challenging social status quos, battling with the powers of evil, overturning the tables in the Temple, and defying theo-political authorities. Jesus's ministry and judgment involve an accounting of individual and social wrongs, injustice, and sin. This accounting inscribes mercy through the exposure of injustice by bringing its absurdity and false claims into the light. As the author of Colossians writes, "He disarmed the rulers and authorities and made a public spectacle of them" (Col. 2:15). God's grace is revealed in judging human sin. In this sense we might be able to maintain the insight of representative and substitutionary models that wish to uphold not only mercy but also justice within God and for the world, without creating divisions within the Godhead whereby Jesus acts as the agent or model of mercy while the Father demands and upholds justice. Judgment is rendered, but it is a judgment of grace. Or as is described in Romans 8, a text altered in Reformed liturgy and used as an assurance of pardon in the prayer of confession, "Hear the good news! Who is in a position to condemn? Only Christ, and Christ died for us, Christ rose for us, Christ reigns in power for us, Christ prays for us . . . In Jesus Christ, we are forgiven." To put this in an Islamic idiom, the master of the day of judgment is none other than Jesus the Christ.

Conclusion

Not only is the move to focus on the resurrection as the primary saving event more biblically coherent and theologically persuasive, but it also offers the conceptual space for further engaging with Muslim understandings of God's vindication of the prophets and their messages, as well as the central confessions of the last judgment, the resurrection of the dead, and even the Second Coming of Jesus. The Christian account that I sketched differs in critical ways from the Islamic tradition, especially insofar as it still includes a representative account of Jesus and divine forgiveness. Jesus remains the one upon whom salvation depends. At the same time, Islam also knows of a divine mercy that overrides strict distributive justice—and a day of judgment that turns to grace. The famous Ḥadīth Qudsī has God proclaiming, "My mercy prevails over my wrath." A similar notion is present throughout the Qurʾān, whether it be in the regular recurrence of the bismillah[54] at the start of all but one Sūra, or most clearly in Sūra al-Anʿām's statement that "Your Lord has prescribed mercy for himself" (6:54). How this divine preference for mercy relates to the accompanying claim that each individual is judged according to their works and faith is not wholly resolved in the Islamic tradition, nor in the Christian for that matter. Still, Mohammad Hassan Khalil has recently argued that the Islamic tradition from al-Ghazali, Rashid

Rida, Ibn 'Arabi, and most surprisingly in Ibn Taymiyya includes a "hermeneutic leap of mercy" that sees divine forgiveness possibly extending to all, even those that refuse the message of the prophet in this life.[55] In Ibn Taymiyya's schema, at least as advanced by Khalil, the end of judgment is not hell but the overcoming of hell. While some may end up in the torments of fire, these torments that they experience will ultimately tip into salvation. The tension between an eschatological weighing up of each individual's life, the real demands for justice, and the overwhelming mercy of God remains a complex nexus for theological reflection in the Islamic tradition as well.

In the context of Muslim judgments against Christian accounts of atonement, Christian theologians find themselves in a position not wholly dissimilar to those earliest Christians. We—like them—must give some account of the meaning of the death of Jesus, a death that is so obviously atrocious, unjust, and scandalous. How can this man and his life and death be the "power of salvation to all who believe" (Rom. 1:16–17)? The addition of two thousand years of theological reflection and nearly fourteen hundred years of diatribe and insightful critique by Muslims only adds to the burden of "giving an account of the hope that is within" us (1 Peter 3:15). What justifies this hope? What grounds Christian claims? How do we know if mercy or justice prevail? We hope in the judgment of God—the same God that vindicated Jesus.

Notes

1. Abū l-Walīd al-Bājī, *"Jawāb al-qāḍi Abū l-Walīd al Bājī ilā risalah rāhib Faransā ilā al-muslimīn,"* in D. M. Dunlop, "A Christian Mission to Muslim Spain in the 11th Century," *Al-Andalus* 17 (1952): 275/299 (pages correspond to the translation and critical edition of the Arabic text). For more on this exchange, see Charles Tieszen, *Cross Veneration in the Medieval Islamic World: Christian Identity and Practice under Muslim Rule* (London: I. B. Tauris, 2017).

2. David Burrell, *Towards a Jewish-Christian-Muslim Theology* (Malden: Blackwell Publishing, 2011), Chapter 7.

3. Mona Siddiqui, *Christians, Muslims and Jesus* (New Haven: Yale University Press, 2013), 242.

4. Mark Swanson, "Folly to the Ḥunafā': The Crucifixion in Early Christian-Muslim Controversy," in *The Encounter of Eastern Christianity with Early Islam*, HCMR, vol. 4, ed. Emmanouela Grypeou et al. (Leiden: Brill 2006), 237–56.

5. Catherine Cornille, *The Im-Possibility of Interreligious Dialogue* (New York: Crossroads, 2008).

6. Seyyed Hossein Nasr, *Islamic Life and Thought* (Albany: SUNY Press, 1981), 210.

7. One comparative strategy, that draws on apologetic methods both early and modern, is to connect the death of Jesus to the Qur'ānic narrative of the near sacrifice by Abraham/Ibrahim of his eldest son. The reasons for this are threefold: First, there are longstanding tropological readings of Jesus's and Abraham's near sacrifice within the Christian interpretative tradition that can be easily drawn upon in this new context. Second, the Qur'ān dubs God's last-minute stay of execution both an act of redemption and a "great sacrifice" (37:17). Finally, the ongoing remembrance of Ibrahim's faith is seemingly enacted every year in 'Eīd al-Aḍḥa. Taken together, these would seem to lend themselves toward comparative exchange. However, this connection remains limited. For instance, there is a recurring Qur'ānic injunction that rejects any view of vicarious guilt or atonement. The sacrifice of 'Eīd al-Aḍḥā does not have a representative function of atoning death as in some practices of Yom Kippur or ancient Israelite religious practices. As such, according to Khaled Abou el Fadl in a recent fatwa on 'Eid al-Aḍḥā, "The sacrifice is not an offering to a deity, and it is not a symbolic reproduction of the atonement offered by Abraham when God instructs him not to kill his son but to slaughter a sheep instead." While broader analysis of repentance, sacrifice, and atonement might be carried out, it would need to move to a more theoretical level than the concreteness of Muslim critiques of the cross would seem to allow. https://www.searchforbeauty.org/2016/06/15/fatwa-on-the-sacrifice-of-eid-al-adha/.

8. For one account of this famous story of early Christian-Muslim dialogue, see Cornell, "The Ethiopian's Dilemma: Islam, Religious Boundaries, and the Identity of God," in Jacob Neusner, Baruch A. Levine, Bruce D. Chilton, and Vincent Cornell, *Do Jews, Christians, and Muslims Worship the Same God?* (Nashville: Abingdon Press, 2012), 85–127.

9. It should not go unnoticed that the Islamic tradition adapts longstanding anti-Jewish discourse from Christianity by employing the trope of Christ killers even as it overturns it—not, however, to negate anti-Jewish rhetoric but to recast it as a new anti-Jewish trope.

10. Todd Lawson, *The Crucifixion and the Qur'an: A Study in the History of Islamic Thought* (London: OneWorld, 2009), 2–6.

11. Ibid., 7–8.

12. Ibid., 15.

13. A. H. Mathias Zahniser, *The Mission and Death of Jesus in Islam and Christianity* (Maryknoll, N.Y.: Orbis, 2008), Chapter 3.

14. Ibn Kathīr al-Qurayshī al-Dimashqī, *Tafsīr al-Qur'ān al-'azīm*, 7 vols. (Beirut: Dar al-fikr, 1970): 2:44.

15. Fakhr dīn al-Razī, *al-Tafsīr al-kabīr* (Beruit:Dar 'Ihya al-Turath al-'Arabi, 1980) vol 11:100.

16. Mahmoud Ayoub, *A Muslim View of Christianity* (Maryknoll, N.Y.: Orbis, 2009), 170.

17. These remain a contested debate within Muslim discourse, as illustrated by a series of fatwa and counter fatwas in the earlier half of the twentieth century in Egypt that began with Shayk Shaltut's claim that Jesus had, in fact, died, although not on the cross. An Arabic copy of the fatwa can be found here: https://ar.m.wikisource.org /wiki/عيسى_نزول/514_العدد/الرسالة_مجلة (accessed Aug. 19, 2018).

18. Lawson, *The Crucifixion and the Qur'an*, 13.

19. In the long history of Christian-Muslim polemics, the cross features less prominently than other key debates around the (tri)unity of God, the incarnation and hypostatic union, and the prophethood of Muḥammad. Metaphysical questions around the in-

carnation of the divine Word, the hypostatic union, and the death of God dominate earlier Muslim critiques of the cross.

20. This is a common apologetic and polemic move and can be seen most clearly in a poem found in *ighātha al lahfān* by Ibn Qayyim al-Jawyizza.

21. Rifaat Ebied and David Thomas, eds., *The Polemical Works of 'Alī al-Ṭabarī* (Leiden: Brill, 2016), 104–5.

22. Ibid.

23. All biblical citations are taken from the New Revised Standard Version, with my own slight alterations of the Greek where noted.

24. Rifaat Ebied and David Thomas, eds., *The Polemical Works of 'Alī al-Ṭabarī*, 124–5.

25. Ibid.

26. Al-Ṭabarī does not use these precise distinctions between "fitting" and "necessary," although he challenges both assumptions. For a classic discussion of the fittingness of the incarnation and crucifixion, see Thomas Aquinas, *Summa Theologica III.1 and III*, trans. Fathers of the English Dominican Province (London: Burns Oates & Washbourne): 46.

27. Ebied and Thomas, eds., *The Polemical Works of 'Alī al-Ṭabarī*, 124–25.

28. Isma'il Ragi al-Faruqi, *Christian Ethics: A Historical Survey and Systematic Analysis of Its Dominant Ideas* (Montreal: McGill University Press, 1967), 223–24.

29. al-Faruqi, *Christian Ethics*, 224.

30. Ibid., 236.

31. Ibid., 230.

32. Ibid., 231.

33. Ibid., 230.

34. Ibid., 231.

35. Ibid.

36. Ibid.

37. Ibid., 226.

38. Ibn Taymiyya writes, "What is the correlation between the crucifixion which is one of the greatest crimes—whether Christ was actually crucified or whether it only appeared so—and between the salvation of these men from Satan?" Thomas Michel, *A Muslim Theologian's Response to Christianity* (Delman: Caravan Books, 1984), 223.

39. For instance, Rashid Riḍa claims that "Muslims do not believe that it is the prophets who, because of their sinlessness, save people from God's punishment and admit them to their standing in God's blessing. They rely but on God alone for that. They believe that salvation depends on true faith and sound action." Simon A. Wood, *Christian Criticisms, Islamic Proofs: Rashid Rida's Modernist Defense of Islam* (Oxford: One World, 2008),133.

40. Mustafa Akyol, *The Islamic Jesus: How the King of the Jews Became a Prophet of the Muslims* (London: St. Martin's Press, 2017) .

41. Friedrich Schleiermacher, *The Christian Faith*, ed. H. R. Mackintosh and J. S. Stewart, trans. D. M. Ballie et al. (London: T&T Clark, 1999), §100.3.

42. al-Faruqi, *Christian Ethics*, 233.

43. "Witness is an act of humble particularity, which is marked by a non-anxious confidence in the One in whom we place our trust, faith, and submission. The central task, then, for both Christians and Muslims, is not to defend religion or protect one's own

religious power or position, but to offer a creative and living witness to God and God's coming just rule. Such a posture of engagement is a sign of faith and trust in the security of God." For more on my approach, see Joshua Ralston, "Bearing Witness: Reframing Christian-Muslim Encounter in light of the refugee crisis," *Theology Today* (2017): 32.

44. Delores S. Williams, "Black Women's Surrogacy Experience and the Christian Notion of Redemption," in *Cross Examinations: Readings on the Meaning of the Cross*, ed. Marit Trelstad (Minneapolis: Fortress Press, 2006), 31.

45. Daniel Madigan, "People of the Word: Reading John with a Muslim," *Review and Expositor* 104 (2007): 81–95.

46. Jerusha Lamptey, *Divine Words, Female Voices: Muslima Explorations in Comparative Feminist Theology* (Oxford: Oxford University Press, 2018), chap. 5.

47. Gabriel Said Reynolds, *The Qur'an and the Bible: Text and Commentary* (New Haven: Yale University Press, 2018), 181.

48. Ingolf Dalferth, *Crucified and Resurrected: Restructuring the Grammar of Christology*, trans. Jo Bennett (Grand Rapids: Baker Academic, 2015), 79.

49. Kathryn Tanner, *Jesus, Humanity and the Trinity* (Minneapolis: Fortress Press, 2001), 15.

50. A longer project would have to engage the metaphors and metaphysical implications found in Paul and Revelation.

51. Jürgen Moltmann, *Theology of Hope*, trans. James W. Letich (Minneapolis: Fortress Press, 1993), 211.

52. Schleiermacher, §104.1, p. 451.

53. The notion of God as righteous judge pervades the Hebrew Bible. Psalm 9 speaks of God sitting "enthroned as a righteous judge" (verse 4) and ruling "the world in righteousness" through judging "the peoples with equity" (verse 8). The psalmists also regularly appeal to and for divine vindication before the people (cf. Psalm 26 or 4). The move in the early Christian hymn of Philippians 2 where Jesus is exalted into a place of power and judgment implies that he will now judge all nations as promised in the Old Testament.

54. In the name of God, the Merciful, the Compassionate.

55. Mohammad Hassan Khalil, *Islam and the Fate of Others: The Salvation Question* (London: Oxford University Press, 2012), 145.

"At One or Not At One?"

CHRISTIAN ATONEMENT IN LIGHT OF BUDDHIST PERSPECTIVES

Leo D. Lefebure

The *Oxford English Dictionary* describes the early history of the English word "atone":

> AT ONE *adv.* in its combined form as representing a simple idea, and 16th cent. pronunciation. Short for the phrase "set or make at one"; compare *to back, to forward, to right*, etc., and the compounds *at-one-maker, at-one making*, under AT ONE *adv.* Assisted by the prior existence of the verb to ONE *v.* = make one, put at one, unite, Latin *unīre*, French *unir*; whence *onement* was used already by Wyclif. From the frequent phrases "set at one" or "at onement," the combined *atonement* began to take the place of *onement* early in 16th cent., and *atone* to supplant *one* verb about 1550. *Atone* was not admitted into the Bible in 1611, though *atonement* had been in since Tyndale.[1]

Used transitively, "to atone" can mean "to set at one, bring into concord, reconcile, unite in harmony," with reference to either persons or differences; used intransitively, the word can mean "to unite, come into unity or concord."[2] The related word "atonement" came a bit later and originally meant "The condition of being *at one* with others; unity of feeling, harmony, concord, agreement," or "The action of setting at one, or condition of being set at one, after discord or strife," or in theology, "Reconciliation or restoration of friendly relations between God and sinners."[3] The word "atonement" first appears in English about 1505–15 with the meaning of "at one ment," and it has been employed and interpreted in many different ways since then.

In the original English usage, being at one was not linked to violence, suffering, sacrifice, or death. While atonement in the sense of reconciliation and harmony after conflict might appear eminently desirable, the history of Christian interpretations of atonement is troubled. Often Christian theologians have interpreted the death of Jesus on the cross as an atoning sacrifice that was in some way necessary for salvation.[4]

When Christians approach atonement in this manner, many Buddhists respond with utter amazement. D. T. Suzuki looked at an image of Jesus on the cross and worried, "The crucified Christ is a terrible sight and I cannot help associating it with the sadistic impulse of a physically affected brain."[5] Suzuki expressed his distaste for Christian language of crucifying the self as well as for the symbolism of eating the flesh of Jesus Christ and drinking his blood:

> Christians would say: This is the way to realise the idea of oneness with Christ. But non-Christians would answer: Could not the idea of oneness be realised in some other way, that is, more peacefully, more rationally, more humanly, more humanely, less militantly, and less violently?[6]

Suzuki viscerally recoiled form the image of crucifixion: "Christ hangs helpless, full of sadness on the vertically erected cross. To the Oriental mind, the sight is almost unbearable."[7] Intellectually, Suzuki grounded his objection to Christian language about crucifying the self in the traditional Buddhist rejection of the notion of a self:

> Buddhism declares that there is from the very beginning no self to crucify. To think that there is the self is the start of all errors and evils. Ignorance is at the root of all things that go wrong. As there is no self, no crucifixion is needed, no sadism is to be practiced, no shocking sight is to be displayed by the road-side.[8]

Suzuki contrasted the image of Jesus on the cross as the climax of suffering with the image of Shakyamuni "Buddha sitting under the Bodhi tree by the river Niranjana. Christ carries his suffering to the end of his earthly life whereas Buddha puts an end to it while living and afterward goes on preaching the gospel of enlightenment."[9] For Suzuki, "What is needed in Buddhism is enlightenment, neither crucifixion nor resurrection."[10]

To many Buddhists, it is very strange to believe that God somehow demands a bloody human sacrifice for atonement and reconciliation to be achieved. It is true that Buddhists have had a long, ambiguous relation to violence, and D. T. Suzuki's own relation to Japanese imperialism has been a topic of dispute.[11] Despite the ambiguities of Buddhist history, Buddhist questions coming from a very different horizon can be illuminating for Christian theologians.

It is striking that Suzuki's questions converge with concerns that many Christians have posed concerning traditional views of atonement. When I was a seminarian, I attended the defense of a doctoral dissertation in theology in which the director of the dissertation challenged the doctoral student about the atoning death of Jesus on the cross: "If this is what God does to those He loves, what does He do to those He doesn't like?" Centuries earlier, Peter Abelard speculated that if God was angry with humans for eating a piece of fruit, one would expect God to be angrier at humans for killing God's Son![12] Various forms of Christian theology and popular piety have viewed God as directly willing the death of Jesus as in some way necessary for atonement to take place. Some perspectives on atonement have appeared to inscribe the rule of violence within the will of God, demanding Jesus's crucifixion and setting dangerous precedents for situations. After surveying the history of Christian perspectives on atonement, Cynthia Crysdale, poses the question of how reconciliation of humans with God comes about:

> To the degree that the answer was "God killed Jesus as a punishment for sin in our place" divine violence began to insert itself into the doctrine. This focus on suffering as itself the agent of salvation carried much of the tradition on atonement doctrine over many centuries, not only at the theoretical level but also in practical piety, art, symbol, and literature.[13]

Viewing suffering as somehow willed by God has given rise to numerous problems and called forth vigorous critiques. If God willed the suffering of Jesus for the sake of some good, could this not be the case for other humans as well? Willie James Jennings notes that at the beginning of the African slave trade in 1440s, Gomes Eanes de Azurar (commonly known as Zurara) probed the mysterious providential will of God by inscribing the suffering of enslaved Africans in the suffering of Jesus. Zurara acknowledged the common humanity that he shared with the enslaved Africans, and he was moved to weep with pity at their sufferings, but he sought to make sense of their enslavement by relating their sufferings to Jesus and to God's inscrutable will. Jennings notes that Zurara's "question [about the meaning of suffering] seeds a problem of theodicy born out of the colonialist question bound to the colonialist project."[14] Jennings explains: "Zurara wrote a passion narrative, one that reads the gestures of slave suffering inside the suffering of the Christ. . . . Both Jesus and the slaves suffer outside the city gates. Outside the city gate for Jesus meant suffering in a place designated by the Roman state for displaying its considerable power over bodies. The parallel with the slaves is remarkable."[15] Jennings sees Zurara adopting a position as observer analogous to the evangelists recounting the suffering of Jesus. In each case, Jennings comments, "The innocent suffer the penalty of the guilty. Like Jesus, these peoples of distant lands are brought to a place where a crucifying identity, slave identity, will be forever fastened like a cross to their bodies."[16] What emerges from the juxtaposition is a justification for the slave trade. Jennings notes that from Zurara's perspective, "We, the Portuguese, will save them. They will become Christians."[17]

Womanist theologian Delores Williams challenges the surrogate suffering of Jesus in relation to the long experience of surrogacy forced upon African American women; she expresses the question of African American women "whether the image of a surrogate-God has salvific power for black women or whether this image supports and reinforces the exploitation that has accompanied their experience with surrogacy.... Can there be salvific power for black women in Christian images of oppression (for example, Jesus on the cross) meant to teach something about redemption?"[18] Williams warns that exhorting women to sacrifice themselves in imitation of Jesus can continue oppressive practices. Feminist scholars Joanne Carlson Brown and Rebecca Parker dramatically accuse traditional theologies of atonement of holding up divine child abuse as an ideal.[19] Identifying atonement with violent abuse of a victim, Brown and Parker insist, "We must do away with the atonement, this idea of a blood sin of the lamb."[20]

One of the gifts that Buddhists bring to Christians is a very different horizon of expectations and assumptions. As D. T. Suzuki noted, Buddhists do not acknowledge a permanent self, though Buddhists have differed in what this teaching means.[21] Nor do they believe in God as Creator of the universe and Redeemer of humankind. Dialogue with Buddhists can prod Christians to view our tradition with different presuppositions than the earlier tradition. Christian theology today is going through a renewed discernment and debate over the meaning of atonement and atoning action. Amid the forceful criticism of traditional theories of atonement, especially of substitutionary punishment, many Christians are looking for new ways to understand atonement. To the ongoing Christian conversation on atonement, I would like to introduce the Shin Buddhist voice of Shinran, especially as presented by Dennis Hirota of Ryukoku University in Kyoto, who led the team that translated the works of Shinran into English.[22] I would like to engage three moments in Shinran's thought: the state of being not at one: the desolation of life under the sway of the three poisons and a calculating mentality; the beginning of Shin Buddhist practice in repentance arising from Other Power; and mature *shinjin*, entrustment-mindedness and life transformed with Amida Buddha. At each point I will draw on Shinran's experience and expressions as presented by Dennis Hirota, and I will reflect on some implications for Christian theology on atonement. My colleagues in this volume, S. Mark Heim and Thierry-Marie Courau, O.P., dialogue primarily with representatives of the rich Indo-Tibetan Buddhist tradition; the voices of the Japanese tradition of Shin Buddhist provide an important contrast and counterpoint, with distinctive points of both convergence and divergence.

Not at One

Discussion of atonement presupposes an awareness of not being at one. Something is awry, a relationship needs to be healed.[23] There is a felt need for reconciliation and forgiveness. Buddhists traditionally describe human suffering as arising from the three poisons of ignorance, craving, and anger. Shinran radicalized the traditional Buddhist analysis by arguing that humans on our own cannot move toward liberation by any means, including religious practices. Shinran believed that "we are full of ignorance and blind passion. Our desires are countless, and anger, wrath, jealousy, and envy are overwhelming, arising without pause; to the very last moment of life they do not cease, or disappear, or exhaust themselves."[24] Religious practices that promise relief actually offer ample opportunity for the poisons to flourish:

> Each of us, in outward bearing,
> Makes a show of being wise, good, and dedicated;
> But so great are our greed, anger, perversity, and deceit,
> That we are filled with all forms of malice and cunning.

> Extremely difficult is it to put an end to our evil nature;
> The mind is like a venomous snake or scorpion.
> Our performance of good acts is also poisoned;
> Hence, it is called false and empty practice.[25]

Heim and Courau both shed light on how other Buddhist traditions view the human predicament. The Japanese Shin tradition is distinctive;

according to Hirota, "The core of Shinran's contribution to the history of Buddhist thought lies in his thoroughgoing problematization of the nature of the subject pursuing the Buddhist path."[26]

> Shinran goes on to radicalize traditional Pure Land thinking, pursuing its awareness of the limitations of the self into the question of whether *any* unenlightened human act or praxis can be self-purifying, or can transcend one's karmic conditionedness and advance one toward awakening. Indeed, for Shinran, the very determination of genuine good is seen as inevitably partial and prone to distortion by the stance of the ego-self.[27]

Shinran views the deepest problem of evil not primarily in moral terms but rather as a religious issue. Yoshifumi Ueda and Dennis Hirota tell us that "while the term 'evil' has moral and ethical implications in his thought, its chief significance is religious; it points to the inability to fulfill any religious practice because of the inveterate self-attachment that pervades one's acts."[28]

Shinran uses the Japanese term "*hakarai*," calculative thinking, to name the role of self-interest in distorting all actions, including religious practice. According to Shinran, *hakarai*, the process of calculation, poisons religious practice and prevents rebirth in the Pure Land: "You cannot be born into the true and real fulfilled land through such self-power calculation."[29] Humans under the sway of *hakarai* can be very clever within its domain, but they lack any accurate standard for true judgment: "Such self-awareness cannot arise through simple reflection, for the intellect alone lacks a standard by which to judge and discern its own profound ignorance and falsity."[30]

Shinran's problematization of the subject poses questions and challenges not only to Buddhist practices but to Christian ones as well. To what degree do Christian actions and reflections in relation to atonement move within the orbit of what Shinran calls *hakarai*? Catholic history features an egregious form of calculation in the sale of indulgences; Renaissance Popes viewed the treasury of merit earned by Jesus Christ as a type of bank account from which they could make endless withdrawals, if appropriately remunerated by the faithful. The crass monetization of release of souls from Purgatory prompted Martin Luther to send his famous 95 Theses to Albrecht of Brandenburg, the Archbishop of Mainz.[31] A particular challenge to a calculating mentality comes in the question that Luther cites from lay persons in thesis 82: if it is true that the Pope can release souls from Purgatory because of the merits of Christ, why doesn't he simply do it out of love for sinners without charging money? I am not aware that any Catholic apologist ever gave a satisfactory reply.

Beyond the most flagrant abuse of selling indulgences to secure entrance into heaven, questions of calculating how to pay a debt run throughout the history of Christian reflection on atonement. In his influential work, *Cur Deus Homo* (*Why God Became Human*), Anselm and his interlocutor Boso considered the perspective of many in the early church who thought the devil had certain rights over humans because of sin. The devil reportedly believed these rights gave power to put Jesus Christ to death, and so the devil overreached. Because the devil had no right to take the life of Jesus, he lost all rights to other humans. Anselm's interlocutor Boso famously rejected this traditional line of thinking, making a good scholastic distinction: while it was just for humans to be punished for sin, it was unjust for the devil to do so.[32] The devil had no rights that God was obligated to respect.

Anselm himself, however, thought that all angels and humans owe a debt to God in the sense of rendering honor to God; when humans failed to do this, they were under obligation to make satisfaction. Being unable to make satisfaction, they faced penalty. Anselm formulated the inexorable demand: *aut satisfactio aut poena* ("either satisfaction or penalty").[33] Humans have violated the honor of God through sin, incurring an infinite debt which they cannot pay. Only humans owe the debt, but only God can pay it; thus a God-human is necessary.[34] Anselm's famous argument turns on the ambiguity of the Latin word "*debeo*," which can mean "I owe" or "I ought." Anselm proposes fitting reasons for Christ to become human, but because it is hard to imagine God not doing what is fitting, there is a slippery slope from what is fitting to what is necessary.[35] By giving his life for the sake of truth and justice, Jesus gives God a gift that was not owed; it is fitting for God to give Jesus a reward, but Jesus as divine is already in possession of all perfections; the one item that Jesus desires but does not yet have is the salvation of humankind.[36] Anselm inscribes human salvation within the gift-giving of the Blessed Trinity.[37] It is a different model of *hakarai* than the theory of the early church; and the argument turns on the overflowing generosity of God; but from a Shin Buddhist perspective, it nonetheless moves within the realm of calculation.

Shin Buddhist perspectives pose the question to many traditional Christian views of atonement: Is a form of calculating appropriate for the mystery of atonement? Do we really become one with God through a calculating mentality? When I hear the words of Shinran, I am aware of the vastly different cosmology of his Buddhist tradition from my Catholic background; but I also find myself in his words. I have two frames of reference, one rooted in Christianity and the other offered by Shinran and the Shin Buddhist tradition. I hear Shinran's warning as a call to examination of conscience that resonates strongly with Jesus's warnings about the danger of religious practice designed to be calculated and seen by other humans (Mt 6:1–6, 16–18). Similar to Shinran's warning against *hakarai* and making a show of virtuous practice, Jesus tells a parable of two men who pray; the prayer of the one who calculates and boastfully compares his virtuous deeds with the failings of others is not received, while the poignant plea for mercy of the other is heard (Lk 18:9–14). Augustine famously describes the problematization of himself as subject: "*mihi quaestio factus sum.*"[38] This could be variously interpreted as becoming a question, a puzzle, a problem, an enigma, or, in the recent translation by Sarah Ruden, "an elaborate investigation to myself."[39] Like Shinran, Augustine found himself at an impasse that he could not understand or resolve. Augustine warns us that when we are in a horizon dominated by sin, even actions that may appear to be good are warped by our self-seeking and pride until we go through a radical conversion effected by divine grace; however, nothing we can possibly do can bring about this conversion.[40]

Peter Abelard famously challenged Anselm's approach, suggesting that the calculation of honor and debt is not the appropriate framework for thinking about atonement. God owes no payment to the devil, and humans could make no payment to God, and so the incarnation of God is not about paying a debt at all. Abelard views Jesus Christ's life and death as a manifestation of the love of God for humans that can elicit a free response of love apart from calculating the repayment of a debt. The motive of God's action to restore us to fellowship is love, and Jesus Christ is the ground and expression of that love.[41] According to Abelard, God acts in Christ to remove the obstacle in our hearts, and we pass from fear to love.[42]

More recently, Bernard Lonergan has described the all-enveloping power of scotosis, systematic blindness that flees from insight and leads to personal, social, and societal decline.[43] Within a horizon of systemic distortion and bias, we can make all kinds of calculations without ever finding what is true and good; our calculations reinforce our sinful condition. For Lonergan, as for the earlier Christian tradition and the Shin

Buddhist tradition, we are powerless to free ourselves through even our most brilliant calculations. One of the most helpful recent analyses is Shawn Copeland's application of Lonergan's analogue of scotosis to racism, sexism, and gender bias in the United States.[44] The analysis of scotosis calls for intellectual, moral, and religious conversion, but on our own we are powerless to do this.

Many figures in the Christian tradition have warned us that on our own apart from divine grace we cannot become at one with ourselves or with God; we are even too sick to call a doctor. Pope Francis recently cited the teaching of the Second Synod of Orange in 529: "Even the desire to be cleansed comes about in us through the outpouring and working of the Holy Spirit."[45] Similar to Shinran warning of the ambiguity of religious practices, Pope Francis quotes St. Theresa of the Child Jesus: "In the evening of this life, I shall appear before you empty-handed, for I do not ask you, Lord, to count my works. All our justices have stains in your sight."[46] Pope Francis warns us about the results of calculative thinking for Catholic life: "Once we believe that everything depends on human effort as channeled by ecclesial rules and structures, we unconsciously complicate the Gospel and become enslaved to a blueprint that leaves few openings for the working of grace."[47] As long as interreligious conversations remain within the horizon of calculating thinking, we risk reproducing the problems of the conflicted world.

The critiques of traditional Christian theologies of atonement that we heard from Suzuki, Jennings, Williams, Brown, and Parker can be understood as articulating problems relating to the application of an instrumental, calculating mentality to Christian theology. As long as thinking about atonement remains within a horizon of calculation, some kind of a bargain must be made with God or by God. All too often it has been thought that someone must suffer for the ultimate good to be obtained.

Becoming at One Through Other Power

Because Shinran insists that humans are completely powerless to escape the rule of the three poisons, he places his entire hope and confidence in Primal Vow of Amida Buddha. Heim and Courau survey other Buddhist approaches to awakening; Shin Buddhists recall that the great bodhisattva Dharmakara performed eons and eons of meritorious action for the sake of liberating all beings and has become Amida Buddha. On the Pure Land Buddhist path, the calculating mind faces a crisis as intellectual and moral efforts reach a point of collapse, but this experience can open us to the compassion of Amida Buddha. This conversion or turnabout is completely impossible from our own resources within any horizon of calculation, and yet it happens because Amida Buddha made the Eighteenth Vow that all beings saying his Name would be born in the Pure Land.[48] Shinran entrusts himself to the Primal Vow of Amida in what he calls *shinjin*; this entrustment is not his autonomous action but rather the working of the compassionate Vow of Amida in him. Shinran tells us the calculating mind cannot grasp this:

> Other Power is entrusting ourselves to the Primal Vow and our birth becoming firmly settled; hence it is altogether without one's own working. Thus, on the one hand, you should not be anxious that Tathagata will not receive you because you do wrong. A foolish being is by nature possessed of blind passions, so you must recognize yourself as a being of karmic evil. On the other hand, you should not think that you deserve to attain birth because you are good. You cannot be born into the true and real fulfilled land through such self-power calculation.[49]

Shinjin is "true, real, and sincere heart and mind," referring to the heart-mind given by Amida Buddha; Shin Buddhists distinguish two aspects of shinjin: "first, it is the act of entrusting oneself to Amida by virtue of the Primal Vow; and second, it is the true and real mind and heart of Amida Buddha. . . . Since this entrusting is all due to true compassion, no room is found for any kind of willful calculation or self-assertion."[50] The classic expression of shinjin is saying the Name, or the nembutsu: *Namu Amida Butsu*: "I take refuge in Amida Buddha." Shinran promises that "saying the Name breaks through all the ignorance of sentient beings and fulfills all their aspirations. Saying the Name is the right act, supreme, true, and excellent."[51] Shinran found this to be the one efficacious practice for him.

Hirota explains that "in Shinran's teaching, practice is accomplished and given by the Buddha, and the practicer is free of instrumental thinking."[52] Amida's Vow offers not only an example or a lure, but also "actively moves toward them. It becomes the source of beings' aspiration for and movement toward the transcendent, and further is identified with the inconceivable goal itself."[53] This dynamic turnaround from impossible impasse to hope resonates with the Apostle Paul who describes the dilemmas created by sin but promises that where sin abounded, grace abounded all the more (Rom 5:20). Coming from a very different cosmology and anthropology than Shinran, Augustine in his debate with Pelagius insisted that divine grace is not only an external example or invitation or lure, but also an internal movement of the will and is the divine goal. For Augustine, good thoughts must precede good actions, but any good we do is the working of God's grace.[54]

Hirota describes the shift in the Pure Land practitioner "as a movement from an interpretation of action in terms of an individual, substantial self and of objective means and goals to a new conception or interpretation of action, one in which attachment to such a self and such goals is constantly undercut by fresh awareness of the self's interrelation with the world of beings, the ocean of all life."[55] In the initial or provisional stage of Pure Land practice, Amida appears as personal to the practitioner. Hirota distinguishes two aspects or dimensions in this transformation: one is teleological and horizontal while the other is interpersonal and vertical.

> The teleological mode—based on the aspiration and will of beings to accord with the good and true that, exceeding their present state, can heal and fulfill their existence by transforming them into itself—develops in the teaching in terms of a dualism between this world and the Pure Land. The interpersonal mode—based on the revelation of the transcendent to us in human terms, making possible both relation to it and movement toward it—develops in terms of a dualism of self and Buddha.[56]

The teleological trajectory maps the horizontal movement from the present world of suffering to the Pure Land; the interpersonal trajectory names the vertical manifestation/appearance of saving grace from a power higher than ourselves. Hirota explains:

> In the initial phase, a person's movement toward the transcendent as goal (Pure Land) is understood to be embraced within a larger teleology (Dharmakara becoming Amida), giving rise to a conception of an interpersonal relationship. Both the teleological and interpersonal images of the transcendent tend to be framed in terms of will and the temporal dimension of its unfolding: self-will to reach the Pure Land through placing oneself in accord with Amida (by reliance, awareness, religious acts, or moral conduct) and Amida's will to save all sentient beings by bringing them to his pure Land.[57]

The terms "teleological" and "interpersonal" have a long history in Christian thought, and Christians can, to a large degree, resonate with

Hirota's description and apply it analogously within a very different context to the Christian path of moving horizontally from sin to the teleological goal of grace; for Christians this movement is made possible because of the vertical, interpersonal relationship with the infinite incomprehensible God manifested in the Person of Jesus Christ. Through both teleological and interpersonal movements, Christians move from estrangement toward being at one with God in Jesus Christ.

We saw that Suzuki challenged the image of Jesus on the cross as the product of sadism, and Jennings and Williams related the historical abuse of this image to racial oppression. For many African American Christians, the crucifixion represents a sadism that resonates deeply with their experience of being lynched. However, the sadism came not from God but from earthly oppressors, whether the Romans or the slave-masters or, more generally, white racists. Karen Baker-Fletcher comments, "God does not *cause* Jesus' death, because God is good. Evil, which is God's adversary, causes Jesus's death. . . . Accompanied by the risen Christ, in the power of the Holy Spirit, men, women, and children are to overcome suffering and evil."[58] She proposes a theology of accompaniment: "Christ as cosufferer accompanies us through our pain and suffering to help us overcome it and to help us live into resurrected life in the power of the Holy Spirit."[59] In a very different cosmological context, Amida Buddha is graciously present to suffering humans through his gracious Vow. Elizabeth Johnson, after critiquing Anselm and other earlier theologies of atonement, proposes a theology of accompaniment that finds salvation in the divine promise to be present: "Redemption comes to mean the presence of God walking with the world through its traumas and travail, even unto death."[60] She finds a double solidarity "of the actual Jesus with all who live, suffer and die, and of the resurrecting God of life with the ministering and crucified Jesus. The two solidarities are actually one as the story takes place."[61]

Hirota notes that various challenges arise in the initial, provisional phase. Some Pure Land practitioners tended to objectify the Vow of Amida; some interpreted the rejection of self-power to exclude any actions toward good in this world; some focused attention only on the Vow's working at the precise moment of one's death.[62] In the initial stage of Pure Land practice, self-power and other-power appear as distinct and opposing activities. If everything depends on the working of Amida's Vow, questions arise concerning what beginning practitioners should actually do in this world. Should they cultivate aspiration for birth in the Pure

Land, or would that be a form of calculating self-power? Should they simply accept the traditional Pure Land teaching, or would that be too me-
chanical? Japanese Shin Buddhists debated these issues very vigorously,
with accusations flying in multiple directions. Hirota describes the Shin
Buddhist controversy known as the "turmoil over religious acts" in the
late eighteenth and early nineteenth centuries in Japan. One prominent
leader, Chido (1736–1805), was arrested, carried to trial in a cage, condemned as a heterodox, and died of an illness while still confined.[63]

Hirota's description of the fierce inner-Shin Buddhist conflicts resonates strongly with Christian debates over grace and free will, which also
involved bitter disputes over what God does and what, if anything,
humans contribute, with endless accusations of heresy flying in many directions. In Christian history, it was not only Protestants and Catholics
who fought with each other over these issues; there were internal divisions within each major communion as well. For example, in Catholic
history after the Reformation, the Dominicans emphasized that divine
grace was all important against the Jesuits who insisted on the role of free
human action as well. Over the course of many years, there were countless disputes until Pope Paul V in 1607 finally ordered both religious
orders under obedience to stop accusing the other of heresy and to wait
for a future papal resolution, which has never appeared! But even this did
not completely stop the controversy. Whether in the Shin Buddhist or
the Christian tradition, as long as we view self-power and other-power
as opposites, challenges continue to arise, which can become full-blown
polemics. We are not yet fully at one with ultimate reality or ourselves.

At One: Shinjin and Jinen in Mature Integrated Practice

Continuing practice on the path of Shin Buddhism leads to transformation of the dualisms of the initial phase. Hirota tells us that in mature,
integrated practice both the teleological dichotomy between this world
and the Pure Land and the interpersonal dichotomy between self and
Amida Buddha are "in some sense overcome, though not eliminated."[64]
Shinjin is the overcoming of duality between self and Other Power:

> When one is free of self-power (the self-centered working of one's intel-
> lect and will to achieve enlightenment), this freedom of one's own heart
> and mind from self-power is itself Other Power. In other words, Other
> Power is the Buddha's power that has become one's own as shinjin. It is

the power of the heart and mind of the person in whom self-power falls away and disappears as oneness with the Buddha's mind is realized.[65]

Shinran describes this as happening through *jinen*, and he explains the components of this word: "*Ji* means 'of itself'—not through the practicer's calculation. It signifies being made so. *Nen* means 'to be made so'—it is not through the practicer's calculation; it is through the working of the Tathagata's Vow."[66] In *jinen*, we become one with Amida Buddha: "Amida loses his character as active subject separate from ourselves (he gives us his sincere mind as a transformation of self)."[67] *Jinen* is both the working of the Vow and also "a term for the ultimate reality of Buddhism, expressing suchness, or things-as-they-are, free from the bondage of birth-and-death. *Jinen* thus signifies that which is beyond form and time and beyond the domain of human intellect and will."[68]

According to Hirota, one of Shinran's major contributions is his articulation of Buddhist existence in which the perspectives of both the teleological and interpersonal dimensions are "integrated in a polarity in which their dualisms are both negated and affirmed."[69] In one sense, the practitioner is still in this world of suffering and is not in the Pure Land; the practitioner is at every moment filled with delusions and is not in any way an enlightened Buddha. Yet in the working of the Vow of Amida, in *jinen*, the practitioner is also beyond any distinctions between this world and the Pure Land or between the unenlightened self and the Buddha. Hirota sees this path as avoiding both monism and theism, with the result that "Shinran develops a perception of present life as the locus of ongoing transformation (presencing of reality in the midst of samsaric existence) that occurs 'of itself' (*jinen*) and that eventually unfolds in full awakening to true reality (which is itself termed '*jinen*')."[70] Shinran writes: "When we entrust ourselves to the Tathagata's Primal Vow, we, who are like bits of tile and pebbles, are turned into gold. Peddlers and hunters, who are like stones and tiles and pebbles, are grasped and never abandoned by the Tathagata's light. Know that this comes about solely through true shinjin."[71] This description resonates with Paul, who wrote to the community in Corinth: "But we have this treasure in clay jars, so that it may be made clear that this extraordinary power belongs to God and does not come from us" (2 Cor 4:7).

The compassion of Amida is directed precisely to fools who in one sense remain fools their entire lives but who become one with Amida; Jesus calls disciples who repeatedly fail to understand him and are described as being "of little faith" (Mt 8:26; 14:31), and to them he entrusts the reign of God. Jesus notes that healthy persons do not need a physician; sick people do (Mk 2:17). Jesus compares the coming of God's rule to the growth of seed: "The kingdom of God is as if someone would scatter seed on the ground, and would sleep and rise night and day, and the seed would sprout and grow, he does not know how. The earth produces of itself, first the stalk, then the head, then the full grain in the head" (Mk 4:26–27). The Greek word translated "of itself" is *automate*, an adjective that is used here as an adverb, a word "used of things that happen without visible cause," here suggesting an unknown divine power producing the growth.[72]

Shinran promises that the transformation worked by Amida takes place in an instant and assures the practitioner of non-retrogression.[73] The transformation is irreversible; it is not, however, total and final, as Hirota cautions: "Although birth is settled, the stance of egocentricity, of attachment and aversion, is not eradicated; thus, impulses towards self-magnifying appropriation of the Vow may arise. Shinran was aware of such feelings in himself."[74] Ueda and Hirota explain the shift: "One sees the self, not with the desperation of one clinging to what must inevitably be lost—what is from the beginning delusive—but with compassion that knows and wisdom that transcends the self."[75]

In light of this development, Hirota reframes the discussion of self-power and other-power: In the initial stage, self-power is "a person's own exertion of effort and will to attain the world of enlightenment (the Pure Land) and other-power [small "o"] denotes the power and working of Amida's Vow, which was undertaken to establish the Pure Land and enable all beings to enter it."[76] Hirota distinguishes between other-power spelled with a small "o," which means "the understanding of the Vow's working as relative to self-power," and Other-Power with a capital "O," which refers to the Vow "as apprehended where self-power has been abandoned in the mature phase of engagement."[77] The distinction between self and other collapses in mature practice. Amida and the practitioner are one and yet not one, identical and yet distinct.

While Catholic theology has often made sophisticated, scholastic distinctions among various dimensions of divine grace and human activity, to pose questions about quantitative contributions of God and humans can be misleading and risks falling into what Shinran called *hakarai*. While their cosmological context is very different from Shinran, Christian theologians describe an analogous process in which Christians are called to become perfectly one with Christ, overcoming duality without ending distinction. At the Last Supper in the gospel of John, Jesus prays to God the Father that his followers "may all be one. As you, Father, are in me and I am in you, may they also be in us. . . . The glory that you have given me I have given them, so that they may be one, as we are one, I in them and you in me, that they may become completely one" (Jn 17:21a, 22–23a). Shin Buddhists become one with Amida by reciting the Name in the Nembutsu; Jesus relates oneness or "atonement" with his disciples to the revelation of the divine name, as he prays to the Father: "I made your name known to them, and I will make it known, so that the love with which you loved me may be in them, and I in them" (Jn 17:26). The Johannine Jesus describes himself as the vine and his followers as the branches (Jn 15:5). The Matthean Jesus promises that the pure in heart will see God (Mt 5:8), and the First Letter of John promises that "when he [Christ] is revealed, we will be like him, for we will see him as he is" (1 Jn 3:2). When the young Saul (Paul) encounters Jesus on the road to Damascus, he hears, "Saul, Saul, why do you persecute me?" (Acts 9:4). Jesus, though ascended into heaven, identifies with his followers whom Saul is persecuting. Paul writes that it is no longer he who lives but Christ who lives in him (Gal 2:20), and he urges the Philippians: "Let the same mind be in you that was in Christ Jesus" (Phil 2:5).

Irenaeus of Lyons and many other early church writers affirm that Jesus, the Word of God became human so humans could become divine.[78] Eastern Christian traditions have long emphasized that the goal of Christian practice is *theosis*, deification, often represented the rays of light of the Transfiguration of Jesus on Mount Tabor. In Catholic sacramental theology, communicants celebrating the Eucharist are transformed into the mystical Body of Christ and become one with Christ. Augustine exhorted his congregation about the Eucharist: "Just as this, when you eat and drink it, becomes part of yourselves, so also you are changed into the body of Christ when you obey the commandments and lead a pious life."[79] As the communicants become one mystical body, the indwelling of the Holy Spirit empowers their actions so that they are performed jointly by the Holy Spirit and the human actor.

We have seen that for Shin Buddhists, the opposition between the practitioner and Amida Buddha is overcome in the Nembutsu. In the ascent of Moses into the cloud atop Mount Sinai, Dionysius the Areopagite finds the prototype for the Christian mystic coming to be at one with God. He describes the state of Moses on the mountain as "here, be-

ing neither oneself nor someone else, one is supremely united by a completely unknowing inactivity of all knowledge, and knows beyond the
mind by knowing nothing."[80] To interpret the puzzling language of
Christian mystics, Bernard McGinn's advises us:

> One thing that all Christian mystics have agreed on is that the experi-
> ence [of God] in itself defies conceptualization and verbalization, in part
> or in whole. Hence, it can only be presented indirectly, partially, by a se-
> ries of verbal strategies in which language is used not so much informa-
> tionally as transformationally, that is, not to convey a content but to assist
> the hearer or reader to hope for or to achieve the same consciousness.[81]

In different ways in each tradition, atonement occurs in the collapse
of the teleological and interpersonal dichotomies, and yet in each tradition distinctions reappear. Hirota describes two poles in mature practice;
"a negative one, in which the dualisms of the two modes of apprehension as they had been construed in the initial phase are dissolved, and a
positive one, in which they are newly established."[82] Christians become
the Body of Christ, but they also remain what medieval Catholic theology called *viatores*, wayfarers or pilgrims. In the respective traditions
there is an identity with Jesus Christ or Amida Buddha and a movement
toward perfect love or compassion, but in this world we are always on
the way. In both traditions, the transformation of life leads to compassion and concern for others. Shin Buddhists describe the return to the
world of suffering. Christians experience transformation in Jesus Christ
as sending them to serve others. It is in the process of becoming at one,
of being transformed and sharing this transformation with others, that
Shin Buddhists and Christians can walk the path together.

Notes

1. *Oxford English Dictionary*, "Atone," https://www.oed-com.proxy.library.georgetown
.edu/view/Entry/12596?.
2. *Oxford English Dictionary*, "Atone."
3. *Oxford English Dictionary*, "Atonement," https://www.oed-com.proxy.library.georgetown
.edu/view/Entry/12599?redirectedFrom=atonement#eid.
4. Martin Hengel, *The Atonement: The Origins of the Doctrine in the New Testament*,
trans. John Bowden (Philadelphia: Fortress Press, 1981); for a survey of views on
atonement, see Ben Pugh, *Atonement Theories: A Way through the Maze* (Eugene,
Ore.: Cascade Books, 2014).
5. Daisetsu Teitaro Suzuki, *Mysticism Christian and Buddhist* (London: Unwin Paperbacks,
1988), 99.

6. Suzuki, *Mysticism*, 100.

7. Suzuki, *Mysticism*, 97.

8. Suzuki, *Mysticism*, 99.

9. Suzuki, *Mysticism*, 97.

10. Suzuki, *Mysticism*, 96.

11. Kemmyo Taira Sato, "D. T. Suzuki and the Question of War," *Eastern Buddhist* 39/1 (2008): 61–120; Kiyohide Kirita, "D. T. Suzuki on Society and the State," in *Rude Awakenings: Zen, the Kyoto School, and the Question of Nationalism*, ed. James W. Heisig and John W. Maraldo (Honolulu: University of Hawai'i Press, 1995), 52–74; Christopher Ives, *Imperial-Way Zen: Ichikawa Hakugen's Critique and Lingering Questions for Zen Ethics* (Honolulu: University of Hawai'i Press, 2008); Brian Victoria, *Zen at War* (Lanham, Md.: Rowman & Littlefield, 2006); Michael K. Jerryson and Mark Juergensmeyer, eds., *Buddhist Warfare* (Oxford: Oxford University Press, 2010).

12. Peter Abelard, *Commentary on the Epistle to the Romans*, trans. Steven R. Cartwright (Washington, DC: Catholic University of America Press, 2011), 166.

13. Cynthia S.W. Crysdale, *Transformed Lives: Making Sense of Atonement for Today* (New York: Seabury Books, 2016), 132.

14. Willie James Jennings, *The Christian Imagination: Theology and the Origins of Race* (New Haven: Yale University Press, 2010), 18.

15. Jennings, *Christian Imagination*, 20.

16. Jennings, *Christian Imagination*, 20.

17. Jennings, *Christian Imagination*, 22.

18. Delores S. Williams, *Sisters in the Wilderness: The Challenge of Womanist God-Talk* (Maryknoll, N.Y.: Orbis Books, 2001), 162.

19. Joanne Carlson Brown and Rebecca Parker, "For God So Loved," in *Christianity, Patriarchy, and Abuse: A Feminist Critique*, ed. Joanne Carlson Brown and Carole R. Bohn (New York: Pilgrim, 1989), 1–30; see also Brown, "Divine Child Abuse,?" *Daughters of Sarah* 18 (1992): 24–28.

20. Brown and Parker, "For God So Loved," 26.

21. Steven Collins, *Selfless Persons: Imagery and Thought in Theravada Buddhism* (Cambridge, UK: Cambridge University Press, 1982).

22. Shinran, *The Collected Works of Shinran*, Vol. I: *The Writings*, Vol. II: *Introductions, Glossaries, and Reading Aids*, trans. Dennis Hirota, Hisao Inagaki, Michio Tokunaga, and Ryushin Uryuzu (Kyoto: Jodo Shinshu Hongwanji-ha, 1997) [henceforth *CWS*].

23. For a variety of different approaches to atonement as reconciliation, see Brandon Lundy, Akanmy Adebayo, and Sherrill Hayes, eds., *Atone: Religion, Conflict, and Reconciliation*, edited by Brandon D. Lundy, Akanmu G. Adebayo, and Sherrill W. Hayes (Lanham, Md.: Lexington Books, 2018).

24. Shinran, *Notes on Once-Calling and Many-Calling*, in *CWS*, 488.

25. Shinran, *Gutoku's Hymns of Lament and Reflection*, 95–96, *CWS* 1:421.

26. Dennis Hirota, "The World of Revelation and Engagement in Shinran," 1; https://docs .google.com/a/georgetown.edu/viewer?a=v&pid=sites&srcid=ZGVmYXVsdGRvbWWF pbnxzaGluY2hyaXNoaWFuXR5aXNsYW18Z3g6Mzk1ZDk2NzcxZDZlNWQzNQ.

27. Hirota, "World of Revelation," 2.

28. Yoshifumi Ueda and Dennis Hirota, *Shinran: An Introduction to His Thought* (Kyoto: Hongwanji International Center, 1989), 154.

29. Ueda and Hirota, *Shinran*, 220, 222.

30. Ueda and Hirota, *Shinran*, 163.

31. Martin E. Marty, *October 31, 1517: Martin Luther and the Day that Changed the World* (Brewster, Mass.: Paraclete Press, 2016).

32. Anselm of Canterbury, *Why God Became Man* 1.7, in *The Major Works*, ed. Brian Davies and G. R. Evans (Oxford: Oxford University Press, 2008), 272–74.

33. Anselm, *Why God Became Man* 1.11, 283–87.

34. Anselm, *Why God Became Man* 2.6, 320.

35. Anselm, *Why God Became Man* 2.16, 338–43.

36. Anselm, *Why God Became Man* 2.18–19, 348–54.

37. Anselm, *Why God Became Man* 2.20, 354.

38. Augustine, *Confessions* 4.4.9, repeated at 10.33.50, trans. Henry Chadwick (Oxford: Oxford University Press, 1992), 57, 208.

39. Sarah Ruden translates: "I became my own elaborate investigation, and I grilled my soul as to why it was sad, and why it threw me into such terrible distress, but it didn't have any answer for me." Augustine, *Confessions*, trans. Sarah Ruden (New York: Modern Library, 2017), 83.

40. Augustine, *The City of God against the Pagans*, ed. and trans. R. W. Dyson (Cambridge, UK: Cambridge University Press, 1998), 19.25; see T. H. Irwin, "Splendid Vices: Augustine for and against Pagan Virtues," *Medieval Philosophy and Theology* 8/2 (1999): 106.

41. Abelard, *Commentary on Romans*, 162–64.

42. Abelard, *Commentary on Romans*, 168.

43. Bernard J. F. Lonergan, *Insight: A Study of Human Understanding*, Collected Works of Bernard Lonergan 3, ed. Frederick E. Crowe and Robert M. Doran (Toronto: University of Toronto Press, 1997), 214–15, 259.

44. M. Shawn Copeland, *Enfleshing Freedom: Body, Race, and Being* (Minneapolis: Fortress Press, 2010).

45. Second Council of Orange, Canon 4, cited by Pope Francis, *Gaudete et Exsultate: On the Call to Holiness in Today's World* 53, http://w2.vatican.va/content/francesco/en/apost_exhortations/documents/papa-francesco_esortazione-ap_20180319_gaudete-et-exsultate.htmll.

46. Theresa of the Child Jesus, "Act of Offering to Merciful Love" (Prayers 6); cited by Pope Francis, *Gaudete et Exsultate* 54.

47. Pope Francis, *Gaudete et Exsultate*, 59.

48. *The Land of Bliss: The Paradise of the Buddha of Measureless Light: Sanskrit and Chinese Versions of the Sukhavativyuha Sutras*, intro. and trans. Luis O. Gomez (Honolulu: University of Hawai'i Press, 1996), 71.

49. Shinran, "Response to an Inquiry from the Nembutsu People of Kasama," *CWS* 1:525–26.

50. *CWS* II, *Introductions, Glossaries, and Reading Aids*, 206, 107.

51. Shinran, *The True Teaching, Practice, and Realization of the Pure Land Way, CWS* 1:17.

52. Dennis Hirota, Introduction to *Toward a Contemporary Understanding of Pure Land Buddhism: Creating a Shin Buddhist Theology in a Religiously Plural World*, 7.

53. Dennis Hirota, "Images of Reality in the Shin Buddhist Path: A Hermeneutical Approach," in *Toward a Contemporary Understanding of Pure Land Buddhism: Creating*

a Shin Buddhist Theology in a Religiously Plural World (Albany: SUNY Press, 2000), 40.

54. Augustine, *On the Free Choice of the Will, On Grace and Free Choice, and Other Writings*, ed. and trans. Peter King (Cambridge, UK: Cambridge University Press, 2010), 7.16; 8.20.

55. Hirota, "Dialogic Engagement and Truth," in *Toward a Contemporary Understanding*.

56. Hirota, "Religious Images of Reality," in *Toward a Contemporary Understanding*, 41.

57. Hirota, "Religious Images of Reality," in *Toward a Contemporary Understanding*, 53.

58. Karen Baker-Fletcher, *Dancing with God: The Trinity from a Womanist Perspective* (St. Louis: Chalice Press, 2006), 137.

59. Baker-Fletcher, *Dancing with God*, 143.

60. Elizabeth A. Johnson, *Creation and the Cross: The Mercy of God for a Planet in Peril* (Maryknoll, N.Y.: Orbis Books, 2018), 106.

61. Johnson, *Creation and the Cross*, 106.

62. Hirota, "Images of Reality," in *Toward a Contemporary Understanding*, 53.

63. Hirota, Introduction to *Toward a Contemporary Understanding*, 10–12.

64. Hirota, "Images of Reality," in *Toward a Contemporary Understanding*, 41.

65. *CWS* 2:207.

66. Shinran, "On *Jinen Honi*," *CWS* 1:427.

67. Hirota, "Images of Reality," in *Toward a Contemporary Understanding*, 59.

68. *CWS* 2:191.

69. Hirota, "Images of Reality," in *Toward a Contemporary Understanding*, 41.

70. Hirota, "Images of Reality," in *Toward a Contemporary Understanding*, 42.

71. Shinran, *Notes on "Essentials of Faith Alone*," *CWS* 1:459–60.

72. John R. Donahue and Daniel J. Harrington, *The Gospel of Mark*, Sacra Pagina Series (Collegeville, Minn.: Liturgical Press, 2002), Vol. 2, 151.

73. *CWS* 2:196.

74. Hirota, "Images of Reality," in *Toward a Contemporary Understanding*, 63.

75. Ueda and Hirota, *Shinran*, 165.

76. Hirota, "Images of Reality," in *Toward a Contemporary Understanding*, 46.

77. Hirota, "Images of Reality," in *Toward a Contemporary Understanding*, 46.

78. Irenaeus of Lyons, *Adversus Haereses*, Book 5, Preface, *Against the Heresies*, Ancient Christian Writers, 3 vols., trans. Dominic J. Unger, John J. Dillon, Matthew Steenberg, and Michael Slusser (New York: Paulist Press, 1992, 2012, 2012).

79. Augustine, *Selected Easter Sermons of Saint Augustine*, introduction, notes, and commentary by Philip T. Weller (St. Louis and London: B. Herder Book Co., 1959), 113.

80. Pseudo-Dionysius the Areopagite, *The Mystical Theology* 1.3, in *Pseudo-Dionysius: The Complete Works*, trans. Colm Luibheid (New York: Paulist Press, 1987), 137.

81. Bernard McGinn, *The Foundations of Mysticism*, vol. I of *The Presence of God: A History of Western Christian Mysticism* (New York: Crossroad, 1991), xvii.

82. Hirota, "Images of Reality," in *Toward a Contemporary Understanding*, 56.

How Empty Is the Cross?

REALIZATION AND NOVELTY
IN ATONEMENT

S. Mark Heim

This essay suggests some ways a theology of the cross can be enriched through a comparative study of the Bodhisattva path and the Christ/disciple path.[1] The Buddhism engaged is a Tibetan-inflected strand of the wider *Mahāyāna* tradition. I center my consideration on an issue that arises with equal force in the center of systematic theological thought and at the heart of Christian spirituality and practice: To what extent are the cross and Christ's redemptive suffering in it paradigmatic? At the systematic end of the theological spectrum, this issue is often debated in terms of the cross as exemplary of divine reality itself. An example would be the discussion about God's suffering, carried on in recent times around Jurgen Moltmann's *The Crucified God*.[2] At the pastoral and cultural end of the theological spectrum, the question relates to the exemplary role of the cross for individuals, and the toxic psychological, spiritual, and social effects that may flow from idealized human conformity to Jesus's suffering.[3] Conversation with Buddhist sources casts these issues into even sharper profile, suggests new perspectives, and supports the theological project of integrating the cross appropriately within the entire work of incarnation and redemption.

My study explores sympathetic or generous Buddhist readings of the cross and their emphasis on a dimension of nondual realization in it. It also reflects on the persisting reservations these same interpreters express, relating to the non-exemplary or novelty features of Jesus's death. I have tried to draw some theological wisdom from both aspects. These points are summarized under three different meanings of "emptiness." The first two relate to central and "salvific" aspects of emptiness in Buddhist understanding. The third relates to a more prosaic sense, in which emptiness represents absence or deficiency. Regarding the first meaning of emptiness, I outline an understanding of "creaturely no-self" guided by Buddhist no-self teaching, in which the cross represents an exemplary realization of this analytical emptiness. On the second count, in reflection on *Mahāyāna* views of Buddha nature and of emptiness as a liberating fullness, I describe a view of divine immanence whose exemplification must be sought in the wider incarnation beyond the cross. And third, I consider emptiness in the sense of the non-exemplary features of the cross and their positive significance for Christian life and thought.

Buddhist Views of the Cross

The cross and the bodhisattva way have a similar focus, an orientation "for others." Christ died for all. The bodhisattva vows to attain enlightenment for the sake of all sentient beings. In both cases, it is a matter not of normal altruism or concern simply amplified in degree but of a radical recasting of the basis for this care. In both cases, these statements are foundational (rooted in the New Testament texts on the one hand and *Mahāyāna* sutras on the other) and yet also on their face expressive of tensions posed in the foundational sources. How can mercy and justice be resolved in the divine salvific act? How can wisdom and compassion coexist? Each preserves and resolves tensions within a wider system, not just an abstract system of thought, but a structure of devotion and practice. As Joseph O'Leary says so succinctly: "If many of the paradoxes of Christianity center on Jesus Christ, who is both true [human] and true God, those of Buddhism often center on the bodhisattvas, in whom *samsaric* and *nirvanic* existence are conjoined."[4]

Christ is a historical and salvific singular event, constitutive of salvation and the believer's practice, but not fully repeatable by the disciple. Bodhisattvas are plural and their path lies open to others to duplicate in its entirety. The second are exhaustively exemplary and replicable in a way that the first is not. Most Buddhist commentators over time have highlighted this as a negative contrast. Jesus's life and, above all, his death, plainly lack the marks of the highest levels of spiritual attainment. The story suffers from an elemental flaw, demonstrated by Christ's disjunctive relationship with God as well as the spiritual agitation and concrete suffering of his death. One author who had reviewed Buddhist comment on Christianity over the last four hundred years, noted that writers often summarized Christian teaching on the cross with little comment or criticism, as though its absurdity were self-evident to anyone: "The message is heard and summarized as a strange story of an angry and unpredictable God who is swayed by his emotions and who is not able to love without seeing blood and suffering."[5]

Buddhist interpreters who take a positive attitude toward Christ and the cross discern there what others had found lacking. Thich Nhat Hanh, for instance, views the cross as representative of an inner, spiritual attitude that realizes no-self.[6] Because each of the things that are not grasped at by Jesus—equality with God, biological life, political status, an independent self—are empty, the focus should be on Jesus's insight in seeing through them and letting them go. A sympathetic Buddhist reading of the cross does not treat it as an event in a historical or personal plot line. It sees it as emblematic of wisdom, a meditative achievement. Jesus's "sacrifice" is an outward sign of an inward disposition, the realization of emptiness. Jesus does not cling to individual existence because Jesus has none and knows it.

On this understanding, death on a cross stands for recognition of something that is always true. Crucifixion marks the death of externally imposed identities and, even more profoundly, of the falsely projected substantial self.[7] Zhang Chunyi, a Chinese scholar who became first Christian and then Buddhist, adopted a program of "Buddhicizing Christianity." He summarized the meaning of the cross under three headings.[8] In the first, more superficial sense, he suggested, it illustrated the kind of altruistic act aspirant bodhisattvas perform. In a second, more profound sense, it illustrated the physical body as a source of suffering.[9] Thich Nhat Hanh, for instance, emphasizes the cross as an instruction in impermanence, its pain a wakeup call to draw us to search for deliverance. Jesus's forgiving spirit can be seen as an instance of the bodhisattva perfection of forbearance.[10] At the highest level, according to Zhang, Jesus's death represented elimination of the defilements attached to an imagined self.[11] The main point is that the "sacrifice" is only apparent. Jesus is not giving up anything as a human being, nor setting aside anything as divine. Masao Abe reads the kenosis of Jesus similarly, as denoting something that is always and everywhere the case, a "single or *nondual function* of self-emptying or self-negation."[12]

Even the most generous Buddhist readings of the cross preserve a lingering and cogent reservation. Is the form of the gospel about Christ, and most especially his passion, really adequate to the truth Buddhists would hope to find in it? The cross is a problematic sign for the spiritual ultimacy of emptiness. Thich Nat Hanh gently puts it this way:

This is a very painful image for me. It does not convey joy or peace, and this does not do justice to Jesus. I hope that our Christian friends will also portray Jesus in other ways, like sitting in the lotus position or doing walking meditation. Doing so will allow us to feel peace and joy penetrating into our hearts when we contemplate Jesus. That is my suggestion.[13]

This reservation points to an absence, to what is not represented in the cross, but might be found at least partially elsewhere. As Seiichi Yagi said in a classic essay on Buddhist interpretation of Christ, the primary point is that "the unconditional given of our existence is that God is with each one of us . . . This is comparable to the fundamental notion of *Mahāyāna* Buddhism that every living thing has a 'Buddha-nature.'"[14] If one is to credit realization of such a nondual identity to Jesus, it would be more apt to look to Jesus "I" statements, especially in the Gospel of John— statements such as "I and the father are one" (John 10:30) or "I am the way, the truth and the life" (John 14:6).[15] Yagi and many Buddhist interpreters take these statements to refer to an identity realization, analogous to the shift in the use of "I" by the bodhisattva from reference to a conditioned particular self to reference to a universal Buddha nature.

Thich Nat Hanh sought an image whose contemplation evokes the state of attainment to which the image is meant to refer. In Buddhism, this state is an experiential nondualism where the disciple follows the model into an unalloyed condition of peace. The bodhisattva is an exemplary figure, representing both the ideal seeker and the fully realized Buddha. The image of the Buddha under the Bodhi tree is a picture of everyone's future, both proximate and final. It directly represents the immediate path to take toward enlightenment and at the same time represents that enlightenment itself. This is so because the fundamental dynamic addressed is that between form and emptiness, the conventional world and the wisdom world. The Dalai Lama explains the coincidence of these two realities this way: "These two truths are like the two sides of a coin. When you look from one side, you see the dependent arising . . . When you look from the other side, you see the emptiness of the phenomenon."[16] Both are absolutely constant in their character, equally available at all times. So they are best represented in terms of simultaneous presence.

But Christ is both exemplary and not exemplary. There are ways in which Jesus is what every Christian wants to be or should be, and ways in which Jesus is not. The image of Jesus on the cross is not a picture of everyone's future. This is Jesus's death. It is factually different from most others, and far from ideal. There are certain aspirations to be "just like Jesus" that Christians will treat as systematically misguided, signs of mental illness or spiritual deformation. But to become part of the body of Christ, to be a "little Christ," to be one with Christ, are all authentic aspirations of disciples.

These differences have to do with the novelty and reconciliation aspects of atonement. I will return to them in our final section. Here I want to recognize that Christians have, in fact, invariably attempted to draw universal and exemplary models from the cross—to take it as a guide to what is always and everywhere so for the believer or God—and are often bedeviled by drawing mistaken ones. Similarly, in seeking to express the uniqueness of Jesus's death, we sometimes insist upon it in a more categorical form than is required (even for the "highest" forms of Christology) for want of some important distinctions.[17] In both respects, I believe we can be instructed by Buddhist teaching to formulate the realization dimension in the cross in a way that brings its own benefit to Christian life, as well as giving greater clarity to Christian thought. This bears particularly on an understanding of the three Christian "registers" of nonduality: apophaticism, immanence, and communion.[18] The first two of these resonate significantly with Buddhist no-self and Buddha nature, respectively, and to these we turn now.

Emptiness Embodied: Creaturely No-Self and the Cross

To be a creature is, by definition, to lack *svabhāva*, the self-existence Buddhist teaching denies to any entity. Athanasius wrote that God granted humanity a share of the divine image, "seeing that by the principle of its [humanity's] own coming into being it would not be able to endure eternally."[19] Creatures are precisely those that do not have existence from their own power or will, those whose continued existence is not in their control. What is more than impermanent in them is loaned from God, not an intrinsic possession.[20] Human life is conditioned on a set of proximate causes and materials that are themselves, likewise, impermanent and not-self existent. This looks like chapter and verse from the Buddhist teaching of dependent co-origination. Karl Barth states it no less emphatically. Humans are not to be regarded as "self-grounded, self-based, self-constituted and self-maintained."[21] Humanity "without God is not; [and] has neither being nor existence."[22]

Barth, famously, has his own vision of "nothingness" as that whose only existence was that it was what God had not chosen. The human effort to make such nothingness actual constituted evil.[23] The sinful is an offshoot of the unreal. But we may say that the positive emptiness that God did choose for all of nature, the emptiness of own-existence, is part and parcel of what it means to be a creature, and of the goodness of being a creature. It is this positive face that Thomas Merton took up on his path into dialogue with Buddhism.[24] Merton summarizes what he found in Barth that resonated so powerfully with his Buddhist exploration: "The great joke is this: having a self that is to be taken seriously, that is to be proved, free, right, logical, consistent, beautiful, successful and in a word 'not absurd'."[25] Merton is deeply moved by Barth's recognition that "the self before God is not *serious*, it is *groundless*. It is not something that exists in its own density and solidity: the self before God is poised on the divine word, the divine communication over an unfathomable abyss."[26] Barth's profound sense of divine freedom and gratuitous election in Christ fosters a frank acceptance of the emptiness and insubstantiality of any projected self. It is not only human religion that Barth so readily questions, but also the presumed selves that pose the problems our constructed religions are to solve. In fact, the two go together.

Christians can acknowledge the Buddhist no-self teaching in what I would call "creaturely no-self." What should Christians expect to find "there" in the direct meditative attention to our individually contained mental contents? Buddhist analysis tells us we will find sensation, succession, distraction, emotion, intention . . . but no permanent self-existent thing doing the experiencing. I see no Christian reason that a creature contemplating itself as a creature would find anything else as the content of immediate awareness.[27]

For Christians, this lack of essential autonomous being is easily and rapidly conflated with something quite distinct, the breaking off from what *is* possible and hoped for: sharing in the divine life and in communion with other creatures. Sin and emptiness are not the same thing, but they can quickly run together. Broken relation and lost communion are something to be remedied, a locus for reconciliation. But pure creatureliness itself is fundamentally good, and so must be the (recovered) realization of it.

This condition of captivity to a world of our own making, which we then further assume is the one true world, is a generative disposition the theological tradition calls original sin. Buddhism holds that ordinary people are born with "mental obscurations carried over from previous lives" and then compound these with "speculative obscurations" acquired in the course of their lives.[28] What Christians call sinners are creatures who have forgotten they are no-thing (in the *svabhāva* sense), whose desires are distorted because their relations are broken. Buddhism calls this state ignorance, a condition that will never allow us to flourish until it is corrected. We could put it another way and say that the condition of original sin we just described is the disposition of taking nothing for something. And the prime example of that nothing taken for something is exactly what Buddhism is speaking of, the no-self taken for a permanent and essential self.

Christianity and Buddhism are in marked agreement on the negative implications of this evasion of no-self. Our failure to accept our own impermanence is a cause of much suffering and evil. Both agree there is value in practices that disrupt the presumed objectivity of the unreal selves we project, whether the disruption comes through confession and repentance or mental analysis. Cultivation and relaxation into this authentic dimension of our creaturely nature offers a positive blessing.

In incarnational terms, for God to assume the nature of a creature is to share the fundamental character of creatures we have been discussing, their lack of any essential self. For Christ to be truly a human being is to be empty of such existence, as all creatures are. Because there is also an apophatic dimension, a dimension of self-emptying, within God's own Trinitarian life, this realization of the emptiness of intrinsic human being at the same time mirrors an emptiness that is proper to God's own character. It is a manifestation of the divine kenosis to take on the creaturely no-self, two overlapping emptinesses. If the incarnation is "creaturehood done right," then Jesus does not cancel this fundamental fact but realizes its great positive potential in the selfless way he lives his life and in the way he gives it up. Jesus gives up his bodily existence, his social world, and even his religious connections altogether. He apparently loses everything that pertains to a self-sustaining creature. Both his life and his death recapitulate what it is to live in the emptiness that belongs to that human nature.

The field of creaturely emptiness is an area of truth and practice where Buddhists got there first and have gone deepest. The emptiness insight enhances Christian awareness of ourselves as creatures. Meditative experience of this simple emptiness has great restorative and constructive value because it cuts through so much that causes inner and outer distress.

There are manifest goods that come from the capacity to accept the momentary emptiness of phenomena. Simply to note the successive variation of our sensations and fleeting thoughts is to loosen the grasp of an assumed, substantial self as the ruling cause or threatened subject of those sensations, for instance. We perceive "that is anger talking," "that is the expression of a false assumption," in a freeing detachment.

This is particularly true, I believe, in dealing with physical pain. From the point of view of the sufferer, Christian responses tend to focus on alleviating the causes of pain, whenever possible, and, in any case, on building a framework of meaning, a network of interpersonal and spiritual support. No-self meditation offers a distinct way to address moment-by-moment bodily suffering. First, mindfulness of this sort diminishes superadded pain. To whatever physical pain is experienced, the focus on substantive selves can gratuitously project even more, adding fear and anxiety about suffering I imagine in the future to that I experience now. Second, it offers concrete bodily relaxation and feedback practices that mitigate the generation of physical pain. These practices today are increasingly detached from Buddhist settings and presented in a purely medical setting. They are also those for which it is easiest to find direct Christian correlatives in forms of repetitive, contemplative prayer. Third, for more extensive practice, this meditation further diminishes the felt or "received" pain, both by weakening our identification with the self that registers the pain and by disaggregating that pain into its smallest, momentary sensory phenomena.[29]

The primary interest of creaturely no-self for our current discussion is that it names a manner in which the cross is exemplary of a universal realization. In the Christian struggle to disentangle the destructive from the liberating in "loss of self," this provides one bright line. With laser-like clarity, we can channel the maximal stress on an exemplary loss of self to the place where it is always fruitful and in order: the place where there never was a self to begin with. This allows us to distinguish more clearly the dimension of the cross that is relational and constitutive in the person-making sphere, but not exemplary in the same manner.

Emptiness Beyond the Cross: Theosis, Bare Awareness, and Buddha Nature

When Buddhists speak of no-self, that which has no inherent existence, they are speaking in a key Christians most readily identify with creatures and the apophatic register of nonduality. When Buddhists speak of Buddha nature as unconditioned and unborn, that which has always been, they are speaking in a key Christians identify with God. In this section we consider an identity realization related to that teaching, bearing on divine immanence.

Christian theology, particularly in its Eastern Orthodox traditions, has developed an understanding of divine immanence as the sharing of the divine energies. There is an incommunicable dimension to the divine life in which God remains unknowable even while in relation. Creatures cannot become the same as God. But what Orthodox theology calls the divine energies are communicable aspects of the divine life. They are the borrowed life of God, supplying what creatures alone cannot. Such uncreated energies are particularly signified by light.[30] The biblical representation of these energies usually takes nonpersonal form, as in the fire of the burning bush, tongues of fire at Pentecost, or the glow surrounding a transfigured Christ.[31] Such energies suffuse all things, particularly all animate things: "All things are permeated and maintained in being by the uncreated energies of God, and so all things are a theophany that mediates his presence. At the heart of each thing is its inner principle or *logos*, implanted within it by the Creator Logos; and so through the *logoi* we enter into communion with the Logos."[32] This vision of the divine energies is simply a realization of what is always present, a removal of obstacles in our sight. As a blade of grass may be thought to have Buddha nature, so it may be thought to be alive with the glory of God.

The uncreated energies are a universal immanence of God in all nature, a universal participation of all nature in God. As such, they constitute a nondual identity. All creation, sentient or not, carries this charge of the divine presence. When shared with creatures that lack subjectivity, such presence might be called vitality or creativity.[33] For creatures with deeper subjectivity the divine energies undergird persons and relations of love, in line with those in the Trinitarian life. They enhance and deepen the relational qualities of persons. So, the light of the nondual energies may be represented in an icon or painting as a halo or mandorla around Christ or other figures. Humans who enter into I-Thou communion with God retain their finite nature as creatures, but they become part of the mutual love in the divine life.[34] Thus, the sharing of the divine life is an unrestricted reality for all creation, but it takes on a distinctive communion dimension for those who are themselves persons. For our purposes, I want to focus on the pre-personal aspect.

The overarching understanding of salvation here is *theosis* or "divinization." We become "by grace (that is to say, in the divine energies), all that God is by nature, save only identity of nature . . ."[35] The saved are "enlightened ones" who have realized the fullness of the divine image that is the watermark of their own being. "Enlightened" here means suffused with divine power or glory. This may be the closest parallel to Buddha nature we can frame: an underlying presence that is of a piece with our own existence. Yet, in the Christian telling, it is a participation, not an exclusive identity.[36]

No-self meditative attainments are rooted in the true emptiness of the creature. Similarly, I believe that Buddha nature meditative attainments point us to the energies of the divine immanence. In all parts of creation, including the less sentient parts, this has the quality of an impersonal glory, which manifests in health or constancy. In more sentient creatures, this underlying presence of divine energies may be only rarely the content of explicit consciousness. It stands to our active mental life somewhat as do the kinds of sensitivity that exist in mental or physical processes below the plane of conscious thought, such as the implicit sense of location in space or an unconscious registering of internal bodily conditions. It may "break out" in spontaneous moments of mystical awareness, but it is not a common experience apart from great meditative focus.

If we think of the immanence of the divine energies from the divine side, we can imagine it as an analogous non-discursive awareness in which the divine mind has an immediate apprehension of the universe from within. At this level, God's perception would be a "view from everywhere," reflecting God's implicit presence in all of creation, a consciousness with no active separated subject (just as our non-conscious modes of awareness need have no explicit subject), but one permeated with beneficence and peace. This is a mode of God's presence in and to the world. A receptive sentient mind can commune with this indwelling as a form of "bare awareness," which is always available underneath the business of communicative consciousness. One can tune in to the carrier wave of divine presence on the frequency of mind, a form of immanent divine energy. We become aware of divine awareness as it genuinely exists, as a dimension inside all that is.

Apophatic nondual experience suspends our false sense of self and gives direct experience of the contingency of our own mental processes, our creaturely no-self. Immanent nondual experience accesses the changeless, limitless qualities of the indwelling divine energies. Buddha nature is what divine immanence looks like in the general field of consciousness. It is a participation in the nonpersonal mind of God, whose quality is the same in all beings at this level, a kind of background radiation of the divine presence. Just as the velocities and trajectories of bodies in space allow us imaginatively to "run the tape" of the universe backwards toward its origin, so this signature immanence has a qualitative vector imparted at its source, an impetus toward creativity and well-being. This is reflected in the marks ("luminous," "vast," "compassion-inducing") attributed to Buddha nature.

We are well aware of types of experience that are not communicative, that involve profound self-forgetfulness through unity with a wider process. Play, sexual ecstasy, athletic absorption, becoming "lost" in nature, attentive perception in making or contemplating art—these are all instances of intense awareness without either contrasting identity or conscious communication. Such states glimpse a divine bare awareness, a wider, luminous, non-personal mind. We experience our distinctive consciousness as continuous or one with this luminous and open presence.

The most characteristic correlative to such nondual awareness, of either the apophatic or immanent types, is not words but silence: the literal silence of stilled voices and quiet minds.[37] Speech can only be a limping sign of such oneness. The communicative speaker-hearer distinction implicitly violates the nondual unity the language may seek to describe. This is less so for personal and communion dimensions of oneness: speech participates to a deeper extent in what it represents, since it is also a medium for establishing and expressing this kind of unity. Critics of such unitive mysticism are mistaken when they suggest that nondual realization itself is outside legitimate Christian spirituality. The realizations of emptiness (creaturely no-self) and immanence (participation in the divine energy) are valid parts of Christian spiritual practice. They have no specific Christian cognitive markers because they have no immediate markers at all.

To look at Jesus through these no-self and immanent awareness lenses is to see something fresh. The identity realization of creaturely no-self is an at-one-ment, God's identification with what is always the case of creatures. We see how the cross is an enactment of this, a transforming instance of relinquishing what is never truly there. This constancy is expressed outwardly as a movement of renunciation, a move away from self-generated objects of desire. The human realization of bare immanence awareness is also an at-one-ment, a human identification with a divine presence that is always the case. It is about uncovering and intensifying energies that are never absent. For images exemplifying this, we should look to the transfiguration and to the resurrection.

Jesus was one with God in these two respects by a nondual realization that is open to all to achieve in the same way. When Christians think about the "ontological" identity of God and Jesus, they do not usually approach it this way, but there is much to recommend such a perspective.[38] In an existential manner, Jesus realized humanity in the image of God, in both the apophatic (related to no-self) and positive (related to Buddha nature) aspects. Any other person who does this does so in the same qualitative manner, leaving behind what constitutes distinctive identity. Buddhists who attained enlightenment were already doing so prior to Jesus.

In these respects, Jesus realized a kind of liberation by recognition (i.e., this is already our nature and this is already God's presence with us).[39] This is Christ at the most bodhisattva-like. The greatness of this oneness with God is precisely its non-uniqueness. Jesus is divine in underlying immanence nature in exactly the same sense that all creatures are, and his realization of that identity is qualitatively the same as any other's realization. Such positive awareness, being without concepts or location, is an identity consciousness no different in Jesus than in anyone else. The divine energies indwell us at a level below cognitive mind and personal interaction, as they indwell all of nature. That presence, a bare "taste of water" awareness, deserves the term "primordial," which Buddhists give it. This dimension of identity with God is not limited to humans. It extends in some proportionate way to all sentient beings and to all of nature. This is a very important point, for it enriches our Christian understanding of God's presence in the natural world. Incarnation is God's participation in humanity and history, but no less in all of nature.

When we consider Christ in light of bodhisattva teaching, we focus on the realization of timeless states: no-self and Buddha nature. We saw that the specific image of the cross or crucifixion works much more effectively in the first case than the second. In regard to the no-self, Jesus's acceptance of death represents the timeless truth of creaturely emptiness and mirrors the emptiness of the divine life. A bare awareness of divine immanence likewise mirrors the positive indwelling of the divine persons in each other. But the cross is not a privileged or sufficient exhibition of that identity. For this we need the transfiguration or the bodily resurrection, the kind of events and images that Thich Nat Hanh sought, which correspond to the full spectrum of a recapitulation view of incarnation such as Athanasius pictures.

Nondual identity with no-self or with the divine energies are rightly facets of Christian spiritual life. They are disciplines of practicing what is already true. In this respect, unitive prayer or meditation are prayer-realization practices that seek God in the specific dimensions in which God's presence can be said to be literally changeless. In the long-running theological battle about what remains intact in humanity after the rupture of our relations with God, neighbor, and nature, I suggest that these two remain: the emptiness of our creaturely selves and the immanence of divine energies. They endure intact because they remain God's work, the continuing activity of creating and sustaining our nature, even while sin and ignorance cloud our access to them.

We might say that within the prayer practice that fulfills Jesus's teaching that we must lose our selves to find ourselves, these are two concrete movements that correspond in greatest purity to the losing. Buddhist wisdom uncovers the fact that rather than simply a painful subtraction preliminary to a subsequent gain, this emptiness is itself already full of blessing. States that we view as the threatening outcomes of following Jesus's injunction—lost control of our identity, phenomenological emptiness—are revealed in Buddhist practice to have a liberative effect in their own right. They not only clear space in which better relations can grow, but they are themselves already a recovered unity with God.

Emptiness of the Cross: Novel and Non-Exemplary

Christian nonduality comes in three primary flavors: apophatic, immanent, and communion. We have so far addressed the first two. No-self, Buddha nature, and *nirvāna* are three distinct terms, but Buddhist analysis powerfully explains how these point to one undifferentiated reality under different names. We cannot say the same thing of creaturely no-self, divine immanence, and communion. Though the first two may be experienced as almost indistinguishable, they differ in that the first is based on the contingent emptiness granted by the creator and the second on the sharing of divine life with the creator. The third, communion, is not only qualitatively different in principle from the first two, but unique in each particular case (whether we are speaking of the communion of two divine persons in the Trinity, two persons with each other, or a creature with God). Reflecting all of these dimensions, Christ is by no means a pure or exclusive vehicle for any one of them. It is this composite character that accounts for Christ's problematic character in Buddhist eyes.

Buddhists may expect nothing finally to be the case but the nondual consciousness of a Buddha, realization of the absolute in immediate experience or knowledge. It appears that for Christians participation in the absolute will always be mediated profoundly by relations, as well as by apophatic and immanent unity. There will always be more than can be comprehended by/in creatures, even as they share in that "more" by their participation in the divine life and the life of other creatures. The purity and coherence in the character of *nirvāna* stand in contrast to the pluralism and composite character in Christian salvation. Human encounters and communion with God come in numberless flavors and qualities. Such novelty and variety persist as a constitutive dimension of the Christian vision of salvation.

This points to another meaning of "emptiness," the deficient or non-exemplary character of the cross. The features that make it an insufficient sign of realization in the Buddhist sense are central to its saving significance in a Christian one. There is an unavoidable element of *wrong* in this event: injustice, cruelty, pain, and abandonment. Buddhist focus turns typically to what is always and everywhere the case, while a Christian focus turns typically to the relational, historical, and social. The bodhisattva's way is emblematic in a sense that the event of the cross is not, hence the "onceness" of the cross and the manyness of bodhisattvas. If everyone's nature were an identical Christ nature and if the cross were a necessary part of that nature's realization, as the bodhisattva path is necessary in every case for the realization of Buddha nature, this would be a nightmare, not a redemption. Replication of Jesus's way would mean replication of the injustice associated with it. Something crucial is lost if we miss the wrongness of the cross, its force precisely for dismantling what it illustrates. The cross is an extreme and decisive event, not the final condition it makes possible. Only the love that animates it is the desired constant.

In comparison to the bodhisattva way, the cross is non-exemplary in three particular ways. First, suffering is unbecoming or inconsistent to attribute to a bodhisattva in that immunity to suffering is the heart of the bodhisattva's realization. One who has truly seen to the bottom of no-self has cut the cord of ignorance, and suffering has no purchase. The fact that Jesus undergoes brute physical pain, personal anguish, and anxiety suggests he lacks this attainment. Buddhists who wish to elevate Jesus's stature are reluctant to credit his suffering as real.

The second failing is that the plan of redemption lacks the appropriate Buddhist grammar of universal identity realization. There is a novelty and contingent quality to the cross that mirrors a wider truth. There is no single path for the Christian aspirant. We cannot say, for instance, that the contemplative approach to God is the final and the necessary path for all, in preference to that of action, or of community or of devotion. A variety of "vehicles" exist even within salvation as well as on the path toward it. The distinctiveness of Jesus's life and person may go beyond that of others, but it reflects the distinctiveness that belongs to each person. Our lives are not identical to any others, as Jesus's life is not identical to ours. It is important that there are some ways in which we are fully, interchangeably one with each other. Creaturely no-self and bare immanence are two such ways whose significance we have been exploring. But that is not the whole story.

The cross is non-exemplary in a third way: It is a social event and not a consciousness event alone. It is cautionary. It illustrates something that is actively wrong as well as models what is right. The wrong it points to is a problem not only with bodies or minds, but also with relations. It represents something among us as much as or more than it represents something inside us. It represents a negative experience, focused on a social world. For Christians, the interpersonal social bonds are themselves the stuff of communion and heaven. Reconciliation in the social world is of a piece with salvation, no less than nondual consciousness.

Crucifixion exposes not only the open wound of the suffering self but also the open wound of the broken community. It is important in Buddhist teaching that the Buddha shared the disease he overcame, extinguishing ignorance and suffering in his own mind. There can be no remedy that is not administered within the deluded perception that must be healed. This is sound from the perspective that the root problem is to be found in mind. But the determinative biblical assumption is that the root problem is found at the social location where our selves intersect, where interpersonal sin is expressed and unevenly borne, as much as in the depths of consciousness. And the crucial position in that nexus is the place of the victim. The key point of the cross as a historical event has to do with what can be seen, and done, only from that location.

In the crucifixion, we are seeing another meaning of no-self entirely: the one who is made into a non-self by the activities of others, by humiliation, abuse, and abandonment. The objects of such persecution are typically quite literally invisible, forgotten, unregistered. Jesus on the cross may exemplify the universal truth of creaturely no-self, and its inner realization. But at the same time, he enacts solidarity with those who are crushed and cast out. The reality of the suffering Jesus activates the interpersonal exchanging of self and other, most particularly with those in the situation of the lost and rejected. Bodhisattvas are a numberless multitude who become one in compassion for the crowd of all beings. Jesus stands in the place where all the crowd focuses its hatred on one being. The cross is a disruptive image, disruptive to the essentialist individual self, and disruptive, too, to the social structures in which victims stay invisible nonentities.

Wonhee Anne Joh, a Korean feminist theologian, expresses this perspective, in which "annihilation of the self" supports a spirituality of resistance and transformation when understood

> as a call to practice emptying out of self so that I might better let a multiplicity of selves into my being in the world. Such emptying out and letting in gives birth to a "co-arising" of many selves in relation with, to and for one another. The annihilation of self then is a call to practice a kind of way of being in the world whose arch is bent toward the other.[40]

In this sense, Jesus's death is about change in what Buddhism regards as a world of projection and convention, but what Christians regard as part and parcel of the kingdom of God. It is an unfinished story, lifting up the visibility of victims and signaling God's disruption of the way the world practices political reconciliation.

The wrongness of Jesus's death is a key part of its significance. The cross is a measure of what is to be changed at the same time it is an event effecting change. The redemptive event of the cross involves God's engagement with the very bad thing that killed Jesus: human scapegoating violence. This tendency to produce victims is what God is freeing us from, "not by overpowering it through an even greater violence, but by graciously 'absorbing' our violence and subverting it from within."[41] If Christian interpretation of the atonement were more univocal on this non-violent logic, the general Buddhist appraisal of it might be different.

To identify with Christ is to identify with those in the victim's place in history, and to build a different kind of history. The resurrection of the crucified one has a significance as the "perfection" of Christ for continuing relation and interaction with creatures. It is a re-arising of Christ's person for continued life within the process whose terms (person-relation) are precisely those within which Buddhism says the problems of suffering cannot be solved. Bodhisattvas liberate beings from a conventional, samsaric realm that itself remains always a theater of suffering. The vision of a new heaven and a new earth is one in which new ways of seeing go hand in hand with changes in the world that is seen. Christ's death and resurrection are not simply about the fate of individuals. Christian theology sees these as cosmic in their scope. Death is not only a biological event but also a pervasive power, and resurrection is not only raised bodies but the instigation of a new heaven and a new earth. To put it in Buddhist terms, it is all of *samsāra* that is to be raised, all of creation to be drawn forward into new and deeper relation.

God encounters us as a particular other and empowers our encounters with one another as creatures precisely to call forth individuals, particularities, and the love that runs across them. God's action not only induces realization of the timeless identities that already obtain. It intends, attracts, and stimulates the quality Duns Scotus named "haecceity," a unique character and calling for different types of creature and, to an increasing extent in the sentient realm, for each individual.[42]

This relational fertility is manifest in person-formation, which Buddhist analysis views as subsumed in the self-arising that is entirely conventional in significance.[43] But such formation manifests a novelty that is inextricable from salvation: the interactions through which people develop their distinctive vocational skills and joys, including their relations with particular persons and dimensions of creation. Becoming a parent, an artist, a skilled craftsperson, a friend—-all these create actual persons in the specific (this child, this craft, this friend). Such emergent additions to the world are part of the divine intention, elements in the world's current and final goodness. What Buddhists regard as the conventional, karmic world exists in the Christian view as the vehicle for this positive purpose.

The Christian view of salvation does not see religious fulfillment as the vanishing point of difference. Diversity is a feature of realization as much as of aspiration. Multiplicity of perspective is part of fulfillment, constitutive of its richness and fullness. Different creatures and the variety of gifts and relations that go with them are as integral to salvation as they are to the path to it.

There is a personal oneness that is an achievement of shared purpose and will, exemplified in the way Jesus and God relate to each other in love. There is also communion oneness, in which the two indwell each other. The value of these types of oneness is bound up with their distinctive textures. Identity oneness is marked by perfect replication, but these kinds of oneness are marked by a rich variety. Jesus is divine in the "hypostatic" or personal union with the divine nature in a manner that is empirically and vocationally unlike anyone else, a sole savior. Others who realize these same dimensions of oneness with God will do so in manners that are also qualitatively and vocationally distinct from his. They share most deeply in Christ's unity with God in these dimensions through a communion with Christ that includes the specificity of their own persons.

When Christians confess Christ to be fully human and fully divine, they are invoking oneness across all the dimensions we have just discussed. There is a nondual identity, as there is a personal unity and a communion oneness. This outlook requires a pluralism in Christian expression, somewhat parallel to skillful means in Buddhism. Here the variety has not so much to do with fitting the teaching to the level of the hearer (that is an important, but distinct question) as it does with expressing these coordinate dimensions. For instance, the personal oneness between Jesus and God involves mutuality and agreement. This is not an ontological condition, but a relational achievement ("not my will but yours be done"). The communion oneness between Jesus and God involves the ability for each to speak or act in the place of the other ("you have heard it said . . . but I say to you"). In these cases, the oneness is relational and not purely nondual in nature.

Conclusion

We can all be what the Buddha is: emptiness and Buddha nature. This universality is the avenue for Christian learning from Buddhism. It is true that none of us belongs to the karmic stream that produced the historical Buddha of this age. We cannot be *who* the Buddha is, in that sense. But that is actually an empty category in any case because in Buddhist perspective such identities relate only to the conditioned world. Our being Buddha is in no way different from any other "one" being Buddha. There is a profound equality and symmetry in that.

We can all become Buddhas, but we cannot all be Christ. We cannot be *who* Christ is. We can share in who Christ is by participation, as we can share all of what Christ is, in that participatory mode. But we cannot be the same one that Christ is. God, by Christian belief, is already three equally good but not identical ways of being. Creatures can become entirely good and entirely happy while still being distinct from each other. There is more than one way to be ultimate, and more than one way to be perfected, because different ones make up the perfection and the good. There is another profound equality and symmetry in that.

In this essay we have seen enriching ways to understand the cross in line with Buddhist wisdom, in terms of creaturely no-self and immanent awareness. We have seen as well that the cross has an enduring significance of another sort, as an intervention in the "conventional" world, for the purpose of transforming that world as a whole and incorporating it finally in an eschatological realized community. The cross in its concreteness is not a model to be replicated, not exemplary for disciples in that respect. Its uniqueness is exemplary of novelty itself as constituent of salvation. We conform to it by avoiding its strict repetition, and by sharing what we each distinctively may become.

Notes

1. It draws on a larger study focused on Śāntideva's work, the *Bodhicaryāvatāra*. See S. Mark Heim, *Crucified Wisdom: Christ and the Bodhisattva in Theological Reflection*, Comparative Theology: Thinking Across Traditions, ed. Loye Ashton and John Thatamanil (New York: Fordham University Press 2018).

2. Jürgen Moltmann, *The Crucified God: The Cross of Christ as the Foundation and Criticism of Christian Theology*, trans. R. A. Wilson and John Bowden (New York: Harper & Row, 1974).

3. As described for instance in Rita Nakashima Brock and Rebecca Ann Parker, *Proverbs of Ashes: Violence, Redemptive Suffering, and the Search for What Saves Us* (Boston: Beacon Press, 2001).

4. Joseph Stephen O'Leary, *Buddhist Nonduality, Paschal Paradox: A Christian Commentary on the Teaching of Vimalakirti* (Leuven: Peeters Publishers, 2017), 17.

5. Notto R. Thelle, "What Do I as a Christian Expect Buddhists to Discover in Jesus?" in *Buddhist Perceptions of Jesus*, ed. Perry Schmidt-Leukel (St. Ottilien EOS-Verlag St. Ottilien, 2001), 146.

6. Thich Naht Hanh, https://www.lionsroar.com/the-fullness-of-emptiness/.On the altar in his hermitage, he reports placing images of both Buddha and Jesus as his spiritual ancestors, *Living Buddha, Living Christ* (New York: Riverhead Books, 1995), 6.

7. For a very thorough exploration of this, see John P. Keenan, *The Emptied Christ of Philippians: Mahāyāna Meditations* (Eugene, Ore.: Wipf & Stock, 2015).

8. Pan-Chiu Lai and Yuen-tai So, "Mahāyāna Interpretation of Christianity: A Case Study of Zhang Chunyi (1871–1955)," *Buddhist-Christian Studies*, no. 27 (2007), 77.

9. A related Buddhist insight would view the cross in terms of the *dukka nanas*. Buddhist texts acknowledge that undertaking the bodhisattva path initially increases suffering.

It does so by making us acutely aware of the true unsatisfactory nature of things and by encouraging us to adopt others' suffering as our own. Both steps may result in difficult stages or experiences, a "dark night" on the way toward enlightenment. These *dukka nanas*, whether times of bodily pain or psychological anguish during meditation, are mapped out to help meditators anticipate and overcome them. Christ's passion can be seen in this light, emblematic of a heightened suffering brought about by heightened insight. See Chapter 3 in Peter Feldmeier, *Christianity Looks East: Comparing the Spiritualities of John of the Cross and Buddhaghosa* (New York: Paulist Press, 2006).

10. These thoughts came from Thich Nhat Hanh's own intensive experience of meditating on a crucifixion image. Thich Nhat Hanh, "Suffering Can Teach Us," http://plumvillage .org/transcriptions/suffering-can-teach-us/.

11. These views are consistent with allegorical or practical spiritual applications of the cross (seeing it as modeling the overcoming of bodily desires for instance) that are widespread in Christian tradition. In this connection, see early Christian use of Plato's observation that humans are "fixed to the body by desire as by a nail" (Donald Senior, *Why The Cross? Reframing New Testament Theology* [Nashville: Abingdon Press, 2014], 7).

12. John B. Cobb, Christopher Ives, and Masao Abe, *The Emptying God: A Buddhist-Jewish-Christian Conversation* (Maryknoll, N.Y.: Orbis Books, 1990), 13.

13. Thich Nhat Hanh, *Going Home: Jesus and Buddha as Brothers* (New York: Riverhead Books, 1999), 46–47.

14. Seiichi Yagi, "'I' in the Words of Jesus," in *The Myth of Christian Uniqueness: Toward a Pluralistic Theology of Religions*, ed. John Hick and Paul F. Knitter (Maryknoll, N.Y.: Orbis Books, 1987), 128.

15. Yagi associates such "spiritually presumptuous" statements by Jesus with those of famous Buddhist figures like Dogen. See Seiichi Yagi and Leonard J. Swidler, *A Bridge to Buddhist-Christian Dialogue* (New York: Paulist Press, 1990), 57.

16. Tenzin Gyatso, "The Practices of Bodhisattvas," in *The Christ and the Bodhisattva*, ed. Donald S. Lopez, Jr., and Steven C. Rockefeller (Albany: SUNY Press, 1987), 218.

17. For instance, the uniqueness of Jesus's death does not require the suffering of the human Jesus to be qualitatively different from that of others. And Jesus's death includes similarity and overlap with kinds of moral and religious attainment that may be present in others—whether moral exemplars or spiritual renunciates—as I am arguing in this paper with specific reference to bodhisattvas.

18. This is my own formulation of material that has been laid out to slightly different effect in David Loy, *Nonduality: A Study in Comparative Philosophy* (Atlantic Highlands, N.J.: Humanities Press, 1997).

19. Athanasius, *On the Incarnation of the Word*, trans. and ed. John Behr (Yonkers, N.Y.: St. Vladimir's Seminary Press, 2012), 52.

20. Though there is no space to develop this here, I argue that a trinitarian God, eternally "co-arising" and coinherent, is not an example of the proscribed *svabhāva* nature.

21. Karl Barth, *Church Dogmatics*, Volume III, Part 2, trans. Thomas F. Torrance, ed. Geoffrey William Bromiley (London, New York: T. & T. Clark International, 2004), 345.

22. Ibid.

23. See Leo Lefebure's fine discussion of Augustine and Buddhist emptiness in Leo D. Lefebure, *The Buddha and the Christ: Explorations in Buddhist and Christian Dialogue*, Faith Meets Faith Series (Maryknoll, N.Y.: Orbis Books, 1993).

24. See Thomas Merton, *Conjectures of a Guilty Bystander* (Garden City, N.Y.: Doubleday, 1966).

25. These are entries from Merton's private journal for June 22, 1966, quoted in Rowan Williams, "Not Being Serious: Thomas Merton and Karl Barth," in *A Silent Action. Engagements with Thomas Merton* (Louisville: Fons Vitae, 2011).

26. This is Williams's summary statement of Merton's text. Ibid.

27. One area where the question is asked is in the monastic dialogue between Buddhists and Christians, and the similarities in contemplative experience described there would seem to support this perspective. See Donald W. Mitchell and James Wiseman, *The Gethsemani Encounter: A Dialogue on the Spiritual Life by Buddhist and Christian Monastics* (New York: Continuum, 1997).

28. See Alan Wallace's note in mtsho Bstan 'dzin rgya and B. Alan Wallace, *Transcendent Wisdom* (Ithaca, N.Y.: Snow Lion Publications, 1994), 140.

29. See Sarah Coakley, Introduction, in *Pain and Its Transformations: The Interface of Biology and Culture*, ed. Sarah Coakley and Kay Kaufman Shelemay (Cambridge: Harvard University Press, 2007), 8–9.

30. The fourteenth-century theological controversy over *hesychasm*, mystical practices associated with the divine energies in the form of light, were as formative in Eastern Christianity as the Reformation in the West. See John Meyendorff, *Byzantine Theology: Historical Trends and Doctrinal Themes* (New York: Fordham University Press, 1974), 76–77.

31. In many cases the word "glory" carries these overtones. For instance, in Romans 6:4 Jesus is said to have been raised from the dead through "the glory of the Father." This can be taken to mean by the power of God, but it also connotes a concrete medium for action through sharing the radiance or energies of God.

32. Bishop of Diokleia Kallistos, *The Orthodox Way* (Crestwood, N.Y.: St. Vladimir's Seminary Press, 1995), 118.

33. "Creativity" here meant in line with Gordon Kaufman's use of "serendipitous creativity." See Gordon Kaufman, "On Thinking of God as Serendipitous Creativity," *The Journal of the American Academy of Religion* 69, no. 2 (2001).

34. See Kallistos Ware, "God Immanent, yet Transcendent: The Divine Energies According to Saint Gregory Palamas," in *In Whom We Live and Move and Have Our Being*, ed. Philip Clayton and A. R. Peacocke (Grand Rapids: Eerdmans 2004), 164.

35. Vladimir Lossky, *The Mystical Theology of the Eastern Church* (Crestwood, N.Y.: St. Vladimir's Seminary Press, 1976), 87.

36. For a sophisticated exploration of this question, including elements in Tibetan Buddhist tradition that could draw the parallel more deeply, see Thomas Cattoi, "What Has Chalcedon to Do with Lhasa? Keenan's and Lai Pai-Chiu's Reflections on Classical Christology and the Possible Shape of a Tibetan Theology of Incarnation," *Buddhist-Christian Studies* 28 (2008).

37. Raimundo Panikkar has effectively expounded this point in various writings. See for instance *The Silence of God: The Answer of the Buddha* (Maryknoll, N.Y.: Orbis Books, 1989).

38. This is the point of John Keenan's commendation of Buddhist categories as alternatives or correctives for the Hellenistic philosophical categories in which this question is traditionally addressed.

39. Rose Drew notes that many of the Buddhist-Christian dual practitioners she treats in her study like to stress that we are already saved/liberated, and that we are living in paradise and don't know it. See *Buddhist and Christian?: An Exploration of Dual Belonging*, Routledge Critical Studies in Buddhism (New York: Routledge, 2011), 120.

40. Wonhee Ann Joh, "Authoring a Multiplicity of Selves and No-Self," *Journal of Feminist Studies in Religion* (2008): 171.

41. The quotation comes from Professor Brian Robinette's fine response to the presentation of this paper at the Boston College conference on comparative theology and atonement. I would like to thank Professor Robinette for that response and our subsequent conversation.

42. On haecceity see John Hare's description in Hare, *God's Command*, Oxford Studies in Theological Ethics (Oxford: Oxford University Press, 2015), 145ff.

43. I suggest that person formation is not the same as the self projection deconstructed by no-self. See the discussion of diversity and person-making in Heim, *Crucified Wisdom*, 237ff.

BIBLIOGRAPHY

Abelard, Peter. *Commentary on the Epistle to the Romans.* Translated by Steven R. Cartwright. Washington, D.C.: Catholic University of America Press, 2011.

Adams, Charles J. "Islam and Christianity: The Opposition of Similarities." In *Logos Islamikos: Studia Islamica in Honorem Georgii Michaelis Wickens,* edited by Roger M. Savory and Dionisius A. Agius, 287–306. Papers in Mediaeval Studies 6. Toronto: Pontifical Institute of Mediaeval Studies, 1984.

Ahmed, Shahab. *Before Orthodoxy: The Satanic Verses in Early Islam.* Cambridge: Harvard University Press, 2017.

Akyol, Mustafa. *The Islamic Jesus: How the King of the Jews Became a Prophet of the Muslims.* London: St. Martin's Press, 2017.

al-Bājī, Abū l-Walīd. "*Jawāb al-qāḍi Abū l-Walīd al Bāji ilā risalah rāhib Faransā ilā al-muslimīn,*" in D. M. Dunlop, *A Christian Mission to Muslim Spain in the 11th Century, Al-Andalus* 17 (1952).

Alexander, Roberts, et al. *The Andti-Nicene Fatheris: The Writings of the Fathers Down to A.D. 325. The Apostolic Fathers with Justyn Martyr and Irenaeus,* Vol. 1. New York: Cosimo Classics, 2007.

al-Razī, Fakhr dīn. *al-Tafsīr al-kabīr.* Cairo: al-Matba'a al-Bahiyya, 1357/1938.

Amaladass, Anand, and Gudrun Löwnew. *Christian Themes in India Art from Mughal Times to the Present.* New Delhi: Manohar, 2011.

Anderson, Carol. *Pain and Its Ending: The Four Noble Truths in the Theravāda Buddhist Canon.* Curzon Critical Studies in Buddhism. Richmond: Curzon, 1999.

Anjum, Ovamir. *Politics, Law, and Community in Islamic Thought: The Taymiyyan Moment.* Cambridge: Cambridge University Press, 2012.

Anselm of Canterbury. *Complete Philosophical and Theological Treatises of Anselm of Canterbury.* Translated with an introduction by Jasper Hopkins and Herbert Richardson. Minneapolis: A. J. Banning Press, 2000.

———. *The Major Works.* Edited by Brian Davies and G. R. Evans. Oxford: Oxford University Press, 2008.

Aquinas, Thomas. *Summa Theologica.* Translated by Fathers of the English Dominican Province. London: Burns Oates & Washbourne, 1920.

Areford, David S. *The Viewer and the Printed Image in Late Medieval Europe.* Surrey and Burlington, Vt.: Ashgate, 2010.

Atisha. *A Lamp for the Path and Commentary*. Translated by R. Sherburne S.J. London: George Allen & Unwin, 1983.

Atisha's *Lamp for the Path to Enlightenment: An Oral Teaching by Geshe Sonam Rinchen*. Translated by R. Sonam. Ithaca, N.Y.: Snow Lion, 1997.

Athanasius. *On the Incarnation of the Word*. Edited and translated by John Behr. Yonkers, N.Y.: St. Vladimir's Seminary Press, 2012.

Augustine. *The City of God Against the Pagans*. Edited and translated by R. W. Dyson. Cambridge, UK: Cambridge University Press, 1998.

———. *Confessions*. Translated by Henry Chadwick. Oxford: Oxford University Press, 1992.

———. *Confessions*. Translated by Sarah Ruden. New York: Modern Library, 2017.

———. *On the Free Choice of the Will, On Grace and Free Choice, and Other Writings*. Edited and translated by Peter King. Cambridge, UK: Cambridge University Press, 2010.

———. *Selected Easter Sermons of Saint Augustine*. Introduction, notes, and commentary by Philip T. Weller. St. Louis and London: B. Herder Book Co., 1959.

Aulén, Gustaf. *Christus Victor: An Historical Study of The Three Main Types of the Idea of Atonement*. Translated by A. G. Herbert. New York: Macmillan, 1951.

Ayoub, Mahmoud. *A Muslim View of Christianity*. Maryknoll, N.Y.: Orbis, 2009.

Baker-Fletcher, Karen. *Dancing with God: The Trinity from a Womanist Perspective*. St. Louis: Chalice Press, 2006.

Barth, Karl. *Church Dogmatics*, Vol. 3, part 2. Edited by Geoffrey William Bromiley. Translated by Thomas F. Torrance. London, New York: T. & T. Clark International, 2004.

Barua, Ankur. "'I am the Living Bread': Ram Mohan Roy's Critique of the Doctrine of the Atonement." *Journal of Hindu-Christian Studies* 30 (2017): 62–71.

Bates, Matthew W. *Salvation by Allegiance Alone: Rethinking Faith, Works, and the Gospel of Jesus the King*. Grand Rapids: Baker Academic, 2017.

Batnizky, Leora. "On the Suffering of God's Chosen: Christian Views in Jewish Terms." In *Christianity in Jewish Terms*, edited by Tikva Frymer-Kensky, David Novak, Peter Ochs, David Fox Samuel, Michael Singer, 203–220. Boulder: Westview Press, 2000.

Baum, Robert M. *West Africa's Women of God: Alinesitoué and the Diola Prophetic Tradition*. Bloomington: Indiana University Press, 2016.

Bausenhart, Guido. "In allem uns gleich außer der Sünde." In *Studien zum Beitrag Maximos' des Bekenners zur altkirchlichen Christologie*, with a commented translation of "Disputatio cum Pyrrho." Mainz: Matthias-Grünewald-Verl, 1992.

Beckin, Bob. "Signs from the Garden: Some Remarks on the Relationship between Eve and Adam in Genesis 2–3." In *Enigmas and Images: Studies in Honor of Tryggve N.D. Metinger*, edited by Goeran Eidevall and Blazenka Scheuer, 22–36. Coniectanea Biblica Old Testament. Winona Lake, Ind.: Eisenbrauns, 2011.

Bediako, Kwame. *Christianity in Africa: The Renewal of a Non-Western Religion*. Edinburgh: University of Edinburgh Press and New York: Orbis Press, 1995.

———. *Theology and Identity: The Impact of Culture Upon Christian Thought in the Second Century and in Modern Africa*. Costa Mesa, Calif.: Regnum Books, 1992.

Benn, Charles. "Daoist Ordination and Zhai Rituals." In *Daoism Handbook*, edited by Kohn Livia, 309–338. Leiden: Brill, 2000.

Berger, David, ed. *The Jewish-Christian Debate in the High Middle Ages: A Critical Edition of the Nizzahon Vetus with an Introduction, Translation, and Commentary*. Philadelphia: Jewish Publication Society of America, 1979.

Berger, David, and Wyschogrod, Michael. *Jews and "Jewish Christianity": A Jewish Response to the Missionary Challenge*. Hoboken, N.J.: KTAV, 1978.

Berkovits, Eliezer. *Faith after the Holocaust*. New York: KTAV, 1973.

Beschi, Constantine Joseph. *Tempāvaṇi: A Garland of Unfading Honey-Sweet Verses*. Translated into English Verse with Sandhi-separated Tamil Text. Translated by M. Dominic Raj. Amazon Inc., 2019.

———. *The Unfading Garlard: Text and Commentary. Tempavani: Mūlamum Uraiyum*. Commentary by Sr. Margaret Bastin, FSJ. Uyir Eḻuttu Patippakam, 2014.

Bidlack, Bede Benjamin. "Daoist Alchemy and the Jesus Prayer Tradition: Comparative Meditation, Contrasting Theology." M.A. thesis, Division of Religious and Theological Studies, Boston University, 2005.

———. *In Good Company: The Body and Divinization in Pierre Teilhard de Chardin, SJ and Daoist Xiao Yingsou, East Asian Comparative Literature and Culture*. Leiden: Brill, 2015.

———. "What Child Is This? Jesus, Lord Lao, and Divine Identity." In *Comparing Faithfully: Insights for Systematic Theological Reflection*, edited by Michelle Voss Roberts, 195–215. New York: Fordham University Press, 2016.

Bokenkamp, Stephen R. "Death and Ascent in Ling-pao Taoism." *Taoist Resources* 1, no. 2 (1989): 1–10.

———. "*Duren jing*." In *Encyclopedia of Taoism*, edited by Fabrizio Pregadio, 394–96. London/New York: Routledge, 2008.

———. *Early Daoist Scriptures*, with a contribution by Peter S. Nickerson. Berkeley: University of California Press, 1997.

———. "Sackcloth and Ashes: Self and Family in the *Tutan zhai*." In *Scriptures, Schools, and Forms of Practice: A Berlin Symposium*, edited by Poul Andersen and Florian Reiter, 33–48. Wiesbaden: Harrassowitz Verlag, 2005.

Bonhoeffer, Dietrich. *The Cost of Discipleship*. New York: Touchstone, 1995.

Boureux, Christophe. "Approche théologale du mensonge." *Lumière et Vie* 218 (1994), 64.

Brock, Rita Nakashima, and Rebecca Ann Parker. *Proverbs of Ashes: Violence, Redemptive Suffering, and the Search for What Saves Us*. Boston: Beacon Press, 2001.

Brown, Joanne Carlson. "Divine Child Abuse?" *Daughters of Sarah* 18 (1992): 24–28.

Brown, Joanne Carlson, and Rebecca Parker. "For God So Loved the World?" In *Christianity, Patriarchy, and Abuse: A Feminist Critique*, edited by Joanne Carlson Brown and Carole R. Bohn, 1–30. New York: Pilgrim, 1989.

Brunner, Hélène. "Maṇḍala and Yantra in the Siddhānta School of Śaivism: Definitions, Description, and Ritual Use." Translated by Raynalt Prévèreau. In *Maṇḍalas and Yantras in the Hindu Traditions*, edited by Gudrun Bühnemann et al., 153–78. Leiden: Brill, 2003.

Bstan 'dzin rgya, mtsho, and B. Alan Wallace. *Transcendent Wisdom*, 2nd ed. Ithaca, N.Y.: Snow Lion Publications, 1994.

Buakasa, T. K. M. *L'impensé Du Discours. "Kindoki" Et "Nkisi" En Pays Kongo Du Zaïre*, 2nd ed. Kinshasa: Facultés Catholiques de Kinshasa, 1980.

Bühnemann, Gudrun. "Maṇḍala, Yantra, and Cakra: Some Observations." In *Maṇḍalas and Yantras in the Hindu Traditions*, edited by Gudrun Bühnemann et al., 13–56. Leiden: Brill, 2003.

Bujo, Bénézet. *Foundations of an African Ethic: Beyond the Universal Claims of Western Morality*. Translated by Brian McNeil. New York: Crossroad, 2001.

Burrell, David. *Towards a Jewish-Christian-Muslim Theology*. Malden: Blackwell Publishing, 2011.

Camus, Albert. *Le mythe de Sisyphe. Essai sur l'absurde*. Paris: Edition Gallimars, 1942.

———. *L'étranger*. Paris: Edition Gallimars, 1957.

Carvalho, Pedro de Moura. *Mir'āt al-quds (Mirror of Holiness): a Life of Christ for Emperor Akbar: a Commentary on Father Jerome Xavier's Text and the Miniatures of Cleveland Museum of Art, Acc. No. 2005.145*. With a translation of the *Mir'āt al-quds* by W. M. Thackston. Leiden: Brill, 2012.

Cattoi, Thomas. "What Has Chalcedon to Do with Lhasa? John Keenan's and Lai Pai-Chiu's Reflections on Classical Christology and the Possible Shape of a Tibetan Theology of Incarnation." *Buddhist-Christian Studies* 28 (2008): 13–25.

Chalier, Catherine. "Le serviteur souffrant: Isaïe 52, 13–15; 53, 1–12." In *Mythe et philosophie: Les traditions bibliques*, edited by Christian Berner, 153–67. Paris: Presses Universitaires de France, 2002.

Chetanananda, Swami. *Ramakrishna as We Saw Him*. Edited and translated by Swami Chetanananda. St. Louis: Vedanta Society of St. Louis, 1990.

Clooney, Francis X. "Christ as the Divine Guru in the Theology of Roberto de Nobili." In *One Faith, Many Cultures*, edited by Ruy Costa, 25–40. Orbis: Maryknoll, 1988. Included as Chapter 1 in *Western Jesuit Scholars in India: Tracing Their Paths, Reassessing Their Goals*. Leiden: Brill, 2020, 19–36.

———. "Finding God in All Things: Some Catholic and Hindu Insights." *Vinayasadhana* d7.1 (2016): 30–44. Reprinted in *Western Jesuit Scholars in India: Tracing Their Paths, Reassessing Their Goals*. Leiden: Brill, 2020, 260–74.

———. *Hindu God, Christian God: How Reason Helps Break Down the Barriers Between Religions*. Oxford: Oxford University Press, 2001.

———. "Passionate Comparison: The Intensification of Affect in Interreligious Reading of Hindu and Christian Texts." *Harvard Theological Review* 98, no. 4 (2005): 367–90.

———. "Renewing the Study of Ramakrishna: A Proposal." *Prabuddha Bharata* 116.1 (2011): 203–8.

———. "Roberto de Nobili's Dialogue on Eternal Life and an Early Jesuit Evaluation of Religion in South India." In *Western Jesuit Scholars in India: Tracing Their Paths, Reassessing Their Goals*. Leiden: Brill, 2020.

Coakley, Sarah. Introduction to *Pain and Its Transformations: The Interface of Biology and Culture*. Edited by Sarah Coakley and Kay Kaufman Shelemay. Cambridge: Harvard University Press, 2007.

Cobb, John B., Christopher Ives, and Masao Abe. *The Emptying God: A Buddhist-Jewish-Christian Conversation*. Maryknoll, N.Y.: Orbis Books, 1990.

Cohn, Norman. *Cosmos, Chaos, and the World to Come: The Ancient Roots of Apocalyptic Faith*. New Haven: Yale University Press, 1993.

Collins, Brian. *Head Beneath the Altar: Hindu Mythology and the Critique of Sacrifice*. East Lansing: Michigan State University Press, 2014.

Collins, Steven. *Selfless Persons: Imagery and Thought in Theravada Buddhism*. Cambridge, UK: Cambridge University Press, 1982.

Cone, James H. *The Cross and the Lynching Tree*. Maryknoll, N.Y.: Orbis Books, 2011.

Copeland, M. Shawn. *Enfleshing Freedom: Body, Race, and Being*. Minneapolis: Fortress Press, 2010.

Cornille, Catherine. *The Im-Possibility of Interreligious Dialogue*. New York: Crossroads, 2008.

———. *Meaning and Method in Comparative Theology*. Chichester: Wiley, 2020.

Cotter, David. *Genesis*. Berit Olam. Collegeville, Minn.: Liturgical Press, 2003.

Crouch, Andrae. "The Blood Will Never Lose Its Power." https://www.azlyrics.com/lyrics/selah/thebloodwillneverloseitspower.html.

Crysdale, Cynthia S. W. *Transformed Lives: Making Sense of Atonement for Today*. New York: Seabury Books, 2016.

Dalferth, Ingolf. *Crucified and Resurrected: Restructuring the Grammar of Christology*. Translated by Jo Bennett. Grand Rapids: Baker Academic, 2015.

Day, Dorothy. "We Mourn Death of Gandhi Non Violent Revolutionary." *The Catholic Worker* (February 1948; accessed online at https://www.catholicworker.org/dorothyday/articles/463.pdf).

de Lange, Nicholas. *Ignaz Maybaum: A Reader*. New York: Berghahn Books, 2001.

de Nobili, Roberto. *Catechism, Third Part (Jñāṇopatecamūntrām Kāṇtam)*. Tamiḷ Ilakkiya Kaḷakam, 1968.

———. *Refutation of Calumnies (Tuṣaṇātikkāram)*. Tamiḷ Ilakkiya Kaḷakam, 1964.

de Saint Cheron, Michael. *Conversations with Emmanuel Levinas, 1983–1994*. Translated by Gary D. Mole. Pittsburgh: Duquesne University Press, 2010.

Desch-Obi, T. J. "Combat and the Crossing of the Kalunga." In *Central Africans and Cultural Transformations in the American Diaspora*, edited by Linda M. Heywood, 353–70. New York: Cambridge University Press, 2002.

Donahue, John R., and Daniel J. Harrington. *The Gospel of Mark. Sacra Pagina*. Series 2. Collegeville, Minn.: Liturgical Press, 2002.

Draguet, René. *Julien d'Harnicasse et sa controverse avec Sévère d'Antioche sur l'incurrupitibilité du corps du Christ: Étude d'histoire littéraire et doctrinale suivie des fragments dogmatiques de Julien* (Texte syriaque et traduction grecque). Louvain, 1924.

Drew, Rose. *Buddhist and Christian?: An Exploration of Dual Belonging*. Routledge Critical Studies in Buddhism. New York: Routledge, 2011.

Dubarle, André-Marie. *Le péché originel. Perspectives théologiques*. Paris: Cerf, 1983.

Dubois, Jean Antoine. *Letters on the State of Christianity in India, in Which the Conversion of the Hindoos Is Considered as Impracticable*. London: Longman, Hurst, Rees, Orme, Brown and Green, 1823.

Du Jarric, Pierre. *Akbar and the Jesuits: An Account of the Jesuit Missions to the Court of Akbar by Father Pierre du Jarric, S.J.* Translated by Charles H. Payne. New York: Harper and Brothers, 1926.

Duparquet, Charles, and Gérard Vieira. *Le Père Duparquet. Tome III, Lettres et Écrits, 1870–1876: De l'exil à Bagamoyo au succès de Landana*. Mémoire D'églises. Paris: Karthala, 2014.

Durand, Emmanuel. *Jésus contemporain. Christologie brève et actuelle*. Paris: Cerf, 2018.

Düzgün, Şaban Ali. "The Capabilities Embedded in to the Human Nature/Fitra." *Journal of Islamic Research* 27, no. 3 (2016): 213–19.

Ebied, Rifaat, and David Thomas, eds. *The Polemical Works of 'Alī al-Ṭabarī*. Leiden: Brill, 2016.

Eckhardt, Alice L. "Suffering: Challenge to Faith, Challenge to God" (1994). http://preserve.lehigh.edu/cas-religion-faculty-publications/12.

Eliade, Mircea. *The Sacred and the Profane: The Nature of Religion*. New York: Harcourt, Brace, 1959.

Elliott, Mark W., ed. *Ancient Christian Commentary on Scripture, Old Testament XI (Isaiah 40–66)*. Downers Grove: Intervarsity Press, 2014.

Eskildsen, Stephen. *Asceticism in Early Taoist Religion*. Albany: SUNY Press, 1998.

Essen, Georg. *Die Freiheit Jesu. Der neuchalkedonische Enhypostasiebegriff im Horizont neuzeitlicher Subjekt- und Personphilosophie*. Regensburg: Pustet, 2001.

Farstad, Mona Helen. "Anthropology of the Qur'ān." In *Encyclopaedia of the Qur'ān*, edited by J. D. McAuliffe. Brill Online, 2016. dx.doi.org/10.1163/1875-3922_q3_EQCOM _050509.

Faruqi, Ismail Raji al-. *Christian Ethics: A Historical and Systematic Analysis of Its Dominant Ideas*. Montreal: McGill University Press, 1986.

———. "Islam and Christianity: Diatribe or dialogue." Reprinted in al-Faruqi, *Islam and Other Faiths*.

———. "Islam and Christianity: Problems and Perspectives." In *The Word in the Third World*, edited by James P. Cotter, 159–81. Washington, D.C.: Corpus Books, 1968.

———. "Islam and Christianity: Prospects for dialogue." *Sacred Heart Messenger*, (September 1967): 29–33.

———. *Islam and Other Faiths*. Edited by Ataullah Siddiqui. Leicester: The Islamic Foundation, 1998.

———. "On the nature of Islamic da'wah." *International Review of Missions* 65, no. 260 (1976): 391–406.

———. "On the Raison d'Être of the Ummah." *Islamic Studies* 2, no. 2 (June 1963): 159–203.

Fee, Gordon. *The First Epistle to the Corinthians*. The New International Commentary on the New Testament, Rev. Edition. Grand Rapids, Mich.: Eerdmans, 2014.

Feldmeier, Peter. *Christianity Looks East: Comparing the Spiritualities of John of the Cross and Buddhaghosa*. New York: Paulist Press, 2006.

Fernandez, James W. "The Cultural Status of a West African Cult Group on the Creation of Culture." In *African Religious Groups and Beliefs—Papers in Honour of William R. Bascom*, edited by Simon Ottenberg, 242–60. Meerut, India: Archana Publications, 1982.

Firey, Abigail. Introduction to *A New History of Penance*, edited by Abigail Firey, 1–18. Leiden: Brill, 2008.

Fletcher, Charles D. "Ismaʿīl al-Faruqi (1921–1986) and Inter-Faith Dialogue: The Man, The Scholar, The Participant." PhD diss., McGill University, 2008.

———. *Muslim-Christian Engagement in the Twentieth Century: The Principles of Interfaith Dialogue and the Work of Ismaʿil Al-Faruqi*. London: I. B. Tauris, 2015.

Flood, Gavin. *The Ascetic Self: Subjectivity, Memory, and Tradition*. Cambridge: Cambridge University Press, 2004.

———. *The Tantric Body: The Secret Tradition of Hindu Religion*. London: I. B. Taurus, 2006.

Fort, Gavin. "Penitents and Their Proxies: Penance for Others in Early Medieval Europe." *Church History* 86, no. 1 (March 2017).

Fromont, Cécile. *The Art of Conversion: Christian Visual Culture in the Kingdom of Kongo*. Virginia: Omohundro Institute of Early American History and Culture and University of North Carolina Press, 2014.

Fuchs, Gotthard. "Glaubenserfahrung—Theologie—Religionsunterricht. Ein Versuch ihrer Zuordnung." In *Katechetische Blätter* 103 (1978): 190–216.

Fudge, Bruce. *Qur'ānic Hermeneutics: al-Tabrisī and the Craft of Commentary*. London: Routledge, 2011.

Funkenstein, Amos. "The Dialectics of Assimilation." *Jewish Social Studies* 1/2 (1995): 1–14.

Gibbs, Robert. "Suspicions of Suffering." In *Christianity in Jewish Terms*, edited by Tikva Frymer-Kensky, David Novak, Peter Ochs, David Fox Samuel, and Michael S. Singer, 221–29. Oxford: Westview Press, 2000.

Girard, Rene. *Sacrifice*. Translated by Matthew Patillo and David Dawson. East Lansing: Michigan State University Press, 2011.

Graham, A. C. *Disputers of the Tao*. La Salle, Ill.: Open Court, 1989.

Greenberg, Irving. "Cloud of Smoke, Pillar of Fire: Judaism, Christianity, and Modernity after the Holocaust." In *Auschwitz: Beginning of a New Era?, Reflections on the Holocaust*, edited by Eva Fleischner, 13–36. New York: KTAV Publishing, 1977.

Gregerman, Adam. "Interpreting the Pain of Others: John Paul II and Benedict XVI on Jewish Suffering in the Shoah." *Journal of Ecumenical Studies* 48 (2013): 443–66.

Greshake, Gisbert. "Der Wandel der Erlösungsvorstellungen in der Theologiegeschichte." In *Erlösung und Emanzipation*, edited by Leo Scheffczyk, 69–101. Freiburg-Basel-Wien: Herder, 1973.

———. "Erlösung und Freiheit: Zur Neuinterpretation der Satisfaktionstheorie Anselms von Canterbury." In *Theologische Quartalsschrift* 153 (1973): 332–45.

Griffith, Sidney. "Syriacisms in the 'Arabic Qur'an': Who Were 'Those Who Said Allāh Is the Third of Three' According to al-Mā'ida 73?" In *A Word Fitly Spoken: Studies in Medieval Exegesis of the Hebrew Bible and the Qur'ān*, edited by Meir M. Bar-Asher et alia, 83–110. Jerusalem, 2007.

Grillmeier, Alois. *Jesus der Christus im Glauben der Kirche*. Bd. 2/2: Die Kirche von Konstantinopel im 6. Jahrhundert, unter Mitarbeit von Theresia Hainthaler. Freiburg-Basel-Wien: Herder, 1989.

Grossman, Avraham. "The Commentary of Rashi on Isaiah and the Jewish-Christian Debate." In *Studies in Medieval Jewish Intellectual and Social History: Festschrift in Honor of Robert Chazan*, edited by David Engel, Lawrence H. Schiffman, and Elliot R. Wolfson, 47–62. Leiden: Brill, 2012.

Guerreiro, Fernão. *Jahangir and the Jesuits, with an Account of the Travels of Benedict Goes and the Mission to Pegu, from the Relations of Father Fernão Guerreiro, S. J.* Translated by Charles H. Payne. London: G. Routledge and Sons, 1930.

Gupta, Mahendranath. *Gospel of Ramakrishna*. Translated by Swami Nikhilananda, Calcutta: Ramakrishna-Vivekananda Center, 1942.

Guwy, France. "Houd van je naaste, dat is wat je zelf bent. Gesprek met Emmanuel Levinas in 1985." In *De ander in ons: Emmanuel Levinas in gesprek: een inleiding in zijn denken*, edited by France Guwy. Amsterdam: Sun, 2008.

Gyatso, Tenzin. "The Practices of Bodhisattvas." In *The Christ and the Bodhisattva*, edited by Donald S. Lopez, Jr., and Steven C. Rockefeller, 217–27. Albany: SUNY Press, 1987.

Hạnh, Thich Nhat. *Going Home: Jesus and Buddha as Brothers*. New York: Riverhead Books, 1999.

———. https://www.lionsroar.com/the-fullness-of-emptiness/.

———. *Living Buddha, Living Christ*. New York: Riverhead Books, 1995.

———. "Suffering Can Teach Us." http://plumvillage.org/transcriptions/suffering-can-teach-us/.

Hare, J. E. *God's Command*. Oxford Studies in Theological Ethics. Oxford: Oxford University Press, 2015.

Harvey, Peter. *Introduction to Buddhism*. New York: Cambridge University Press, 2013.

Hastings, Adrian. *The Church in Africa 1450–1950*. Oxford: Clarendon Press, 1994.

Hefling, Charles. "Why the Cross?: God's At-One-Ment with Humanity." *The Christian Century* 130, no. 6 (2013): 24–27.

Heim, S. Mark. *Crucified Wisdom: Christ and the Bodhisattva in Theological Reflection* Comparative Theology: Thinking across Traditions. Edited by Loye Ashton and John Thatamanil. New York: Fordham University Press 2018.

Held, Shai. *Abraham Joshua Heschel: The Call of Transcendence*. Bloomington and Indianapolis: Indiana University Press, 2013.

Hengel, Martin. *The Atonement: The Origins of the Doctrine in the New Testament*. Translated by John Bowden. Philadelphia: Fortress Press, 1981.

Heschel, Abraham Joshua. *Heavenly Torah as Refracted Through the Generations*. Edited and translated by Gordon Tucker. New York: Continuum, 2005.

———. *The Prophets*. New York: Harper & Row, 1962.

Hirota, Dennis, ed. *Toward a Contemporary Understanding of Pure Land Buddhism: Creating a Shin Buddhist Theology in a Religiously Plural World*. Albany: SUNY Press, 2000.

———. "The World of Revelation and Engagement in Shinran." https://docs.google.com/a/georgetown.edu/viewer?a=v&pid=sites&srcid=ZGVmYXVsdGRvbWFpbnxzaGluY2hya XNoaWFuaXR5aXNsYW18Z3g6Mzk1ZDk2NzcxZDZlNWQzNQ, accessed July 5, 2018.

Hoffman, Lawrence A. "Jewish and Christian Liturgy." In *Christianity in Jewish Terms*, edited by Tikva Frymer-Kensky et al., 175–89. Oxford: Westview Press, 2000.

Howard, Damian. "Christians and Muslims in Tomorrow's Europe." *Studies: An Irish Quarterly Review* 105, no. 419 (Autumn 2016): 294–308.

Hudson, Wm. Clarke. "Spreading the Dao, Managing Mastership, and Performing Salvation: The Life and Alchemical Teachings of Chen Zhixu." PhD diss., Department of Religious Studies, Indiana University, 2007.

Ibn Kathīr al-Qurayshī al-Dimashqī, *Tafsīr al-Qurʾān al-ʿazīm*, 7 vols. Beirut: Dar al-fikr, 1970.

Ide, Pascal. *Une théo-logique du don. Le don dans la trilogie de Hans Urs von Balthasar*. Leuven: Peeters, 2013.

Irenaeus of Lyons. *Against the Heresies*. Ancient Christian Writers. 3 vols. Translated by Dominic J. Unger, John J. Dillon, Matthew Steenberg, and Michael Slusser. New York: Paulist Press, 1992, 2012, 2012.

Irwin, T. H. "Splendid Vices: Augustine For and Against Pagan Virtues." *Medieval Philosophy and Theology* 8, no. 2 (1999): 105–27.

Ives, Christopher. *Imperial-Way Zen: Ichikawa Hakugen's Critique and Lingering Questions for Zen Ethics*. Honolulu: University of Hawai'i Press, 2008.

Izutsu, Toshihiko. *Ethico-Religious Concepts in the Qur'ān*. Montreal: McGill University Press, 1966.

Jacob of Serug, *On the Mother of God*. Translated by Mary Hanbury. Introduction by Sebastian Brock. Crestwood, N.Y.: St. Vladimir Seminary Press, 1998.

Jaeger, John. "Abraham Heschel and the Theology of Jurgen Moltmann." *Perspectives in Religious Studies* 24, no. 2 (1997): 167–79.

Jantzen, Grace. *Julian of Norwich: Mystic and Theologian*, 2nd ed. London: SPCK, 2000 [1987].

Jennings, Willie James. *The Christian Imagination: Theology and the Origins of Race*. New Haven, Conn.: Yale University Press, 2010.

Jerryson, Michael, and Mark Juergensmeyer, eds. *Buddhist Warfare*. Oxford: Oxford University Press, 2010.

Johnson, Elizabeth A. *Creation and the Cross: The Mercy of God for a Planet in Peril*. Maryknoll, N.Y.: Orbis Books, 2018.

Joh, Wonhee Ann. "Authoring a Multiplicity of Selves and No-Self." *Journal of Feminist Studies in Religion* (2008): 169–72.

Joslyn-Siemiatkoski, Daniel. *Christian Memories of the Maccabean Martyrs*. New York: Palgrave Macmillan, 2009.

———. "Comparative Theology and the Status of Judaism: Hegemony and Reversals." In *The New Comparative Theology: Interreligious Insights from the Next Generation*, edited by Francis X. Clooney, 89–108. New York: Continuum, 2010.

———. *The More Torah, the More Life: A Christian Commentary on Mishnah Avot*. Leuven: Peeters Publishers, 2018.

———. "The Mother and Seven Sons in Late Antique and Medieval Ashkenazi Judaism: Narrative Transformations and Communal Identity." In *Dying for the Faith, Killing for the Faith: Old Testament Faith-Warriors (1 and 2 Maccabees) in Historical Perspective*, edited by Gabriela Signori, 127–46. Leiden: Brill, 2012.

Julian of Norwich. *Showings*. Translated from the critical text by Edmund Colledge and James Walsh. Mahwah, N.J.: Paulist Press, 1978.

———. *The Writings of Julian of Norwich: A Vision Showed to a Devout Woman and a Revelation of Love*. Edited by Nicholas Watson and Jacqueline Jenkins. University Park: Pennsylvania State University Press, 2006.

Kabwita, Kabolo Iko. *Le Royaume Kongo Et La Mission Catholique (1750–1838). Du Déclin À L'extinction*. Edited by Paul Coulon. Mémoire D'églises. Paris: Karthala, 2004.

Kaegi, Walter E. *Heracliu: Emperor of Byzantium*. Cambridge: Cambridge University Press: 2003.

Kallistos, Bishop of Diokleia. *The Orthodox Way*. Crestwood, N.Y.: St. Vladimir's Seminary Press, 1995.

Kant, Immanuel. *Religion Within the Limits of Reason Alone*. Translated by Theodore M. Greene and Hoyt H. Hudson. New York: Harper & Row: 1794/1960.

Kaufman, Gordon. "On Thinking of God as Serendipitous Creativity." *The Journal of the American Academy of Religion* 69, no. 2 (2001): 409–25.

Keenan, John P. *The Emptied Christ of Philippians: Mahāyāna Meditations*. Eugene, Ore.: Wipf & Stock, 2015.

Khalil, Mohammad Hassan. *Islam and the Fate of Others: The Salvation Question.* London: Oxford University Press, 2012.

Khorchide, Mouhanad, and Klaus von Stosch. *Der andere Prophet. Jesus im Koran.* Freiburg-Basel-Wien: Herder, 2018.

Kirita, Kiyohide. "D.T. Suzuki on Society and the State." In *Rude Awakenings: Zen, the Kyoto School, and the Question of Nationalism,* edited by James W. Heisig and John W. Maraldo, 52–74. Honolulu: University of Hawai'i Press, 1995.

Kleeman, Terry F. *Celestial Masters: History and Ritual in Early Daoist Communities.* Harvard-Yenching Institute Monograph Series. Cambridge: Harvard University Asia Center, 2016.

Kohn, Livia. *Cosmos and Community: The Ethical Dimension of Daoism.* Cambridge, Mass.: Three Pines Press, 2004.

———. *Health and Long Life: The Chinese Way.* Cambridge, Mass.: Three Pines Press, 2005), 23–29.

———. *Hsiao tao lun: Laughing at the Tao Debates among Buddhists and Taoists in Medieval China.* Princeton, N.J: Princeton University Press, 1995.

———. "The Symbolism of Evil in Traditional China." In *Living with the Dao: Conceptual Issues in Daoist Practice.* Cambridge, Mass.: Three Pines Press, 2006.

———. *The Taoist Experience.* Albany: SUNY Press, 1993.

Krell, Marc A. "Comparative Philosophical Approaches to Salvation: An Examination of a Particular Instance of an Interreligious Experience." *Shofar: An Interdisciplinary Journal of Jewish Studies* 16 (1998): 71–83.

Krings, Hermann. *System und Freiheit. Gesammelte Aufsätze.* Freiburg-München: Alber, 1980 (Praktische Philosophie; 12).

Kṣemarāja. *Bhairavānukaraṇastava.* In *Language of Images: Visualization and Meaning* by Sthaneshwar Timalsina, 145–57. New York: Peter Lang, 2015.

Lagerway, John. *Taoist Ritual in Chinese Society and History.* New York: Macmillan, 1987.

———. *Wu-shang pi-yao: Somme Taoiste du VIe siècle, Publications de l'Ecole française d'Extrême-Orient.* Paris: Ecole française d'Extrême-Orient, 1981.

Lai, Pan-Chiu, and Yuen-tai So. "Mahāyāna Interpretation of Christianity: A Case Study of Zhang Chunyi (1871–1955)." *Buddhist-Christian Studies,* 27 (2007): 67–87.

Lamptey, Jerusha. *Divine Words, Female Voices: Muslima Explorations in Comparative Feminist Theology.* Oxford: Oxford University Press, 2018.

The Land of Bliss: The Paradise of the Buddha of Measureless Light: Sanskrit and Chinese Versions of the Sukhavativyuha Sutras. Introduced and translated by Luis O. Gomez. Honolulu: University of Hawai'i Press / Kyoto: Higashi Hongani Shinshu Otani-Ha, 1996.

Langenfeld, Aaron. *Das Schweigen brechen. Christliche Soteriologie im Kontext Islamischer Theologie.* Paderborn: Ferdinand Schöningh, 2016.

Lawson, Todd. *The Crucifixion and the Qur'an: A Study in the History of Islamic Thought.* London: OneWorld, 2009.

Lefebure, Leo D. *The Buddha and the Christ: Explorations in Buddhist and Christian Dialogue.* Faith Meets Faith Series. Maryknoll, N.Y.: Orbis Books, 1993.

———. *True and Holy: Christian Scripture and Other Religions.* Maryknoll, N.Y.: Orbis Books, 2014.

Leontius of Byzantium. *Complete Works*. Edited by Brian E. Daley. Oxford: Oxford University Press, 2017.

Lerch, Magnus. *Selbstmitteilung Gottes: Herausforderungen einer freiheitstheoretischen Offenbarungstheologie*. Regensburg: Pustet, 2015 (ratio fidei; 56).

Levinas, Emmanuel. *Difficult Freedom: Essays on Judaism*. London: Athlone, 1990.

———. "L'inspiration religieuse de l'alliance." *Paix et droit* 8 (1935): 4.

———. "Useless Suffering." In *The Provocation of Levinas: Re-Thinking the* Other, edited by Robert Bernasconi and David Wood, 156–67. London: Routledge, 1988.

Lonergan, Bernard J. F. *Insight: A Study of Human Understanding*. Collected Works of Bernard Lonergan 3. Edited by Frederick E. Crowe and Robert M. Doran. Toronto: University of Toronto Press, 1997.

Longenecker, Richard. *The Epistle to the Romans: A Commentary on the Greek Text*. The New International Greek Testament Commentary. Grand Rapids, Mich.: Eerdmans, 2016.

Lossky, Vladimir. *The Mystical Theology of the Eastern Church*. Crestwood, N.Y.: St. Vladimir's Seminary Press, 1976.

Louth, Andrew. *Introducing Eastern Orthodox Theology*. Downer's Grove, Ill.: Intervarsity Press, 2013.

Lovell, Nadia. *Cord of Blood—Possession and the Making of Voodoo*. London and Sterling, Va.: Pluto Press, 2002.

Loy, David. *Nonduality: A Study in Comparative Philosophy*. Atlantic Highlands, N.J.: Humanities Press, 1997.

Loyola, Ignatius. *The Constitutions of the Society of Jesus and Their Complementary Norms*. Institute of Jesuit Sources, 1996.

———. *The Spiritual Exercises*. Translated by Elder Mullan, S.J. P.J. Kennedy and Sons, 1914.

Lü, Pengzhi. "Daoist Rituals." In *Early Chinese Religion*, edited by John Lagerwey and Marc Kalinowski, 1245–1353. Leiden: Brill, 2009.

Lundy, Brandon, Akanmy Adebayo, and Sherrill Hayes, eds. *Atone: Religion, Conflict, and Reconciliation*. Lanham, Md.: Lexington Books, 2018.

Lutgendorf, Philip. *The Life of a Text: Performing the Ramcaritmanas of Tulsidas*. Berkeley: University of California Press, 1991.

MacGaffey, Wyatt. *Religion and Society in Central Africa: The Bakongo of Lower Zaire*. Chicago: University of Chicago Press, 1986.

Madigan, Daniel. "People of the Word: Reading John with a Muslim." *Review and Expositor* 104 (2007): 81–95.

———. *The Qur'ān's Self-Image: Writing and Authority in Islam's Scripture*. Princeton: Princeton University Press, 2001.

Mana, Kä. *La Nouvelle Évangélisation En Afrique*. Chrétiens En Liberté. Paris/Yaoundé: Clé/Karthala, 2000.

Marcus, Joel. *Jesus and the Holocaust. Reflections on Suffering and Hope*. Grand Rapids, Mich.: Eerdmans, 2017.

Marshman, Joshua. *A Defence of the Deity and Atonement of Jesus Christ, in Reply to Ram-Mohun Roy of Calcutta*. Kingsbury, Parbury, and Allen, 1822.

Marty, Martin E. *October 31, 1517: Martin Luther and the Day That Changed the World*. Brewster, Mass.: Paraclete Press, 2016.

Martyn, J. Louis. *Galatians: A New Translation with Introduction and Commentary.* The Anchor Bible, Vol. 33A. New York: Doubleday, 1997.

Masaaki, Tsuchiya. "Confession of Sins and Awareness of Self in the *Taiping jing.*" In *Daoist Identity History, Lineage, and Ritual,* edited by Livia Kohn and Harold David Roth. Honolulu: University of Hawai'i Press, 2002.

Maspero, Henri. *Mélanges posthumes sur les religions et l'histoire de la Chine.* 3 vols., *Publications du Musée Guimet Bibliothèque de diffusion.* Paris: Civilisations du Sud, S.A.E.P, 1950.

Maududi, Sayed Abul A'la. *The Political Theory of Islam.* Lahore: Islamic Publications Limited, 1968.

Maybaum, Ignaz. *A Reader. Edited and with an Introduction by Nicholas de Lang.* New York: Berghahn Books, 2001.

Mbiti, John S. *Bible and Theology in African Christianity.* Nairobi: Oxford University Press, 1986.

McDougall, Joy Ann. *The Pilgrimage of Love: Moltmann on the Trinity and Christian Life.* Oxford: Oxford University Press, 2005.

McGinn, Bernard. *The Foundations of Mysticism,* Vol. 1, *The Presence of God: A History of Western Christian Mysticism.* New York: Crossroad, 1991.

McGrath, Alister. *Christian Theology. An Introduction.* Oxford: Blackwell Publishers, 1994.

McLain, Charles E. "A Comparison of Ancient and Medieval Jewish Interpretations of the Suffering Servant in Isaiah." *Calvary Baptist Theological Journal* 6 (1990): 2–31.

Melion, Walter S. "The Art of Vision in Jerome Nadal's Annotationes et meditationes in evangelia." Introduction to *Jeronimo Nadal, Annotations and Meditations on the Gospels.* Translated and edited by Frederick A. Homann, S.J. Philadelphia: St. Joseph's University Press, 2003, 1–32.

Merkle, John C. "Heschel's Theology of Divine Pathos." In *Abraham Joshua Heschel: Exploring His Life and Thought,* edited by John C. Merkle, 66–83. New York: Macmillan, 1985.

Merton, Thomas. *Conjectures of a Guilty Bystander.* Garden City, N.Y.: Doubleday, 1966.

Mettinger, Tryggve. *The Eden Narrative: A Literary and Religio-Historical Study of Genesis 2–3.* Winona Lake, Ind.: Eisenbrauns, 2007.

Metz, Johannes Baptist. "Facing the Jews: Christian Theology After Auschwitz." In *The Holocaust as Interruption, Concilium* 175, edited by Elisabeth Schüssler Fiorenza and David Tracy, 43–52. Edinburgh: T. & T. Clark, 1984.

Meyendorff, John. *Byzantine Theology: Historical Trends and Doctrinal Themes.* New York: Fordham University Press, 1974.

Michel, Thomas. *A Muslim Theologian's Response to Christianity.* Delman: Caravan Books, 1984.

Mitchell, Donald W., and James Wiseman. *The Gethsemani Encounter: A Dialogue on the Spiritual Life by Buddhist and Christian Monastics.* New York: Continuum, 1997.

Mohamed, Yasien. "The Interpretations of Fiṭrah." *Islamic Studies* 34, no. 2 (1995): 129–51.

Moltmann, Jürgen. *A Broad Place.* Translated by Margaret Kohl. Minneapolis: Fortress, 2008.

———. *The Crucified God: The Cross of Christ as the Foundation and Criticism of Christian Theology.* Translated by R. A. Wilson and John Bowden. New York: Harper & Row, 1974.

———. *History and the Triune God: Contributions to Trinitarian Theology.* Translated by John Bowden. New York: Crossroads, 1992.

———. *Theology of Hope,* translated by James W. Letich. Minneapolis: Fortress Press, 1993.

———. *The Way of Jesus Christ: Christology in Messianic Dimensions.* Translated by Margaret Kohl. New York: HarperCollins, 1990.

Moo, Douglas. *The Letter to the Romans.* The New International Commentary on the New Testament, 2nd edition. Grand Rapids, Mich.: Eerdmans, 2018.

Moyaert, Marianne. "Comparative Theology after the Shoah: Risks, Pivots and Opportunities of Comparing Traditions." In *How to Do Comparative Theology,* edited by Francis X. Clooney and Klaus von Stosch, 174–87. New York: Fordham University Press, 2017.

Nasr, Seyyed Hossein. *Islamic Life and Thought.* Albany: SUNY Press, 1981.

Neusner, Jacob, Baruch A. Levine, Bruce D. Chilton, and Vincent Cornell. *Do Jews, Christians, and Muslims Worship the Same God?* Nashville: Abingdon Press, 2012.

Nietzsche, Friedrich. "Die fröhliche Wissenschaft." In *Kritische Studienausgabe, Vol. 3: Morgenröte. Idyllen aus Messina, Die fröhliche Wissenschaft,* edited by Giorgio Colli and Mazzino Montinari, 343–651. München: dtv, 1999.

Olayiwola, David O. "Aladura Christianity in Dialogue with African Traditional Religion (the Yoruba Example)." *Studia Missionalia* 43 (1994): 345–62.

O'Leary, Joseph Stephen. *Buddhist Nonduality, Paschal Paradox: A Christian Commentary on the Teaching of Vimalakirti.* Leuven: Peeters, 2017.

Orthodox Rabbinic Statement on Christianity. *To Do the Will of Our Father in Heaven: Toward a Partnership between Jews and Christians,* 3 December 2015. http://cjcuc.com /site/2015/12/03/orthodox-rabbinic-statement-on-christianity/.

Osborne, Kenan B. *Reconciliation and Justification: The Sacrament and Its Theology.* New York: Paulist Press, 1990.

Ouro, Roberto. "The Garden of Eden Account: The Chiastic Structure of Genesis 2–3." In *Andrews University Seminary Studies* 40.2 (2002), 219–43.

Padoux, André. "Maṇḍalas in Abhinavagupta's Tantrāloka." In *Maṇḍalas and Yantras in the Hindu Traditions,* edited by Gudrun Bühnemann et al., 225–38. Leiden: Brill, 2003.

———. "The Śrīcakra According to the First Chapter of the Yoginīhṛdaya." In *Maṇḍalas and Yantras in the Hindu Traditions,* edited by Gudrun Bühnemann et al., 239–50. Leiden: Brill, 2003.

Panikkar, Raimundo. *The Silence of God: The Answer of the Buddha.* Faith Meets Faith Series. Maryknoll, N.Y.: Orbis Books, 1989.

Pannenberg, Wolfhart. *Systematische Theologie,* Vol. 2. Göttingen: Vandenhoeck & Ruprecht, 1991.

Parrinder, Edward Geoffrey. "Le Mysticisme Des Médiums En Afrique Occidentale." In *Réincarnation Et Vie Mystique En Afrique Noire,* edited by Dominique Zahan and Roger Bastide, 130–42. Paris: Presses Universitaires de France, 1965.

Pope Francis. *Gaudete et Exsultate: On the Call to Holiness in Today's World.* Apostolic Exhortation, 2018.

———. *Laudato si': On Care for Our Common Home.* Encyclical Letter, 2015.

Pope, John Paul II. "Reconciliatio et Paenientia: Reconciliation and Penance." Liberia Editrice Vaticana. http://w2.vatican.va/content/john-paul-ii/en/apost_exhortations /documents/hf_jp-ii_exh_02121984_reconciliatio-et-paenitentia.html.

Prieto, Andrés. "The Perils of Accommodation: Jesuit Missionary Strategies in the Early Modern World." *Journal of Jesuit Studies* 4 (2017): 395–414.

Pröpper, Thomas. *Erlösungsglaube und Freiheitsgeschichte: Eine Skizze zur Soteriologie*, 3rd ed. München: Kösel, 1991.

——. *Theologische Anthropologie*, Vols. 1–2. Freiburg-Basel-Wien: Herder, 2011.

Pseudo-Dionysius. *The Complete Works*. Translated by Colm Luibheid. New York: Paulist Press, 1987.

Pugh, Ben. *Atonement Theories: A Way Through the Maze*. Eugene, Ore.: Cascade Books, 2014.

Rahner, Karl. *Foundations of Christian Faith: An Introduction to the Idea of Christianity*. New York: Crossroad, 1978.

Ralston, Joshua. "Bearing Witness: Reframing Christian-Muslim Encounter in Light of the Refugee Crisis." *Theology Today* (2017): 22–35.

Rapp, Claudia. "Spiritual Guarantors at Penance, Baptism, and Ordination in the Late Antique East." In *A New History of Penance*, edited by Abigail Firey, 121–48. Leiden: Brill, 2008.

Ravasi, Gianfranco. "Uberschattet vom Baum der Erkenntnis: Hermeneutische Anmerkungen zu Genesis 2–3." *Internationale katholische Zeitschrift: Communio* 20, no. 4 (July 1991): 294–304. Translation in English: "Hermeneutical Comments on Gn 2–3." *Theology Digest* 39 (1992): 241–47.

Rembaum, Joel. "The Development of a Jewish Exegetical Tradition Regarding Isaiah 53." *The Harvard Theological Review* 75, no. 3 (1982): 289–311.

Reynolds, Gabriel Said. *The Qur'an and the Bible: Text and Commentary*. New Haven: Yale University Press, 2018.

Richardson, Cyril C. *Early Christian Fathers*. Translated by Cyril C. Richardson. New York: Touchstone, 1996.

Ricœur, Paul. *Aux frontières de la philosophie*. Paris: Seuil, 1994.

——. *The Conflict of Interpretations: Essays in Hermeneutics*. Evanston: Northwestern University Press, 2007.

——. "Herméneutique des symboles et réflexion philosophique (1)." In *Le conflit des interprétations. Essais d'herméneutique I*. Paris: Seuil, 1969, 283–310.

——. "Le mal: un défi à la philosophie et à la théologie." In *Lectures 3: Aux frontières de la philosophie*. Paris: Seuil, 1994, 211–33.

——. "Le 'péché originel': étude de signification." In *Le conflit des interprétations. Essais d'herméneutique I*. Paris: Seuil, 1969, 265–82.

Riḍā, Muḥammad Rashīd, and Simon Wood. *Christian Criticisms, Islamic Proofs: Rashīd Riḍā's Modernist Defence of Islam*. Oxford: Oneworld, 2008.

Roberts, Alexander, et al. *The Anti-Nicene Fathers: The Writings of the Fathers Down to A.D. 325*, Vol. 1—*The Apostolic Fathers with Justin Martyr and Irenaeus*. New York: Cosimo Classics, 2007.

Rosny, Eric de. "For a Mission of Vision—a Testimony." In *Africa: Towards Priorities of Mission—Acts of the Inter-Continental Congress of the Spiritan International School of Theology (Sist), Attakwu, Enugu, Nigeria, November 11–17 1996*, edited by P. Ikechukwu Odozor, Chinedu Amadi-Azuogu, and Elochukwu Uzukwu, 95–100. Enugu: SIST Publications, 2000.

———. *Healers in the Night*. Translated by Robert R. Barr. New York: Orbis, 1985.

———. *Les Yeux De Ma Chèvre: Sur Les Pas Des Maîtres De La Nuit En Pays Douala*. Paris: Plon, 1981.

Roy, Rammuhun. *A Treatise on Christian Doctrine, Being the Second Appeal to the Christian Public, in Defence of "Precepts of Jesus."* The British and Foreign Unitarian Association, 1834 (second edition).

Ryliskyte, Ligita. *Cur Deus Cruciatus?: Lonergan's Law of the Cross and the Transpositions of "Justice over Power."* PhD diss. in Systematic Theology at Boston College, 2020.

Sacks, Jonathan. *The Dignity of Difference*. New York: Continuum, 2003.

Saeed, Abdullah. *Reading the Qur'ān in the Twenty-First Century: a Contextualist Approach*. Abingdon: Routledge, 2014.

Sahi, Jyoti. *Stepping Stones: Reflections on the Theology of Indian Christian Culture*. Bangalore: Asian Trading Corporation, 1986.

———. "Yoga and the Wounded Heart." *Religion and the Arts* 12 (2008): 42–76.

Saiving, Valerie. "The Human Situation: A Feminine View." In *Womanspirit Rising: A Feminist Reader in Religion*, edited by Carol P. Christ and Judith Plaskow, 25–42. New York: Harper & Row, 1979.

Sanderson, Alexis. "Maṇḍala and Āgamic Identity in the Trika of Kashmir." In *Mantras et Diagrammes Rituels Dans L'Hindouisme*, edited by André Padoux, 169–214. Paris: Centre National de la Recherche Scientifique, 1986.

Sarrió Cucarella, Diego. *Muslim-Christian Polemics Across the Mediterranean: The Splendid Replies of Shihāb al-Dīn al-Qarāfī (d. 684/1285)*. The History of Christian-Muslim Relations 23. Leiden: Brill, 2015.

Saso, Michael R. *Taoism and the Rite of Cosmic Renewal*. Pullman: Washington State University Press, 1990.

Sato, Kemmyo Taira. "D. T. Suzuki and the Question of War." *Eastern Buddhist* 39, no. 1 (2008): 61–120.

Schäfer, Peter. *Jesus in the Talmud*. Princeton, N.J.: Princeton University Press, 2007.

Schleiermacher, Friedrich. *The Christian Faith*. Edited by H. R. Mackintosh and J. S. Stewart. Translated by D. M. Ballie et al. London: T & T Clark, 1999.

Schneiders, Sandra. "The Lamb of God and the Forgiveness of Sin(s) in the Fourth Gospel." *The Catholic Biblical Quarterly* 73 (2011): 1–29.

Schreiter, Robert J., ed. *Faces of Jesus in Africa*. Faith and Cultures Series. Maryknoll, N.Y.: Orbis Books, 1991.

Schweig, Graham M. "The Crucifixion and the Rāsa Maṇḍala: A Comparative Sketch of Two Great Symbols of Divine Love." *Journal of Vaishnava Studies* 21, no. 2 (Spring 2012): 171–85.

———. *Dance of Divine Love: The Rāsa Līlā of Krishna from the Bhāgavata Purāṇa, India's Classic Sacred Love Story*. Delhi: Motilal Banarsidass, 2007 [2005].

Seidel, Anna. "Post-Mortem Immortality or: The Taoist Resurrection of the Body." In *Gilgul: Essays on Transformation, Revelation, and Permanence in the History of Religions*, edited by Shaul Shaked, David Dean Shulman, and Gedaliahu A. G. Stroumsa, 223–37. Leiden: Brill, 1987.

Senior, Donald. *Why the Cross? Reframing New Testament Theology*. Nashville, Tenn.: Abingdon Press, 2014.

Sen, Keshab Chunder. *Asia's Message to Europe. A Lecture Delivered on the Occasion of the Fifty-Third Anniversary of the Brahmo Somaj at the Town Hall, Calcutta, on Saturday the 20th January, 1883.* Calcutta: R. S. Bhatta, 1883.

Shinran. *The Collected Works of Shinran.* Vol. 1: *The Writings.* Vol. 2: *Introductions, Glossaries, and Reading Aids.* Translated by Dennis Hirota, Hisao Inagaki, Michio Tokunaga, and Ryushin Uryuzu. Kyoto: Jodo Shinshu Hongwanji-ha, 1997.

Siddiqui, Mona. *Christians, Muslims and Jesus.* New Haven: Yale University Press, 2013.

Ska, Jean-Louis. "Genesis 2–3 Some Fundamental Questions." In *Beyond Eden: The Biblical Story of Paradise (Genesis 2–3) and Its Reception History,* edited by Konrad Schmid and Christoph Riedweg, 1–27. Tubingen: Mohr Siebeck, 2008.

———. *Introduction à la lecture du Pentateuque: Clés pour l'interprétation des cinq premiers livres de la Bible.* Bruxelles: Lessius, 2000.

Sobhānī, Ğ. *Forūğe abadīyyat.* Tehran 1993.

Soulen, R. Kendall. *The God of Israel and Christian Theology.* Minneapolis: Augsburg Fortress, 1996.

Stephens, Thomas. *Kristapurāṇa.* Edited and translated by Nelson Falcao, SDB. Kristu Jyoti Publications, 2012.

Stinton, Diane B. *Jesus of Africa—Voices of Contemporary African Christology.* Maryknoll, N.Y.: Orbis, 2004.

Stordalen, Terje. "Man, Soil, Garden: Garden Basic Plot in Genesis 2–3 Reconsidered." *Journal for the Study of the Old Testament* 53 (1992): 3–26.

Stosch, Klaus von. "Jesus als Gott der Sohn? Eine Auseinandersetzung mit der Christologie von Karl-Heinz Menke." In *Die Wahrheit ist Person: Brennpunkte einer christologisch gewendeten Dogmatik,* edited by Julia Knop, Magnus Lerch, and Bernd J. Claret, 1129–49. FS K.-H. Menke, Regensburg: Pustet, 2015.

———. *Trinität.* Paderborn: UTB/Ferdinand Schöningh, 2017 (Grundwissen Theologie).

———. "Über Erlösung reden." In *Religionsunterricht an höheren Schulen,* Vol. 52 (2009): 80–87.

———. "Wunder Kinder. Was es bedeutet, Kinder zu haben." In Herder Korrespondenz Spezial: *Kinder, Kinder. Ethische Konflikte am Lebensanfang* (2017): 4–6.

Stump, Eleonore. *Atonement.* Oxford: Oxford University Press, 2018.

Surgy, Albert de. *L'église Du Christianisme Céleste—Un Exemple D'église Prophétique Au Bénin.* Paris: Karthala, 2001.

Suzuki, Daisetsu Teitaro. *Mysticism Christian and Buddhist.* London: Unwin Paperbacks, 1988.

Swami Chetanananda. *Ramakrishna as We Saw Him.* Vedanta Society of St. Louis (1990 edition).

Swami Saradananda. *Ramakrishna and His Divine Play* (The Great Master). Translated by Swami Chetanananda. Vedanta Society of St. Louis, 2003.

Swami Vivekananda. *Christ the Messenger.* Boston: Vedanta Centre, 1900.

———. "History of the Aryan Race." In *The Complete Works of Swami Vivekananda.* Calcutta: Vedanta Press & Bookshop, 1947.

———. "Lecture on the Kathopanishad," Saturday, July 27, 1895. *The Complete Works of Swami Vivekananda,* Vol. 7. Accessed at https://en.wikisource.org/wiki/The_Complete _Works_of_Swami_Vivekananda/Volume_7/Inspired_Talks/Saturday,_July_27.

Swanson, Mark. "Folly to the Ḥunafā': The Crucifixion in Early Christian-Muslim Controversy." In *The Encounter of Eastern Christianity with Early Islam*, HCMR, Vol. 4, edited by Emmanouela Grypeou et al. Leiden: Brill, 2006.

Tanner, Kathryn. *Christ the Key*. Cambridge: Cambridge University Press, 2010.

———. *Jesus, Humanity and the Trinity*. Minneapolis: Fortress Press, 2001.

Teilhard de Chardin, Pierre S.J. *The Divine Milieu*. Translated by Siôn Cowell. East Sussex: Sussex Academic Press, 2004.

Terrell, JoAnne Marie. *Power in the Blood? The Cross in the African American Experience*. Maryknoll, N.Y.: Orbis, 1998.

Thelle, Notto R. "What Do I as a Christian Expect Buddhists to Discover in Jesus?" In *Buddhist Perceptions of Jesus*, edited by Perry Schmidt-Leukel, 142–57. St. Ottilien EOS-Verlag St. Ottilien, 2001.

Thiselton, Anthony C. *The First Epistle to the Corinthians: A Commentary on the Greek Text*. The New International Greek Testament Commentary, 2000/2013. Grand Rapids, Mich.: Eerdmans.

Thompson, Robert Farris. *Flash of the Spirit: African and Afro-American Art and Philosophy*. New York: Random House, 1983.

Thornton, John K. *Africa and Africans in the Making of the Atlantic World, 1400–1680*. Studies in Comparative World History. New York: Cambridge University Press, 1992.

———. *The Kongolese Saint Anthony: Dona Beatriz Kimpa Vita and the Antonian Movement, 1684–1706*. New York: Cambridge University Press, 1998.

———. "Religious and Ceremonial Life in the Kongo and Mbundu Areas, 1500–1700." In *Central Africans and Cultural Transformations in the American Diaspora*, edited by Linda M. Heywood, 71–90. New York: Cambridge University Press, 2002.

Tidjani, A. Serpos. "Rituels." *Présence Africaine* 8–9, no. Spécial "Le Monde Noir" dirigé par Théodore Monod (1950): 297–305.

Tieszen, Charles. *Cross Veneration in the Medieval Islamic World: Christian Identity and Practice under Muslim Rule*. London: I. B. Tauris, 2017.

Tillard, Jean-Marie-Roger. *L'Église locale—Ecclésiologie de Communion et Catholicité*. Paris: Cerf, 1995.

Tillich, Paul. "The Religious Symbol." *Daedalus* 87 (1958): 3–21.

———. *Systematic Theology*. Chicago: University of Chicago Press, 1967.

Timalsina, Sthaneshwar. "A Cognitive Approach to Tantric Language." *Religions* 7, no. 12 (2016): 139ff.

———. *Language of Images: Visualization and Meaning in Tantras*. New York: Peter Lang, 2015.

Tsong-kha-pa; Lam Rim Chen Mo. *The Great Treatise on the Stages of the Path to Enlightenment*. Translated by the Lamrim Chenmo Translation Committee. Edited by J. W. C. Cutler and G. Newland. Ithaca, N.Y.: Snow Lion Publications, I: 2000, II: 2004, III: 2002.

Tsoukalas, Steven. *Kṛṣṇa and Christ*. Milton Keynes: Paternoster, 2006.

Ueda, Yoshifumi, and Dennis Hirota. *Shinran: An Introduction to His Thought*. Kyoto: Hongwanji International Center, 1989.

Uhalde, Kevin. "Juridical Administration in the Church and Pastoral Care in Late Antiquity." In *A New History of Penance*, edited by Abigail Firey, 97–120. Leiden: Brill, 2008.

Umeh, John Anenechukwu. *After God Is Dibia.* 2 vols. Vol. 1: *Igbo Cosmology, Divination &*
Sacred Science in Nigeria. London: Karnak House; Lawrenceville, N.J.: U.S. distributors,
Red Sea Press, 1997.

Upadhyay, Brahmabandhab. *The Writings of Brahmabandhab Upadhyay.* 2 vols. (English
writings). Edited and annotated by Julius Lipner and George Gispert-Sauch. Bangalore:
United Theological College, 1991, 2002.

Uthemann, Karl-Heinz. *Christus, Kosmos, Diatribe: Themen der frühen Kirche als*
Beiträge zu einer historischen Theologie. Berlin; New York: De Gruyter, 2005 (Arbeiten
zur Kirchengeschichte; 93).

———. "Kaiser Justinian als Kirchenpolitiker und Theologe." In *Augustinianum* 33 (1999):
5–83.

Uzukwu, Elochukwu E. *God, Spirit, and Human Wholeness: Appropriating Faith and*
Culture in West African Style. Eugene, Ore.: Pickwick Publications, 2012.

van Riessen, Renée. *Man as a Place of God: Levinas' Hermeneutics of Kenosis.* Dordrecht:
Springer, 2007.

van Wolde, Ellen. *A Semiotic Analysis of Genesis 2–3: A Semiotic Theory and Method of*
Analysis to the Story of the Garden of Eden. Studia Semitica Neerlandica 25. Assen: Van
Gorcum, 1989.

Vasubandu, *Abhidharmakośa,* L. de La Vallée Poussin, trans. Paris: P. Geuthner; Louvain:
J.-B. Istas, 6 vols., 1923–1931.

Victoria, Brian Daizen. *Zen at War.* Lanham: Rowman & Littlefield, 2006.

Viezure, Dana. "Philoxenus of Mabbug and the controversies over the 'Theopaschite'
Trisagion." *Studia Patristica* 47 (2010): 137–46.

Vogels, Walter. "L'être humain appartient au sol. Gn 2,4b–3,24," *NRT* 105 (1983).

———. *Nos Origines. Genèse 1–11.* Montreal: Bellarmin, 1992/2000.

Ware, Kallistos. "God Immanent, yet Transcendent: The Divine Energies According to
Saint Gregory Palamas." In *In Whom We Live and Move and Have Our Being,* edited by
Philip Clayton and A. R. Peacocke. Grand Rapids: Eerdmans, 2004.

Wenger, Antoine. "Les interventions de Marie dans l'église orthodoxe et l'histoire de
Byzance." In *De primordiis cultus Mariani,* edited by Ponteficia Academia Mariana
Internationalis, Rome 1970, 423–31.

Westerlund, David. "Spiritual Beings as Agents of Illness." In *African Spirituality: Forms,*
Meanings, and Expressions, edited by Jacob Obafemi Kehinde Olupona. World
Spirituality, 152–75. New York: Crossroad, 2000.

Westermann, Claus. *Genesis 1–11: A Continental Commentary.* Translated by J. J. Scullion.
Minneapolis: Augsburg Fortress, 1990.

Whaling, Frank. *The Rise of the Religious Significance of Rama.* Preface by Daniel H.
Ingalls. Delhi: Motilal Banarsidass, 1980.

Wijsen, Frans Jozef Servaas. *There Is Only One God: A Socio-Scientific and Theological*
Study of Popular Religion and Evangelization in Sukumaland, Northwest Tanzania.
Nijmegen: Uitgeverij Kok-Kampen, 1993.

Williams, Delores S. "Black Women's Surrogacy Experience and the Christian Notion of
Redemption." In *Cross Examinations: Readings on the Meaning of the Cross,* edited by
Marit Trelstad, 19–32. Minneapolis: Fortress Press, 2006.

———. *Sisters in the Wilderness: The Challenge of Womanist God-Talk.* Maryknoll, N.Y.: Orbis Books, 2001.

Williams, Rowan. "Not Being Serious: Thomas Merton and Karl Barth." In *A Silent Action. Engagements with Thomas Merton,* 69–82. Louisville: Fons Vitae, 2011.

Willits, Catherine. "The Obfuscation of Bodily Sight in the *Showings* of Julian of Norwich." *Journal of Literary and Cultural Disability Studies* 8, no. (2014): 81–96.

Wilson, Monica. "Nyakyusa Ritual and Symbolism." *American Anthropologist* 56, no. 2 (1954): 228–41.

Wood, Simon A. *Christian Criticisms, Islamic Proofs: Rashid Rida's Modernist Defense of Islam.* Oxford: One World, 2008.

Wright, N. T. *The Climax of the Covenant: Christ and the Law in Pauline Theology.* Minneapolis: Fortress Press, 1991.

Wyschogrod, Michael. *Abraham's Promise: Judaism and Jewish-Christian Relations.* Grand Rapids: Eerdmans, 2004.

Yagi, Seiichi. "'I' in the Words of Jesus." In *The Myth of Christian Uniqueness: Toward a Pluralistic Theology of Religions,* edited by John Hick and Paul F. Knitter. Faith Meets Faith, 117–36. Maryknoll, N.Y.: Orbis Books, 1987.

Yagi, Seiichi, and Leonard J. Swidler. *A Bridge to Buddhist-Christian Dialogue.* New York: Paulist Press, 1990.

Yamada, Toshiaki. "The Lingbao School." In *Daoism Handbook,* edited by Livia Kohn, 225–55. Leiden: Brill, 2000.

———. "*Tutan zhai*: Mud and Soot Retreat." In *Encyclopedia of Taoism,* edited by Fabrizio Pregadio, 1001. New York: Routledge, 2008.

Young, Jason R. *Rituals of Resistance: African Atlantic Religion in Kongo and the Lowcountry South in the Era of Slavery.* Baton Rouge: Louisiana State University Press, 2007.

Zahniser, A. H. Mathias. *The Mission and Death of Jesus in Islam and Christianity.* Maryknoll, N.Y.: Orbis, 2008.

Zhang, Dainian. *Key Concepts in Chinese Philosophy.* Translated by Edmund Ryden. New Haven: Yale University Press, 2002.

Zürcher, Erik. *The Buddhist Conquest of China: The Spread and Adaptation of Buddhism in Early Medieval China.* 3rd ed. with a foreword and edited by Stephen F. Teiser. Leiden: Brill, 2007.

CONTRIBUTORS

BEDE BENJAMIN BIDLACK is an Associate Professor of Theology at Saint Anselm College in Manchester, New Hampshire. He publishes in the areas of comparative theology, Daoist studies, theological anthropology, interreligious dialogue, and philosophy. He is the author of *In Good Company: The Body and Divinization in the Thought of Pierre Teilhard de Chardin, SJ and Daoist Xiao Yingsou* (2015).

FRANCIS X. CLOONEY, S.J., is the Parkman Professor of Divinity and Professor of Comparative Theology at Harvard Divinity School. His primary areas of Indological scholarship are theological commentarial writings in the Sanskrit and Tamil traditions of Hindu India. He has also written on the Jesuit missionary tradition, particularly in India, on the early Jesuit pan-Asian discourse on reincarnation, and on the dynamics of dialogue and interreligious learning in the contemporary world. His most recent books are *Reading the Hindu and Christian Classics: Why and How Deep Learning Still Matters* (2019) and *Western Jesuit Scholars in India: Tracing their Paths, Reassessing Their Goals* (2020).

CATHERINE CORNILLE is Professor of Comparative Theology at Boston College, where she holds the Newton College Alumnae Chair of Western Culture. Her areas of research focus on theology of religions, interreligious dialogue, and religious hybridity. She is the author of *The Im-Possibility of Interreligious Dialogue* (2008) and *Meaning and Method in Comparative Theology* (2020), and she has edited numerous books in the area of interreligious dialogue.

THIERRY-MARIE COURAU, O.P., is a Catholic theologian and Honorary Dean at the Faculty of Theology and Religious Sciences—*Theologicum,* at the Catholic Institute of Paris, France (2011–2017). A member of the Dominican Order, he specializes in Tibetan Buddhism studies. He is President of the International Journal of Theology, *Concilium*. His most recent books are *Le dialogue des rationalités culturelles et religieuses* (2019), *Le salut comme dialogue* (2018), and *La succession des exercices vers l'Éveil bouddhique* (2017).

S. MARK HEIM is the Samuel Abbot Professor of Christian Theology at Andover Newton Seminary at Yale Divinity School. He has written extensively on issues of religious pluralism, atonement, and Christian ecumenism. His books include *Salvations: Truth and Difference in Theology* (1995), *The Depth of the Riches: A Trinitarian Theology of Religious Ends* (2001), *Saved from Sacrifice: A Theology of the Cross* (2006), and most recently, *Crucified Wisdom: Christ and the Bodhisattva in Theological Reflection* (2018).

DANIEL JOSLYN-SIEMIATKOSKI is the Duncalf-Villavaso Professor of Church History at Seminary of the Southwest in Austin, Texas. He works in the fields of comparative theology, Jewish-Christian relations, and Anglican studies. He is most recently the author of *The More Torah, The More Life: A Christian Commentary on Mishnah Avot* (2018). He is an ordained priest in the Episcopal Church.

LEO D. LEFEBURE is the inaugural holder of the Matteo Ricci, S.J., Chair of Theology at Georgetown University. He is the author of the forthcoming work *Interreligious Relationships Transformed: Catholic Responses to Religious Pluralism in the United States*; he is also the author of *True and Holy: Christian Scripture and Other Religions* (2014) and the co-author of *The Path of Wisdom: A Christian Commentary on the Dhammapada* (2011). He is President of the Society for Buddhist-Christian Studies, Research Fellow of the Chinese University of Hong Kong, and Trustee Emeritus of the Council for a Parliament of the World's Religions.

DANIEL A. MADIGAN, S.J., is Jeanette W. and Otto J. Ruesch Family Distinguished Jesuit Scholar, Associate Professor and Director of Graduate Studies in the Department of Theology and Religious Studies, Senior Fellow of the Al-Waleed Center for Muslim-Christian Understanding, and Faculty Fellow of the Berkley Center for Religion, Peace and World Affairs at Georgetown University. He is also an Honorary Professorial

Fellow of Australian Catholic University. From 2000 to 2007, Madigan was the founder and director of the Institute for the Study of Religions and Cultures at the Pontifical Gregorian University. Since 2012, he has been Chair of the Building Bridges Seminar, an annual week-long study session for Muslim and Christian scholars invited from all over the world.

MARIANNE MOYAERT is Professor at the Free University of Amsterdam, where she holds the Fenna Diemer Lindeboom Chair in Comparative Theology and the Hermeneutics of Interreligious Dialogue. She is the author of *In Response to the Religious Other: Ricoeur and the Fragility of Interreligious Encounters* (2014) and editor of *Interreligious Dialogue and Ritual Participation: Boundaries, Transgressions and Innovations* (2015).

JOSHUA RALSTON is Reader in Christian-Muslim Relations at the University of Edinburgh and founder and director of the Christian-Muslim Studies Network. He is the author of *Law and the Rule of God: A Christian Engagement with Shariʿa* and co-editor of *Church in the Age of Global Migration: A Moving Body* (2015). He has published numerous essays and book chapters on Protestant theology, Christian-Muslim dialogue, and political theology.

ELOCHUKWU UZUKWU is the Rev. Pierre Schouver C.S.Sp. Endowed Chair in Mission at Duquesne University. His research interests are in the areas of liturgy-sacraments, ritual studies, ecclesiology, missiology, and contextual theology, with particular focus on continental Africa and Africa in the diaspora. He is author of *God, Spirit, and Human Wholeness: Appropriating Faith and Culture in West African Style* (2012) and *Family of God: Africa's Treasure, Reinventing Christianity and the World* (in progress).

KLAUS VON STOSCH holds the Schlegel Chair in Systematic Theology at Bonn University. His areas of research are comparative theology; faith and reason; the problem of evil; Christian theology responsive to Islam, especially Christology; and theology of the Trinity. His most recent books are *Herausforderung Islam. Christliche Annaherungen* (2016) and *The Other Prophet: Jesus in the Qurʾan* (2019).

MICHELLE VOSS ROBERTS is Professor of Theology and Principal at Emmanuel College, a multireligious theological school at the University of

Toronto. Her published work in comparative theology includes *Dualities: A Theology of Difference* (2010), *Tastes of the Divine: Hindu and Christian Theologies of Emotion* (2014), and *Body Parts: A Theological Anthropology* (2017). With Chad Bauman, she is also the editor of the *Routledge Handbook of Hindu-Christian Relations*.

INDEX

Comparative / Thinking Across
Theology / Traditions

Loye Ashton and John Thatamanil, series editors

Hyo-Dong Lee, *Spirit, Qi, and the Multitude: A Comparative Theology for the Democracy of Creation*

Michelle Voss Roberts, *Tastes of the Divine: Hindu and Christian Theologies of Emotion*

Michelle Voss Roberts (ed.), *Comparing Faithfully: Insights for Systematic Theological Reflection*

Francis X. Clooney, S.J., and Klaus von Stosch (eds.), *How to Do Comparative Theology*

F. Dominic Longo, *Spiritual Grammar: Genre and the Saintly Subject in Islam and Christianity*

S. Mark Heim, *Crucified Wisdom: Theological Reflection on Christ and the Bodhisattva*

Martha L. Moore-Keish and Christian T. Collins Winn (eds.), *Karl Barth and Comparative Theology*

John J. Thatamanil, *Circling the Elephant: A Comparative Theology of Religious Diversity*

Catherine Cornille (ed.), *Atonement and Comparative Theology: The Cross in Dialogue with Other Religions*